for Service and Support CNE

The Cram Sheet

This Cram Sheet contains the distilled, key facts about the Service and Support exam. Review this information last thing before you enter the test room, paying special attention to those areas where you feel you need the most review. You can transfer any of these facts from your head onto a blank piece of paper before beginning the exam.

TROUBLESHOOTING

1. The troubleshooting model consists of four steps: investigation, diagnosis, repair, and documentation.

2. Simple troubleshooting solutions include:
   - Making sure the user hasn't made an error
   - Verifying all network components
   - Backing up the data—especially if storage devices are involved
   - Restarting the devices involved
   - Removing and/or not loading unnecessary components to simplify the system
   - Investigating security and access permissions
   - Evaluating the versions of the software pieces

3. Troubleshooting procedures should include:
   - Collecting the basic information about the events, software, and hardware components.
   - Developing a problem-isolation plan and prioritizing the possible solution actions.
   - Executing the solution plan.
   - Documenting solutions' specific problems.

ELECTROSTATIC DISCHARGE (ESD)

4. Static electricity is an electrical discharge caused by an imbalance of electrons on a material's surface.

5. ESD is the transfer of the charge between bodies at different electrical potentials. 20 to 30 volts can potentially damage electronic components.

6. ESD of 3,000 volts can be felt.

7. Small discharges of static electricity over time cause degradation of equipment, which shortens the equipment's lifetime, leads to earlier failures, and causes 90 percent of damage to components.

ESD CONTROL PROGRAM

8. An ESD control program has many benefits, including reduced hardware inventory, downtime, and service calls; fewer intermittent hardware problems; and happier customers.

9. Preventing ESD is a key component to protecting your equipment. To prevent ESD:
   - Ground equipment and yourself.
   - Don't touch circuit boards by their leads or connectors.
   - Don't allow other people to touch you while you're working on the equipment.
   - Use undamaged static-shielding bags.
   - Keep nonconductive materials such as Styrofoam cups or synthetic fabrics which can hold a static charge and discharge, away from components.
   - Don't place the electronic components on conductive material, such as metal.
   - Try to keep the humidity above 70 percent.

NETWORK DOCUMENTATION

10. First, document the components of the LAN, including:
    - **Network map** Physical topology of the network.
    - **LAN inventory** List of various network components.
    - **Network cabling documentation** Label all wall-plate and wiring closet connectors to make tracing the physical connections easier.
    - **Server** and **workstation documentation** Use a management product such as ManageWise.

- **Change log** Document all changes to the LAN.

11. Also document the history of the LAN, including Business environment, user information, past problems, baseline information, and usage patterns.

12. Also document resources used within the LAN, such as:
    - **Technologies** Routing tables, protocol information, DNS architecture, and so on
    - **Technical support** Who to contact for support of each network component

DIAGNOSTIC SOFTWARE

13. WinCheckIt, CheckIt Pro, and MSD (Microsoft System Diagnostics)

NOVELL INTERNET SERVICES

14. The requirements to access Novell Internet services are an Internet connection, TCP/IP on the workstation oran IPX to IP gateway, and an ISP or online provider.

NOVELL SUPPORT CONNECTION

15. Go to Support Connection on the Web at **http://support.novell.com** for the KnowledgeBase, patches, fixes, updates, technical information documents (TIDs), and incident tracking.

16. Support Connection on the Web includes forums, incident tracking, TIDs and KnowledgeBase, and file downloads.

17. Support Connection CD requires is a monthly subscription and includes the AppNotes and Developer Notes.

18. The following table compares the elements of the Support Connection Web site and CD-ROM.

Content	Web	CD
Product information	Yes	Yes
Patches/updates	Yes	Yes
TIDs	Yes	Yes
Novell Labs reports	Yes	Yes
Product Manuals	No	Yes
Support Forums	Yes	No
Application Notes	optional	Yes
Developer Notes	optional	Yes

SUPPORTSOURCE AND THE MTL

19. SupportSource is a CD-ROM containing extensive hardware documentation and patches including the Micro House Technical Library.

20. It contains supplementary information such as common disk problems, cabling information for different topologies, and so on.

21. Main tool bar includes the Document Viewer Pane (which contains the Document, Summary, and Company tabs), the Query Pane, and the Data Tree.

PC ARCHITECTURE TYPES

22. ISA is 16-bit bus operating at 8 to 10MHz.

23. MCA is a 32-bit bus operating at 10MHz.

24. An MCA bus requires software to configure the hardware settings; files are Adapter Definition Files (ADFs).

25. EISA is a 32-bit bus operating at 8MHz.

26. An EISA bus requires software to configure the hardware settings; custom configuration file (that ends with the CFG extension).

27. Video Electronics Standards Association VLB buses (originally designed for video boards; runs at 32MHz).

28. PCMIA cards are credit-card size and used for laptops. Also called PC Cards.

29. PCI is a 32-bit bus and can share interrupts. You can connect up to 10 devices per computer.

PLUS AND PLAY BIOS

30. The Plug and Play system requires the BIOS and system manufacturers to work closely with the operating system vendors.

INTERRUPT REQUESTS (IRQS)

31. IRQs send notice to the system board and CPU that a device needs service. Default interrupt settings are:
    - **IRQ 0** Used by the system timer only.
    - **IRQ 1** Used by keyboard input only.
    - **IRQ 2** Linked to IRQs 8-15. Can also be used by some modems and video boards.
    - **IRQ 3** Typically used by COM2 serial ports and may be available. Can also be used by COM4 ports, network boards, and sound cards.
    - **IRQ 4** Typically used by COM1 serial port, but can be used by COM3 ports.
    - **IRQ 5** Used by LPT2 parallel ports, usually available, and use varies widely. Can be used by sound cards and network boards.
    - **IRQ 6** Typically used by a floppy-disk controller, but can be used by tape accelerator cards.
    - **IRQ 7** Used by the LPT1 parallel port, which is usually the printer port.
    - **IRQ 8** Used by the realtime clock timer only.

for Service and Support CNE

Melanie Hoag
Gary Novosel

Exam Cram for Service And Support CNE

© 1999 The Coriolis Group. All Rights Reserved.

Limits Of Liability And Disclaimer Of Warranty

The author and publisher of this book have used their best efforts in preparing the book and the programs contained in it. These efforts include the development, research, and testing of the theories and programs to determine their effectiveness. The author and publisher make no warranty of any kind, expressed or implied, with regard to these programs or the documentation contained in this book.

The author and publisher shall not be liable in the event of incidental or consequential damages in connection with, or arising out of, the furnishing, performance, or use of the programs, associated instructions, and/or claims of productivity gains.

Trademarks

Trademarked names appear throughout this book. Rather than list the names and entities that own the trademarks or insert a trademark symbol with each mention of the trademarked name, the publisher states that it is using the names for editorial purposes only and to the benefit of the trademark owner, with no intention of infringing upon that trademark.

The Coriolis Group, LLC
14455 N. Hayden Road, Suite 220
Scottsdale, Arizona 85260

480/483-0192
FAX 480/483-0193
http://www.coriolis.com
Hoag, Melanie
    Exam cram for service and support CNE / by Melanie Hoag and Gary Novosel.
        p. cm.
    ISBN 1-57610-354-4
    1. Electronic data processing personnel--Certification.   2. Novell software--Examinations Study guides.   3. Computer Networks--Examinations Study guides.   I. Novosel, Gary.   II. Title.
QA76.3.H65   1999
004.6--dc21   99-32113
                                                                  CIP

Printed in the United States of America
10 9 8 7 6 5 4 3 2 1

Publisher
Keith Weiskamp

Acquisitions Editor
Shari Jo Hehr

Marketing Specialist
Cynthia Caldwell

Project Editor
Don Eamon

Technical Reviewer
Randy Grein

Production Coordinator
Wendy Littley

Cover Design
Jesse Dunn

Layout Design
April Nielsen

CORIOLIS

14455 North Hayden Road, Suite 220 • Scottsdale, Arizona 85260

Coriolis: The Training And Certification Destination™

Thank you for purchasing one of our innovative certification study guides, just one of the many members of the Coriolis family of certification products.

Certification Insider Press™ has long believed that achieving your IT certification is more of a road trip than anything else. This is why most of our readers consider us their *Training And Certification Destination*. By providing a one-stop shop for the most innovative and unique training materials, our readers know we are the first place to look when it comes to achieving their certification. As one reader put it, "I plan on using your books for all of the exams I take."

To help you reach your goals, we've listened to others like you, and we've designed our entire product line around you and the way you like to study, learn, and master challenging subjects. Our approach is *The Smartest Way To Get Certified™*.

In addition to our highly popular *Exam Cram* and *Exam Prep* guides, we have a number of new products. We recently launched Exam Cram Live!, two-day seminars based on *Exam Cram* material. We've also developed a new series of books and study aides—*Practice Tests Exam Crams* and *Exam Cram Flash Cards*—designed to make your studying fun as well as productive.

Our commitment to being the *Training And Certification Destination* does not stop there. We just introduced *Exam Cram Insider*, a biweekly newsletter containing the latest in certification news, study tips, and announcements from Certification Insider Press. (To subscribe, send an email to **eci@coriolis.com** and type "subscribe insider" in the body of the email.) We also recently announced the launch of the Certified Crammer Society and the Coriolis Help Center—two new additions to the Certification Insider Press family.

We'd like to hear from you. Help us continue to provide the very best certification study materials possible. Write us or email us at **cipq@coriolis.com** and let us know how our books have helped you study, or tell us about new features that you'd like us to add. If you send us a story about how we've helped you, and we use it in one of our books, we'll send you an official Coriolis shirt for your efforts.

Good luck with your certification exam and your career. Thank you for allowing us to help you achieve your goals.

Keith Weiskamp
Keith Weiskamp
Publisher, Certification Insider Press

About The Authors

Melanie Hoag, Ph.D., holds MCNI, MCNE, MCT, and MCP certifications and is a Senior Technical Training Consultant for Productivity Point International, Inc. (PPI) in Austin, TX. Melanie began her computer career in 1983 at Drexel University in Philadelphia. She was involved in a variety of activities and projects ranging from software design and construction, courseware development, and technical presentations to consulting. Between the time at Drexel and PPI, Melanie ran a small software-development company with her husband. Melanie is currently teaching Novell authorized courses covering the entire NetWare 5 and NetWare 4.11 CNE and CNA certification tracks and selected MCNE courses. In addition to teaching, she's also involved in network-related issues and projects within PPI. When not associated with networking "things," Melanie and her family run a small ranch near Hutto, TX. They raise and show prize-winning Texas Longhorn cattle.

Gary Novosel is an MCSE, MCP+ Internet, and MCT. He is currently employed as an IM Project Manager with Compaq Computer Corporation in Houston, TX. He started building PCs and networks in 1983, has expertise in Unix, NetWare, and Windows NT, and is an expert in distributed document management. Gary served nine years in the Navy stationed aboard submarines and as a nuclear instructor at Knolls Atomic Power Laboratory in upstate New York.

Acknowledgments

Several people have helped with the development of this book and without them, it would not have been possible.

First, a very special thanks and love to my family, my husband and partner, Bob Bliss, and our daughter, Lee Ann Bliss. Putting together this second book has put a lot of burden on our lives together, and I thank you both for your understanding, help, and encouragement. I would also like to thank my parents, Bill and Doris, who taught me that "you'll never know if you can do it until you have tried." And to my brother, David, whose skills as a screenwriter inspired me to make the plunge into writing. Thanks also to all my friends, who constantly lend a helping hand and are always there when needed the most.

I would like to offer a special thanks to Mary Burmeister; her wonderful editing skills produce smooth and polished products. Mary was also an efficient project manager and kept me in "line" before I drifted too far away! Also, thanks to Ed Tittel and the rest of the crew at LANWrights for giving me the opportunity to do this book, and to James Gaskin and Todd Meadors whose contributions and comments helped make the book possible.

Finally, a big thanks to all my fellow instructors and employees at Productivity Point Int'l, Inc. (PPI). Being both friends and coworkers makes PPI a fun place to "work" and to share our "geekdom!"

Finally, I must not forget all of my students, both past and future, who make teaching fun. Sharing your experiences, both good and bad, enhances all our skill sets and makes for lively discussions!

God bless,
—Melanie Hoag

One of my recent students said he wished he someday knew what I know now. If I have somehow misguided my students into thinking I know it all, then it certainly must be time to raise my consulting rates. Any instructor (or anyone, for that matter) who tells you they know it all is either correct or delusional. I have not yet met anyone that was correct and, unfortunately, that includes me. If you wish you had more experience or knowledge than you do now, then you've jumped the first hurdle—procrastination.

I'd like to apologize to my family and friends. For the past several months, you've asked for my attention and gotten an answer like "I'll be writing this weekend, let's reschedule." Thank God I have a great family and friends. You've said you understand, and I can only hope you did. Thanks for not abandoning me. I'd especially like to thank my wife, Yvete. The past year has been intense, and I believe if we weren't going to be married at least 100 more years, you would have left me by now. You are the love of my life.

To my Mom; while you probably don't understand what's in this book, you can now show everybody what I do for a living. Thanks for being my Mom. Finally, to my grandson Matthew. You allow me to correct all the mistakes I've made in dealings with other people and help me realize the virtue of unconditional love of another. I will always, always be there; especially for you.

—*Gary Novosel*

Contents At A Glance

Table Of Contents

Introduction

Welcome to *Exam Cram for Service and Support CNE*! This book aims to help you get ready to take—and pass—Novell certification Test 050-635, "Service and Support." This Introduction explains Novell's certification programs in general and discusses how the *Exam Cram* series can help you prepare for Novell's certification tests.

Exam Cram books help you understand and appreciate the subjects and materials you need to pass Novell certification tests. *Exam Cram* books are aimed strictly at test preparation and review. They do not teach you everything you need to know about a topic, such as how to configure each type of network board or which topology to use. Instead, we (the authors) present and dissect the questions and problems we've found that you're likely to encounter on a test. We've worked from Novell's own training materials, preparation guides, and tests, and from a battery of third-party test preparation tools. Our aim is to bring together as much information as possible about Novell certification tests.

Nevertheless, to completely prepare yourself for any Novell test, we recommend that you begin by taking the Self-Assessment immediately following this Introduction. The Self-Assessment will help you evaluate your knowledge base against the requirements for a CNE under both ideal and real circumstances.

Based on what you learn from that exercise, you might decide to begin your studies with some classroom training or by reading one of the many study guides available from The Coriolis Group, Novell Press (an imprint of IDG Books Worldwide), or third-party vendors. We strongly recommend that you install, configure, and fool around with any software that you'll be tested on— especially NetWare 5 and Micro House SupportSource—because nothing beats hands-on experience and familiarity when it comes to understanding questions you're likely to encounter on a certification test. Book learning is essential, but hands-on experience is the best teacher of all.

Novell Professional Certifications

Novell's various certifications currently encompass six separate programs, each of which boasts its own special acronym (as a would-be certificant, you need to have a high tolerance for alphabet soup of all kinds):

➤ **CNA (Certified Novell Administrator)** This is the least prestigious of all the certification tracks from Novell. Candidates can demonstrate their skills in any of a number of areas of expertise. This certification requires passing one test in any of five tracks (three are specific to NetWare versions 3.x, 4.x, and 5; two are specific to GroupWise versions; for the purposes of this book, we assume that the NetWare 5 track is the one for you). Table 1 shows the required test for the CNA certification. For more information about this program and its requirements, visit **http://education.novell.com/cna**.

➤ **CNE (Certified Novell Engineer)** This is the primary target for most people who seek a Novell certification of one kind or another. Candidates who want to demonstrate their skills in installing and managing NetWare networks make up its primary audience. This certification is obtained by passing six or seven tests, including five or six (depending on which track you pursue) required core tests and a single elective. Table 1 shows the required and elective tests for CNE certification in the NetWare 5 track. For more information about this program and its requirements, visit **http://education.novell.com/cne**.

➤ **MCNE (Master CNE)** Candidates for this certification program must first prove their basic expertise by obtaining CNE certification. To obtain MCNE status, candidates must pass four to six additional tests in any of seven specialized areas. This is Novell's most elite certification. For more information about this program and its requirements, visit **http://education.novell.com/mcne**.

➤ **CIP (Certified Internet Professional)** This certification program is designed for individuals who seek to step into one or more of a variety of professional Internet roles. These roles include that of Certified Internet Business Strategist, Certified Web Designer, Certified Web Developer, Certified Internet Manager, and Certified Internet Architect. To qualify, candidates must pass anywhere from one to five required tests, depending on which role they seek to fill. For more information about this program and its requirements, visit **www.netboss.com**.

Table 1 Novell CNA And CNE Requirements*

CNA

Only 1 test required	
Test 050-639	NetWare 5 Administration

CNE

All 5 of these tests are required	
Test 050-639	NetWare 5 Administration
Test 050-632	Networking Technologies
Test 050-640	NetWare 5 Advanced Administration
Test 050-634	NDS Design and Implementation
Test 050-635	Service and Support
Choose 1 elective from this group	
Test 050-629	Securing Intranets with BorderManager
Test 050-628	Network Management Using ManageWise 2.1
Test 050-641	Network Management Using ManageWise 2.6
Test 050-636	intraNetWare: Integrating Windows NT
Test 050-618	GroupWise 5 Administration
Test 050-633	GroupWise 5.5 System Administration

* This is not a complete listing. We have included only those tests needed for the NetWare 5 track. If you are currently a CNE certified in NetWare 4, you need only take the CNE NetWare 4.11 to NetWare 5 Update test (Test 050-638) to be certified in NetWare 5.

➤ **CNI (Certified Novell Instructor)** Candidates who want to teach any elements of the Novell official curriculum (and there's usually an official class tied to each of the Novell certification tests) must meet several requirements to obtain CNI certification. They must take a special instructor training class, demonstrate their proficiency in a classroom setting, and take a special version of the test for each certification topic they plan to teach to show a higher level of knowledge and understanding of the topics involved. For more information about this program and its requirements, visit **http://education.novell.com/cni**.

Novell also offers a Master CNI (MCNI) credential to exceptional instructors who have two years of CNI teaching experience, and who possess an MCNE certification as well.

➤ **CNS (Certified Novell Salesperson)** This is a newer Novell certification and focuses on the knowledge that sales professionals need to master to present and position Novell's various networking products accurately and professionally.

To obtain this certification, an individual must pass a self-study class on sales skills and Novell products, as well as take regular product update training when it becomes available. This level of certification is intended to demonstrate a salesperson's ability to position and represent Novell's many products accurately and fairly. For more information about this program and its requirements, visit **http://education.novell.com/ powersell**.

Certification is an ongoing activity. When a Novell product becomes obsolete, Novell certified professionals typically have 12 to 18 months during which they may recertify on new product versions. If individuals do not recertify within the specified period, their certifications become invalid. Because technology keeps changing and new products continually supplant old ones, this should come as no surprise to anyone. Certification is not a one-time achievement, but rather a commitment to a set of evolving tools and technologies.

The best place to keep tabs on Novell's certification program and its various certifications is on the Novell Web site. The current root URL for all Novell certification programs is **http://education.novell.com/certinfo**. If, however, this URL doesn't work, try using the Search tool on Novell's site with "certification" or "certification programs" as a search string. You will then find the latest, most up-to-date information about Novell's certification programs.

Taking A Certification Exam

Alas, testing is not free. Each computer-based Novell test costs $95, and if you don't pass, you may retest for an additional $95 for each try. In the United States and Canada, tests are administered by Sylvan Prometric and by Virtual University Enterprises (VUE). Here's how you can contact them:

➤ **Sylvan Prometric** Sign up for a test through the company's Web site at **www.slspro.com**. In the United States or Canada, call 800-233-3382; outside that area, call 612-820-5706.

➤ **Virtual University Enterprises** Sign up for a test or get the phone numbers for local testing centers through the Web page at **www.vue.com**. In the United States or Canada, call 800-511-8123 or 888-834-8378; outside that area, call 612-897-7370.

To sign up for a test, you need a valid credit card, or you need to contact either company for mailing instructions to send them a check (in the U.S.). Only when payment is verified, or a check has cleared, can you actually register for a test.

To schedule a test, call the number or visit either of the Web pages at least one day in advance. To cancel or reschedule a test, you must call before 7 P.M. Pacific standard time, the business day before the scheduled test time (or you may be charged, even if you don't show up for the test). To schedule a test, please have the following information ready:

➤ Your name, organization, and mailing address.

➤ Your Novell Test ID. (Inside the United States, this means your Social Security number; citizens of other nations should call ahead to find out what type of identification number is required to register for a test.)

➤ The name and number of the test you plan to take.

➤ A method of payment. (As we've already mentioned, a credit card is the most convenient method, but alternate means can be arranged in advance, if necessary.)

After you sign up for a test, you'll be informed as to when and where the test is scheduled. Try to arrive at least 15 minutes early. You must supply two forms of identification—one of which must be a photo ID—to be admitted into the testing room.

All tests are completely closed-book. In fact, you will not be allowed to take anything with you into the testing area, but you will be furnished with a blank sheet of paper and a pen or, in some cases, an erasable plastic sheet and an erasable pen. We suggest that you immediately write down all the information you've memorized for the test. In *Exam Cram* books, this information appears on a tear-out sheet inside the front cover of each book. You'll have some time to compose yourself, to record this information, and even to take a sample orientation test before you begin the real thing. We suggest you take the orientation test before taking your first test, but because they're all more or less identical in layout, behavior, and controls, you probably won't need to do this more than once.

After you complete a Novell certification test, the software will tell you whether you've passed or failed. Results are broken into topical areas that map to the test's specific test objectives. Even if you fail, we suggest you ask for—and keep—the detailed report that the test administrator should print for you. You should use this report to help you prepare for another go-round, if needed.

If you need to retake a test, you'll have to schedule a new test with Sylvan Prometric or VUE and pay another $95.

 The first time you fail a test, you can retake the test the next day. However, if you fail a second time, you must wait 14 days before retaking that test. The 14-day waiting period remains in effect for all retakes after the first failure.

Tracking Novell Certification Status

As soon as you pass one of the applicable Novell tests, you'll attain Certified NetWare Administrator (CNA) status. Novell also generates transcripts that indicate which tests you have passed and your certification status. You can check (or print) your transcript at any time by visiting the official Novell site for certified professionals through its login page at **http://certification. novell.com/pinlogin.htm**. As the name of the Web page (pinlogin) is meant to suggest, you need an account name and a Personal Identification Number (PIN) to access this page. You'll receive this information by email about two weeks after you pass any exam that might qualify you for CNA or CNE status.

At the Novell certification site, you can also update your personal profile, including your name, address, phone and fax numbers, email address, and other contact information. You can view a list of all certifications that you've received so far and check a complete list of all exams you've taken.

Benefits Of Novell Certification

After you pass the necessary set of tests (one for CNA, six or seven for CNE, four to six more for the MCNE), you'll become certified (or obtain an additional certification). Official certification usually takes anywhere from four to six weeks, so don't expect to get your credentials overnight. When the package for a qualified certification arrives, it includes a set of materials that contain several important elements:

➤ A certificate, suitable for framing, along with an official membership card.

➤ A license to use the appropriate Novell certified professional logo, which allows you to use that logo in advertisements, promotions, and documents, and on letterhead, business cards, and so on. As part of your certification packet, you'll get a logo sheet, which includes camera-ready artwork. (Note that before using any artwork, individuals must sign and return a licensing agreement that indicates they'll abide by its terms and conditions.)

➤ A subscription to the *NetWare Connection* magazine, which provides ongoing data about testing and certification activities, requirements, and changes to the program.

➤ Access to a special Web site, commensurate with your current level of certification, through the **http://certification.novell.com/pinlogin.htm**

login page. You'll find more than your own personal records here—you'll also find reports of new certification programs, special downloads, practice test information, and other goodies not available to the general public.

Many people believe that the benefits of Novell CNA or CNE certification go well beyond the perks that Novell provides to newly anointed members of these elite groups. For years, job listings have included requirements for CNA, CNE, and so on, and many individuals who complete the program can qualify for increases in pay and/or responsibility. As an official recognition of hard work and broad knowledge, any of the Novell certifications is a badge of honor in many IT organizations, and a requirement for employment in many others.

How To Prepare For An Exam

Preparing for any NetWare-related test (including "Service and Support") requires that you obtain and study materials designed to provide comprehensive information about the product and its capabilities that will appear on the specific test for which you're preparing. The following list of materials will help you study and prepare:

➤ The objectives for the course that relates to Test 050-635 appear in the information that Novell provides for Course 580, "Service and Support." You can read these objectives on the Novell Web site at **http:// education.novell.com/testinfo/objectives/580tobj.htm**. These will also define the feedback topics when you take the test, so this document should be an essential part of your planning and preparation for the exam. You might even want to print a copy and use it along with your other study materials.

➤ General information about Novell tests is also available. This information includes what type of test will be delivered for each topic, how many questions you'll see on any given test, the minimum passing score (which Novell calls a *cut score*) for each test, and the maximum amount of time allotted for each test. All this information is compiled in a table called "Test Data" that you can read at **http://education.novell.com/ testinfo/testdata.htm**.

Additionally, you'll probably find any or all of the following materials useful as you prepare for the "Service and Support" test:

➤ **Novell Course 580: Service and Support** Novell Education offers a five-day class that covers the materials for this test at a level intended to permit anyone who's taken the 560 class (NetWare 5 Administration), the 565 class (Networking Technologies), the 570 class (NetWare 5

Advanced Administration), and the 575 class (NDS Design and Implementation) to completely master this material. Although Novell recommends these courses as prerequisites, they are not required to sign up for 580 (or to take the corresponding exam, 050-635).

➤ **The Novell Support Connection CD** This monthly CD-ROM-based publication delivers numerous electronic titles on topics relevant to NetWare and other key Novell products and topics, primarily, "Monthly Update" CD-ROMs (there are two at the time of this writing). Offerings on these CD-ROMs include product facts, technical articles and white papers, tools and utilities, and other information.

A subscription to the Novell Support Connection costs $495 per year (a $100 discount is available to all CNEs and MCNEs as one of the benefits of certification), but it is well worth the cost. Visit **http://support.novell.com** and check out the information under the "Support Connection CD" menu entry for details.

➤ **Classroom Training** Although you'll find Novell Authorized Education Centers (NAECs) worldwide that teach the official Novell curriculum, unlicensed third-party training companies (such as Wave Technologies, American Research Group, Learning Tree, Data-Tech, and others) offer classroom training on Service and Support as well. These companies aim to help you prepare to pass Test 050-635. Although such training runs upwards of $350 per day in class, most of the individuals lucky enough to partake (including your humble authors, who've even taught such courses) find them to be quite worthwhile.

➤ **Other Publications** You'll find direct references to other publications and resources in this book, but there's no shortage of information available about service and support. To help you sift through the various offerings available, we end each chapter with a "Need To Know More?" section that provides pointers to more complete and exhaustive resources covering the chapter's subjects. This should give you some idea of where we think you should look for further discussion and more details, if you feel like you need them.

By far, this set of required and recommended materials represents a nonpareil collection of sources and resources for service and support and for related topics. We anticipate that you'll find that this book belongs in this company. In the following section, we explain how this book works, and we give you some good reasons why this book counts as a member of the required and recommended materials list.

About This Book

Each topical *Exam Cram* chapter follows a regular structure, along with graphical cues about important or useful information. Here's the structure of a typical chapter:

➤ **Opening Hotlists** Each chapter begins with a list of the terms, tools, and techniques that you must learn and understand before you can be fully conversant with that chapter's subject matter. We follow the hotlists with one or two introductory paragraphs to set the stage for the rest of the chapter.

➤ **Topical Coverage** After the opening hotlists, each chapter covers a series of topics related to the chapter's subject title. Throughout this section, we highlight topics or concepts likely to appear on a test using a special Exam Alert layout, like this:

 This is what an Exam Alert looks like. Usually, an Exam Alert stresses concepts, terms, software, or activities that are likely to relate to one or more certification test questions. For this reason, we think any information found offset in Exam Alert format is worthy of unusual attentiveness on your part. Indeed, most of the information that appears on The Cram Sheet appears as Exam Alerts within the text as well.

Pay close attention to any material flagged as an Exam Alert. Although all the information in this book pertains to what you need to know to pass the exam, we flag certain items that are especially important. You'll find what appears in the meat of each chapter to be worth knowing, too, when preparing for the test. Because this book's material is highly condensed, we recommend that you use this book along with other resources to achieve the maximum benefit.

In addition to the Exam Alerts, we provide tips that will help you build a better foundation for service and support knowledge. Although the information may not be on the exam, it's certainly related and will help you become a better test-taker.

 This is how tips are formatted. Keep your eyes open for these, and you'll become an Service and Support expert in no time!

➤ **Practice Questions** Although we talk about test topics throughout each chapter, this section presents a series of mock test questions and explanations for both correct and incorrect answers. We also try to point out especially tricky questions by using a special icon, like this:

➤ Ordinarily, this icon flags the presence of a particularly devious inquiry, if not an outright trick question. Trick questions are calculated to be answered incorrectly if not read more than once, and carefully, at that. Although they're not ubiquitous, such questions make occasional appearances on the Novell tests. That's why we say test questions are as much about reading comprehension as they are about knowing your material inside out and backwards.

➤ **Details And Resources** Every chapter ends with a "Need To Know More?" section, which provides direct pointers to Novell and third-party resources offering more details on the chapter's subject. Additionally, this section tries to rank or at least rate the quality and thoroughness of the topic's coverage by each resource.

If you find a resource you like in this collection, use it, but don't feel compelled to use all the resources we cite. On the other hand, we recommend only resources we use on a regular basis, so none of our recommendations will waste your time or money. But purchasing them all at once probably represents an expense that many network administrators and would-be CNAs, CNEs, and MCNEs might find hard to justify.

The bulk of the book follows this chapter structure slavishly, but there are a few other elements that we'd like to point out. Chapter 13 includes a sample test that provides a good review of the material presented throughout the book to ensure you're ready for the exam. Chapter 14 presents an answer key to the sample test that appears in Chapter 13. We suggest you take the sample test when you think you're ready for the "real thing," and that you seek out other practice tests to work on if you don't get at least 75 percent of the questions correct. Additionally, you'll find a Glossary that explains terms and an index that you can use to track down terms as they appear in the text.

Finally, the tear-out Cram Sheet attached next to the inside front cover of this *Exam Cram* book represents a condensed and compiled collection of facts and tips that we think you should memorize before taking the test. Because you can dump this information out of your head onto a piece of paper before taking the exam, you can master this information by brute force—you need to remember it only long enough to write it down when you walk into the test room. You might even want to look at it in the car or in the lobby of the testing center just before you walk in to take the test.

Novell Terms

While studying for your Service and Support test, you may come across terms that we represent a certain way in our material, but that are represented differently in other resources. Some of these are as follows:

➤ **NetWare Administrator** You may see this referred to as NWAdmin in some resources; however, NWAdmin is not acknowledged by Novell as a copyrighted term. Try not to confuse NetWare Administrator with NETADMIN, which is the text-based version of NetWare Administrator available in earlier versions of NetWare.

➤ **Network board** A network board is also called a *network interface card* (NIC), *network adapter*, *network card*, and *network interface board*. Novell uses the term *network board* most often. However, the network board vendors usually refer to network boards as *NICs*.

➤ **Novell Directory Services (NDS)** You may also see this service referred to as NetWare Directory Services (it even appears as such on Novell's own Web site, **www.novell.com**). However, the official trademark name is Novell Directory Services.

➤ **NDS tree** The NDS tree is also called the Directory tree and sometimes it's simply referred to as the Directory (with a capital D).

One general source of confusion (as is the case with NDS) is that sometimes an "N" in an acronym is thought to stand for "NetWare" when it really stands for "Novell." As long as you know how to work the utility, you should be okay—the name isn't a huge issue.

As you'll notice while reading this book, a wide variety of acronyms are associated with service and support. Many of these acronyms have numerous expansions that mean the same thing. We'll insert notes pointing out some of these, and others will be mentioned in the Glossary.

How To Use This Book

If you're prepping for a first-time test, we've structured the topics in this book to build on one another. Therefore, some topics in later chapters make more sense after you've read earlier chapters. That's why we suggest you read this book from front to back for your initial test preparation. If you need to brush up on a topic or you have to bone up for a second try, use the index or table of contents to go straight to the topics and questions that you need to study. Beyond helping you prepare for the test, we think you'll find this book useful as a tightly focused reference to some of the most important aspects of the "Service and Support" test.

Given all the book's elements and its specialized focus, we've tried to create a tool that will help you prepare for—and pass—Novell Test 050-635, "Service and Support." Please share your feedback on the book with us, especially if you have ideas about how we can improve it for future test-takers. We'll consider everything you say carefully, and we'll respond to all suggestions.

Send your questions or comments to us at **cipq@coriolis.com**. Please remember to include the title of the book in your message; otherwise, we'll be forced to guess which book you're writing about. Also, be sure to check out the Web pages at **www.certificationinsider.com**, where you'll find information updates, commentary, and certification information.

Thanks, and enjoy the book!

Self-Assessment

Based on recent statistics from Novell, as many as 400,000 individuals are at some stage of the certification process but haven't yet received a CNA, CNE, or other Novell certification. We also know that easily twice that number may be considering whether to obtain a Novell certification of some kind. That's a huge audience!

The reason we included this Self-Assessment in this *Exam Cram* book is to help you evaluate your readiness to tackle CNE (and even MCNE) certification. It should also help you understand what you need to master the topic of this book—namely, Exam 050-635, "Service and Support." But before you tackle this Self-Assessment, let's discuss concerns you may face when pursuing a CNE and what an ideal CNE candidate might look like.

CNEs In The Real World

In the following section, we describe an ideal CNE candidate, knowing full well that only a few real candidates will meet this ideal. In fact, our description of that ideal candidate might seem downright scary. But take heart: Although the requirements to obtain a CNE may seem pretty formidable, they are by no means impossible to meet. However, you should be keenly aware that it takes time, requires some expense, and consumes substantial effort to get through the process.

More than 160,000 CNEs are already certified, so it's obviously an attainable goal. You can get all the real-world motivation you need from knowing that many others have gone before, so you'll be able to follow in their footsteps. If you're willing to tackle the process seriously and do what it takes to obtain the necessary experience and knowledge, you can take—and pass—all the certification tests involved in obtaining a CNE. In fact, we've designed these *Exam Crams* to make it as easy on you as possible to prepare for these exams. But prepare you must!

The same, of course, is true for other Novell certifications, including:

➤ **MCNE (Master CNE)** This certification is like the CNE certification but requires a CNE, plus four to six additional exams, across eight different tracks that cover topics such as network management, connectivity, messaging, Internet solutions, and a variety of hybrid network environments.

➤ **CNA (Certified Novell Administrator)** This entry-level certification requires passing a single core exam in any one of the five possible NetWare tracks, which include NetWare 3, NetWare 4/intraNetWare, and NetWare 5, plus GroupWise 4 and GroupWise 5.

➤ **Other Novell certifications** The requirements for these certifications range from two or more tests (Certified Novell Instructor, or CNI) to many tests, plus a requirement for minimum time spent as an instructor (Master CNI).

The Ideal CNE Candidate

To give you some idea of what an ideal CNE candidate is like, here are some relevant statistics about the background and experience such an individual might have. Don't worry if you don't meet—or don't come that close to meeting—these qualifications, this is a far from ideal world, and where you fall short is simply where you'll have more work to do:

➤ Academic or professional training in network theory, concepts, and operations. This includes everything from networking media and transmission techniques to network operating systems, services, protocols, routing algorithms, and applications.

➤ Four-plus years of professional networking experience, including experience with Ethernet, token ring, modems, and other networking media. This must include installation, configuration, upgrade, and troubleshooting experience, plus some experience in working with and supporting users in a networked environment.

➤ Two-plus years in a networked environment that includes hands-on experience with NetWare 4.x and, hopefully, some training on and exposure to NetWare 5 (which only started shipping in August 1998, so nobody outside Novell has years of experience with it—yet). Some knowledge of NetWare 3.x is also advisable, especially on networks where this product remains in use. Individuals must also acquire a solid understanding of each system's architecture, installation, configuration, maintenance, and troubleshooting techniques. An ability to run down and research information about software, hardware components, systems, and technologies on the Internet and elsewhere is also an essential job skill.

➤ A thorough understanding of key networking protocols, addressing, and name resolution, including the Transmission Control Protocol/Internet Protocol (TCP/IP) and Internetwork Packet Exchange/Sequenced Packet Exchange (IPX/SPX). Also, some knowledge of Systems Network Architecture (SNA), Digital Equipment Corporation Network (DECnet), Xerox Network System (XNS), Open Systems Interconnection (OSI), and NetBEUI is strongly recommended.

➤ A thorough understanding of Novell's naming methods, Directory services, and file and print services is absolutely essential.

➤ Familiarity with key NetWare-based TCP/IP-based services, including Hypertext Transfer Protocol (HTTP) Web servers, Dynamic Host Configuration Protocol (DHCP), Domain Name System (DNS), plus familiarity with one or more of the following: BorderManager, NetWare MultiProtocol Router (MPR), ManageWise, and other supporting Novell products and partner offerings.

➤ Working knowledge of Windows NT is an excellent accessory to this collection of facts and skills, including familiarity with Windows NT Server, Windows NT Workstation, and Microsoft implementations of key technologies, such as Internet Information Server (IIS), Internet Explorer, DHCP, Windows Internet Name Service (WINS), and Domain Name Service (DNS).

Fundamentally, this boils down to a bachelor's degree in computer science, plus three or more years of work experience in a technical position involving network design, installation, configuration, and maintenance. We believe that less than half of all CNE candidates meet these requirements, and that, in fact, most meet less than half of these requirements—at least, when they begin the certification process. But because all 160,000 people who already have been certified have survived this ordeal, you can survive it too—especially if you heed what our Self-Assessment can tell you about what you already know and what you need to learn.

Put Yourself To The Test

The following series of questions and observations is designed to help you figure out how much work you must do to pursue Novell certification and what types of resources you should consult on your quest. Be absolutely honest in your answers, or you'll end up wasting money on exams you're not yet ready to take. There are no right or wrong answers, only steps along the path to certification. Only you can decide where you really belong in the broad spectrum of aspiring candidates.

Two things should be clear from the outset, however:

➤ Even a modest background in computer science will be helpful.

➤ Hands-on experience with Novell products and technologies is essential for certification success. If you don't already have it, you'll need to get some along the way; if you do already have it, you still need to get more along the way!

Educational Background

1. Have you ever taken any computer-related classes? [Yes or No]

   If Yes, proceed to question 2; if No, proceed to question 4.

2. Have you taken any classes on computer operating systems? [Yes or No]

   If Yes, you'll probably be able to handle Novell's architecture and system component discussions. If you're rusty, brush up on basic operating system concepts, especially virtual memory, multitasking regimes, program load and unload behaviors, and general computer security topics.

   If No, consider some basic reading in this area. We strongly recommend a good general operating systems book, such as *Operating System Concepts*, by Abraham Silberschatz and Peter Baer Galvin (Addison-Wesley, 1997, ISBN 0-201-59113-8). If this title doesn't appeal to you, check out reviews for other, similar titles at your favorite online bookstore.

3. Have you taken any networking concepts or technologies classes? [Yes or No]

   If Yes, you'll probably be able to handle Novell's networking terminology, concepts, and technologies (brace yourself for occasional departures from normal usage). If you're rusty, brush up on basic networking concepts and terminology, especially networking media, transmission types, the OSI reference model, networking protocols and services, and networking technologies, such as Ethernet, token ring, Fiber Distributed Data Interface (FDDI), and wide area network (WAN) links.

   If No, you might want to read several books in this topic area. The two best books that we know of are *Computer Networks, 3rd Edition*, by Andrew S. Tanenbaum (Prentice-Hall, 1996, ISBN 0-13-349945-6) and *Computer Networks and Internets*, by Douglas E. Comer (Prentice-Hall, 1997, ISBN 0-13-239070-1). We also strongly recommend Laura Chappell's book *Novell's Guide to LAN/WAN Analysis* (IDG/Novell

Press, 1998, ISBN 0-7645-4508-6), because of its outstanding coverage of NetWare-related protocols and network behavior. In addition, Sandy Stevens and J.D. Marymee's *Novell's Guide to BorderManager* (IDG/ Novell Press, 1998, ISBN 0-7645-4540-X) is also worth a once-over for those who wish to be well-prepared for CNE topics and concepts.

Skip to the next section, "Hands-On Experience."

4. Have you done any reading on operating systems or networks? [Yes or No]

   If Yes, review the requirements stated in the first paragraphs after Questions 2 and 3. If you meet those requirements, move on to the next section, "Hands-On Experience."

   If No, consult the recommended reading for both topics. A strong background will help you prepare for the Novell exams better than just about anything else.

Hands-On Experience

The most important key to success on all Novell tests is hands-on experience, especially with NetWare 4.x, intraNetWare, and NetWare 5, plus the many system services and other software components that cluster around NetWare and appear on many of the Novell certification tests. These system services and software components include GroupWise, Novell Directory Services (NDS), Netscape FastTrack Server, and Micro House SupportSource. If we leave you with only one realization after taking this Self-Assessment, it should be that there's no substitute for time spent installing, configuring, and using the various Novell and ancillary products upon which you'll be tested repeatedly and in depth.

5. Have you installed, configured, and worked with:

   ➤ NetWare 3.x? NetWare 4.x? NetWare 5? [Yes or No]

   The more times you answer Yes, the better off you are. Please make sure you understand basic concepts as covered in Test 050-639, "NetWare 5 Administration" and advanced concepts as covered in Test 050-640, "NetWare 5 Advanced Administration."

   You should also study the NDS interfaces, utilities, and services for Test 050-635, and plan to take Course 580, "Service and Support," to prepare yourself for Test 050-635. To succeed on this last exam, you must know how to use the Micro House SupportSource product, which costs more than $1,000 for a yearly subscription, but to which you'll have a week's exposure and after-hours access in Course 580. (You can obtain a seven-day trial version of SupportSource from **www.supportsource.com**.)

 You can download objectives, practice exams, and other information about Novell exams from the company's education pages on the Web at **http://education.novell.com**. Use the "Certification|Test Info" link to find specific test information, including objectives, related courses, and so on.

If you haven't worked with NetWare, NDS, and whatever product or technology you choose for your elective subject, you must obtain one or two machines and a copy of NetWare 5. Then, you must learn the operating system and IPX, TCP/IP, and whatever other software components on which you'll be tested.

We recommend that you obtain two computers, each with a network board, and set up a two-node network on which to practice. With decent NetWare-capable computers selling for under $600 each, this shouldn't be too much of a financial hardship. You can download limited use and duration evaluation copies of most Novell products, including NetWare 5, from the company's Web page at **www.novell.com/catalog/evals.html**.

 For all of the Novell exams, check to see if Novell Press (an imprint of IDG Books Worldwide) offers related titles. Also, David James Clarke IV has recently completed NetWare 5 upgrades to his outstanding *CNE Study Guide* series. These books should be essential parts of your test preparation toolkit. Also, you can check our Web site at **www.coriolis.com** to see the many NetWare titles we have available.

6. For any specific Novell product that is not itself an operating system (for example, GroupWise, BorderManager, and so on), have you installed, configured, used, and upgraded this software? [Yes or No]

If the answer is Yes, skip to the next section, "Testing Your Exam-Readiness." If it's No, you must get some experience. Read on for suggestions on how to do this.

Experience is a must with any Novell product test, be it something as simple as Web Server Management or as challenging as NDS installation and configuration. Here again, you can look for downloadable evaluation copies of whatever software you're studying at **www.novell.com/catalog/evals.html**.

If you have the funds or if your employer will pay your way, consider checking out one or more of the many training options that Novell offers. This could be something as expensive as taking a class at a Novell Authorized Education Center (NAEC), or as cheaper options that include Novell's Self-Study Training programs, video- and computer-based training options, and even classes that are now available online. Be sure to check out the many training options that Novell itself offers, and the options it authorizes third parties to deliver, at **http://education. novell.com/general/trainopt.htm**.

Before you even think about taking a Novell test, make sure you've spent enough time with the related software to understand how it may be installed and configured, how to maintain such an installation, and how to troubleshoot that software when things go wrong. This will help you in the exam, and in real life!

Testing Your Exam-Readiness

Whether you attend a formal class on a specific topic to get ready for an exam or use written materials to study on your own, some preparation for the Novell certification exams is essential. At $95 a try, pass or fail, you want to do everything you can to pass on your first try. That's where studying comes in.

We have included a practice test in this book, so if you don't score that well on the first test, you need to study more and then locate and tackle a second practice test. If you still don't hit a score of at least 75 percent after two or more tests, keep at it until you get there.

For any given subject, consider taking a class if you've tackled self-study materials, taken the test, and failed anyway. The opportunity to interact with an instructor and fellow students can make all the difference in the world, if you can afford that privilege. For information about Novell courses, visit Novell Education at **http://education.novell.com** and follow the "Training|Training Options" link.

If you can't afford to take a class, visit the Novell Education page anyway, because it also includes pointers to a CD-ROM that includes free practice exams (it's called "The Guide" CD, and you can read more about it at **http://education.novell.com/theguide**). Even if you can't afford to spend much, you should still invest in some low-cost practice exams from commercial vendors, because they can help you assess your readiness to pass a test better than any other tool. The following Web sites offer practice exams online for less than $100 apiece (some for significantly less):

➤ **www.bfq.com** Beachfront Quizzer

➤ **www.certify.com** CyberPass

➤ **www.stsware.com** Self-Test Software

7. Have you taken a practice exam on your chosen test subject? [Yes or No]

If Yes, and your score meets or beats the cut score for the related Novell test, you're probably ready to tackle the real thing. If your score isn't above that crucial threshold, keep at it until you break that barrier.

If No, obtain all the free and low-budget practice tests you can find (see the previous list) and get to work. Keep at it until you can break the passing threshold comfortably.

Taking a good-quality practice exam and beating Novell's minimum passing grade, known as the *cut score*, is the best way to assess your test readiness. When we're preparing ourselves, we shoot for 10 percent over the cut score—just to leave room for the "weirdness factor" that sometimes shows up on Novell exams.

Assessing Readiness For Exam 050-635

Beyond the general exam-readiness information in the previous section, there are several things you can do to prepare for the "Service and Support" exam. As you're getting ready for Exam 050-635, visit the Novell Education forums online. Sign up at **http://education.novell.com/general/forumlogin.htm** (you'll need to agree to their terms and conditions before you can get in, but it's worth it). Once inside these forums, you'll find discussion areas for certification, training, and testing. These are great places to ask questions and get good answers or simply to watch the questions that others ask (along with the answers, of course).

You should also cruise the Web, looking for "braindumps" (recollections of test topics and experiences recorded by others) to help you anticipate topics you're likely to encounter on the test. The Novell certification forum at **http://www.saluki.com:8081/~2/** is a good place to start, as are the Forums at **www.theforums.com**, and you can produce numerous additional entry points by visiting Yahoo! or Excite and entering "NetWare braindump" or "Novell braindump" as your search string.

When using any braindump, it's OK to pay attention to information about questions. But you can't always be sure that a braindump's author will always be able to provide correct answers. Therefore, use the questions to guide your studies, but don't rely on the answers in a braindump to lead you to the truth. Double-check everything you find in any braindump.

Novell exam mavens also recommend checking the Novell Support Connection CD-ROMs for "meaningful technical-support issues" that relate to your test's topics. Although we're not sure exactly what the quoted phrase means, we have also noticed some overlap between technical support questions on particular products and troubleshooting questions on the tests for those products. For more information on these CD-ROMs, visit **http://support.novell.com** and click on the "Support Connection CD" link on that page.

Onward, Through The Fog!

After you've assessed your readiness, undertaken the right background studies, obtained the hands-on experience that will help you understand the products and technologies at work, and reviewed the many sources of information to help you prepare for a test, you'll be ready to take a round of practice tests. When your scores come back positive enough to get you through the exam, you're ready to go after the real thing. If you follow our assessment regime, you'll not only know what you need to study, but when you're ready to make a test date at Sylvan or VUE. Good luck!

Novell
Certification
Exams

Terms you'll need to understand:

√ Radio button

√ Checkbox

√ Exhibit

√ Multiple-choice question formats

√ Careful reading

√ Process of elimination

√ Adaptive tests

√ Form (program) tests

√ Simulations

Techniques you'll need to master:

√ Assessing your exam-readiness

√ Preparing to take a certification exam

√ Making the best use of the testing software

√ Budgeting your time

√ Guessing (as a last resort)

Exam taking is not something that most people anticipate eagerly, no matter how well prepared they may be. In most cases, familiarity helps offset test anxiety. In plain English, this means you probably won't be as nervous when you take your fourth or fifth Novell certification exam as you'll be when you take your first one.

Whether it's your first exam or your tenth, understanding the details of exam taking (how much time to spend on questions, the environment you'll be in, and so on) and the exam software will help you concentrate on the material rather than on the setting. Likewise, mastering a few basic exam-taking skills should help you recognize—and perhaps even outfox—some of the tricks and snares you're bound to find in some of the exam questions.

This chapter, besides explaining the exam environment and software, describes some proven exam-taking strategies that you should be able to use to your advantage.

Assessing Exam-Readiness

Before you take any more Novell exams, we strongly recommend that you read through and take the Self-Assessment included with this book (it appears just before this chapter). The Self-Assessment can help you gauge how your knowledge base stacks up against the requirements necessary for obtaining a CNE. Further, it can help you pinpoint areas of your background or experience that may be in need of improvement, enhancement, or further learning. If you get the right set of basics under your belt, obtaining Novell certification will be that much easier.

After you've gone through the Self-Assessment, you can remedy those topical areas where your background or experience may not measure up to an ideal certification candidate. What's more, you can also tackle subject matter for individual tests at the same time, so you can continue making progress while you're catching up in some areas.

After you've worked through an *Exam Cram*, reviewed the supplementary materials, and taken the practice test, you'll probably know when you're ready to take the real exam. We strongly recommend that you keep practicing until your practice scores top the 75 percent mark (although you might want to give yourself some margin for error, because in a real exam situation, stress plays more of a role than when you practice). When you can consistently earn high scores on practice tests, you should be ready to go. If you get through the practice exam in this book without attaining 75 percent, you should continue to take other practice tests and study the materials until you master the information. You'll find details about other practice test vendors in the Self-Assessment, along with pointers about how to study and prepare. But for now, let's discuss what happens on exam day.

The Exam Situation

When you arrive at the testing center where you scheduled your exam, you'll need to sign in with an exam coordinator. The coordinator will ask you to show two forms of identification, one of which must be a photo ID. After you sign in and your time slot arrives, you'll be asked to deposit any books, bags, cell phones, pagers, or other items you brought with you. Then, you'll be escorted into a closed room. Typically, the room will be furnished with anywhere from one to half a dozen computers, and each workstation will be separated from the others by dividers designed to keep you from seeing what's happening on someone else's computer.

You'll be furnished with a pen or pencil and a blank sheet of paper or, in some cases, an erasable plastic sheet and an erasable pen. You're allowed to write down anything you want on both sides of this sheet. Before the exam, you should memorize as much of the material that appears on The Cram Sheet (in the front of this book) as possible. You can then write that information on the blank sheet as soon as you're seated in front of the computer. You can refer to your rendition of The Cram Sheet anytime you like during the test, but you'll have to surrender the sheet when you leave the room.

Most test rooms feature a wall with a large picture window. This allows the exam coordinator to monitor the room, to prevent exam-takers from talking to one another, and to observe anything out of the ordinary that might go on. The exam coordinator will have preloaded the appropriate Novell certification test—for this book, that's Test 050-635—and you'll be permitted to start as soon as you're seated in front of the computer.

All Novell certification exams allow a certain maximum amount of time in which to complete your work (this time is indicated on the exam by an on-screen counter/clock, so you can check the time remaining whenever you like). Test 050-635, "Service and Support," is what Novell calls a *form test* or a *program test*. This test consists of a set of 79 questions and you may take up to 120 minutes to complete it. The cut score, or minimum passing score, for this test is 602 out of 800 (or 75 percent).

All Novell certification exams are computer-generated and use a combination of questions that include several multiple-choice formats, interactive illustrations (sometimes called *exhibits*), and simulations. In short, Novell provides plenty of ways to interact with the test materials. These tests not only check your mastery of facts and figures about network service and support, but they also require you to evaluate multiple sets of circumstances and requirements. Sometimes, you're asked to give more than one answer to a question (in these cases, though, Novell almost always tells you how many answers you need to choose). Sometimes, you're asked to select the best or most effective solution to a problem from a range of choices, all of which may be correct from a technical standpoint. Taking such a test is quite an adventure, and it involves real thinking. This book shows you what to expect and how to deal with the potential problems, puzzles, and predicaments.

Many Novell tests, but *not* the "Service and Support" exam, employ more advanced testing capabilities than might immediately meet the eye. Although the questions that appear are still multiple choice, the logic that drives them is more complex than form or program tests (like this exam), which use a fixed sequence of questions. Most Novell tests, including "Service and Support," that cover specific software products employ a sophisticated user interface, which Novell calls a *simulation*, to test your knowledge of the software and systems under consideration in a more or less "live" environment that behaves just like the original.

Eventually, most Novell tests will employ *adaptive testing*, a well-known technique used to establish a test-taker's level of knowledge and product competence. Adaptive exams look the same as form tests, but they interact dynamically with test-takers to discover the level of difficulty at which individual test-takers can answer questions correctly. Normally, when new tests are introduced in beta form (and for some time even after the beta is over), they are form tests. Eventually, most of these tests will be switched to an adaptive format. That is, after Novell has run its question pool past enough test-takers to derive some statistical notion of how to grade the questions in terms of difficulty, it can then restructure the question pool to make a test adaptive.

On adaptive exams, test-takers with differing levels of knowledge or ability see different sets of questions. Individuals with high levels of knowledge or ability are presented with a smaller set of more difficult questions, whereas individuals with lower levels of knowledge are presented with a larger set of easier questions. Even if two individuals answer the same percentage of questions correctly, the test-taker with a higher knowledge or ability level will score higher because his or her questions are worth more.

Also, the lower-level test-taker will probably answer more questions than his or her more-knowledgeable colleague. This explains why adaptive tests use ranges of values to define the number of questions and the amount of time it takes to complete the test. Sooner or later, we expect this test, 050-635, to become adaptive as well.

Adaptive tests work by evaluating the test-taker's most recent answer. A correct answer leads to a more difficult question (and the test software's estimate of the test-taker's knowledge and ability level is raised). An incorrect answer leads to a less difficult question (and the test software's estimate of the test-taker's knowledge and ability level is lowered). This process continues until the test determines a test-taker's true ability level (presenting a minimum of 15 questions to all test-takers). A test concludes when the test-taker's level of accuracy meets a statistically acceptable value. In other words, the test ends when the taker's performance demonstrates an acceptable level of knowledge and ability) or when the maximum number of items has been presented (in which case, the test-taker is almost certain to fail; no adaptive Novell test presents more than 25 questions to any test-taker).

Novell tests come in one form or the other—either they're a form test or an adaptive test. Therefore, you must take the test in whichever form it appears; you can't choose one type over another. If anything, it pays off even more to prepare thoroughly for an adaptive test than for a form test. The penalties for answering incorrectly are built into the test itself on an adaptive test, whereas the layout remains the same for a form test, no matter how many questions you answer incorrectly.

In the following section, you'll learn more about what Novell test questions look like and how they must be answered.

Exam Layout And Design

Some exam questions require you to select a single answer, whereas others ask you to select multiple correct answers. The following multiple-choice question requires you to select a single correct answer. Following the question is a brief summary of each potential answer and why it's either right or wrong.

Question 1

Ethernet is described as a contention-based system. Because of this, several devices may transmit simultaneously, which causes which of the following to be generated?

○ a. Collisions

○ b. Packet bursts

○ c. Large Internet Packets (LIPs)

○ d. Crosstalk

○ e. Merging of data packets with the same destination address

The correct answer is a. Several devices transmitting simultaneously cause collisions. Packet Burst is another protocol that permits several packets to be sent to the same destination in a burst. Therefore, answer b is incorrect. LIPs are designed for travel across routers. Therefore, answer c is incorrect. Crosstalk occurs when copper wires placed in parallel are used to transmit electrical energy. Therefore, answer d is incorrect. Because answer a is correct, there cannot be merging of data. Therefore, answer e is incorrect.

This sample question format corresponds closely to the Novell certification test format—the only difference on the test is that questions are not followed by answers. In the real test, to select an answer, you position the cursor over the radio button next to the correct answer (in this case, answer a) and then click the mouse button to select the answer.

Let's examine a question that requires choosing multiple answers. This type of question provides checkboxes rather than radio buttons for marking all appropriate selections.

Question 2

What are the main components of the Novell Client for Windows NT? [Choose the four best answers]

❏ a. NIOS.VXD

❏ b. NWFS.SYS

❏ c. CLIENT32.NLM

❏ d. NDIS or ODI drivers

❏ e. TCP/IP and/or IPX/SPX

The correct answers are b, c, d, and e. NIOS.VXD is the companion NWFS.SYS component found on a Windows 95/98 machine running the Novell Client. Therefore, answer a is incorrect.

For this type of question, more than one answer is required. As far as the authors can tell (and Novell won't comment), such questions are scored as wrong unless all the required selections are chosen. In other words, a partially correct answer does not result in partial credit when the test is scored. For Question 2, you have to check the boxes next to items b, c, d, and e to obtain credit for a correct answer. Notice that picking the right answers also means knowing why the other answers are wrong.

Although these two basic types of questions can appear in many forms, they constitute the foundation on which most of Novell's certification test questions rest. More complex questions include *exhibits*, which are usually screenshots of some kind of network diagram or topology, or *simulations*, which mock some NetWare administrative utility, installation program, or other system component. (This test, 050-635, contains both simulations and exhibits.) For some of these questions, you'll be asked to make a selection by clicking on a checkbox, entering data into a text entry box, or clicking on a radio button on a simulated screen. For others, you'll be expected to use the information displayed on a graphic to guide your answer to a question. Because software is involved, familiarity with important NetWare 5 administrative tools and utilities, as well as Micro House SupportSource, is the key to choosing the correct answer(s).

Other questions involving exhibits use charts or network diagrams to help document a workplace scenario that you'll be asked to troubleshoot or configure. Careful attention to such exhibits is the key to success. Be prepared to toggle frequently between the exhibit and the question as you work.

Test-Taking Strategy For Form And Adaptive Tests

When it comes to either kind of Novell test—be it a form test or an adaptive test—one principle applies: Get it right the first time. You cannot elect to skip a question and move on to the next one when taking either of these types of tests. In the form test, the testing software forces you to go on to the next question, with no opportunity to skip ahead or turn back. In the adaptive test, the adaptive testing software uses your answer to the current question to select whatever question it plans to present next. In addition, you can't return to a question after you've answered it on an adaptive test, because the test software gives you only one chance to answer each question.

On an adaptive test, testing continues until the program settles into a reasonably accurate estimate of what you know and can do, taking anywhere between 15 and 25 questions. On a form test, you have to complete an entire series of questions, which usually takes an hour or longer and involves many more questions than an adaptive test (79 questions for Test 050-635).

The good news about adaptive tests is that if you know your stuff, you'll probably finish in 30 minutes or less; in fact, Novell never schedules more than 60 minutes for any of its adaptive tests. The bad news is that you must really, really know your stuff to do your best on an adaptive test. That's because some questions are difficult enough that you're bound to miss one or two, at a minimum, even if you do know your stuff. Therefore, the more you know, the better you'll do on an adaptive test, even accounting for the occasionally brutal questions that appear on these exams.

Of course, it's also true on a form test that you must know your stuff to do your best. But for us, the most profound difference between a form test and an adaptive test is the opportunity to cover a broader range of topics and questions on the form test versus the randomness of the adaptive test. If the adaptive test engine happens to hit a hole in your knowledge base early in the testing process, it can make it harder for you to pass because the test engine probes your knowledge of this topic. On a form test, if some questions hit a hole, you can assume that other questions will appear that you'll be able to answer.

Either way, if you encounter a question on an adaptive test or a form test that you can't answer, you must guess an answer immediately. Because of the way the adaptive software works, you may have to suffer for your guess on the next question if you guess right, because you'll get a more difficult question next. On a form test, at least a lucky guess won't cost you in terms of the difficulty of the next question (but that doesn't mean the next question won't be a real skull-buster, too).

Test-Taking Basics

The most important advice about taking any test is this: Read each question carefully. Some questions may be ambiguous, whereas others use technical terminology in incredibly precise ways. Your authors have taken numerous Novell exams—both practice tests and real tests—and in nearly every instance, we've missed at least one question because we didn't read it closely or carefully enough.

Here are some suggestions on how to deal with the tendency to jump to an answer too quickly:

➤ Make sure you read every word in the question. If you find yourself jumping ahead in the question impatiently, read the question again.

➤ As you read, try to restate the question in your own terms. If you can do this, you should be able to pick the correct answer(s) much more easily.

➤ Some questions may be long and complex, to the point where they fill up more than one screen's worth of information. You might find it worthwhile to take notes on such questions and to summarize the key points in the question so you can refer to them while reading the potential answers to save yourself the effort of ping-ponging up and down the question as you read.

➤ Some questions may remind you of key points about NetWare tools, terms, or technologies that you might want to record for reference later in the test. Even if you can't go back to earlier questions, you can indeed go back through your notes.

Above all, try to deal with each question by thinking through what you know about NetWare 5, Micro House SupportSource, and troubleshooting networks. By reviewing what you know (and what you've written down on your information sheet), you'll often recall or understand things sufficiently to determine the answers to the questions you'll encounter on the test.

Question-Handling Strategies

Based on exams we've taken, some interesting trends have become apparent. For those questions that take only a single answer, usually two or three of the answers will be obviously incorrect, and two of the answers will be plausible—of course, only one can be correct. Unless the answer leaps out at you (if it does, reread the question to look for a trick; sometimes those are the ones you're most likely to get wrong), begin the process of answering by eliminating those answers that are most obviously wrong.

Things to look for in obviously wrong answers include spurious menu choices or utility names, nonexistent software options, and terminology you've never seen. If you've done your homework for an exam, no valid information should be completely new to you. In that case, unfamiliar or bizarre terminology probably indicates a totally bogus answer. In fact, recognizing unlikely answers is probably the most significant way in which preparation pays off at test-taking time.

Numerous questions assume that the default behavior of some particular utility is in effect. If you know the defaults and understand what they mean, this knowledge will help you cut through many potentially tricky problems.

Mastering The Inner Game

In the final analysis, knowledge breeds confidence, and confidence breeds success. If you study the materials in this book carefully and review all the practice questions at the end of each chapter, you should become aware of those areas where additional learning and study are required.

Next, follow up by reading some or all of the materials recommended in the "Need To Know More?" section at the end of each chapter. The idea is to become familiar enough with the concepts and situations you find in the sample questions that you can reason your way through similar situations on a real test.

If you know the material, you have every right to be confident that you can pass the test.

You should also visit (and print or download) the Test Objectives page for Course 580: Service and Support (**http://education.novell.com/testinfo/ objectives/580tobj.htm**). Here, you'll find a list of 33 specific test objectives that will help guide your study of all the topics and technologies that Novell thinks are relevant to the 050-635 test. In fact, you can use this list as a type of road map to help guide your initial studying and to help you focus your efforts as you gear up to take your practice test(s)—and then, for the real thing when you're ready.

After you work your way through this book and the Test Objectives page, take the practice test in Chapter 13. This will provide a reality check and help you identify areas to study further. Make sure you follow up and review materials related to the questions you miss on any practice test before scheduling a real test. Only after you've covered all the ground and feel comfortable with the scope of the practice test should you take the real one.

 If you take the practice test and don't score at least 75 percent correct, you'll want to practice further. Novell provides free practice tests on its "The Guide" CD. To obtain this CD, you must contact a local NetWare Authorized Education Center (NAEC) and request that one be sent to you. For more information on how to obtain this CD, you can use the Training Locator on the Novell certification pages at **http://education.novell.com** to locate the NAEC(s) nearest you.

Armed with the information in this book and with the determination to augment your knowledge, you should be able to pass the "Service and Support" test. However, you need to work at it; otherwise, you'll spend the exam fee more than once before you finally pass. If you prepare seriously, you should do well. Good luck!

Additional Resources

A good source of information about Novell certification tests comes from Novell itself. Because its products and technologies—and the tests that go with them—change frequently, the best place to go for test-related information is online.

If you haven't already visited the Novell Education site, do so right now. The Novell Education home page resides at **http://education.novell.com** (see Figure 1.1).

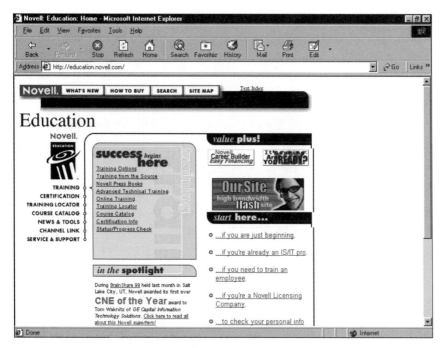

Figure 1.1 The Novell Education home page.

Note: This page might not be there by the time you read this, or it might be replaced with something new and different, because information changes on the Novell site. Should this happen, please read the sidebar titled "Coping With Change On The Web."

The menu options on the left side of the home page point to the most important sources of information in these pages. Here are some suggestions of what to check out:

➤ **Training** Use this link to locate an NAEC in your vicinity, to learn more about available training, or to request "The Guide" CD (which includes practice tests, among other materials).

➤ **Certification** This option is the ultimate source of all information about the various Novell certifications. Use this menu entry to find a list of the courses and related tests, including test objectives, test data, a testing FAQ (a list of frequently asked questions about Novell's testing policies, strategies, and requirements), and more.

➤ **News & Tools** Check this item to get news about new tests, updates to existing tests, obsolete tests that have been retired, and information about software and practice tests.

These are just the high points of what's available on the Novell Education pages. As you browse through them—and we strongly recommend that you do—you'll probably find other informational tidbits mentioned that are every bit as interesting and compelling.

The following vendors offer practice tests for Novell certification topics:

➤ **www.certify.com** is the Cyber Pass Web site. This company makes "CNEQuizr."

➤ **www.stsware.com** is the Self-Test Software Web site. This company makes practice tests for most of the Novell curriculum.

➤ **www.bfq.com** is the Beach Front Quizzer Web site. This company makes practice tests for most of the Novell curriculum.

➤ **www.syngress.com** is the Syngress Software Web site. This company has a set of NetWare 5 practice exams in the works. Visit the Web site for more information.

You can find still more sources of practice exams on the Internet if you're willing to spend some time using your favorite search engines.

Here's the bottom line about testing readiness: If you don't score 75 percent or better on the practice test in this book, you'll probably be well served by buying one or more additional practice tests to help you prepare for the real thing. It may even be cheaper than taking the Novell test more than once, and it will certainly increase the pool of potential questions to use as practice.

Coping With Change On The Web

Sooner or later, all the information we've shared with you about the Novell Education pages and the other Web-based resources mentioned throughout the rest of this book will go stale or be replaced by newer information. In some cases, the URLs you find here might lead you to their replacements; in other cases, the URLs will go nowhere, leaving you with the dreaded "404 File Not Found" error message. When this happens, don't give up.

There's always a way to find what you want on the Web if you're willing to invest some time and energy. Most large or complex Web sites—and Novell's qualifies on both counts—offer a search engine. On all of Novell's Web pages, a Search button appears along the top edge of the page. As long as you can get to Novell's Web site (it should stay at **www.novell.com** for a long time), you can use this tool to help you find what you need.

The more focused you can make a search request, the more likely the results will include information you can use. For example, you can search for the string

```
training and certification
```

to produce a lot of data about the subject in general, but if you're looking for the objectives for Test 050-635, "Service and Support," you'll be more likely to get there quickly if you use a search string similar to the following:

```
050-635 AND objectives
```

Also, feel free to use general search tools—such as **www.search.com**, **www.altavista.com**, and **www.excite.com**—to look for related information. Although Novell offers great information about its certification tests online, plenty of third-party sources of information and assistance are available that need not follow Novell's party line. Therefore, if you can't find something where the book says it lives, start looking around. If worse comes to worst, you can always email us. We just might have a clue.

What Is Service And Support?

Terms you'll need to understand:

√ Electrostatic discharge (ESD)

√ intraNetWare

√ SupportSource

√ Local area network (LAN)

√ Terminate-and-stay-resident (TSR)

√ Baseline data

√ Protocol analyzers

Techniques you'll need to master:

√ Configuring hardware, such as hard disks, network boards, and disk controllers

√ Configuring server and other networking software

√ Explaining the troubleshooting model, including investigating, diagnosing, fixing, and documenting the problem

√ Understanding and preventing electrostatic discharge (ESD)

√ Describing good service and support techniques

√ Using diagnostic and system support software

Support in a networking environment is nothing unique to Novell. In typical network troubleshooting and maintenance, one may tend to overlook procedures and poorly document actions. This chapter focuses on basics that apply to network and computer management, such as breaking down a troubleshooting hypothesis into the smallest reasonable, testable concepts.

This chapter focuses on Novell's service and support. In this chapter, you learn the tasks related to service and support, including using Novell's troubleshooting model and diagnostic tools, understanding network documentation, and learning about electrostatic discharge (ESD) and its prevention.

Service And Support Introduction

This chapter explains Novell's model of service and support to provide you with a foundation for further study. Service and support, as defined by Novell, is the installing, configuring, maintaining, and troubleshooting of hardware and software on a NetWare network. Your responsibilities vary, depending on the size and complexity of your organization's network.

You need to understand the concepts covered in this chapter to gain a solid knowledge of Novell's initiative for service and support. A solid foundation in troubleshooting and documentation is essential for computer and network support. The remainder of this book expands on these concepts and how each plays into the service and support ideal.

Troubleshooting Model For Networks

Troubleshooting, in general terms, is the process of investigation, diagnosis, repair, and documentation of problems. In this section, we explore each of these phases in detail. Troubleshooting always comes back to these four stages. The order of the troubleshooting model is also important. Imagine a doctor diagnosing you with the flu before he even takes your vital signs. Although this may sound silly, how many times have you seen someone jump to an incorrect diagnosis of why a computer cannot connect to another without investigating the problem? Both the order of the process and the elements of the process are equally important for productive and accurate service and support.

We troubleshoot hardware and/or software in an attempt to restore them to working condition in a timely manner. Troubleshooting isn't magic—it's more of a methodical art. As an artist becomes better with experience, so does a troubleshooter.

The basic troubleshooting process is similar to structured programming. Structured programming involves taking the goal of a project and breaking it into subprojects, further dissecting each subproject into the smallest possible chunks. Troubleshooting is nearly identical to that process in that the "big picture" problem generally cannot be attacked until it's divided, then conquered.

Stages Of Troubleshooting

Before you even begin formal troubleshooting, you need to gather data. You must understand what the desired outcome of the action should be. For example, the desired outcome might be when the user clicks on an icon, a Web browser launches and opens the user's home page. When a user says something isn't working correctly, there are generally three possibilities:

➤ The user has accidentally done something incorrectly.

➤ The process is working but it's taking longer than normal.

➤ The hardware and/or software has failed and there's an actual problem.

Let's examine the three possibilities. First, the user has accidentally done something incorrectly. The user could be clicking the wrong icon, or maybe the user is at a different workstation and hasn't logged in to the network. Isolating and eliminating the user as the source of the problem is crucial because the user generates the greatest likelihood of fault.

The second condition is that the process is working, but the user does not recognize it. It's possible that the Web page is indeed launching, but it's taking twice the amount of time as it usually does. This doesn't mean that something has failed entirely, but the user believes it has failed. The important element to grasp is to effectively manage the expectation of the user and establish how the item used to work and why he or she believes it's not working now.

The third condition invokes formal troubleshooting because something is really not working. You arrive at this step by eliminating the first two. Problem elimination occurs when the original condition is no longer impacting the user.

Formal Troubleshooting Procedure

When troubleshooting a network, there are simple solutions and more complex solutions. The following is literally a simple procedure for troubleshooting; however, it's important to remember that you're also trying to isolate and then solve the problem:

1. **Make sure the user hasn't made an error.** Walk the user through the problem. Ask questions such as, "When did you first notice this?" or

"Has anything been installed or changed on this computer?" to attempt to narrow the troubleshooting focus. Sometimes, when someone else is watching, everything works fine, but as soon as you walk away, the problem reoccurs. Make sure both you and the user can perform the task successfully. The problem is not resolved until the user says the problem is resolved.

2. **Check all the network components.** If the computer case was opened for a maintenance task, see if a cable was bumped loose. The computer may have been moved recently and something jostled loose in the process. Check whether the cables are connected upside down. Newer cable connectors attempt to prevent this, but it's still a possibility with older systems. Check that the component indicating a failure is actually installed. This may sound silly, but instances do occur when you try to figure out why sound on a computer isn't working, for example, only to discover the computer doesn't have a sound card installed.

3. **If storage devices are included, back up your data.** Always have a back-up plan. Never assume a software install that you've done a thousand times will work this time. Never assume that simply moving a hard drive from one computer to another will not lose data. Hard drives can sometimes mysteriously disappear from your desk. Prior to working any storage-related issue, you should back up your data. Along with backups, you should test restoring data. Just because it's backed up doesn't mean you can restore it. Prove it.

4. **Reboot the equipment.** There comes a realization in computing that sometimes you just need to reboot the machine. Networking and computing are not ideal worlds. Programs leak memory, dynamic link libraries (DLLs) fail to be dynamic, and sometimes programs do not work well together. When this happens, you should reset the hardware. Some systems running in corporate environments are rebooted on a scheduled basis because the administrators recognize that things can fail after a given runtime. Sometimes, problems just go away following a reboot.

5. **Simplify the system.** Simplifying the system happens in one of two ways. Using a computer for an example, boot the computer using the bare-bones configuration by eliminating terminate-and-stay-resident (TSR) programs, any automatically loaded programs, and any optional components added during the life of the computer. Then, gradually introduce each of these back into the system until the failure occurs. The second option is to gradually eliminate component by component until the problem is identified. Using either option, only add or reduce a single item at a time during the problem isolation phase. If you remove

five components, reboot, and the problem is gone, you can't identify which of the five components caused the problem. Although you have possibly narrowed the scope, you still must reintroduce each item individually to isolate the cause.

6. **Investigate security and permissions.** Let's say you can run one program but not another. Alternatively, let's say you can access one network drive but not another. The problem may involve either system security or object permissions (also called *rights*). If a user cannot print to a printer, ask the user to try printing to another printer. Should one work and the other fail, security or permissions could be the culprit.

7. **Evaluate program versions.** When we say to *evaluate program versions*, we imply that a particular version of a software product may have a known bug or quite possibly lack the feature the user is trying to execute. The version of software installed on the user's desktop may be incompatible with a server version of accompanying software. Version checking is not inherently obvious and is often overlooked.

After you've checked everything in the previous list, it's time to get serious. The following sections should be followed, in order, to provide you with an effective troubleshooting procedure.

1. Collect The Basic Information

Information gathering is the process of collecting relevant information to aid in troubleshooting. Let's use a sample troubleshooting scenario. A user, Laura, calls and complains that she cannot log in to the network. At this point, you need to gather information. Understand that Laura might be upset over this event or under pressure to produce a report located on a network drive, and may be reluctant to answer questions. Ask her when the problem started. Ask her how she knows she's not logged in to the network. Another unrelated error might have popped up and she assumed she wasn't logged in. Ask her if anyone else is experiencing the problem. If she says she's the only one who cannot log in, try to determine the approximate time of the failure. Was she able to log in yesterday or the day before? Most modern network software provides extensive error-logging capabilities and may provide clues.

2. Develop A Problem Isolation Plan

You're still working with the user who cannot connect to the network, and you're beginning to put together a troubleshooting plan. Using your networking and computer knowledge, attempt to narrow the focus of the investigation. Try to determine what caused this problem, build a list of two or three possible errors (such as the network, a user error, or failed software), and include them in a list.

Now that you have a list, prioritize it to determine the order in which to work on them. One method is to list the problems in the order of likelihood. If one problem is more likely than another, it makes sense to work on that one first. For example, an unplugged cable is more likely than a broken network backbone; therefore, determine if the cable is unplugged first. Work prioritization should also consider ease of implementing the fix. If your first guess will take two hours to investigate, but the second only takes two or three minutes, do the second one first.

3. Execute The Plan

Now that you've planned the work, it's time to work the plan. If the first choice is a failed network connection, divide that item into smaller and smaller items. Your goal here is similar to making your first list. List all the components that make up the big-picture task and evaluate the likelihood of occurrence and the ease of implementation. It's much easier to check the computer cable connection than it is to put a packet sniffer on the network.

Using the list you made for the user who cannot connect to the network, one guess was to check network connectivity itself. The following is a list of digestible tasks related to network connectivity to check:

➤ Is the network cable connected to the computer?

➤ Is the network cable connected to the LAN jack in the wall?

➤ Is the cable damaged in any way?

➤ Is a networking protocol loaded?

➤ If you're using TCP/IP, can you ping other servers?

 Connectivity checks can (and must) be made with all network protocols, not just ping for TCP/IP. Also, ping checks just low-level functionality on IP—use more advanced utilities to make sure there's more than just a functioning IP stack on the destination. (This is a common error in troubleshooting Windows NT networks—NT often crashes with just a functioning partial IP stack running. Ping works, but nothing else.)

Using the task list we developed, change one item at a time and try to connect to the network again. Remember never to change more than one item at a time, so you don't complicate the problem.

When troubleshooting a problem such as network connectivity, you can choose two directions. One direction is away from the client, and the other is toward the client. The direction away from the client is known as *forward chaining*, and the direction toward the client is known as *reverse chaining*. Because the problem seems to be isolated to an individual client, use forward chaining in an attempt to work the problem from the client out to the network.

Related to testing, use only tested tools and software to troubleshoot the problem. Imagine troubleshooting this problem only to determine the cable from the computer to the wall outlet is bad or the cable-testing tool used to troubleshoot the network is malfunctioning.

4. Solution Documentation

The most frequently overlooked troubleshooting tool is information—using it, recording it, and updating it. Many engineers spend hours troubleshooting a problem only to find out that others already knew about it and failed to document it. A mileage log is a great example of something used to record information. It's easy to maintain, but somehow it's never complete when it's needed. After you identify a problem and its solution, document both the problem and the solution. If no formal documentation system exists, write the information down in a notebook. Preferably, the information regarding problems and solutions is recorded in a database or problem-tracking system. Maintaining the information in this manner allows you to search the information for possible solutions and track the time spent on troubleshooting problems. This information could then be used to identify possible causes of failure, which could then result in the replacement of the failed components or user training classes. Even if all you have is a notebook, it's better suited to retain information than your memory. Remember to document *everything*.

Examples of appropriate documentation are baseline information and statistical analysis. When a server is installed and used normally, you should perform a baseline analysis. A baseline analysis establishes a basis for trends and future planning. For example, if you place a server into production today, you would want to establish some baseline data about that server, such as percent processor utilization gathered every 15 minutes over the course of 48 hours. This data shows explicitly when CPU utilization was high and how high it was, as well as when it was low and how low it was. If you gather this data once a month, you'll begin to see processor trends and anticipate when the CPU will require upgrading.

 The Novell Support Connection CD and Web site are invaluable resources for troubleshooting Novell networks. You can order the CD and peruse the Support Connection Web site at **http:// support.novell.com**.

Electrostatic Discharge

We've all experienced static electricity before. Someone glides across the carpet, then a touch of the hand, and *zap*. The zap you feel when this happens is more than sufficient to incapacitate electronic components. This section addresses electrostatic discharge (ESD), how to avoid it, and how to develop and implement an ESD prevention plan.

What Is Electrostatic Discharge?

Static electricity is an electrical charge caused by an imbalance of electrons on the surface of material. This imbalance of electrons produces an electric field that's measurable and that can influence other objects at a distance. *ESD* is the transfer of the charge between bodies at different electrical potentials.

To feel ESD, it must reach approximately 3,000 volts. How much is 3,000 volts? If you simply move your foot, you can generate about 1,000 volts, which is not enough to even notice. To do damage to an electronic component, only 20 to 30 volts are actually required. Because this voltage is less than perceptible, in an ESD-managed environment, we are actually doing damage to every electronic component we touch. If we're doing so much damage, why do things keep working?

 Tiny ESDs of 20 to 30 volts represent a hazard to electronic devices. Remember that ESDs are a potential cause of component failure.

Amazingly, direct physical contact is not required for a static charge to build. A static charge can develop on a physical component or on the equipment and personnel directly related to the manufacturing, packaging, delivery, and installation of the component. These little ESDs of 20 to 30 volts, although not perceptible by humans, are detectable by sensitive measuring instruments. This slight voltage can actually degrade the electronic components over time instead of instantly. Of course, if we zap a network board with 30,000 volts, we might get a pile of goo, but only 20 to 30 volts will be imperceptible. The damage, of course, occurs over time. Ninety percent of the time, damage incurred by electronic components is gradual rather than instantaneous.

ESD Control Program Benefits

As a Novell professional, it's important that you support ESD programs and encourage your customers to do the same. In case your customer is not aware of the benefits of an ESD control program, we've listed some here:

➤ Reduced hardware inventory

➤ Reduced downtime

➤ Fewer intermittent hardware problems

➤ Reduced service calls

➤ Happier customers

Preventing Electrostatic Discharge

The key to protecting equipment from ESD is to prevent static electricity from occurring. Although you can't eliminate static electricity completely, you can greatly reduce its occurrence and effect. Novell has some rules that can help mitigate the effects of static electricity:

➤ Ground equipment and ground yourself. Do this before working on any printed circuit board or electronic component. Accomplish grounding using grounding wrist straps and mats. Computer systems generally have grounded plugs, but they do not guarantee ground connections. Test all grounds daily to ensure personal devices and equipment stay properly grounded.

   Note: Wrist straps should not be used when working on monitors. Monitors carry a large voltage capable of reaching you through the wrist strap, which can cause shock and possible injury.

➤ Never touch circuit boards or any electronic component by its leads or connectors.

➤ Other people should not touch you while you're working on circuit boards or any electronic components.

➤ Use static-preventing (also called *static-shielding*) bags when storing or moving electronic components. If the bag has one little hole, it's no good. If in doubt, throw it out. Note that there are other types of bags called *antistatic bags*. These are usually blue or pink and don't protect against external static fields.

➤ Keep nonconductive materials away from electronic components. Polyester clothing, Styrofoam cups, and plastics generate significant static charges quickly.

➤ Never directly place an electronic component on another conductive material, such as metal. It's very easy to place memory chips on top of the server you're working on and zap them without even knowing it.

➤ Regulate the humidity. Keep humidity levels between 70 and 90 percent. Lower humidity levels exacerbate static buildup.

There are several key aspects of an ESD program to monitor on an ongoing basis. Elements of inspection should include storage areas, the technicians themselves, shipping and receiving areas, and the actual work areas. Technicians shouldn't wear jewelry, keep objects in their pockets (such as pocket pens), or wear static-prone clothing (such as polyester).

 Common ESD program violations include leaving a Styrofoam cup or a polyester tie next to open computer components.

Documentation

An old saying states that history repeats itself. Previously in this chapter, we discussed troubleshooting. Information that's both readily available and accurate aids the troubleshooting process. In this section, we discuss how to manage and collect documentation and the types of information you need to keep. Whether your network is large or small, documentation will justify the time investment required to produce the documentation. According to Novell, you should document the components, history, and resources of your LAN.

Documenting The Components Of The LAN

You should document LANs using manual methods or software automation tools, such as Novell's ManageWise. Documenting a LAN helps you troubleshoot and resolve networking problems. The following documentation categories will help you troubleshoot your network.

Network Map

A *network map* is just like a state map of Florida. The map of a state identifies cities, state boundaries, county boundaries, bodies of water, coastlines, and tourist attractions. A network map does the same thing, except with networking components. It's a representation of the physical locations and layouts of networking components within a floor or building. Generally, a network map is a scaled, graphical representation of the actual layout of the equipment. The network map simply helps you find the location of a component. If you have a very large network, you understand the benefit. You should include users and workstations on your network map.

Applications are available to help you create network maps. These include ManageWise, Visio, and OpenView.

LAN Inventory

A *LAN inventory* is a list of components. You should keep an inventory so you never have to guess whether something has possibly been stolen or is missing. The components you should inventory include printers, computers, monitors, and software. If you know the serial number, model number, description, and location of the missing component, it'll be easier to find. Asset management is performed either manually by recording this information for each piece of equipment or software or though applications that interrogate the machine and retrieve serial number and software configuration information.

Network Cabling Documentation

Wiring closets can be a nightmare. No teenager's room can possibly compare to a wiring project gone bad. Cabling documentation should include a point-to-point drawing of the wiring. A crisis is the wrong time to determine where a cable is *supposed* to go. Additionally, you should label and color-code network cables.

Wiring is color coded so you can trace color and cable, not simply a sea of yellow or red. Many manufacturers sell hand-held label printers specifically designed for network cable. Labels are installed every few feet of a run so when you're staring at a bundle of wires, you can determine which one is which.

There's a standard for wiring in commercial buildings—the Electronic Industries Association/Telecommunications Industry Association (EIA/TIA) Commercial Building Wiring Standard. For more information, search for EIA/TIA with your favorite Web browser.

Workstation Documentation

Workstation documentation, except in the smallest of networks, is gathered through automated means. Several software products are available to gather this information, such as ManageWise from Novell, Systems Management Server (SMS) from Microsoft, and HP OpenView from Hewlett-Packard.

Each product allows you to periodically examine network clients and gather specific information about them—for example, type and speed of processor, amount and type of memory, and so on. This information is used when considering system upgrades or for inventory management.

Change Log

Which version of NetWare is running on each of your 500 servers? When were patches applied and who applied them? When did you upgrade your Web server's memory, and how much did it have before the upgrade? All this information is captured in a change log. A *change log* is exactly that: a record of changes made to a component. That change may be software or hardware, but the log includes who, what, when, where, and why. Keeping track of this information starts a history of significant life events that is essential in maintaining a computing environment.

Documenting The History Of The LAN

You need to know who owns the Web server on the second floor, and why you have six Web servers when you thought you only needed four. If you documented the history of the LAN, you'd know. You need to record the history so you don't keep repeating the same mistakes. Keeping a history of the LAN gives you distinct advantages. This information aids you when you must justify why memory is needed or when a processor upgrade is considered. If you have a server that needs a memory upgrade within 60 days or it'll exceed capacity and you need to justify the upgrade, you'll have a much stronger argument if you have facts to support it. LAN history enables you to manage the information decision-makers require to make a large capital expenditure.

The Business Environment

The way a company does business dictates how it uses its network. Although we sometimes look at a network from the technology perspective, the business drives why we build it and what we build. It's important to document not only the network but also the business drivers and justifications of why it's the way it is. Understanding the business requirements helps define the human factors involved for more informed troubleshooting.

User Information

User information is the most difficult to obtain and is therefore gathered the least often. User information may be a list of all the training courses each user attended or the physical location of the user and his or her phone number. This information is not just valuable as a type of phone book, it also helps you understand the levels of computer training your users have.

Past Problems

Problems will repeat. Maybe not in the exact manner as before, but usually they will be so similar that the solution found the first time will work the second and third times a problem occurs. Problem documentation needs to include not only the problem but also a solution. These are referred to as *problem/resolution pairs*. Each problem should have an associated solution, date, and location, as well as enough additional information so a person unfamiliar with the problem can re-create it. This information also benefits ongoing problem analysis to pinpoint problem equipment or software (or users).

Baseline Information

Remember when you rode in your first new car? Remember the smell and the odometer reading 16 miles? The information your brain recorded is a baseline. When anything happened to that car, you mentally compared it to your baseline information. You started to see degrading performance and poorer gas mileage. *Baseline information* in a computer system is the initial measurement to which you refer back and compare the present operating conditions. You do this to evaluate changing conditions over time. This helps us identify problems that will occur before they occur.

 Search your favorite Web browser for "help desk software" for various types of software you can use to help you document this information.

Usage Patterns

Let's go back to the car example again. Let's say your dad knew you drove to and from school every day, which was exactly 12 miles, round trip. He also knew something was awry when 42 miles registered when only 12 were expected. Dad determined a usage pattern for your car. Without that, he would never have known that 42 miles happened to be abnormal. Usage patterns for a network help us predict peak periods of bandwidth utilization. You could compensate by rescheduling administrative jobs to run during other periods or by scheduling a software upgrade during the lowest use period of a month. Usage patterns help you understand how your systems are used as well as when and how much.

Documenting Resources Used With A LAN

Resources used with a LAN can be anything not previously mentioned, such as firewall configurations and domain routing tables. Tracking resources allows you to find them when you need them. Novell divides the resources into two general areas: technology and technical support.

Technology

Routing tables, protocol information, LAN architectures, Domain Name Service architectures, and extranet configurations are all examples of technologies you need to document. This information refers more to the technological aspects of how you do the things you do rather than simply the identification of a router or firewall. The method you use for intrusion prevention is an excellent example of technology documentation.

Technical Support

This category is simplest, but one of the most underused. It's 2:00 A.M. and your ecommerce Web server dies. Who do you call? This is where the documentation of available technical support comes in handy. A technical support list can consist of people to call, their pager numbers, immediate and supplementary actions for problems, and a URL list for technical support Web sites. Anything referenced to technically support a system should be included in this category.

Diagnostic Software

Diagnostic software has been around for some time, and many different types are available. As with any software, each differs in price, functionality, and quality. Novell references two specific titles of system and diagnostic software: WinCheckIt and CheckIt Pro (DOS-based). For reference, WinCheckIt is now available in a Windows 98 version. Microsoft includes Microsoft System Diagnostics (MSD) with DOS 6.22 and higher. All three of these products offer similar functionality and perform the following functions:

➤ Determine facts about the hardware and operating system

➤ Inventory internal components

➤ Perform system benchmarking

➤ Check and list interrupt requests (IRQs), Direct Memory Access (DMA), I/O addresses, and memory settings

➤ Edit the complementary metal oxide semiconductor (CMOS)

➤ Collect system information to determine software conflicts

➤ Employ hardware-testing tools to diagnose system components

➤ Provide memory tune-up tools

➤ Have uninstall utilities

➤ Have unused file clean-up utilities

Practice Questions

Question 1

> What is the minimum level of ESD that will cause equipment damage?
>
> ○ a. 50,000 volts
>
> ○ b. 20 to 30 volts
>
> ○ c. 200 to 300 volts
>
> ○ d. 2,000 to 3,000 volts

The correct answer is b. Only 20 to 30 volts are required to do damage to an electronic component. If you want to melt an electronic component, 50,000 volts would do the job. Therefore, answer a is incorrect. 200 to 300 volts would definitely do some damage, but it's not the minimum. Therefore, answer c is incorrect. For a human to feel ESD, it must reach approximately 3,000 volts. Therefore, answer d is incorrect.

Question 2

> What information does a network map provide? [Choose the two best answers]
>
> ❑ a. User locations
>
> ❑ b. Protocol implementations
>
> ❑ c. Equipment locations
>
> ❑ d. Equipment configuration

The correct answers are a and c. A network map is a scaled, graphical representation of the actual layout of the equipment. The network map helps you find the location of a component. When you have a lot of equipment, you'll understand the benefit. Users and workstations are often included on a network map. Protocol implementations are part of technology documentation. Therefore, answer b is incorrect. Equipment configuration information is kept in the workstation documentation. Therefore, answer d is incorrect.

Question 3

> What basic information should you collect prior to beginning system trouble-
> shooting? [Choose the three best answers]
>
> ❑ a. The existing symptoms and users affected
>
> ❑ b. Network logs to determine baseline performance
>
> ❑ c. Configuration logs from all computers in the server room
>
> ❑ d. Usage and activity levels

The correct answers are a, b, and d. Basic troubleshooting begins with an in-
formation-gathering phase. In this phase, determination of affected users,
identification of symptoms, baseline component performance, system usage,
and activity levels are all essential to problem identification. It's not necessary
to gather logs from all computers in the server room, because log-gathering is
a time-consuming and unnecessary task for this situation. Therefore, answer c
is incorrect.

Question 4

> Which of the following statements regarding ESD is false?
>
> ○ a. About 90 percent of the time, ESD causes components to degrade
> but not immediately fail.
>
> ○ b. Normal movements, such as lifting a chair, can generate static
> charges of 1,000 volts.
>
> ○ c. Low humidity of 20 to 30 percent will minimize static buildup.
>
> ○ d. Computer components are damaged with ESD as low as 20 to
> 30 volts.

The correct answer is c. You're more likely to experience getting shocked in
cold conditions because the humidity is very low. Have you ever been on a
tropical beach and been shocked? Humidity levels of 70 to 90 percent will
minimize static buildup. Answers a, b, and d are all true regarding ESD and are
therefore incorrect.

Question 5

Which of the following is an appropriate method for transporting a network board?

○ a. In a shipping box with Styrofoam packing material

○ b. In an antistatic bag

○ c. Network boards are not affected by ESD

○ d. In a static-shielding bag

The correct answer is d. The gray/silver static-shielding bags protect their contents from ESD. Styrofoam in any form exacerbates the buildup of static electricity. You should not ship electronic components in any Styrofoam material. Therefore, answer a is incorrect. Antistatic bags are not static-shielding bags and do not protect electronic components from ESD. Antistatic bags are generally tinted pink or blue and should not be used to transport electronic components. Therefore, answer b is incorrect. All electronic components are susceptible to ESD, including network boards. Therefore, answer c is incorrect.

Question 6

Which two diagnostic software programs could you use to gather information on your system's IRQs, I/O addresses, and memory addresses?

❑ a. CheckIt Pro

❑ b. WinCheckIt

❑ c. Novell Support Connection

❑ d. CheckWare

The correct answers are a and b. Novell Support Connection is a service provided by Novell that includes very valuable information for troubleshooting networks, but it's not used to gather information on your system's IRQs, I/O addresses, and memory addresses. Therefore, answer c is incorrect. CheckWare is not a software program currently in existence. Therefore, answer d is incorrect.

Need To Know More?

 Clarke, David James IV. *Novell's CNE Study Set: Guide to IntranetWare/NetWare 4.11 and Guide to Core Technologies.* Novell Press, San Jose, CA, 1997. ISBN 0-76454-533-7. This is one of the few books available with good coverage of service and support.

 www.microhouse.com is Micro House's SupportSource page. It's an excellent resource for vendor specifications and troubleshooting information.

 http://support.novell.com is Novell's Support Connection Website. Search by using the keyword "troubleshooting" for a plethora of information about troubleshooting.

Troubleshooting Tools

. . . .

Terms you'll need to understand:

√ Browser

√ Internet Service Provider (ISP)

√ Knowledgebase

√ Novell Support Connection Web site and CD-ROM

√ File Transfer Protocol (FTP)

√ Uniform Resource Locator (URL)

√ SupportSource

√ Micro House Technical Library (MTL)

Techniques you'll need to master:

√ Accessing the Internet

√ Accessing the Novell Support Connection Web site

√ Searching for files and technical documents on the Web site

√ Installing and querying the SupportSource application

√ Installing and querying the MTL

√ Choosing the appropriate tool for research based on the project

√ Understanding the differences between Support Connection on CD-ROM and on the Web

Finding the correct information transforms troubleshooting from a painful exercise to a less painful experience. Troubleshooting always takes more time and resources than planned, because the very nature of troubleshooting is dealing with the unplanned, unscheduled, and unknown.

If experience is the ability to recognize a mistake the second time you make it, then this troubleshooting tools chapter will help you gain experience more quickly than you can blundering around on your own.

Novell provides a wide variety of information to help you deal with the complexities of NetWare. Third parties also make help available, such as this book full of NetWare information. Line your troubleshooting resources up early and you can avoid panic situations later. The resources you'll learn about in this chapter include Novell reference materials on CD-ROM and its Web site, as well as the third-party CD-ROM database by SupportSource. We'll also briefly cover some other tools, including LANalyzer.

Available Novell Internet Services

Chances are the Internet is probably already part of your daily life. The Internet is a worldwide, high-speed, publicly accessible collection of networks based on the Internet Protocol (IP), which is a communications protocol. Almost every technology company is on the Internet, including Novell, and the day when every company in the world must have Internet access to conduct its business isn't too far away. Novell's Web site has a plethora of information on it. Here's a list of just some of what you can find:

➤ Files, patches, fixes, and updates

➤ Novell's Buyer's Guide

➤ Technical information documents (TIDs)

➤ User forums for exchanging information with peers

What You Need To Access Online Troubleshooting Tools

The technical world is quickly moving from paper documentation to online documentation. There are several prerequisites to accessing Novell's troubleshooting trove of information. First, of course, you must get there (the Novell Web site), meaning you must have access to the Internet and experience with a Web browser.

Connecting To The Internet

Before worrying about specific Web sites, you must have access to the Internet in general. Several methods, with attendant prerequisites, provide Internet access. Some of the methods available include the following:

➤ **TCP/IP on your workstation** This is the protocol of the Internet and the only protocol suite allowed on the Internet since January 1, 1983. Microsoft Windows 95/98 and Windows NT include TCP/IP acceptable for Internet access. Unix, Linux, OS/2, BeOS, and any other up-and-coming operating systems now must provide Internet access and a full TCP/IP suite.

➤ **An IPX-to-TCP/IP gateway** Several companies, including Novell, make gateways that convert IPX packets on the local network into TCP/IP packets for travel across the Internet. Security is increased with this method, because outsiders cannot see past the IPX-to-IP gateway into your network. However, the market has declared TCP/IP to be the protocol of choice for local and Internet traffic, so Novell now offers full TCP/IP protocol support for client-to-server communications, eliminating the need for the gateway. Of course, the security advantage is eliminated as well, but we won't cover that in this chapter.

➤ **Internet Service Provider (ISP)** A company that links customers who connect to its site via dial-up phone lines, dedicated lines, Integrated Services Digital Network (ISDN), Frame Relay, or some other method to the Internet at large. Once reaching the ISP, users are authenticated and passed upstream to the Internet. These companies normally charge users a monthly fee rather than a per-hour connection charge.

Note: Novell Directory Services (NDS) version 8 was scaled up to work for the number of users supported by ISPs.

➤ **Major online provider (such as America Online)** Millions of computer users reach the Internet through AOL or CompuServe. These services were once the entire online world for their users, but now they provide access to the Internet through built-in or third-party Web browsers. There are limitations with this approach, mostly in the limited download and email formats supported. These companies normally charge each user a monthly fee, although some pricing plans start charging per hour after a connection time limit has been reached.

The requirements for Novell Internet services are an Internet connection, TCP/IP on the workstation or IPX to IP gateway, and an ISP or online provider (CompuServe or AOL).

The standard Internet connection for medium to large companies is a network-based router that links to an ISP. Every network client then has access to the Internet.

Small companies are moving toward the same model, and many products are aimed at the small and home office markets for growth and new product sales. Costs have dropped so drastically for network connection hardware that even the smallest company can afford to reach the Internet with some type of pooled service, rather than connecting modems to each computer.

Web Browser Operation

A *browser* is an application that reads Web page text and graphics over a network connection of some type and formats the information for proper display. Although browser technology is invading corporate networks at a tremendous rate, browsers were originally developed for Internet use.

Mosaic was the first publicly available browser and defined the new technology in early 1994. Today, Mosaic and all other browsers are victims of the war between Microsoft Internet Explorer and Netscape Navigator, now owned by America Online.

Browsers of all types work by interpreting hyperlinks—special code on Web pages that connects the viewer to files. Those other files may be text, graphics, or even application-type files that perform a function, such as downloading a file. The most common method of indicating a hyperlink of some type is to change the cursor to a hand with a pointing finger when the cursor moves over a hyperlink on a Web page. Text hyperlinks are almost always in a different color and are underlined to stand out.

Hyperlinks, when followed (left-clicked once when the cursor is in finger-pointing mode), may do any of the following:

➤ Connect to additional text

➤ Display an explanatory graphic

➤ Begin a file download

➤ Start a search through a database

➤ Open a form for user input and storage on the Web site

After a hyperlink is followed, all browsers offer a back (left) arrow to return to the linking page. Good Web page design instructs Web designers to include navigational tools on every page, making it easy for users to go forward, backward, or back to the start of a section (home).

A helpful menu pops open for most browsers with a right-click of the mouse. The Back option moves back a page to the linking page, just like the left-pointing arrow that should be placed on the page by the designer.

Bookmarks are virtual updates of the paper bookmark, which tracks your place for easy location later. A browser bookmark does the same thing by copying the address into a file kept on your local system and maintained by the browser application. Your browser menu will offer Bookmarks or Favorites (or something similar) and will display all the saved bookmarks when prompted. Useful troubleshooting sites and information sources should be bookmarked so you can easily access them the next time you're troubleshooting a problem.

Web addresses usually follow the **www.***something*.com format. This is called a Uniform Resource Locator (URL), sometimes pronounced U-R-L and sometimes "earl." The **www** part of the URL is not mandatory.

Novell's Web Site

Novell's main Web site, **www.novell.com**, offers a wide range of information about Novell products and the company itself. As you might expect, the information leans heavily toward presales, but that makes sense for the main Web page. Although the Novell Web site continually changes, there are some constant elements. For example, there are four hyperlink buttons across the top of the screen (see Figure 3.1). Although the layout might change, chances are the following selections will be available on the Novell Web site for quite a while:

➤ **What's New** This is an excellent place to start. This selection leads you to the latest press releases, Webcasts, news about Novell clipped from computer, business, and consumer magazines and papers, and plenty of corporate information.

➤ **How To Buy** This selection links to lists of resellers by location, online resellers, products direct from Novell, and even Novell-logo merchandise in case you need another computer-company T-shirt. Packaged solution descriptions for various types of companies help lead customers and prospects in the proper direction.

➤ **Search** This selection allows you to search all of **www.novell.com** or all the product documentation. Several of the most popular search topics are gathered and hyperlinked for you, such as Year2000, Client32, and Technical Support.

Figure 3.1 The Novell home page.

➤ **Site Map** A well-designed site makes it easy to get around, and Novell is no exception. The Site Map shortcuts plenty of locations by providing headlines that should lead you to what you want.

The good thing about these four hyperlink buttons is that they're currently available on every Novell Web site screen. Any time you feel the need to search, you're only one click away.

Along the left side of the screen is a series of hyperlinks that changes based on the primary screen display, similar to menus and submenus. Currently—and these are subject to change (see the "Coping With Change On The Web" sidebar in Chapter 1)—the hyperlink menu choices are as follows:

➤ Products And Solutions

➤ Technical Support

➤ Partners

➤ Developers

➤ Company Information

➤ Training & Services

➤ Promotions & Events

➤ Free Downloads

➤ Year 2000

➤ International Sites

Many of these links hide completely different Web sites, such as Developers and Training & Services. Also, the Technical Support selection links directly to **http://support.novell.com**, which is the focus of this chapter.

Feature stories rotate regularly, as do the links for Novell In The News and the like. However, the hyperlink buttons across the top and down the left side stay the same—at least for the vast majority of Novell Web pages.

Technical Support From The Novell Support Connection

You can reach the Novell Support Connection site from the main Web page or by going directly to **http://support.novell.com**. You should bookmark this Web site to save those few seconds next time you're in troubleshooting mode.

The Novell Support Connection CD (a monthly subscription and update service) is not as current as the Web site because the content posted to the Web site is not shipped in CD-ROM form until the following month. However, the Support Connection CD program includes a complete set of AppNotes and Developer Notes. These virtual magazines might not troubleshoot your particular problem, but they do provide valuable information about all Novell products.

Site Assistant

If you're new to the Novell Support Connection, your first stop should be the Site Assistant link. The hyperlink is (currently) the top-right choice under the main headline banner. Once clicked, you'll see the following options (as shown in Figure 3.2):

➤ **Frequently Asked Questions** This includes how to find the latest clients, files, patches, and technical information.

➤ **Sound Advice via RealPlayer audio clips** This provides you with audio information about the Support Connection site. The RealPlayer download button is also available for you to download and install the RealPlayer software if you don't currently have it.

As you scroll down the Site Assistant page, you'll see a listing of all Frequently Asked Questions (FAQs) and their answers. This is for those users who prefer to scroll rather than hyperlink on the same long page.

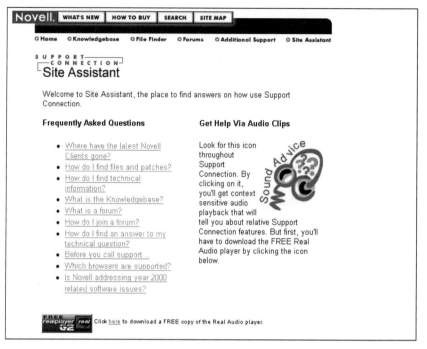

Figure 3.2   The Site Assistant in the Support Connection Web site.

The Site Assistant contains valuable information for anyone new to Support Connection. It's an excellent place to start when you're searching for critical information.

Forums

Across the top line near the middle is the Forums hyperlink, where veteran System Operators (SysOps) answer thousands of questions per week. Many of the SysOps are Novell employees, and all SysOps are experienced and willing to help.

The Forums area is also a good place to locate other NetWare administrators facing the same types of problems as you. Knowing others are in a similar predicament will make your plight less lonely. Additionally, the problem you're facing this week may be one several compatriots solved last week.

Incident Tracking

Once an issue is started with Novell support, the status can be checked electronically. Using the personal identification number (PIN) provided by the support person during the initial call, a user can log in to the Incident Tracking page by providing his or her last name, email address, and password, if one was assigned.

Technical Information And Knowledgebase

Finding information about particular problems is facilitated in two ways that overlap somewhat: the product manuals and technical information documents (TIDs). The Knowledgebase hyperlink, up on the top of the screen near the Forums and Site Assistant hyperlinks, shows a huge range of technical documents, each solving a particular problem. As you can see in Figure 3.3, you can search by product and by topic. Additionally, if you pull down the menu in number 2, you can choose to search the product manuals or the product manuals and TIDs.

File Downloads Galore

One of the best ways to fix a problem is to update the software causing the problem. With a software application as large and complex as NetWare, multiple patch files may be required.

The Knowledgebase often recommends files for downloading, and a text-input search window can be accessed using the File Finder selection next to the Knowledgebase selection at the top of the Support Connection page. On the File Finder screen, you'll see several ways to find your file, such as:

➤ Enter Filename

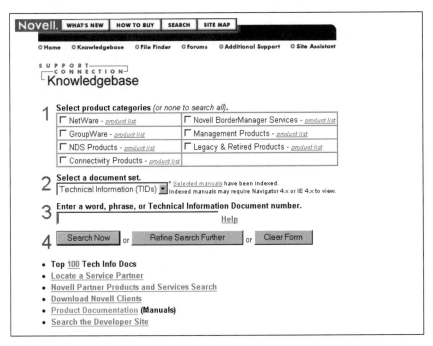

Figure 3.3 The Novell Support Connection Knowledgebase site.

➤ Browse Files By Product

➤ Minimum Patch List (also reachable from the home page)

➤ New Files This Week

➤ Novell Downloadable Software Index

➤ Download Novell Clients

There should be no file that escapes detection with all these options. All files are thoroughly scanned for viruses before being put on the Web site.

Before Calling Support

Chances are very slim that you'll ever have a problem that no one else in the NetWare world has had. Additionally, in the heat of a troubleshooting moment, some obvious answers may be overlooked. This is why Novell puts a hyperlink on the Support Connection home page called Before Calling Support.

It's funny to hear stories about users who didn't have electrical power and called tech support because their system didn't work, or the ones who broke a cupholder. This won't happen to you, but sometimes details are overlooked. Sometimes, Novell describes a procedure that doesn't work exactly as advertised.

When you click on the Before Calling Support hyperlink, you'll find listings for each main product area. For instance, there are areas for BorderManager, Directory Services, ManageWise, client issues, and instructions for installing the five-user Oracle test software. Check these out before calling technical support. Better yet, check these out before you start feeling like you have to fix everything in the world all at one time.

 If you do end up calling Novell tech support, remember to have your credit card in hand because Novell does charge for its tech support.

Chasing Files

A common exercise in troubleshooting, as well as helping customers, is downloading files for some reason. Let's take a standard scenario and step through how you would find and download several different files to solve several different problems.

There are several ways to accomplish the same thing. Our way is just one of many. Novell intentionally puts a variety of paths to each answer into its Web site. If you find the file you need, you're successful, no matter which path you take.

Finding NetWare 5 Client Files

A customer needs the latest NetWare 5 client files for a new Windows 98 workstation. In this section, we'll cover two ways you can accomplish this. In this first example, it takes seven steps to access those files:

1. Start your browser and load **http://support.novell.com**.

2. Click on File Finder.

3. Click on Download Novell Clients.

4. Scroll down to Clients - Network.

5. Click on Client v3.1 for Windows 95/98 English.

6. Read the information to verify this is the correct file.

7. Click on Proceed To Download.

However, there's a shorter way:

1. Start your browser and load **http://support.novell.com**.

2. Click on the drop-down list box that shows Product Specific Support and scroll down to Novell Client v3.0 For Windows 95/98.

3. Look down the page until you see the Download Novell Software button and click on it.

4. Read the information to verify this is the correct file.

5. Click on Proceed To Download.

We shaved two steps off our search, which won't save all that much time, but it does show that there are at least two ways to reach the same download screen. True, the front screen isn't as current as the actual file on the download screen, but the Novell Webmasters did lead us to the most current file.

Always look closely at the screen for hints on quick ways to find what you need. Don't always jump at the first likely option you see.

Self-Test

In this section, we're going to provide an example that will help you become familiar with the Knowledgebase documents. A customer is having trouble getting his NetWare Dynamic Host Configuration Protocol (DHCP) to recognize the intelligent uninterruptible power supply (UPS). There's a document in the Knowledgebase that addresses this issue. To find it, you would follow these steps:

1. Access **http://support.novell.com**.

2. Click on the Knowledgebase label near the top of the screen.

3. Type the words "DHCP UPS" in the search field (upper- or lowercase).

4. Peruse the list offered by the search engine.

The first item covers a PS/2 Model 70 problem; however, you don't have a Model 70 problem. Therefore, you wouldn't need to read this TID. The second TID, titled "Disaster Prevention and Recovery," however, does cover the problem. When in doubt, check the most current article first. Sometimes, the process won't be this easy, and you may need to refine several searches before finding a solution.

Micro House's SupportSource

NetWare (as does any network) relies on a large number of hardware parts from a mind-numbing number of vendors, and Novell can't keep up with the details for every single part. Luckily, several third-party vendors have made up-to-date technical information their specialties.

For years, Novell has encouraged the use of the Micro House Technical Library (MTL) along with its SupportSource CD set. Updated quarterly, these CD-ROMs offer the best information available on virtually every hardware component used in any PC.

Micro House Technical Library (MTL)

The SupportSource CD contains the search engine and interfaces used to access and query installed Knowledge Modules. These Knowledge Modules contain various types of data, including the MTL. Novell recommends use of the MTL to research hardware details. The MTL contains databases of information separated into the following categories:

➤ **Hard Drive Controller Cards** Contains diagrams, documentation, jumper settings, performance specifications, and component locations on over 1,500 various hard drive controllers

➤ **Hard Drives** Covers information on over 4,000 hard drives, such as number of heads, size, cylinders, write precompensation, tracks per sector, and Mean Time Between Failures (MTBF)

➤ **Optical Drives** Contains details on over 400 types of CD-ROM and CD-RW (Read/Write) drives

➤ **Tape Drives** Contains details on almost 300 types of tape drives, including interface, format, and size information

➤ **Mainboards** Covers information on over 7,000 motherboards, such as diagrams, documentation, connections, cache configuration settings, memory configurations, jumper settings, and component locations

➤ **Data Communications Devices** Contains information on over 2,500 types of LAN boards, WAN boards, specifications, and jumper settings

➤ **Telecommunications Devices** Contains information on over 2,000 types of modems, ISDN adapters, and other telecom devices

➤ **Video Controller Cards** Contains details on over 1,500 types of video boards

➤ **Miscellaneous I/O Controller Cards** Contains information on thousands of I/O interfaces, as well as serial, parallel, and sound devices and their configuration information and jumper settings

➤ **Micro House Technical Guide Series** Contains documents from the Modem, Hard Disk, and Network Technical Guides

➤ **Manufacturers** Contains nearly 4,000 vendor company details, including Web site addresses

➤ **FCC ID Locator** Contains a reverse directory listing of manufacturers by checking the FCC ID numbers

Remember that the SupportSource CD and the MTL databases are two separate items, at least officially. The standard interface, until recently, has been a two-paned window with tabbed information for easy access to text and graphics. The screen display may be modified to suit the user by arranging window placement and toolbars.

The included search engine has always been able to query any installed Knowledge Modules. SupportSource provides an Internet server that facilitates database searches on hundreds of other hardware-related Web sites. Access to manufacturer's Web sites is also part of the package.

Believe it or not, there are network boards that are not included in the MTL list. However, Novell certainly encourages a rather narrow list of hardware proven to do an outstanding job, and these will almost always be included. Client components are a different matter, of course, because the performance demands are less. The closer you stick to mainstream brands of PCs, the more luck you'll have finding the components listed in the MTL. Only when you wander off into the strangest clones will you run across hardware missing from the MTL.

Component details can be printed from the SupportSource display interface. You should print out the pages that describe the components you use and keep them handy to speed up troubleshooting.

Extra Neat Stuff In The MTL

Filling up a component database is hard when sticking only to actual components. Because Micro House understands the people using its materials, it added some background and references pieces, such as the following:

➤ Searchable glossaries on general networking terms, modems, and hard disks

➤ A searchable database that contains detailed information on various manufacturers

➤ A node ID setting quick reference

➤ A document containing ways to resolve common disk problems

➤ An appendix that contains details about the specific cabling used for various network topologies

Notice that many of the previous items are searchable. Having data such as this on a CD-ROM or on a Web site makes it much easier to search than notebooks. Besides, carrying four fat notebooks full of technical documentation is much harder than carrying a CD-ROM and a laptop computer on which to run it.

Hardware Requirements For SupportSource

The mention of a laptop in the previous section brings up the minimum hardware requirements needed to run the SupportSource CD. You shouldn't find these requirements a problem, although the practical recommendations follow the minimums, which are as follows:

➤ 8MB RAM (16MB recommended)

➤ 10MB hard disk space available (50MB recommended)

➤ 486 CPU (Pentium of some type)

➤ 4X CD-ROM (faster is recommended)

➤ Mouse

➤ VGA (800 by 600 mode or higher)

➤ Windows 3.1 or above (Windows 95 and above or Windows NT recommended)

You'll have no trouble finding a laptop to meet these requirements. In fact, your executives may have thrown systems better than these into the junk closet a year or two ago. Dig one out and dedicate it for traveling administrators, and you'll be in good shape.

Know the hardware requirements necessary to run SupportSource.

SupportSource Installation

SupportSource is moving to a Web-based mode with a browser interface. However, you do need to know how to install the MTL in the CD-ROM version. But first, we're going to cover the installation of the SupportSource CD-ROM itself. You can set up the SupportSource CD-ROM as a NetWare volume or install it on a local PC.

To install the SupportSource CD-ROM as a NetWare volume, follow these steps:

1. Map two drives—one to the server volume that will hold the Support-Source application and one to the CD-ROM volume (this is for installation purposes).

2. Double-click on the SETUP.EXE file from the SupportSource CD-ROM.

3. Specify the drive to use for installation (the server volume you specified in Step 1) and the name of the installation directory.

4. Answer any other questions presented.

When completed, your local machine will have a SupportSource program group. Other machines must map a drive to the SupportSource directory and run the WSETUP.EXE file to copy the local programs, including the program group information, to their systems.

The first station running the SupportSource program must provide registration information. You must provide at least the first and last names of the primary user, the company, and the registration number. The Knowledge Module, separate applications (remember), must be unlocked for all to uses them.

The modules are locked to guard against piracy. To install and unlock a Knowledge Module, follow these steps:

1. Start SupportSource by clicking on the SOURCE.EXE file in the location you chose.

2. Choose Add|Edit Knowledge Modules from the File menu.

3. In the Knowledge Modules dialog box, click on Add.

4. Select the appropriate SSM (Support Source Module) files from the CD-ROM. (Choose MTL.SSM for the Micro House Technical Library.)

5. Provide the correct Knowledge Module serial number in the Knowledge Modules dialog box (see Figure 3.4) and click on Done.

6. Accept the license agreement, and you're ready to go.

   Note: *The SupportSource screenshots in this chapter are taken from the trial version. The version you receive may be slightly different, but the general concepts will be the same.*

Quarterly updates are installed in a similar manner. The updates can't keep up with every new board immediately but will match up as soon as possible.

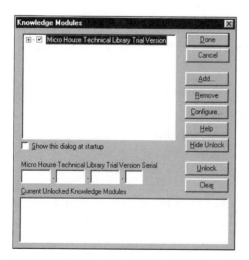

Figure 3.4   The Knowledge Modules dialog box requiring the serial number.

Operating SupportSource

As one might expect from an electronic information database, the help is online rather than in thick manuals. When necessary, hit the F1 key, click the Help menu item, *or* drag the question mark to the item confusing you.

There are three primary screen sections that you can access in SupportSource:

➤ **Document Viewer** There are three tabs available in the Document Viewer pane (see Figure 3.5):

  ➤ Document

  ➤ Summary

  ➤ Company

  You use the zoom pointer to increase or decrease illustration or document magnification—use a right-click to decrease the magnification and a left-click to increase it. Any available diagrams are shown in the Document section.

➤ **Data Tree** This pane allows you to browse the data tree and look for general information or specific documents.

➤ **Query Assistant** This pane allows you to search through the database in an organized manner. The Query Assistant is accessed by choosing Search|Show Query Assistant. (We cover the Query Assistant in the following section.)

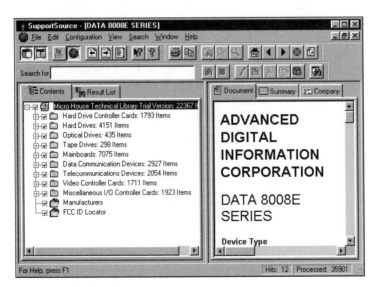

Figure 3.5   The Document Viewer view.

When you open a new document, the previous document does not automatically close. You must manually close a document by clicking on the X in the upper-right corner of the document window or choosing Close from the File menu.

Note: *As with other applications, if you click the X in the top-most right corner of the screen, you close the application completely.*

Searching SupportSource

A CD-ROM holds far too much information to put what you're looking for at the moment on the front page. This is especially true because you'll most likely be looking for something different every time you access SupportSource.

The Data Tree view shows a hierarchical list of documents in the database. General documents and reference information may actually be found more quickly this way than using the other search options. Specific hardware details require more specific searches, however. You use the Query Assistant to do this.

The Query Assistant assembles a query by providing a dialog box to help you narrow the search parameters (see Figure 3.6). The dialog box is a tabbed page, with the following tabs:

➤ Hard Drive Controller Cards

➤ Hard Drives

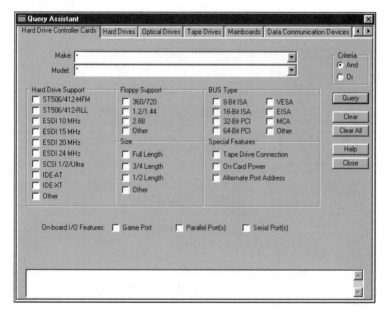

Figure 3.6 The Query Assistant.

➤ Optical Drives

➤ Tape Drives

➤ Mainboards

➤ Data Communication Devices

➤ Telecommunication Devices

➤ Video Controller Cards

➤ Miscellaneous I/O Controller Cards

➤ FCC ID Locator

Each tabbed page provides varying numbers of checkboxes. You left-click in each checkbox that represents an important requirement for the primary item being searched. There are also drop-down lists that contain manufacturers and model numbers.

For example, if you're looking for information about the jumpers on a Seagate hard drive model number ST510808, you would perform the following steps:

1. In the Query Assistant, select the Hard Drive tab.

2. In the Make menu, scroll down until you find Seagate Technology Inc. and select it.

3. In the Model menu, scroll down until you find the model number ST51080A.

4. Click on Query.

Figure 3.7 shows the correct selections made in the Query Assistant. The results are shown in the Result List tab (see Figure 3.8), and if you browse the Document tab's information, you'll see a table that contains the jumper information.

If you're looking for a hard drive controller from Adaptec, you would choose the Hard Drive Controller Cards tab, choose Adaptec, Inc. from the Make menu, and then choose any other necessary specifications, such as the type of drive to support and the system bus available.

The more you narrow your search, the faster the search happens. Why churn through hundreds of hard drive controllers that don't include a serial I/O port if you really need the I/O port on your system? Verify what you need and make your queries as specific as possible.

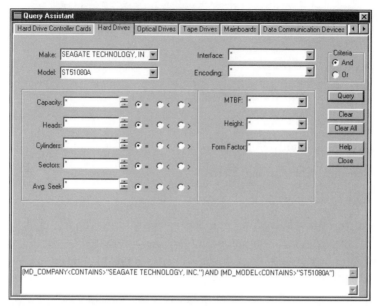

Figure 3.7 The correct selections made in the Query Assistant.

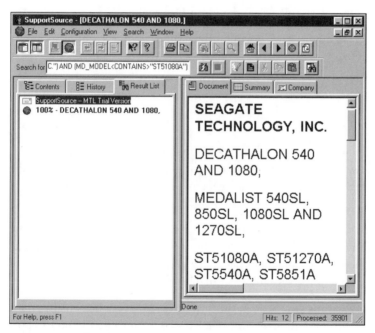

Figure 3.8 The results as shown in SupportSource.

When you have a document that might answer your question, use the Find dialog box to hunt for specific text strings in the document.

Here are some tips that can help you create more efficient searches:

➤ When long-winded queries turn up no matches, reduce the number of words in the search.

➤ Pick the proper section of the Knowledge Module to search.

➤ Verify that all other databases are excluded from your search.

➤ Use Boolean operators (the default is AND).

➤ Clear existing queries before you start a new one.

When you have a chance to use a SupportSource CD, play around a bit. Find all the reference items and check out important additions, such as the Manufacturer Directory.

 We suggest that you download the trial version of SupportSource (**www.supportsource.com/mtltrial/whatis.htm**) and spend some time familiarizing yourself with the Query Assistant. Give yourself little tests. How many platters does the hard drive in your server have? Are there any jumpers to set on your video controller board? How many memory banks are available on 350MHz or above motherboards? Play around a little and indulge your curiosity.

SupportSource Goes To The Web

These changes aren't reflected in the Novell course materials available during the writing of this *Exam Cram* book, but SupportSource and the MTL have undergone many changes recently.

First, SupportSource 2.1 includes automatic updating of directories from the SupportSource Web site. CD-ROM updates are no longer necessary.

Second, Micro House was acquired by EarthWeb Inc. in late March of 1999. EarthWeb includes the Developer.com and ITKnowledge.com services, as well as Datamation. ITKnowledge, for example, contains hundreds of technical books online, including full text and code samples.

Finally, the ubiquity of the Web (it's everywhere) makes it possible to eliminate the use of CD-ROMs for large amounts of reference material. A Java-based applet running on any Netscape Navigator or Microsoft Internet Explorer browser (version 4 or above) will handle all the same duties done by the CD-ROM version.

No client installation process will be required for the new version of Support-Source, labeled SupportSource 2000, except for the browser to support the Java applet. All data will remain online on the SupportSource Web site, meaning changes and updates are available immediately without the need to create and deliver CD-ROM update disks.

Looking For Answers In All The Right Places

Network administrators are rarely given the luxury of a leisurely search for answers when the network is down. It's hard to relax and take it slow when people are upset because they can't reach the network resources they need for their jobs.

Knowing which research resources have the type of information you'll likely need to solve a problem can save valuable time. Each of the resource areas discussed so far has its strengths and weaknesses, and we'll cover each in this section.

The three research resources we'll examine are the following:

➤ Novell's Support Connection Web site

➤ Novell's Support Connection CD

➤ SupportSource and MTL

Advantages And Disadvantages Of Each Research Tool

Troubleshooting is not a zero-sum game in which only one resource has the correct answer. The goal of this section is to help you look in the most likely place to find the correct answer to a problem in the shortest time possible. Sometimes, the choice is made for you. If you're going to a customer site that may not have Internet access, online resources won't do you much good. However, if you're working from the office with a fast Internet connection, it may actually be faster to download driver files than look for the latest CD-ROM and search it.

Novell Support Connection

As you might guess, the content of Novell's Support Connection CD and Web site overlap quite a bit. Realize that the same information may be found in each place. However, they do have some differences, which you'll learn about in this section.

The Novell Support Connection Web site has many advantages:

➤ It's very easy to use because of its browser-based interface.

➤ It contains more information on Novell than any other resource.

➤ You can interact with other administrators through newsgroups, mailing lists, and forums on the site.

➤ It always contains the most up-to-date drivers, files, patches, and news about Novell products.

The advantages of the Support Connection Web site definitely outweigh the disadvantages. Here are the only disadvantages that can occur with the Web site:

➤ You must have a modem.

➤ If you have an ISP that still charges on a per-minute basis, the cost could get quite high.

Advantages of the Novell Support Connection CD include the following:

➤ Like the Support Connection Web site, the CD-ROM version is also very easy to use. It has a browser-based interface that's familiar to most NetWare administrators.

➤ Internet access is not required because it's on a CD-ROM, which also makes it portable.

➤ A single-license fee allows unlimited use.

➤ You can keep previous copies of the CD-ROM, which contain drivers and patches for older equipment and installations.

Once again, the advantages out weigh the disadvantages. The disadvantages of the Novell Support Connection CD include the following:

➤ Because the CD-ROM can't be updated like the Web site, it's out-of-date the minute it leaves Novell.

➤ You can't interact with other administrators through CD-ROM like you can the Web site.

➤ CD-ROMs are easy to lose.

Table 3.1 provides you with a quick reference that shows you which features are available on the Support Connection Web site and CD-ROM.

The first four items in Table 3.1 are common to both the Support Connection Web site and the CD-ROM. The last four vary back and forth. Remember

Vital Table 3.1 A yes/no feature chart for the Support Connection Web site and CD-ROM.		
Content	**Web**	**CD-ROM**
Product information	Yes	Yes
Patches/updates	Yes	Yes
Technical information documents	Yes	Yes
Novell Labs reports	Yes	Yes
Product manuals	No	Yes
Support forums	Yes	No
Application Notes	Optional	Yes
Developer Notes	Optional	Yes

that the Support Connection Web site is free, whereas the CD-ROM set, which gets updated each month, requires a subscription fee.

 At the time the Novell tests and this book were written, Novell documentation was only available on the Support Connection CD-ROM. However, the product documentation is now available online.

Both the Application Notes and Developer Notes newsletters are available for order through the Novell Web site. For that matter, so is the Support Connection CD yearly license.

SupportSource

The other reference material we discussed was Micro House's SupportSource CD. The advantages of the SupportSource CD include the following:

➤ It contains an almost complete listing of computer hardware.

➤ The excellent diagrams contained in the Document section of the descriptions make it easy to identify the hardware in question.

➤ The SupportSource CD is portable.

Disadvantages of the SupportSource CD include the following:

➤ As with other CD-ROM-based reference materials, it's out-of-date the minute it leaves SupportSource.

➤ Again, CD-ROMs can be lost or forgotten, which makes the information unavailable to an offsite administrator.

➤ If the CD-ROM is accessed via the network, the information may be unavailable to an offsite administrator.

Like many research databases, SupportSource is moving to a 100 percent browser-based model with the SupportSource 2000 version. The vast majority of the research databases will maintain both online and CD-ROM versions, but time and CD lag-time will push everyone to the Web sooner or later.

One extra advantage of Web access for research tools is the reach beyond your primary research targets to the rest of the world. SupportSource and Novell's Support Connection both update their files quickly, but the vendors always have the files first. Using the Internet as your primary research resource means you'll be able to check a vendor's Web site directly if SupportSource and Support Connection don't have what you need.

Sample Troubleshooting Scenarios

Everyone needs some practice using research tools, so in this section, we'll provide you with some sample troubleshooting scenarios. Remember that answers can come from a variety of different places and still be correct.

Upgrading Directory Services

You have a customer with a NetWare 4.11 server who needs to upgrade the DS.NLM file and support files. What's the easiest and quickest way to obtain this file (or files)?

> *Note: It's not fair, unless you're in marketing, to suggest the customer upgrade to NetWare 5. That's a valid point in real life, but not for this situation.*

See if you can do this in six steps or less:

Step 1: _____

Step 2: _____

Step 3: _____

Step 4: _____

Step 5: _____

Step 6: _____

Did you find the necessary file(s)? Let's see one way to solve this research problem:

1. Open your browser and load the **http://support.novell.com** Web site.

2. From the menu on the left of the page, click on Minimum Patch List.

3. In the Table Of Contents, click on NetWare.

4. Under NetWare 4.11, read about DS411Q.EXE, the NDS Update for NetWare 4.11/4.2.

5. Click on the file name and read the description.

6. Click on the file name in the description to begin downloading the file.

This file may be on the Support Connection CD, but at the time of this writing, the DS411Q.EXE file was less than a month old—a file that new would most likely not be on the Support Connection CD, unless the CD-ROM arrived recently. The most recent files will always be on the Web site.

Replacing And Upgrading A Hard Disk

A customer calls who has a Quantum hard disk that died in a server. Luckily, this is a little-used volume, so you don't have to hire an ambulance to race across town. He wants a drive with a 3.5" form factor, no higher than 3H, to fit in the space of the last drive. The interface is IDE(AT). The old drive was 2GB, but he wants to add some space because he has to spend the money anyway. He has decided he wants 6GB or more.

How many steps will it take to find a suitable drive? Try for six again:

Step 1: _____

Step 2: _____

Step 3: _____

Step 4: _____

Step 5: _____

Step 6: _____

Let's see one acceptable method for finding a suitable replacement drive:

1. Load SupportSource.

2. Open the Query Assistant and choose the Hard Drives tab.

3. Select Quantum from the Make field and IDE(AT) in the Interface field.

4. Select 3H in the Height field and 3.50 in the Form Factor field.

5. Click on Query. The results are shown.

6. Read about the Fireball SE 6.4AT (6,448MB).

Is there any sense in looking at Novell's Support Connection, either CD or Web site, for this information? None at all, because third-party hardware details aren't included in Support Connection. Specific hardware details, such as the jumper settings for the Fireball SE drive (if that's the drive chosen), are not available in the NetWare information. If you scroll down in the Document section of the board, you'll see a diagram of it. All the jumpers and connectors are shown, so your installation will go smoothly.

Help From LANalyzer And Other Sources

There are more tools than just the Support Connection Web site and CD and SupportSource available to explore troubleshooting details. Vendors are getting much better about posting helpful information on Web sites, and there are books that deal with troubleshooting exclusively by examining each network system and looking at ways to verify proper operation.

Novell provides a wonderful program for network troubleshooting as part of its LANalyzer for Windows (LZFW) product. Called the *NetWare Expert Tutorial*, the program uses some artificial intelligence techniques to provide network recommendations.

Documentation with NetWare also provides some troubleshooting help. Many times, a problem is a typo or missed setting in one of the many configuration fields rushed through during installation or reconfiguration. Tracking steps from the beginning will help verify all configuration details.

The most critical part of network troubleshooting is the user. Whenever a problem occurs, the user must answer one simple question, "What changed?" Something always changes before a problem starts, even if the change seems simple and unlikely to be the culprit.

Practice Questions

Question 1

> Which item is not included on Novell's Support Connection Web site?
>
> ○ a. Software patches
>
> ○ b. The Novell Buyer's Guide
>
> ○ c. User forums
>
> ○ d. Hard drive configuration details
>
> ○ e. Technical information documents (TIDs)

The correct answer is d. Novell includes little specific hardware information on its Web site or Support Connection CD, leaving that to third-party vendors. The Novell Support Connection Web site contains software patches, the Novell Buyer's Guide, user forums, and TIDs. Therefore, answers a, b, c, and e are incorrect.

Question 2

> Which of the following are true concerning connecting to the Internet? [Choose the two best answers]
>
> ❏ a. You must have an Ethernet NIC in your computer.
>
> ❏ b. TCP/IP is not necessary if you have an IPX-to-TCP/IP gateway.
>
> ❏ c. You can't reach the Internet from AOL.
>
> ❏ d. ISPs provide Internet service based on a security profile.
>
> ❏ e. TCP/IP is an extra-cost option for Windows 95 and Windows 98.

The correct answers are b and d. An IPX-to-TCP/IP gateway from Novell or a third party connects networked systems to the Internet while utilizing only IPX for local network communications. ISPs provide access based on a login name and password (a security profile). You can have other types of network boards in your computer to access the Internet. Therefore, answer a is incorrect. AOL is an ISP for nearly 20 million users, all of whom may reach the Internet through AOL. Therefore, answer c is incorrect. TCP/IP, albeit a bare-bones implementation, is included with Windows 95 and 98. Therefore, answer e is incorrect.

Question 3

> Which of the following are *not* true statements? [Choose the two best answers]
>
> ❑ a. The Novell Support Connection CD and Web site are identical.
>
> ❑ b. FAQs answer many common problems and are a good place to start looking for answers.
>
> ❑ c. Novell employees are not allowed to participate in the forums.
>
> ❑ d. Open support questions can be checked on the Support Connection Web site.

The correct answers are a and c. Some substantial differences exist between the Support Connection Web site and the CD-ROM, such as the inclusion of the Developer Notes and AppNotes within the CD-ROM. Novell not only allows employees to be involved with the forums, it also pays many to spend a large part of their time in that area. The statements in answers b and d are true and therefore incorrect.

Question 4

> Which of the following is *not* true about SupportSource?
>
> ○ a. The SupportSource query engine and interface are separate from the MTL.
>
> ○ b. Network boards are not included in the MTL.
>
> ○ c. The MTL has an FCC ID lookup database.
>
> ○ d. Extra glossary, background, and reference information is included with SupportSource.
>
> ○ e. SupportSource 2000 will be an online-only product.

The correct answer is b. Network boards are included with the SupportSource database, not in the MTL. Almost every piece of hardware used in a personal computer or server can be found in SupportSource, and all include their FCC ID number for searching. Plenty of helpful information may be found beyond hardware details, such as a complete glossary and other references. Plans call for SupportSource 2000 to be browser-based and only available through the Web. Therefore, answers a, c, d, and e are true and, therefore, incorrect.

Question 5

You receive a call from a customer who needs to download the most recent client files for a Windows NT Workstation machine attached to a NetWare 5 server. Which of the following is the best resource in which to find this information? [Choose the best answer]

○ a. SupportSource

○ b. The Microsoft Web site

○ c. The Novell online documentation

○ d. The Novell Support Connection Web site

○ e. The Novell Support Connection CD

The correct answer is d. The best place to find this information is the Novell Support Connection Web site, because it will have the most up-to-date files. The SupportSource CD contains detailed hardware information, not software information. Therefore, answer a is incorrect. You wouldn't be able to obtain NetWare client downloads from the Microsoft Web site. Therefore, answer b is incorrect. The Novell online documentation may eventually tell you the name of the file you need and the location, but it's not the most efficient resource. Therefore, answer c is incorrect. The Novell Support Connection CD may contain the files, but they may not be the most current. Therefore, answer e is incorrect.

Question 6

You want to find out the default status of jumpers on your Microscience International ESDI FH-21200 hard drive. Which of the following are the best resources in which to find this information? [Choose the two best answers]

❏ a. SupportSource

❏ b. The vendor's Web site

❏ c. The Novell Support Connection Web site

❏ d. The Novell Support Connection CD

The correct answers are a and b. The best places to find this information are the SupportSource CD and the vendor's Web site. The Novell Support Connection Web site and CD-ROM contain software-related information. Therefore, answers c and d are incorrect.

Need To Know More?

 Dayley, Brady and Rich Jensen. *Novell's Guide to Resolving Critical Server Issues*. Novell Press, San Jose, CA, 1998. ISBN 0-7645-4550-7. This entire book contains valuable troubleshooting information.

 Shafer, Kevin. *Novell's Guide to Networking Hardware*. Novell Press, San Jose, CA, 1998. ISBN 0-7645-4553-1. This book contains valuable information about troubleshooting networking hardware. This would be a handy book to have around in addition to SupportSource.

 www.techweb.com/encyclopedia contains a useful online encyclopedia of more than 11,000 computer terms and concepts. Many include illustrations. This site is a good place to verify details and definitions.

 www.supportsource.com is the SupportSource Web site. You can download the SupportSource seven-day trial version from this site or order the CD-ROM.

Basic Hardware Primer

Terms you'll need to understand:

√ Network board

√ Industry Standard Architecture (ISA)

√ Extended Industry Standard Architecture (EISA)

√ Peripheral Component Interconnect (PCI)

√ Interrupt request (IRQ)

√ Direct Memory Access (DMA)

√ Input/output (I/O) address (port)

√ Memory address

√ Dual in-line package (DIP) switch

√ Jumper

√ Plug and play

Techniques you'll need to master:

√ Understanding the differences in various buses

√ Knowing which buses you're most likely to encounter

√ Identifying and configuring IRQs

√ Recognizing jumpers and how to enable and disable them

√ Recognizing and configuring DIP switches

√ Recognizing and using custom configuration utilities

√ Understanding the limitations of plug and play

Understanding the basics of computer hardware is essential to the service and support of any network. In this chapter, we cover the various types of network boards and offer a brief summary of their installation. You'll also learn about the various types of buses available, including Industry Standard Architecture (ISA), Micro Channel Architecture (MCA), Extended Industry Standard Architecture (EISA), Video Electronics Standards Association (VESA), Local Bus (VLB), Personal Computer Memory Card International Association (PCMCIA), CardBus, and Peripheral Component Interconnect (PCI). We'll finish the section on PC architecture with the configuration information that's needed to install network boards.

Later in the chapter, you'll learn how to configure hardware, including jumpers and dual in-line package (DIP) switches. Then, we'll cover the details of installing network boards and discuss the details of configuration software.

Personal Computer Architecture

Architecture is basically a fancy term that refers to the inside design of a computer. Like most discussions of system architecture in the PC world, we'll concentrate on bus architecture. (If you are interested in a more comprehensive review, you can search through electrical engineering and systems-design magazines for information on different types of system architectures.)

Variations for every computer bus type exist because network boards have become more intelligent over time. Advances in the computer operating systems (Windows in most cases) also support newer, more intelligent network boards. Backward compatibility, until now, has demanded that even the newest servers include a few slots that support the oldest network board types. However, the 1999 Windows reference platform calls for the elimination of the ISA and EISA slots, as well as serial and parallel ports.

> *Note: A network board is also called a network interface card (NIC), network adapter, network card, and network interface board. Novell uses the term network board most often. However, network board vendors usually call it a NIC.*

A PC does not become part of a network until a network board is installed, configured, and connected to the proper network cabling (as described in Chapter 6). Network boards vary, depending on the type of computer architecture inside the server or workstation to be networked.

Network Board Types

All interface cards in a PC, but particularly network boards, must be configured in some way to communicate properly with the host PC. From old to new, here are the general network board types you'll encounter:

➤ **Configured manually** With DIP switches and jumper blocks

➤ **Configured via software** Provided with the network board

➤ **Configured automatically by the operating system** Plug and play

Early network boards required hardware manipulation to configure various board parameters. This hardware approach led to much trial and error because early installers would try various jumper settings to find the one that did not conflict with existing PC settings. Although time-consuming and difficult to change, the manual configuration method was bearable for small networks but grew progressively more difficult to support as the networks grew.

Software-configured boards replaced hardware jumpers and switches with intelligent controls on the physical board and in configuration software. Vendor-supplied software runs on the PC and communicates with the network board. Settings made in the software are saved to nonvolatile memory on the network board; therefore, they are kept after the PC is turned off. This type of software is a huge improvement over manually configured network boards.

Plug-and-play systems allow the operating system (Windows 95/98—and to a very limited extent, Windows NT) to communicate and negotiate the proper settings with the network board. No manual configuration is necessary, and Microsoft supports most of the major network board manufacturers by including their plug-and-play details in the Windows operating systems.

> *Note:* *Plug and play received a truly appalling reputation during its first generation in PCs. This reputation was so common that most technicians have heard, if not used, the satiric "plug and pray." This reputation was especially harsh when compared to the smooth running plug and play Apple had built into the Macintosh years before. Current hardware has improved, but problems still occur.*

Some network boards require software from the vendor to inform Windows about the configuration parameters of the network board. Plug and play is great when it works, but when Windows fails to handle configuration settings properly, it's difficult to troubleshoot.

Plug-and-play support is great, but don't get complacent. You need to have a full working knowledge of manual configuration. Additionally, you'll probably have to work with legacy hardware for *years* to come. You'll also need this knowledge to manually configure the system when it can't resolve conflicts on its own.

General Network Board Installation Steps

When installing network boards, you should note that certain steps are common for all board types. Knowing these steps can be very helpful when you're troubleshooting network boards, because it's often necessary to go back to the earliest steps possible to verify settings. Here are the basic network-board installation steps:

1. Pick the proper network board for the network cabling scheme, network topology, and PC architecture. The network board must handle the installed cabling, the network topology (Ethernet, token ring, and so on), and must fit into a bus provided by the PC.

2. Determine whether the board is manually configured, software configured, or plug and play.

3. If necessary, configure the board via jumpers and/or DIP switches before installing it into the PC. (See the "Configuring Hardware" section later in this chapter.)

4. If the network board is software configured, find the proper software and have it close at hand.

5. Physically install the board into the PC and make sure the proper bus type is used.

6. Configure the board with vendor-supplied software, if necessary. If the board is plug and play, the operating system should handle the configuration.

7. Reboot the system.

These steps may look elementary, but they can lead to confusion. An Ethernet PCI NIC for twisted-pair cabling looks almost exactly like a token ring PCI NIC for twisted-pair cabling. Verify what type of board you have before continuing your installation.

Realize that most network board vendors offer several models for each PC architecture type (covered in the following section). Software-configured models are sold alongside plug-and-play models and are often identical except for the configuration type supported. Then, factor in whether the popular PC architecture supports plug-and-play boards (which depends on the PC motherboard) or software-configured network boards.

As mentioned, network boards must be chosen to fit the existing network cabling and topology as well as the PC architecture of the server or workstation that will host the network board. If these criteria aren't met, the network boards won't work properly.

PC Architecture Types

A *bus* is a common channel, or *pathway*, in a computer that connects multiple devices. There are several buses inside a PC, including the *processor bus*, which provides a parallel data path between the central processing unit (CPU), main memory, and the peripheral buses. Other buses include the memory, input/output (I/O), and address buses. The term *bus* is applied to these paths because the signal stops at each device—just like a bus stops at every designated stop. The six common buses used in IBM-compatible personal computers are discussed in the following sections.

Industry Standard Architecture (ISA)

The ISA (pronounced *eye-suh*) bus appeared with the first IBM Advanced Technology (AT). ISA is a 16-bit bus operating at 8 to 10MHz (occasionally pushed to 16MHz, but often unstable at that speed), an upgrade from the 8-bit bus that appeared in the IBM PC back in 1981. Most 8-bit boards will fit into the first connector of a 16-bit ISA slot, leaving the extension connector empty.

Putting an 8-bit card into a modern computer should be avoided if at all possible, because the performance will degrade all other system components. A few 8-bit boards have a *skirt* (a board area that drops down to the motherboard level past the connector fingers) that makes it impossible to fit them into a 16-bit ISA slot.

The limitations of the 16-bit adapters force the PC operating system to break down each 32-bit piece of information into two pieces to match the data width of the ISA card. This, as you might expect, drops performance considerably. It's significant to note that serial and parallel ports, unless enhanced, operate as 8-bit ISA devices and provide considerable system-performance degradation during use.

The AT form factor, with the taller case size, allowed ISA boards to be 4.8 inches tall. Today's smaller cases top out at 4.2 inches; therefore, most ISA board manufacturers stick with the shorter form factor.

Today, 16-bit ISA boards are still popular but are gradually giving way to cards for the PCI bus (discussed later in this section). Network servers using an ISA bus can support small networks but should be replaced with a PCI bus and adapters if the CPU utilization stays above 50 percent. This indicates the server is working too hard. The likely cause of this is a combination of 16- and 32-bit data transfers (which are rather slow) combined with the almost total lack of bus mastering and co-processing in ISA boards.

 ISA is 16-bit bus operating at 8 to 10MHz.

Micro Channel Architecture (MCA)

The newfangled 386DX processor that followed the IBM AT and 286 Intel chip demanded a new and wider bus. IBM jumped on its design horse and created MCA—a 32-bit, 20MHz specification that covered both 16-bit and 32-bit MCA interface cards.

Like the ISA connectors, the longer MCA connectors used an extension for the 32-bit boards. This left a small gap between the finger tabs, similar to the gap on 16-bit ISA boards. The spacing and pin size for MCA ensured no ISA board could be plugged in by mistake, and vice versa.

First shipped in 1987, MCA boards transfer data at speeds ranging from 20Mbps to 80Mbps, and they accounted for much of the PS/2 performance boost over the AT. (Contrast this with the 16Mbps raw transfer rate of the AT bus.) What seemed like a winning combination floundered when IBM tried to force the computer world to pay high licensing fees for using MCA for boards and PCs. The industry balked, and IBM discontinued MCA products in 1996 in favor of the PCI bus.

You probably won't encounter any MCA buses or cards in installations today, and you probably won't see any legacy systems with the MCA bus either.

Extended Industry Standard Architecture (EISA)

Forcing the computer industry to pay high licensing fees for MCA led directly to the development of the EISA (pronounced *ee-suh*) bus. Pushed primarily by Compaq Computer Corporation, which also shipped the first 386-based personal computer, the EISA bus was released in early 1988. Because the EISA bus runs at the ISA standard rate of 8MHz, it can support legacy ISA cards. However, mixing 16-bit and 32-bit cards in one computer lowers overall performance.

The 32-bit cards built for the EISA bus were taller than even the AT cards, measuring a full 5 inches. Special software is required to configure EISA cards plugged into the EISA bus. You should avoid using an EISA bus computer and card today, especially in a server, because PCI is much faster and easier to use—not to mention less expensive.

VESA Local Bus (VLB)

Mashing acronyms, the Video Electronics Standards Association committee provided its VESA Local Bus (sometimes called *VL-Bus*) to handle 486 processors in 1992. The VESA group, established by NEC, aimed to make a compatible, open standard for high-performance video boards and monitors.

VLB interface cards show a series of two more extension connector fingers past the 32-bit connectors that appear in ISA cards. This extension bus is tied directly to the CPU so the VLB interface card can take full advantage of the 486 CPU address space. A theoretical speed of 66MHz gave way to the practical limit of 32MHz to avoid problems.

Because applications such as Computer Aided Design (CAD) were gaining in popularity, the VLB idea caused many problems. Event timing between the CPU and VLB boards is tricky, and the inclusion of more than one VLB slot in computers makes things even more difficult.

Luckily, VLB slots are backward compatible with both ISA 8-bit and 16-bit cards. However, VLB systems have disappeared in favor of PCI or Accelerated Graphics Port (AGP) slots—another video-only bus connector. (Note that even AGP has been tagged for additional uses beyond video.)

 VESA buses are for video boards and operate at 32MHz.

Personal Computer Memory Card International Association (PCMCIA) Or PC Card

The credit-card size PC Card (or *PCMCIA*) offers a way to tie peripherals into a computer bus without opening the computer and plugging the board into a connector on the motherboard. First provided for laptop computers, which have no room for typical connectors, the PC Card standard uses a 16-bit interface that's configured automatically by the host system.

 PCMCIAs are credit-card size and used for laptops.

There are no DIP switches or jumpers because there's no room for either. PC Card slots are used for network adapters, modems, sound cards, extra hard drives, and anything else a vendor wants to attach to a laptop. Although PC Card slots are available for desktop PCs, the market penetration is nonexistent. A large part of the reason for this is the lack of performance—the PC Card bus is limited to 2Mbps.

If you can't remember the correct acronym for PCMCIA, try "Personal Computer Makers Can't Invent Acronyms," or you can just call it a *PC Card*.

The logical extension of the PC Card bus to 32 bits is known as CardBus, and has become quite common in new laptops. This is largely driven by the ubiquity of Fast Ethernet. CardBus is theoretically PCI in a different form factor, but in reality, performance falls short. However, it's still far in advance of its PCMCIA ancestor. CardBus slots are visually the same as PCMCIA, and will accept PCMCIA peripherals.

Peripheral Component Interconnect (PCI)

The PCI bus is the bus taking us into the future. All high-end PCs have PCI architectures now, and the cost and market penetration makes the PCI bus the choice of even low-cost computer systems.

Intel introduced the PCI bus in 1992 as a 32-bit bus supporting a speed of 33MHz. The network and disk controllers of PCI are on separate buses for better throughput. Peak bandwidth is up to 132Mbps at 33MHz. PCI version 2.1 calls for a doubling of speed—up to 66MHz—(also doubling throughput). When necessary, PCI specifications can be scaled up to 64-bits at 66MHz, which quadruples throughput to a burst rate of 528Mbps.

Similar to Hardware Abstraction Layer (HAL) found in Windows NT, the PCI specification separates the CPU and peripherals. Updates to CPU technology will not require changes in the PCI specifications. Processors supported by PCI include the Intel 486, Pentium, Pentium workalikes, the RS/600 by IBM, and even the PowerPC (yes, from Apple Computer and IBM).

Sharing is big in the PCI world. Up to eight functions can be built into one peripheral board, meaning network interface, sound, video, and game port cards are possible on the same board—if not particularly practical. PCI also shares interrupts, which eases the constriction of IRQs claimed by ISA cards. As long as one IRQ remains for the PCI bus, all the PCI-connected devices can share the interrupt and work correctly. Up to 10 devices per computer can be supported by the PCI architecture.

 PCI is a 32-bit bus that can share interrupts. You can connect up to 10 devices per computer.

Configuration Information Required For Board Installation

There are five areas that you can possibly configure for any board installed in a personal computer:

➤ Interrupt request (IRQ)

➤ Direct Memory Access (DMA)

➤ Input/Output (I/O) address (port)

➤ Base memory (shared memory)

➤ Slot number

Each interface board installed into a PC requires one or all of these bits of information. Certain buses, such as PCI, share scarce resources such as IRQs. The combination of plug-and-play-enabled operating systems with the PCI bus would seem to eliminate every problem involved with peripheral board installation and use. Alas, as shown by the extensive previous chapter on troubleshooting tools, this is not so.

Interrupt Requests (IRQs)

Also called a *hardware interrupt*, an IRQ sends notice to the system board and CPU that a device needs service. Literally, there are 16 separate, physical lines or traces leading from the ISA or PCI bus. The adapter requiring attention raises voltage on its dedicated IRQ line to request processor attention (also called *generating an interrupt*). The CPU puts other services on hold after an interrupt, then services the device that triggered it. This request-driven model allows external devices to be acknowledged and serviced immediately when necessary, but the CPU doesn't need to waste time checking on them periodically. When an external device such as a network board needs the system's attention, it requests that attention using an IRQ.

To describe IRQs more clearly, we'll use a meeting analogy. While the manager conducts the meeting, the attendees sit quietly and pay attention. If someone raises his or her hand for attention, the manager stops, listens, gives an answer (if only the postponement of a decision), and then continues with the meeting. The manager was working, was interrupted, handled the interruption, then went back to working. This is exactly like the CPU and the network board.

There are 16 interrupt lines available in a PC. The PC AT used two interrupt controller chips (which means the number of interrupt lines has doubled since the first PC model). Those 16 lines are arranged in two banks of eight interrupts each. IRQ 2 is the link between the first eight and the second eight and is therefore not available to service add-on devices. First bank IRQs are considered more valuable than those in the second bank, because older ISA boards may not be able to use the higher interrupt numbers.

This brings us to a problem: Many of the IRQs are spoken for by system devices and are not available for important items such as network boards. The following list shows the IRQ numbers and their standard assignments:

➤ **IRQ 0** Used by the system timer only.

➤ **IRQ 1** Used by keyboard input only.

➤ **IRQ 2** Linked to IRQs 8 to 15. This IRQ can also be used by some modems, Attached Resource Computer Network (ARCnet), and video boards.

➤ **IRQ 3** Typically used by a COM2 serial port and may be available. It can also be used by COM4 ports, network boards, and sound cards.

➤ **IRQ 4** Typically used by a COM1 serial port but may be used by a COM3 port.

➤ **IRQ 5** Used by an LPT2 parallel port and is usually available. It can also be used by sound cards and network boards. The use of this port varies widely.

➤ **IRQ 6** Typically used by a floppy disk controller but can be used by tape accelerator cards.

➤ **IRQ 7** Used by the LPT1 parallel port, which is usually the printer port.

➤ **IRQ 8** Used by the realtime clock timer only.

➤ **IRQ 9** Linked to IRQ 2 and is sometimes used by video graphics array (VGA) or 3270 Emulation.

➤ **IRQ 10** Available. It's the default choice for many network boards.

➤ **IRQ 11** Available. It can be used fby r sound boards, network boards, VGA cards, PCI devices, and more.

➤ **IRQ 12** Used for PS/2 mouse. It can be used by sound boards, network boards, VGA cards, PCI devices, and more.

➤ **IRQ 13** Used by the math coprocessor. This port is for system use only.

➤ **IRQ 14** Used by a hard disk controller, the primary IDE channel. It can also be used by SCSI host adapters.

➤ **IRQ 15** Available. However, it's usually used by a secondary disk controller. It can also be used by SCSI host adapters and network boards.

 IRQs send notice to the system board and CPU that a device needs service. Know the default interrupt settings.

If a computer system has more than two serial ports, COM3 shares the same interrupt as COM1, and COM4 shares IRQ 4 with COM2. Add-on serial port boards will use controller chips to share one interrupt for the interface board among all the serial ports attached to the board.

Interrupts work more like Ethernet—a station with a packet to transmit tries to take control of the network long enough to send the packet, without waiting for any kind of polling mechanism or token. The opposite of interrupts is *polling*, which is when the CPU goes to each and every device and asks whether the device needs to be serviced. You can compare this to token ring, in which the token goes to every station.

Interrupt service routine (ISR) software lies in low memory on the PC and provides the link between the IRQ and the sequence of events triggered by the subsequent CPU interruption. These ISRs are stored by the system board in the interrupt vector tables at the bottom of low memory. You'll never have to find or configure these addresses, but you will regularly fight for IRQs until you move to PCI systems and interface cards exclusively. Even then, it's possible to have IRQ problems, and these problems will be with us until a better system, such as I2O, eliminates interrupts entirely.

Direct Memory Access (DMA)

Engineers developed DMA so certain devices could bypass the CPU and communicate directly with system memory. Keeping the CPU out of the byte-transfer business makes communication between device memory and system memory much faster.

First, there were only four DMA channels. Then, the 286-based IBM AT systems started using eight DMA channels, linking the second four to the first four, much like the IRQ banks are linked. In other words, one of the DMA channels is the bridge to channels 5, 6, and 7. The following list details the DMA channels and their assignments:

➤ **DMA 0** Used by Dynamic RAM (DRAM) refresh only.

➤ **DMA 1** Used by hard disk controllers.

➤ **DMA 2** Used by a floppy disk controller. It can also be used by tape accelerator cards.

➤ **DMA 3** Available. It can be used by sound boards (low DMA), network boards, SCSI host adapters, and more.

➤ **DMA 4** A bridge to the first group of DMA channels (controller cascade) only.

➤ **DMA 5** Available. It's generally used by sound boards.

➤ **DMA 6** Available. It can be used by sound and network boards.

➤ **DMA 7** Available. It can be used by sound and network boards.

Some boards allow DMA to be disabled. Even though sending every byte via the CPU slows performance, some systems still do not use DMA. Using a board that allows DMA to be disabled may be a potential workaround when faced with a DMA conflict. If you find a system that does not use DMA, upgrade it.

 DMA is a channel used so certain devices can bypass the CPU and communicate directly with system memory. Know the DMA settings.

I/O (Input/Output) Address (Port)

An I/O address is often called a *port address* or *base I/O address*. A *port* is a specified memory address used by other programs to communicate with a host program. In this case, the I/O address is the memory address used by external devices, such as network boards, to communicate with the CPU. The external device places data at the port address and interrupts the CPU, and then the CPU fetches the data at the address.

If you have conflicting port addresses, the wrong data will be waiting at a port address. These conflicts lead to system problems, so each device needs a unique port address for CPU data exchange.

The I/O address is set by the manufacturer, but the motherboard manufacturers allow the address to be changed to accommodate the need for flexibility. Changes in port memory addresses are made using DIP switches, jumpers, or configuration software.

A PC operating system such as NetWare must know the I/O addresses to avoid conflicts and system crashes. If you have Microsoft Office 97, the System Information menu choice under About Microsoft on the Help menu shows every detail of your hardware resources—including I/O, IRQs, DMA, and memory.

The following list provides the common I/O addresses and their assignments. Each interface card lists available addresses, and none of the following should be used:

➤ **000-0FF** Used by the system only

➤ **1F0-1F8** Used by hard disks

➤ **200-207** Used by the game port

➤ **278-27F** Used by the LPT2 parallel port

➤ **2F8-2FF** Used by the COM2 serial port

➤ **378-37F** Used by the LPT1 parallel port

➤ **3F0-3F7** Used by the floppy disk controller

➤ **3F8-3FF** Used by the COM1 serial port

An I/O address is the memory address used by external devices such as network boards to communicate with the CPU. Know the I/O settings.

This information often accompanies interface boards in the section discussing I/O addresses and how to set them. Configuration software is often not smart enough to block out these addresses automatically, so the manufacturer trusts you, the installer, to read the chart and avoid the commonly used addresses.

Base Memory

Interface boards with read-only memory (ROM) included to control operations must link to an address space in the main system memory to do their jobs. If a network board needs to control some portion of system memory because of RAM requirements on the board, the point of system memory used is called *base memory* or *shared memory*. Two resources cannot share a base memory address, and the base memory addresses can't overlap.

Boards using ROM addresses normally let you configure the memory address via jumpers or configuration software. If this address overlaps an existing base memory address claimed by any other device, the board will not function.

The upper memory address space between 640KB and 1MB is a point of contention for many external devices and system needs. Many computers automatically claim this address space for internal needs, blocking it from use by any external device, such as network adapters. This address space is called *base memory*, even though base memory addresses accommodate board-based ROM software routines.

Memory manager software, included with Windows of various flavors since 3.1, will block out memory addresses for use by the operating system. By using a combination of memory manager settings and configurations for the interface board in question, a safe memory address can usually be located. However, trial and error is not uncommon. Table 4.1 shows the normal base memory allocation.

 If a network board needs to control some portion of system memory because of RAM requirements on the board, the point of system memory used is called *base memory* or *shared memory*.

Again, interface boards will allow configuration changes through jumpers, DIP switches, or software to change the starting memory address to match available memory in the host PC. When possible, start looking in the CA000 to DFFFF area for room.

Vital Table 4.1	Shared memory blocks and typical assignments.
Address	**Typical Assignment**
00000 to 9FFFF	System memory
A0000 to AFFFF	Enhanced graphics adapter (EGA)/VGA video graphics
B0000 to B7FFF	Monochrome display
B8000 to BFFFF	Color graphics adapter (CGA), EGA, VGA, and VGA text
C0000 to CFFFF	EGA/VGA basic input/output system (BIOS)
C8000 to C87FF	PC/XT hard disk controller
CA000 to DFFFF	Available for drivers and the Expanded Memory Specification (EMS) page frame
E0000 to EFFFF	Used on PC/AT and compatibles as well as PS/2 systems
F0000 to FFFFF	PC system BIOS, PS/2 system, and VGA BIOS

Slot Number

Some PCI and EISA adapters (as well as MCA) are recognized by their slot number during configuration. This greatly simplifies identifying the board because the slot number is physical—two boards cannot occupy the same slot. However, the system board must still assign resources as before and arbitrate conflicts; the ugly parts are just hidden from casual view.

Remember that although the slot number is based on a physical slot, the numbering scheme used varies from motherboard manufacturer to manufacturer, and embedded boards are fairly common. Always check the documentation.

Checking Resources

It's a good idea to make a resource area map for computers, indicating which resources are available and where installed boards have been set. Novell recommends you check the System icon under Control Panel in Windows 95/98, but to get an overall picture, you much check each item and see the resources used. Go back to the instructions for checking system information within Microsoft Office's Help screen to start; then, use the System icon resource information to fill in the blanks if necessary.

Most of the diagnostic tools for PCs will show available resources. CheckIT (**www.checkit.com/index.htm**) is a popular diagnostic tool recommended by Novell, but other utilities will provide the information as well. Many of the network management packages show this information in their reports on client stations, such as BindView (**www.bindview.com**), NetCensus (**www.netinfobuilder.com/tally/netcensus/prodlist.html**), AimIT, the MSD utility that comes with Windows 3.1 and 3.11, WinLAND, and Gasp.

Configuring Hardware

Now that you know why you must perform address contortions to find available resources for interface cards, let's talk about the physical contortions you may have to perform to configure the hardware in question. The move toward completely software-controlled motherboards and peripheral interface cards is underway but has not taken over completely—yet. There are many boards—motherboards and otherwise—that will present jumpers, DIP switches, or a combination of the two, and you must be able to configure them.

 Buy software-configurable motherboards and plug-and-play peripheral cards. Then, keep your motherboard configuration software disk in a very safe place. You may also want to make multiple copies of this disk and make sure they are clearly labeled.

Here are some common items to configure on motherboards:

➤ COM ports used

➤ System memory configuration

➤ Hard disk controller on/off

➤ Enabling a secondary hard disk controller

Here are some common items to configure on interface cards:

➤ IRQ used

➤ I/O address

➤ Speed of network transmission (for example, 4/16 token ring)

➤ DMA channel used

➤ Base memory address for onboard ROM

Again, the number of jumpers and DIP switches used is dropping, but it's not gone. In the following sections, we look at the two hardware configuration options and how to deal with them.

Understanding And Setting Jumpers, Jumper Pins, And Jumper Blocks

If you look closely at many motherboards, you'll see groups of pins sticking up. Sometimes there are only two pins, sometimes more, and each set of two pins is about a quarter-inch apart. These are *jumper pins*.

 Each set of two pins represents a logic circuit on the mother-board. If the pins are covered with a jumper, or *shunt*, the electrical connection between the two pins is made and the circuit is complete.

If there is no jumper on the pin, the circuit is broken. Jumpers themselves are small, flat pieces of plastic, usually black, with an internal metal sleeve that electrically connects the two pins when put in place. You must be careful when installing the jumpers.

Do not throw away (or lose) the jumpers you think you don't need—as soon as you do, you'll need them again. Place unneeded jumpers on a single pin of the pair, letting half the jumper hang out over the motherboard. The circuit will not be completed and will not interfere with anything else.

Jumpers can go bad, but not often. If adding a jumper doesn't make the change you expect, verify the metal sleeve is still inside the plastic case. Then, try another jumper just in case.

DIP Switch Settings

Dual in-line package (DIP) switches are being phased out and are rarely included on interface cards and motherboards now. Electrically, the jumper and DIP switch handle the same function. However, DIP switches are able to pack more connections into a smaller board space.

Unfortunately, DIP switches don't have a clear on/off setting like the jumpers do. If there's no jumper, there is no connection. With DIP switches, you must read the documentation to see whether Up is Off or On.

Some DIP switch packages use little sliding switches that are impossible to set without the aid of a sharp, pointed object. Others use an Up or Down switch, which again requires a sharp point, because fingers will mash down more switches than you want mashed. Some even use little rocker switches, like tiny seesaws on the motherboard.

Avoid using a pencil point, no matter how tempting. Graphite inside the switch mechanism can cause problems.

Be aware that instructions are not always as clear as one would hope. Up and Down is pretty straightforward, but not when used in relation to the sliding switches. On and Off is even more confusing, because the terms apply to the electrical connection, which is not visible to the naked eye. Read the documentation closely, and cross your fingers for a good illustration.

Often, instructions are given for the entire set of DIP switches at one time—for example, On-On-Off-On or Up-Down-Up-Up-Down. Verify the settings with the documentation and illustration at least twice before performing the task.

DIP switches are electrically the same concept as a jumper. You can either close a circuit or leave it open.

Board Installation

Once interface boards and host computer motherboards are configured, one must be installed into the other. Common sense steps, and your experience, should make this simple:

1. Turn the computer off and then remove the computer case.

2. Lay the computer flat on a sturdy surface so you don't twist, bend, or drop the system. Bad news comes with all those actions. Twisting the motherboard may break small circuit connections that render the system inoperable, and because you can't see the broken electrical trace, you'll go crazy trying to fix a dead motherboard. These boards are tough, but not bulletproof.

3. Firmly place the interface card into the proper slot and apply even pressure along the length of the board to seat the board into the slot. Do not force the board—if it won't go in, look to make sure the board fingers are lined up correctly with the slot opening. You should not rock the board back and forth in the slot. This can damage the board as well as the slot.

4. Use the mounting screw to connect the board's mounting bracket properly to the system case. This provides support when plugging cables into and out of the board, and it grounds the interface board to the system case.

Network Boards And Configuration Software

Configuration software is an ever-advancing technology that's quickly replacing jumpers and DIP switches. Unfortunately, this is not always an advantage. Experienced users will admit it's just as easy to lose a critical disk as it is to lose the only instructions for a particular motherboard or network board.

All things considered, software is an easier way to go, if for no other reason than the ability to change network board settings without having to pull the board out of the computer. Of course, each brand of board uses a different software and configuration routine, but there are enough common activities to support a quick overview.

MCA Network Board Configuration

Most MCA bus boards are manufactured by IBM and must come with the reference diskette, which contains all the system programs for that particular board type. Configuration through these software utilities is much easier than peering at tiny DIP switches.

Many of the necessary files are adapter definition files (ADFs) that come with the board. (You can copy these ADFs to the reference diskette or to the hard disk for easy access.) ADFs resolve conflicts, such as two boards both claiming IRQ 10. The ADFs set the new board to avoid the conflict, much like changing jumpers or DIP switches, but without requiring you to open the computer.

MCA is a 32-bit bus operating at 10MHz. An MCA bus requires software to configure the hardware settings; the files have an ADF extension.

The EISA Configuration Utility

Just as the MCA boards ship with a configuration diskette, so do EISA boards. A standardized configuration utility was developed by Micro Computer System (MCS), Inc., to handle EISA board configurations—appropriately named the *EISA Configuration Utility* (ECU).

> *Note:* *Novell tends to refer to the ECU as simply the configuration utility.*

ISA boards, which fit into the backward-compatible EISA slots, do not respond to the ECU commands. However, ECU can provide advice about common ISA boards and configure the EISA boards around the default values of pre-existing ISA boards.

Each EISA board ships with a custom configuration file (which ends with the CFG extension), describing the board characteristics and how to modify the configuration. Compaq provides some CFG files for boards that didn't ship with the proper CFG files from their vendors.

The ECU also has two other interesting features: Verification Mode and Lock/Unlock. Verification Mode checks the board and host system to ensure both have maintained a valid configuration. Lock/Unlock secures the resources allocated to a particular board. When new boards are added to the system, they're not able to take one of the resource assignments of a locked board. This reduces flexibility just a bit, but at least the existing system configuration won't be changed to mush by an aborted installation of a new board.

EISA is a 32-bit bus operating at 8MHz. An EISA bus requires software to configure the hardware settings' custom configuration file (that ends with the CFG extension).

Custom ISA And VLB Configuration Options

New boards, especially the continuing flood of ISA boards, are now often configurable through vendor-supplied software. Unlike MCA, where IBM called the shots, or EISA, where a group of vendors worked out the configuration details together, ISA vendors are on their own.

Each ISA configuration utility is developed by each vendor, customized for a particular board or family of boards, and has little or nothing to do with any other configuration utility for any other board. For example, 3Com provides a consistent DOS-menu program for its EtherLink network board family, but the files holding the board details vary with each board. The configuration file from one 3Com board will not work on another 3Com board (such as trying an EtherLink II program on an EtherLink III board), and it certainly won't work on any other vendors' Ethernet interface cards. Additionally, most of these utilities must run under DOS, which creates problems for Windows 95/98 workstations and huge problems for Windows NT machines. NetWare servers, which boot to DOS first, are easy to deal with should you need to use such an ISA board.

Software-configurable ISA and VLB boards use a special Electrically Erasable Programmable Read Only Memory (EEPROM) chip to hold configuration details. Details about IRQ, I/O, and DMA settings are written to the EEPROM chip and saved when the host computer is turned off—and even when the board is removed from the computer.

Plug And Play Advances In Automatic Configuration

Plug and Play, which was pushed by Microsoft, enables you to plug a board into a computer and have the computer recognize the board and automatically find the right resource settings for the board to fit with the other boards.

Specifications exist for PCI, PCMCIA, ISA, and MCA buses. Realistically, PCI carries the most load for desktop systems, although enough ISA bus manufacturers are getting involved to make ISA buses work most of the time. PCMCIA has the advantage of starting without legacy systems to consider, so it works most reliably. Unfortunately, these advances have yet to invade desktop systems.

Three components make up the full Plug and Play system:

➤ **Plug and Play operating systems** Windows 95, Windows 98, and OS/2 are Plug and Play ready. Windows NT almost is—extra modules are needed to make Windows NT systems fully compatible with plug-and-play components. The operating system must warn the user whenever the BIOS is unable to force plug-and-play components to work together.

➤ **Plug and Play boards** Compatible boards must follow the Plug and Play specifications so they can communicate with the system BIOS and request acceptable resources. When the BIOS responds with approved resource settings, the board must be able to configure itself to match the resource list provided.

➤ **Plug and Play BIOS** This is the heart of the Plug and Play system. It requires the BIOS and system manufacturers to work closely with the operating system vendors. During the power-on self test (POST), a system BIOS always discovers available resources and checks to see what type of hardware or software services are using those resources. A Plug and Play-enabled BIOS then reads the resource settings stored on each plug-and-play board, checks those against available resources, and assigns resources accordingly.

 | Plug and Play BIOS is the heart of the plug-and-play system. It requires the BIOS and system manufacturers to work closely with the operating system vendors.

No board settings or special configuration software are necessary for Plug and Play systems—if they work correctly. If they don't, which is the case far too often, the Control Panel and System Settings will become very familiar. Difficult cases often respond to a BIOS upgrade—first check with the system manufacturer.

Practice Questions

Question 1

> The modern ISA bus first appeared in which system?
>
> ○ a. Compaq 386
>
> ○ b. The original IBM PC
>
> ○ c. IBM AT
>
> ○ d. IBM XT
>
> ○ e. IBM PS/2

The correct answer is c. The modern ISA bus first appeared in the IBM AT system. Compaq pushed the EISA bus. Therefore, answer a is incorrect. The original IBM PC and IBM XT used 8-bit buses, which were expanded for the AT to the modern ISA bus. Therefore, answers b and d are incorrect. The PS/2 introduced the MCA bus. Therefore, answer e is incorrect.

Question 2

> Which of the following is a true statement?
>
> ○ a. EISA boards are always shorter than ISA boards.
>
> ○ b. Compaq released the EISA board before IBM released MCA.
>
> ○ c. EISA was released with the first 386 computer from IBM.
>
> ○ d. VLB provided great improvements in graphical applications.
>
> ○ e. PCMCIA (PC-Card) devices have small DIP switches on the outside
>   edge.

The correct answer is d. VLB provided great improvements in graphical applications. EISA boards took advantage of the larger case for the IBM AT and were 5 inches tall (in contrast to ISA boards at 4.2 inches). Therefore, answer a is incorrect. IBM released MCA before Compaq and partners could counter with EISA, which first shipped with the Compaq 386. Therefore, answers b and c are incorrect. There are no DIP switches on PCMCIA cards. Therefore, answer e is incorrect.

Question 3

Which of the following is *not* a true statement?

○ a. Intel introduced the PCI bus in 1992.

○ b. The PCI bus has a peak bandwidth of 132Mbps at 33MHz.

○ c. Up to 10 functions can be built into a single PCI interface board.

○ d. PCI boards share IRQs.

○ e. A PCI bus can scale up to 66MHz.

The correct answer is c. Up to eight functions can be built onto a single PCI interface card, but up to 10 devices per computer can be supported by the PCI architecture. All other answers are true statements and are therefore incorrect.

Question 4

Which of the following are valid IRQ descriptions? [Choose the best answers]

❑ a. There are eight IRQ lines in an IBM PC.

❑ b. There are 16 IRQ lines in an IBM AT.

❑ c. IRQs are used by devices to interrupt the processor for service.

❑ d. IRQ 2 is the link between the first and second bank of IRQs.

The correct answers are a, b, c, and d. All answers are valid descriptions of IRQs and are therefore correct.

Question 5

Which of the following are *not* true of I/O addresses? [Choose the three best answers]

❑ a. I/O addresses are randomly assigned by the BIOS upon booting.

❑ b. I/O address 378-37F is always reserved for LPT1 and cannot be changed.

❑ c. There's no way to get a listing of I/O addresses in use on a particular computer.

❑ d. I/O addresses specify where data from external devices is waiting for the CPU.

The correct answers are a, b, and c. I/O addresses are set by the motherboard configuration and given to the BIOS. Therefore, answer a is correct. Addresses can be changed; common addresses are listed for convenience. Therefore, answer b is correct. Several programs, including Microsoft Office 97 Help, provide a listing of I/O addresses in use. Therefore, answer c is correct. I/O addresses specify where data from external devices is waiting for the CPU. Therefore, answer d is true and incorrect.

Question 6

Which of the following is *not* true about jumpers?

○ a. Connecting jumper pins with the jumper completes an electrical circuit.

○ b. The plastic housing on jumpers covers a metal sleeve.

○ c. All motherboards have jumpers in the same place.

○ d. Jumpers can go bad, but this is unusual.

The correct answer is c. Motherboards follow no standard placement of jumper blocks—some don't even have jumpers. A metal sleeve inside the plastic covering on a jumper connects the two pins electrically to complete a circuit. Therefore, answer a is incorrect. Jumpers can go bad and not work, which almost always means the metal sleeve has fallen out of the plastic housing. Therefore, answers b and d are incorrect.

Question 7

Which of the following are *not* true about DIP switches? [Choose the four best answers]

❏ a. Electrically, DIP switches and jumpers complete an electrical circuit.

❏ b. DIP switches always use Up and Down switches.

❏ c. It's easy to tell which setting is On and Off for DIP switches.

❏ d. Pencil points are recommended tools for setting DIP switches.

❏ e. Careful attention to the documentation when setting DIP switches isn't necessary.

The correct answers are b, c, d, and e. Careful attention to the documentation is critical for setting DIP switches, because it's difficult to tell which setting is

On or Off on the various types of switch levers, sliders, and seesaws. Therefore, answers b, c, and e are correct. Graphite from pencils can cause switch problems and should be avoided. Therefore, answer d is correct. DIP switches and jumpers complete an electrical circuit. Therefore, answer a is true and incorrect.

Question 8

Which IRQ is always used by the keyboard?

O a. IRQ 13

O b. IRQ 8

O c. IRQ 1

O d. IRQ 0

The correct answer is c. IRQ 1 is used by the keyboard only. IRQ 13 is used for the math coprocessor. Therefore, answer a is incorrect. IRQ 8 is used by the realtime clock timer only. Therefore, answer b is incorrect. IRQ 0 is used by the system timer only. Therefore, answer d is incorrect.

Question 9

Plug and Play specifications exist for which of the following? [Choose the four best answers]

❑ a. PCI buses

❑ b. MCA buses

❑ c. ISA buses

❑ d. BIOS buses

❑ e. PCMCIA buses

The correct answers are a, b, c, and e. Plug and Play specifications exist for PCI, MCA, ISA, and PCMCIA buses. The BIOS is not a bus. It reads settings for each plug-and-play board during the boot process. Therefore, answer d is incorrect.

Need To Know More?

Mueller, Scott. *Upgrading & Repairing PCs, Eighth Edition.* Que Corporation, Indianapolis, IN, 1997. ISBN 0-7897-1295-4. Chapter 5, "Bus Slots and I/O Cards," contains information relevant to the material covered in this chapter.

www.techweb.com/encyclopedia/ contains a useful online encyclopedia of more than 11,000 computer terms and concepts, many of which include illustrations. This site is a good place to verify details and definitions.

Storage Devices

Terms you'll need to understand:

- √ Small Computer System Interface (SCSI)
- √ Integrated Device Electronics (IDE)
- √ Modified frequency modulation (MFM)
- √ Run length limited (RLL)
- √ Enhanced Small Device Interface (ESDI)
- √ Termination
- √ Host Bus Adapter (HBA)
- √ Low-level formatting
- √ Partitions
- √ Disk mirroring and duplexing
- √ Redundant Array of Inexpensive Disks (RAID)

Techniques you'll need to master:

- √ Describing hard disk principles
- √ Installing hard disks
- √ Configuring and troubleshooting hard disks
- √ Terminating SCSI devices
- √ Attaching disk cables
- √ Creating partitions, volumes, disk spans, and fault-tolerant devices
- √ Installing and configuring a CD-ROM as a NetWare volume

This chapter concentrates on the basics of computer storage devices. It covers how a hard disk works, the different types of disk interfaces, and how to install, configure, and troubleshoot storage devices. In addition, this chapter also discusses fault-tolerant strategies for disk management.

Storage Device Basics

A *storage device* is any component capable of storing information. Storage device types include memory, CD-ROMs, hard disks, optical drives, and tape devices. This chapter focuses strictly on hard disks and CD-ROMs, including installing, configuring, and troubleshooting them.

A hard disk provides data storage and retrieval functions. Hard disks 15 years ago weren't very reliable. Today's hard disks, however, deliver extremely high reliability, fast performance, a small footprint, and reasonable pricing. Hard disks are also sealed units. The end user cannot repair one in the event of a failure. The inside of a hard drive resembles a stack of dinner dishes, or *platters*. Above and below each platter is an arm that can move between the platters. Each arm has a read/write head that records and reads data from each platter. These drive components are sealed within a case. When the drive operates, the platters spin and the read/write heads move from the edge to the center of each platter—reading and writing information along the way.

The platters of a hard disk are similar to a running track—with each platter divided into circles. Each circle on a platter is called a *track*. A track is then further subdivided into *sectors*. A sector is really just a part of one of the circular tracks. Within each sector, DOS stores files in organizational units called *clusters*. A single cluster is the minimum space DOS allocates for storage. Hard drive manufacturers specify performance information about the hard drives they make. Two specific measures of performance are seek time and latency. *Seek time* is the time it takes the drive to locate a requested track. Seek time is measured in milliseconds. *Latency* is the time it takes the data to spin under a read/write head immediately after the correct track is located.

Here's the order of what happens: An application makes a data request, the drive controller sends the request to the hard drive, the read/write heads move to the correct track, and the computer waits for the requested data on the selected track to spin under the read/write heads. Because data is spread over different sections of the drive, the read/write heads move quickly and all over the disk's surface without actually making physical contact with it. Drive speed measurement is advertised as *access time*. Access time equals seek time plus latency—it's the total amount of time required to access a particular piece of data.

You may also hear about other common terms related to hard disks. *Settling* is the amount of time required for the read/write head to stabilize after motion. A *block* is the minimum unit of space used on a drive by NetWare. (A block for NetWare is analogous to a DOS *cluster*.) Finally, the *cylinder* is a distinct, concentric ring of storage on a hard disk.

Currently, two major types of hard disks are sold: Integrated Device Electronics (IDE) and Small Computer System Interface (SCSI). The difference between these two types is that the controller electronics for IDE are on the disk itself, whereas the SCSI electronics are separated from the physical drive. Each has advantages and disadvantages, which we'll discuss in the following sections. While working with various networks, you'll be exposed to many drive types; therefore, it's important for you to understand how to make different drive types coexist.

ST-506 Basics

ST-506 is an old standard developed by Seagate. The ST-506 standard was first developed for Seagate's 5MB disk drives. We briefly cover ST-506 in this chapter because you may encounter a drive of this type on an older machine. Two different encoding schemes pertain to this drive type: run length limited (RLL) and modified frequency modulation (MFM). RLL offers increased data density on the hard disk and is advantageous over the MFM scheme. MFM and RLL are not drive types—they're just encoding schemes. For example, an IDE or SCSI drive can use an RLL encoding scheme (however, more modern encoding schemes are used today). Floppy disks and some small hard disks use MFM encoding. It's beyond the scope of this book to explore each type; however, you can visit **www.seagate.com** to find more information.

The Enhanced Small Device Interface (ESDI) is ST-506's more powerful replacement. Both ST-506 and ESDI require a disk, cable, and a compatible controller. ESDI is rarely used: SCSI, IDE, and EIDE are used instead.

SCSI Basics

SCSI (pronounced *scuzzy*) is a high-speed, parallel drive standard. SCSI is also an ANSI standard and is characterized by both higher speeds and higher cost compared to other subsystem specifications. SCSI allows up to seven SCSI devices to be daisy-chained on a single cable. SCSI interfaces provide faster data transmission rates (up to 80Mbps) than standard serial and parallel port input/output (I/O) transmissions. Additionally, you can attach many devices to a single SCSI port; therefore, SCSI is really an I/O bus rather than simply an interface. Although SCSI is an ANSI standard, there are many variations of it; therefore, two SCSI interfaces may be incompatible.

For years, SCSI was the standard interface for Macintoshes, PC servers, and virtually all minicomputers and high-end workstations. However, PCs also support a variety of interfaces in addition to SCSI. These include IDE, Enhanced IDE (EIDE), Enhanced Small Device Interface (ESDI) for mass storage devices, and Centronics interfaces for printers. You can attach SCSI devices to a PC by inserting a SCSI interface board in one of its expansion slots. Many new computers come with SCSI built in. However, the long evolution of the SCSI standard means that some devices may not work with all SCSI expansion boards, and some devices may not work well together on the same SCSI bus. SCSI is available in several variants, some of which are shown in Table 5.1.

When a SCSI drive is installed in a computer system, it's assigned a SCSI ID. SCSI devices are either manually or automatically configured, depending on the configuration. The computer can then identify each component on a SCSI chain by its SCSI ID. SCSI devices, unlike IDE devices, must be terminated. (*Termination* is the process of closing off or ending a cable.) SCSI terminators are attached to the end of the data cable to make the cable appear continuous to the attached SCSI devices.

 Approximately 95 percent of all SCSI-related problems are attributed to improper or lack of termination, or the improper configuration of a SCSI ID.

Table 5.1 SCSI variations.		
Type	**Description**	**Data Transfer Rates**
SCSI-1	Uses an 8-bit bus	Up to 5Mbps
SCSI-2	Same as SCSI-1 but uses a 50-pin connector instead of a 25-pin connector and supports multiple devices	Up to 10Mbps
Wide SCSI	68-pin cable for 16-bit transfers	Up to 104Mbps
Fast SCSI	8-bit bus; double clock rate	Up to 10Mbps (rarely seen)
Fast-Wide SCSI	16-bit bus	Up to 20Mbps
Ultra SCSI	8-bit bus	Up to 20Mbps
SCSI-3 (Ultra-Wide)	16-bit bus	Up to 40Mbps
Ultra2 SCSI	8-bit bus	Up to 40Mbps
Wide Ultra2 SCSI	16-bit bus	Up to 80Mbps

When a computer starts, the SCSI controller polls all the attached SCSI devices and reestablishes connections. This discovery and registration process occurs during the power on self-test (POST) and delays the start of the computer system. A failure of all SCSI devices during the discovery process would indicate improper cable termination or possible conflicting SCSI IDs.

IDE Basics

The Integrated Device Electronics (IDE) specification is an industry attempt to move all drive electronics off the controllers and onto the drives themselves. IDE uses only run length limited (RLL) encoding for its drives. Enhanced IDE (EIDE) is an enhancement to the IDE standard. It was developed to support drive sizes greater than 528MB and higher data transfer rates (up to 13.3Mbps). EIDE has an upgraded Basic Input/Output System (BIOS) that allows a higher drive capacity, which addresses the currently limiting standard IDE drives. NetWare can only address the first 528MB of an IDE drive's physical space but can fully utilize the capacity of an EIDE drive. EIDE drives are often referred to as *ATA drives* or *AT Attachment drives*.

 NetWare, like most other operating systems, can only access 528MB of space on an IDE drive, regardless of the physical size of the hard disk. EIDE drives and compatible controllers allow you to attach drives larger than 528MB.

Standard IDE controllers support two or four drives configured with one or two physical drives per cable connection. IDE drives do not require termination like SCSI drives, are less expensive than their SCSI counterparts, and are not as fast as SCSI drives.

> *Note:* *These controllers are effectively paired single controllers—they take two sets of interrupt request (IRQ) and I/O port resources. Also note that IDE drives require CPU processing time, which is not generally required by a bus mastering SCSI adapter. This is an important consideration when designing a server or high performance workstation.*

Preparing A Disk Subsystem

Different types of hard disks mandate different installation methods. For this reason, we'll discuss general hard disk installations first, and then we'll cover IDE and SCSI installations in depth.

Know how to use Micro House's SupportSource (**www. supportsource.com**) to look up the steps needed to set up a drive or other computing device.

The installation of hard disk storage requires three components: the disk itself, a controller, and a cable to connect them. First, you must install a hard disk and then prepare the disk for use. Computer manufacturers provide various methods of containing a hard disk within a computer. There's no trick here other than finding some way to mount the disk within the case. Next, you must install a controller board, known as a *Host Bus Adapter (HBA)*. Finally, you must install a cable that connects the two devices. IDE and SCSI drives use different sets of drives, controllers, and cables. An IDE cable will not physically fit into a SCSI drive, making it difficult to attach the wrong cable to the wrong drive.

Host Bus Adapter (HBA) Installation

Although many newer computer systems come with an HBA, you may still have to install one. HBAs are associated with SCSI devices. Remember that IDE devices contain their own electronics, so an HBA is not required for them. Installing an HBA is no different from installing any other card in a computer—it's simply inserted into an available slot. With SCSI, every device on the bus must have a SCSI ID, and the HBA is no exception. It's standard to assign a SCSI ID of 7 to the HBA. The settings on the HBA can be set through dual in-line package (DIP) switches, jumpers, or a wheel-like dial on the back plane of the card.

Most newer SCSI devices and cards are configured using the manufacturers setup software and do not require manual configuration.

HBAs may also require termination. Each end of a SCSI bus is terminated. Depending on your drive location and configuration, either the HBA, the last drive in a chain, or the end point of the SCSI cable is terminated. Finally, each HBA or interface installed into a computer must have the following configured or verified: IRQ channel, Direct Memory Access (DMA) channel, I/O address, and base memory address. After you install the HBA interface card, you can connect the drive cable to the HBA. Impedance-matched cables are recommended for external SCSI subsystems for increased data reliability and performance.

Finally, you must configure the complementary metal oxide semiconductor (CMOS) to recognize the SCSI drive. Set the drive type to either 0 or Not Installed. This is required because SCSI disks do not require CMOS settings.

IDE Installation

IDE drives assume one of three roles: single, master, or slave. IDE drive manufacturers ship drives configured as single drives. If you're only going to have a single drive in the system, no jumper changes are required. If your system is going to have two drives, one is designated a master and the other is designated a slave. Whichever drive you boot from is the *master drive*. On the rear of the physical drive near the power connection are jumpers used for configuring the drive type. The *slave drive* is the drive not used as the boot device. Some EIDE drives automatically determine whether they're a slave or master without requiring manipulation of jumpers or switches.

 The older IDE specification fails to support tape devices and optical disks; it imposes a 528MB limitation without special BIOS, does not support bus mastering to offload work from the CPU, and does not support multitasking input/output.

To begin an IDE installation, first install the drive in the case. Although the drive electronics are physically located on the drive, the drive cable can be connected either to the motherboard directly or to a network board. Newer computers have the IDE connectors built directly into the motherboard, which alleviates the need for adapter cards. An IDE cable has two device connectors on the cable, which allow two drives to be installed on the same cable. One drive is a master, and the second drive is a slave.

A *jumper* is a tiny plastic-coated metal connector used to connect pins located on the rear of a hard drive. The jumper is *on* when it connects two pins and *off* when it does not connect them. A DIP switch (acting like a light switch) can be set to on or off without the use of a jumper. Either of these may be present on your drive. The manufacturer assigns the functions to these items and includes a listing of them with the hard drive's documentation. After you connect a drive to the interface card, you can plug a power cable into the drive. The power cables are inside the computer case and connected to the power supply.

 Older IDE drives restrict drive sizes to 528MB without a special BIOS chip on either the drive or a special IDE controller.

Factors Affecting An IDE Drive Installation

Use a setup program to configure IDE drives. If a setup program is not available, you must provide drive information to CMOS. CMOS requires the drive size in megabytes, the number of drive heads, and the number of drive cylinders. Occasionally, write precompensation settings are required—depending on the drive. As tracks move closer to the center of the disk, the size of the tracks decreases. Write precompensation makes up for this difference. This information is usually labeled on the physical drive itself. The SupportSource disk also provides drive configuration information. If you cannot find the settings for a particular drive, you can guess. For example, the drive is 40MB but you have no idea how many heads or cylinders the drive contains. You could pick a type approximately the same physical capacity as your drive and test it. More often than not, you'll guess correctly enough to allow the drive to function.

Installing An IDE Subsystem

Use the following procedure to install and configure the IDE subsystem within a computer:

1. Unplug the computer.

2. Install the drive interface card.

3. Set IDE drive jumpers for Master, Slave, or Single drive.

4. Physically install the IDE drive.

5. Connect the data cable from the drive to the drive interface card.

6. Connect power to the drive.

7. Power on the computer.

8. Open the CMOS setup and set the disk type using SupportSource or the manufacturer's documentation.

9. Save the setting and exit CMOS setup.

SCSI Installation

For a SCSI drive installation, you have to first install the drive in the case. With SCSI devices, the cable is different than the IDE standard. A SCSI cable can connect up to seven SCSI devices to the same controller—Wide SCSI can support up to 15 devices (the controller is the eighth or sixteenth device and is usually not counted). The other major difference is termination. Terminators are like cable end-caps that indicate the end of the cable. An improperly terminated cable is one of the most likely failures of SCSI subsystems. SCSI devices do not have to connect to the cable in any order. When the computer boots, the SCSI controller interrogates all connected SCSI devices and assigns a SCSI ID. ID contention is the second most likely cause of SCSI subsystem failure. The SCSI hardware adapter gets the SCSI ID of 7.

Note: If different devices share the same SCSI ID, you may receive a warning, such as "WARNING: There is possible SCSI bus contention. A reboot may correct the problem when SCSI interrogation occurs." Otherwise, you may see the same device on all available SCSI addresses, see only one device when several are installed, or the controller may not boot.

Factors Affecting A SCSI Drive Installation

The following is a list of things you should be aware of or do that could affect the installation of a SCSI device:

➤ Route drive cables as far away as possible from the power supply or other sources of electromagnetic interference.

➤ The cable marked with red indicates pin 1 on a connector.

➤ SCSI cables and floppy cables are similar but different sizes. Be careful not to interchange them.

➤ SCSI connectors on a cable run must be at least 18 inches apart.

➤ SCSI connectors can be either 25 pins or 50 pins. Wide SCSI connectors are 68 pins.

 Be wary of using adapters to mix wide and narrow devices. It can be done, but they may not always function correctly. If you must mix narrow and wide (or SCSI speeds), you should test them first, and be aware of the possibility of intermittent problems.

Installing A SCSI Subsystem

Use the following procedure to install and configure the SCSI subsystem within a computer:

1. Unplug the computer.

2. Configure and terminate the HBA.

3. Terminate the SCSI drive.

4. Physically install the SCSI drive.

5. Connect the SCSI cable from the disk to the HBA.

6. Connect power to the SCSI drive.

7. Power on the computer.

8. Open the CMOS setup and set Disk Type to 0 or NOT INSTALLED.

9. Save the setting and exit CMOS setup.

Hard Drive Preparation

Almost every computer system is used for a different purpose, and the hard disks within computer systems have different uses too. It's important to determine whether a fault-tolerant strategy is necessary or if performance is a consideration for your system. These factors determine how you configure a system's physical drives.

In the "Storage Device Basics" section of this chapter, we discussed tracks and sectors, which determine how information is physically located on the drive's surface. Tracks and sectors do not just happen; they're configured when a drive is formatted. Formatting determines the physical layout of the tracks and sectors on a drive. There are two types of formatting: high level and low level. Imagine an old vinyl LP record—low-level formatting is the process of making the circle and punching the hole in the middle. It also makes sure the record's surface is free of imperfections by checking its surface. Low-level formatting also makes the grooves. For a hard disk, this is the process of defining tracks and sectors. This low-level stage of formatting identifies bad sectors and prevents information from being written to those locations. Finally, low-level formatting determines the interleave ratio and writes temporary information to each sector as a type of placeholder for later use.

 Low-level formatting is a destructive process that completely and permanently deletes all information from a drive. Low-level formats cannot be undone. Low-level formatting is not recommended on IDE drives unless required by the drive manufacturer.

After a drive completes a low-level format, you can partition it. *Partitioning* divides the drive into logical sections, similar to the way cubicles divide office space. FDISK is one of many DOS-based utilities used to partition drives.

When you're installing NetWare, only a small DOS partition is required, and it should exceed the amount of RAM installed in the computer itself by at least 50MB. NetWare automatically partitions and formats the remaining drive space during the installation process.

Hard disks are built with multiple platters. A partition can take up space on several physical platters on the same disk. Use partitioning to create logical devices rather than physical ones. For example, if your system contains two physical drives, each drive can be partitioned into multiple logical drives. A physical drive can contain multiple logical partitions, and each partition can be assigned a drive letter. Your system can then have C:, D:, and E: logical drives all on the same physical disk.

You would perform a low-level format in the following instances:

➤ When there's an indication of a large number of disk errors

➤ When you want to destroy all information on a drive

➤ When interleave values need to be changed

➤ When you install a new drive or controller (not always required)

After partitions are created, high-level formatting occurs. High-level formatting double-checks the success of the low-level format and scans the drive for bad sectors a second time. During this stage, the File Allocation Table (FAT) is created. The FAT functions as a lookup list. When you write files to the drive, the recorded locations of the file's sectors go into the FAT. High-level formatting can also copy DOS system files. The system files are required if you want to make a drive bootable. The command **FORMAT C: /S** performs a high-level drive format, tests the disk read/write heads, creates tracks and sectors, assigns sector IDs, sets the drive's interleave ratio, temporarily fills each sector, and marks bad sectors to keep the drive from writing data to them. Also, the transferred DOS system files make the C: drive a bootable disk.

Preparing NetWare Drives

Preparing a NetWare drive differs somewhat from creation of a DOS drive. A NetWare drive contains a small primary DOS partition and NetWare partition.

 Only one NetWare partition can exist on a single drive—except in NetWare 5. However, NetWare can have different partitions on the same physical drive if different versions of NetWare inhabit each partition.

NetWare considers the DOS partition to be the first logical partition and NetWare, itself, the second. The logical numbering of partitions starts with zero; therefore, the DOS partition is partition 0, and the NetWare partition is partition 1. The NetWare volume also contains a Hot Fix Redirection Area. When a write attempt occurs on the NetWare volume, the operating system determines whether the destination block is bad. If so, the operating system writes the data to the Hot Fix Redirection Area rather than to the bad block.

Physical Vs. Logical Partitions

So far, your drive has a DOS partition and a NetWare partition. What kind of partitions are they really? A *physical partition* relates to the physical division of space on a hard drive, whereas a *logical partition* may be made up of several physical partitions to form an apparently larger drive. Logical drives have perceived structure, whereas physical drives are fixed in size and can be removed from a system and held in your hand. NetWare uses logical partition numbers in fault-tolerant disk strategies, such as disk mirroring, to identify drives. The data area space of a physical partition is also known as a *logical partition*. Physical partition numbers are used to keep track of how NetWare records bad blocks to the Hot Fix Redirection Areas.

Volumes

Volumes are storage containers that represent the highest level of organization in NetWare. The first volume created on a NetWare server is the SYS volume. During the installation process, NetWare creates this SYS volume, which is initially nothing more than a container. Volumes possess the following characteristics:

➤ Up to 64 can exist on the same server.

➤ Volumes can be as large as 1 terabyte (TB) with a theoretical maximum capacity of 32TB.

➤ Can be created from any part of a NetWare partition.

➤ Can contain a complete NetWare partition.

➤ Can contain more than one NetWare partition spanning more than one physical disk.

➤ Capable of supporting up to 2,048 physical disks.

➤ Can have names between 2 and 15 characters long.

➤ Can have the same name only if they don't reside on the same server.

➤ Names can't contain special characters or spaces.

➤ Names must end with a colon (:).

Fault-Tolerant Strategies

A Redundant Array of Inexpensive Disks, or *RAID*, specifies disk configurations within a computer system using two or more physical drives. RAID configurations, as they're referred to, offer both fault-tolerant and non-fault-tolerant strategies. Key benefits of RAID are improved speed and fault tolerance. Table 5.2 lists common RAID configurations, descriptions, and benefits.

 To check the current state of a duplexed or mirrored drive set, use the NWCONFIG or INSTALL utility. (The INSTALL utility has been replaced by the NWCONFIG utility in NetWare 5.)

The most common RAID configurations are RAID 0, RAID 1, and RAID 5. RAID 0, also known as *disk striping*, combines multiple logical drives into a stripe set. When data is read or written from a stripe set, simultaneous reads or writes occur to each of the drives in the set, reading and writing data to each of the three disks at the same time.

Disk striping with parity (RAID 5) simultaneously reads from and writes to multiple drives. In addition, RAID 5 duplicates the information written on one drive to another drive within the set. Although slower than RAID 0, a RAID 5 set can sustain a loss of a single drive without incurring data loss. A single drive failure in RAID 0, on the other hand, causes the loss of the entire drive set. Therefore, RAID 0 provides no fault tolerance, and RAID 5 does. RAID 5 does have a slight downside—it requires you to add the additional drive for parity. Figure 5.1 illustrates the comparison of the configuration of RAID 1 to RAID 5.

Table 5.2	RAID configurations and descriptions.	
RAID	**Description**	**Benefits**
RAID 0	Disk striping	Performance
RAID 1	Disk mirroring/duplexing	Fault tolerance
RAID 2	Data striping with interleave	Performance
RAID 3	Bit interleave striping with parity	Fault tolerance and speed in single-tasking systems
RAID 4	Block interleave striping with parity	Fault tolerance and speed in some conditions
RAID 5	Disk striping with parity	Fault tolerance and speed

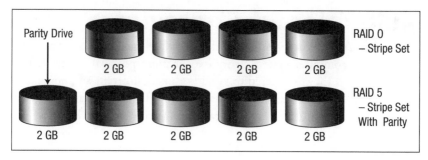

Figure 5.1 Comparison of RAID 1 to RAID 5.

Each array in Figure 5.1 supports 8GB of total storage. You may wonder why the five 2GB drives in the RAID 5 configuration equal 8GB of storage, not 10GB. Although the RAID 5 configuration has 10GB of drive space, one drive in a RAID 5 array is lost to parity. A common mistake is the belief that the extra drive is the parity drive, and that's simply not the case. The formula $T=(N-1) * drive\ size$ explains this concept, where T is the total available drive space, N is the number of drives, and *drive size* is the size of each of the drives. In RAID 5, each drive must be identical in size.

Drive Parity

Figure 5.2 illustrates the principle of parity and shows data written to Drives A and B. Parity data, or the same data, is simultaneously written to Drives B and C. The data written to Drive A has parity on Drive B. The initial data written to Drive B has parity on Drive C. To discover how fault tolerance works, pretend Drive A fails. Do you lose your data? The answer is no. When Drive A failed, you lost the first part of the data write on Drive A, and that parity data was simultaneously written to Drive B. Therefore, the data still exists on Drive B and Drive C. For data to be lost in RAID 5, two drives must fail. In this scenario, however, if you were running RAID 0, data would be lost.

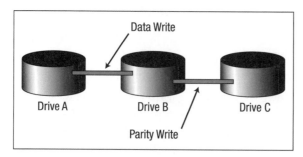

Figure 5.2 Overview of drive parity.

When a drive fails in RAID1, fail over to the backup drive is automatic and occurs with no user interaction. Additionally, with both drives functioning, reads are satisfied from either disk—roughly doubling multitasking read performance.

Two additional fault-tolerant strategies fall under RAID 1: disk mirroring and disk duplexing. Disk mirroring and disk duplexing both require two hard disks. Disk mirroring requires a single disk controller, whereas disk duplexing requires two. Both strategies are fault tolerant for disk failure, but only disk duplexing is fault tolerant for both the drive and the HBA. Both strategies simultaneously write data to both disks. Data is automatically accessed from the second disk in the event of failure of the first. Disk duplexing offers additional protection because two HBAs write data individually to two drives. Either the controller or the drive could fail with no downtime. The disadvantage of RAID 1 is cost. If you need support for 10GB of data in RAID 1 configuration, it requires two 10GB drives. Effective storage is only 50 percent of the total drive capacity compared with the much higher capacity offered by RAID 5.

When using RAID 1, Novell makes the following recommendations:

➤ Load disk drivers in the same order and load internal controllers first.

➤ Keep a log of hard disk device codes for reference during configuration or troubleshooting.

➤ Fault-tolerant strategies do not replace reliable and tested backups and restores.

➤ Use the INSTALL or NWCONFIG utility to monitor mirroring and duplexing status.

Disk Spanning

Disk spanning, or RAID 0, creates a single volume from multiple disks. The benefit of disk spanning is the creation of a single larger disk volume from two or more smaller, and possibly less useful, disk spaces. Data is saved over multiple physical drives, so the likelihood of data loss is high.

Novell recommends you mirror spanned disks for fault tolerance, because the loss of a single drive space in a disk span loses the entire volume.

CD-ROM

Compact Disk Read Only Memory (CD-ROM) is an ISO 9660 optical, read-only storage standard. CD-ROM technology has virtually eliminated vinyl LP records and the floppy disk in today's music and computing environments, respectively. CD-ROMs are capable of storing about 680MB of information on a single disk, which roughly equals 472 1.44MB floppy disks. Until recently, producing CD-ROM media was cost prohibitive, but low-priced CD-ROM burners are now available for the consumer market. Media prices hover around one dollar per disk. Additionally, CD-RW (read/write) drives have evolved, allowing multiple writes on the same disk for about five dollars per disk.

Current formats of both CD-ROM and CD-RW are standardized so nearly any CD reader can read them. The CDs themselves are not only very light-weight but also inexpensive to reproduce, based on their vast data-storage capabilities. With early CD-ROM drives, speed was a disadvantage; however, newer high-speed CD-ROM drives virtually eliminate this argument. Remember that older CD-ROM drives employed a caddy mechanism to house the CD for insertion into the physical drive. Modern CD-ROMs overcome this with a built-in automatic tray or a trayless input slot similar to a pay phone coin slot or a car-cup holder.

NetWare 5, as well as NetWare 4.11 and 3.12, support the CD-ROM technology on either IDE or SCSI buses. Architecturally, a CD-ROM drive should be on a separate disk controller to minimize I/O bus contention with the disk subsystem. If you do otherwise, you risk volume dismounts, such as media change, during CD ROM access. You install a CD-ROM just as you would any permanent storage device. Drives are mounted in a similar manner to fixed disks. The following procedure details CD-ROM drive installation and configuration but assumes that the drive is physically installed in a computer running NetWare server software. To install a CD-ROM, take these steps:

1. Load the HBA drive for the CD-ROM drive, preferably from the STARTUP.NCF file.

2. If you're installing on NetWare 3.12, load the AFTER311 and NPA312 drives from the Support Connection Web site (**http://support.novell.com**).

3. Load any CD-ROM drivers specified by the manufacturer.

4. Load the most recent CDROM.NLM (NLM stands for NetWare Loadable Module).

To determine whether the CD-ROM driver actually loaded, execute the **CD DEVICE LIST** command at the NetWare server console. If the CD-ROM isn't in the list, unload and reload the driver or install a third-party CD-ROM driver. With NetWare, you may be forced to set disk buffers for the CD-ROM. This is performed with the following command:

```
SET RESERVED BUFFERS BELOW 16 MEG=200
```

As an option, a third-party product called SCSI Express can be used for SCSI-based CD-ROMs as well as other SCSI devices.

 If a CD-ROM drive isn't working, first make sure it's in the device list with the **CD DEVICE LIST** command. Then, reload the CDROM.NLM and issue the command **SET RESERVED BUFFERS BELOW 16 MEG=200** from STARTUP.NCF.

When you're networking with a CD-ROM, remember that a CD-ROM may cause the system to lock when you're copying NetWare installation files to a NetWare volume. In these instances, you have several options: You can move the drive to another physical drive controller, re-create the SYS volume on another system hard disk rather than on the subsystem disk, or use the parallel to SCSI adapter instead of using the SCSI bus directly. These recommendations are potential solutions for a misbehaving CD-ROM drive running in a networked environment.

Troubleshooting Storage Devices

This section investigates common reasons for storage device failure and problems common in NetWare. It covers SCSI, IDE, and CD-ROM subsystems.

SCSI Subsystem Troubleshooting

In the "Preparing A Disk Subsystem" section earlier in this chapter, we covered failure points that can occur when working with SCSI subsystems. Let's put those potential problems to the test and explore some symptoms and likely solutions. The possible causes of why you cannot boot up on a SCSI drive and possible solutions are as follows:

➤ **No power** Does the computer have power connected? The power cable to the drive may have been accidentally disconnected or not connected during installation.

➤ **Improper termination** If the drive is spinning, it has power. Check for proper termination. Are both the start and end points terminated? Are the HBA and the drive itself in single-drive configurations?

➤ **Cable not connected to drive** Is the drive spinning? If it's spinning, it has power. Is the SCSI cable between the drive and the HBA connected? The drive may be perfect but unable to transfer data to the computer.

➤ **Operating system not installed** If the drive is spinning and the cable is connected, is the operating system installed? This would certainly prevent a computer from booting.

➤ **SCSI ID conflict** Are you getting a WARNING: POSSIBLE SCSI BUS CONTENTION error message? It's possible some SCSI devices have the same SCSI ID. Check and change the offending piece of equipment.

➤ **HBA configured incorrectly** If SCSI bus contention is a problem, it may be your HBA. Verify its SCSI ID is set to 7 and no devices have the same ID. Now is also a good time to check the HBA controller interrupt, base memory settings, base I/O address, and DMA channel.

➤ **SCSI BIOS not enabled** Are you getting DRIVE NOT READY - ERROR or COMPUTER CANNOT START errors? SCSI BIOS must be enabled for the drive to boot.

➤ **Cable placement** Is the SCSI cable installed near a high electromagnetic-field generation source? It might be conflicting with the data transfer from the drive. Reroute the SCSI data cable.

➤ **Installation software** Did the drive or HBA come with setup software? If all else fails, reinstall the software.

➤ **Termination power** Some older devices are sensitive to the amount and source of termination power. Usually, this is provided by the HBA and at least one other device. Check the documentation for each component for termination power limits and enable or disable one or more devices as needed.

IDE Subsystem Troubleshooting

This chapter also covered possible failure points for IDE subsystems in the "Factors Affecting An IDE Drive Installation" section. We'll review those potential failure points and review possible solutions. If you cannot boot up on an IDE drive, some possible problems and their solutions may be as follows:

➤ **No power** Does the computer have power connected? The power cable to the drive may have been accidentally disconnected or not connected during installation.

➤ **Improperly set jumpers** What's the role of the drive and is more than one installed? Remember that an IDE drive is set as a master, slave, or single drive. On the rear of the drive, you'll see a jumper. If you have a single drive only, the jumper will be set to master or single. Set the jumper to slave only if two drives are installed and it's not the boot drive.

➤ **Cable not connected to drive** Is the drive spinning? If it's spinning, it has power. Check the IDE cable between the drive and the drive-interface board. The drive may be working fine but unable to transfer data to the computer.

➤ **Operating system not installed** If the drive is spinning and the cable is connected, is the operating system installed? This would certainly prevent a computer from booting.

➤ **Cable placement** Is the IDE cable installed near a high electromagnetic-field generation source? It might be conflicting with the data transfer from the drive. Reroute the IDE data cable away from the electromagnetic field source.

➤ **Drive adapter configured incorrectly** Verify settings for the controller interrupt, base memory, base I/O address, and DMA channel in the STARTUP.NCF file. The symptom of an incorrect configuration would be a disk controller failure.

CD-ROM Subsystem Troubleshooting

This chapter also covered possible failure points for CD-ROM subsystems in the CD-ROM section. We'll review those potential failure points and review possible solutions. Some likely reasons why your CD-ROM drive might not be working are as follows:

➤ **Drive mounting** Is the drive actually mounted? Use the **CD DEVICE LIST** command to check drive mounting. If the drive isn't mounted, issue the **CD MOUNT** *volume_name* command to mount the drive.

➤ **Drive adapter configured incorrectly** Verify settings for the controller interrupt, base memory, base I/O address, and DMA channel in the STARTUP.NCF file. The symptom of an incorrect configuration would be a disk controller failure. You may try setting the drive buffers in the STARTUP.NCF file. Add the following entry:

```
SET RESERVED BUFFERS BELOW 16 MEG=200
```

➤ **Installation software** Did the drive or controller come with setup software? Use the Support Connection CD and reload the CD-ROM driver. Your CD-ROM may use a nonstandard driver. Check with the drive manufacturer for a NetWare-compatible driver.

➤ **No power** Are the computer's components getting power? The power cable to the drive may have been accidentally disconnected or not connected during installation.

➤ **Improperly set jumpers** What's the role of the drive and is more than one installed? Remember that an IDE drive is set as a master, slave, or single drive. This pertains not only to hard drives but IDE CD-ROMs as well. On the rear of the drive, you'll see a jumper. If you have a single drive only, the jumper will be set to master or single. If the CD-ROM is on the same cable as an IDE hard drive, the CD-ROM jumper will be set to slave.

➤ **Operating system not installed** If the drive is spinning and the cable is connected, is the operating system installed? This would certainly prevent a computer from booting.

➤ **Installation software** Did the drive or controller come with setup software? If all else fails, reinstall the software.

➤ **Bus sharing** Is the CD-ROM drive sharing the SCSI or IDE bus with another device? If problems continue, give it a dedicated bus.

Practice Questions

Question 1

> A customer reports a SCSI disk is not working correctly on his or her NetWare
> server. What would you check first?
>
> ○ a. Disk spindle
>
> ○ b. Disk read/write heads
>
> ○ c. SCSI ID
>
> ○ d. Drive RPM

The correct answer is c. SCSI drives generally suffer failures because of conflicting SCSI IDs, improper termination, or improper cabling (listed in order of occurrence). Disk spindle (answer a) and disk read/write heads (answer b) are internal to the physical drive. The drive is a sealed unit and should never be opened by untrained technicians. Therefore, answers a and b are incorrect. Drive RPM is difficult to measure without equipment designed specifically to measure it. Although a possibility, drive RPM is not the first thing you should check according to Novell. Therefore, answer d is incorrect.

Question 2

> You're troubleshooting a SCSI drive. What three things can you quickly check?
>
> ❏ a. Termination
>
> ❏ b. SCSI address
>
> ❏ c. Cable connections
>
> ❏ d. Termination resistance

The correct answers are a, b, and c. Termination of the SCSI bus, SCSI ID address conflict, and proper cable installation are the likely candidates for SCSI failure. Although termination is a possible cause, determining the termination resistance is not something quickly checked or even likely. Therefore, answer d is incorrect and the reason this is a trick question.

Question 3

> A user, John, calls you claiming that he cannot access his CD-ROM drive. What actions can he take to investigate and correct this problem? [Choose the three best answers]
>
> ❏ a. Enter the **CD DEVICE LIST** command at the Server Console to see if the volume name appears.
>
> ❏ b. Restart the server.
>
> ❏ c. Mount the CD-ROM drive using the **CD MOUNT** *volume_name* command.
>
> ❏ d. Add the command **SET RESERVED BUFFERS BELOW 16 MEG=200** in the STARTUP.NCF file.

The correct answers are a, c, and d. The **CD DEVICE LIST** command shows the current volume names the system is aware of and indicates whether the drive is physically mounted. If the drive is not mounted, you must mount the drive. This is performed with the **CD MOUNT** *volume_name* command, where *volume_name* is the actual name of the disk volume. It may also be necessary to set the memory buffers for NetWare. This is done in the STARTUP.NCF file with the **SET RESERVED BUFFERS BELOW 16 MEG=200** command. Restarting the server is not likely to cure a CD-ROM-related problem. Therefore, answer b is incorrect.

Question 4

> Which of the following RAID levels offer fault tolerance in a personal computer? [Choose the two best answers]
>
> ❏ a. Stripe set (RAID 0)
>
> ❏ b. Disk duplexing (RAID 1)
>
> ❏ c. Data striping with data interleave (RAID 2)
>
> ❏ d. Disk striping with parity (RAID 5)

The correct answers are b and d. Disk duplexing (RAID 1) provides fault tolerance in two ways: It provides an additional disk as well as an additional controller. Any single component could fail with no consequences. A controller and its associated disk could fail, and the system would simply fail over to the redundant components. Disk striping with parity, or RAID 5, writes parity information (a copy of the information) to another drive within the array such that at any time, two drives share the same information and no single drive solely possesses any information. RAID 5 supports a loss of a single drive with no corresponding loss of data. RAID 0 is a stripe set. Data is written to multiple drives simultaneously. RAID 0 does not write parity information. Although fast, it does not offer fault tolerance. A loss of a single drive in a RAID 0 array causes complete data loss. Therefore, answer a is incorrect. RAID 2 is a trick answer because RAID 2 is not supported on any computer platform. Therefore, answer c is incorrect.

Question 5

What are the requirements of disk duplexing?

- ○ a. One drive and two controllers
- ○ b. Three controllers and one drive
- ○ c. Two drives and two controllers
- ○ d. One controller and two drives

The correct answer is c. Disk duplexing (RAID 1) ensures fault tolerance by simultaneously writing data to two different drives. As compared to disk mirroring, disk duplexing uses dual disk controllers rather than just a single controller. With duplexing, either drive or either controller could individually fail with no adverse system effects. Disk duplexing requires two drives and two controllers. Therefore, answers a and b are incorrect. One controller operating two drives in the RAID 1 configuration is disk mirroring, where a single controller simultaneously writes to two drives. Therefore, answer d is incorrect.

Question 6

Which of the following tasks is *not* a requirement when working with mirrored or duplexed disks?

- ○ a. Loading disk drivers in the same order
- ○ b. Performing regular backups
- ○ c. Running **FDISK /S** on the secondary duplexed drive following backups
- ○ d. Keeping a record of device codes of the hard disks

The correct answer is c. **FDISK /S** formats a drive and makes it bootable by copying system files. This is not a requirement. The only time a high-level format is necessary is to identify and mark suspected bad blocks on a disk. Answers a, b, and d are all requirements when working with RAID 1 configuration and are therefore incorrect.

Question 7

> Which of the following items must you configure when installing an HBA?
> [Choose the three best answers]
>
> ❑ a. SCSI ID
>
> ❑ b. Drive type jumper
>
> ❑ c. Termination
>
> ❑ d. Base memory and controller interrupt addresses

The correct answers are a, c, and d. SCSI HBAs have a SCSI ID of 7. You should verify this setting does not conflict with the setting of other SCSI devices. Both ends of a SCSI bus must be terminated, and the HBA is almost always one end. Termination is a requirement in any SCSI bus installation. HBA base memory, controller interrupt address, as well as base I/O memory and the DMA channel must be set for the HBA. This is often performed via a software utility provided by the manufacturer. HBAs are used for SCSI devices. IDE devices use a motherboard connection or an interface board rather than an HBA. Therefore, answer b is incorrect.

Question 8

> Which of the following items cannot be contained in a NetWare volume?
>
> ○ a. Partitions from multiple disks
>
> ○ b. A portion of a NetWare partition
>
> ○ c. Another volume
>
> ○ d. An entire NetWare partition

The correct answer is c. A volume can contain partitions from multiple disks (spanning) and all or part of a partition. A volume set is a group of partitions combined to make a larger logical device, but it cannot contain another volume. Answers a, b, and d can all be part of a volume and are therefore incorrect.

Question 9

> Your server is running RAID 1 mirrored drives. A file being saved encounters a bad block on one of the drives. Where is the data written?
>
> ○ a. It's not written anywhere. The user will receive a drive write error.
>
> ○ b. It's only written to one drive.
>
> ○ c. It's written to the Hot Fix Redirection Area on the good drive.
>
> ○ d. It's written to the Hot Fix Redirection Area on the drive with the bad block.

The correct answer is d. NetWare disks typically contain a partition table, a DOS partition, a NetWare partition with a Hot Fix Redirection Area, and a data area. During a write event, if the drive controller encounters a bad block, the data writes to the Hot Fix Redirection Area (and, in this case) in addition to writing to the normal location on the good drive. Data loss is not acceptable in any environment. NetWare doesn't just abandon the data to the bit-bucket. Therefore, answer a is incorrect. Mirroring writes data simultaneously to two drives. Data would only be written to one drive if the other drive failed. Therefore, answer b is incorrect. The Hot Fix Redirection Area is specific to the drive exhibiting the bad block, not the good one. Therefore, answer c is incorrect.

Question 10

> What are volumes containing partitions from multiple disks called?
>
> ○ a. SYS
>
> ○ b. Sparing
>
> ○ c. Spanning
>
> ○ d. Spamming

The correct answer is c. Spanning takes multiple partitions from multiple physical disks and combines them into a single, larger logical drive. Spanning is not fault tolerant. When you're operating with spanned drives, Novell recommends mirroring the volume. The SYS volume is the first volume created on a NetWare server. Therefore, answer a is incorrect. *Sparing* is not a valid term related to partitions. Therefore, answer b is incorrect. *Spamming* is the sending of mass unsolicited email. Therefore, answer d is incorrect.

Need To Know More?

 Mueller, Scott. Upgrading & Repairing PCs, Eigth Edition. Que Corporation, Indianapolis, IN, 1997. ISBN 0-7897-1295-4. Chapters 14, 15, 16, and 17 contain detailed information about the material in this chapter.

 Siyan, Karanjit. *NetWare Training Guide: NetWare 4 Administration*. New Riders Publishing, Indianapolis, IN, 1994. ISBN 1-56205-240-3. Chapter 3 provides some of the best coverage of NetWare 4.1 file system structures and organization available.

 www.supportsource.com is Micro House's page for SupportSource, an excellent resource for vendor specifications and troubleshooting information.

Network Boards And Cabling

Terms you'll need to understand:

√ Twisted-pair, Fiber-optic, and Coaxial cable

√ Ethernet

√ Token ring

√ Fiber Distributed Data Interface (FDDI)

√ Asynchronous Transfer Mode (ATM)

√ Category 1, 2, 3, 4, and 5 cables

√ IBM Type 1, 2, 3, 6, 8, and 9 cables

√ Cladding

√ Light emitting diodes (LEDs) and injection laser diodes (ILDs)

√ RG-58, RG-59, RG-62

√ Plenum

√ Carrier Sense Multiple Access with Collision Detection (CSMA/CD)

√ 10BaseT, 10Base2, 100BaseT, 1000BaseT, 10Base5

√ Multistation Access Unit (MSAU) and Controlled Access Unit (CAU)

√ IBM 8228

√ Beaconing

√ Autoreconfiguration

√ Early token release

Techniques you'll need to master:

√ Describing and understanding unshielded twisted-pair (UTP) and shielded twisted-pair (STP) cable composition

√ Describing fiber-optic and coaxial cable composition

√ Matching the correct resistance terminator with the specified cable type

√ Outlining the purpose of fire ratings for cables

√ Describing how Ethernet and token ring work

√ Describing briefly how FDDI and ATM work

One of the most important physical components of a network is the transmission media. A network can have a mixture of wire and fiber cable or wireless media. In this chapter, we cover the three most common types of cable found in today's networks. We also discuss the physical characteristics of twisted-pair cable, fiber-optic cable, and coaxial cable.

Other important considerations in networking include the various networking architectures. In this chapter, we cover the two most common architectures: Ethernet and token ring. Additionally, we briefly discuss FDDI and ATM.

Finally, we outline troubleshooting techniques for addressing transmission media problems and protocol issues.

Types Of Network Cables

The majority of networks that reside in buildings use some type of cable. Because of this, over 50 percent of failures that occur on a network are cable related. Having a good understanding of the types of cables and the configuration requirements can help you troubleshoot cable-related problems.

Three of the most common types of cables used in today's networks are twisted-pair, fiber-optic, and coaxial cable. Twisted-pair and coaxial are copper-wire cables and transmit data on electrical signals that have been modulated. Fiber-optic cable transmits data that's encoded with bursts of light.

Understanding Twisted-Pair Cable

Twisted-pair network cable is one of the most common types of transmission media used in buildings. It's inexpensive and has been used for many years. These features, combined with its physical flexibility and its light weight, make twisted-pair cable very easy to work with.

Twisted-pair cable uses copper wire that carries electromagnetic energy. The cable is usually made of 22 or 24 gauge copper wires that are each covered with insulation. The insulation prevents the wires from touching each other. Two wires are then twisted around each other, and usually two or four pairs of these twisted pair sets are twisted around each other, and then encased in some type of plastic sheath. This plastic sheath is what you usually see on the network, and the encasement can come in different media types to fulfill requirements such as local fire codes.

It's also very important that network cable implementations observe the maximum length requirements. As electrical energy travels down copper wire, the strength of the signal decreases as the distance increases. This behavior is referred to as *attenuation* and is measured in decibels (dB) per kilometer. When the signal strength becomes too weak, the quality of the data in the signal is unreliable and/or inaccurate.

The reason for twisting two wires around each other is to reduce the effects of *crosstalk* and/or *inductance*. If you take two copper wires, place them so they are parallel to each other, and pass an electrical current around the two wires, electromagnetic fields are generated around each cable. The force in these electromagnetic fields can affect the electrical currents carrying data on the wire. If you twist the wires around each other, the electromagnetic fields will cancel each other out. It's also important that the twists are present along the entire length of the cable all the way to the connection points. To maintain the quality of the cable, the rating of the connectors must match the rating of the cable. For example, if you attach a Category 2 cable jack to a Category 5 cable, the rating of the cable is Category 2. Also, bending the cable too far stresses the copper wires and can damage the cable. A general rule is to not create a bend in the cable that is greater than 10 times the diameter of the cable. For example, if the cable is 1/4 inch in diameter, don't create a bend in the cable greater than 25 degrees.

Twisted-pair cable used on networks is configured in two forms: unshielded twisted pair (UTP) and shielded twisted pair (STP). UTP is very popular and is typically used for interior building telephone wires. The second form is STP, and it has an additional shield around the wires to further reduce the effects of external electromagnetic fields. Figure 6.1 shows a UTP cable, and Figure 6.2 shows an STP cable.

The numbers of twists per foot produces different categories of twisted-pair cable. Categories 1 and 2 are typically used to carry voice information over the

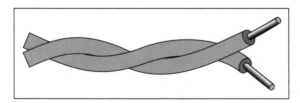

Figure 6.1   UTP cable.

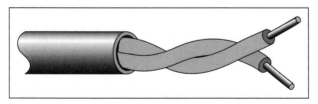

Figure 6.2   STP cable.

wire and are typically found in conventional household telephone cable. Category 1 cannot be used for data transmission; Category 2 can be used for data, but only up to 1Mbps. Category 3 is generally considered the lowest category useable for data. Category 3 cables can handle data rates up to 16Mbps and can be either unshielded or shielded. This type of cable has been used for 10BaseT, Attached Resource Computer Network (ARCNet), and 4Mbps token ring implementations. Category 4 can handle data up to 20Mbps and has been used in 16Mbps token ring configurations. Category 5 is probably the most common type used for network cables. It allows transmission speeds up to 100Mbps and is commonly used for 10BaseT and 100BaseTX implementations.

IBM technologies use twisted-pair cables, and for those implementations, the terms for the types of cables are different. IBM Type 1 cable is 22 American Wire Gauge (AWG) copper wires twisted in two pairs and surrounded by a braided shield. This type is typically used to connect terminal devices with distribution panels. It's also used in conduits in the same building and between wiring closets. Adding four additional twisted pairs to a Type 1 cable makes a Type 2 cable. Type 2 cables are used for the same type of wiring situations as Type 1 cables. IBM Type 3 is an unshielded cable composed of 22 or 24 AWG copper wire. The wire pairs are twisted together with at least two twists for every foot. This type of cable is very inexpensive; however, because of the low number of twists per foot, it's more susceptible to noise and crosstalk and therefore cannot be used for long distances. IBM Type 6 cables are shielded and have more twists per foot. This permits longer distances and more reliability. Type 6 cables are commonly found in extension and patch cables within a building. IBM Type 8 and Type 9 cables are designed for special uses. Engineers designed Type 8 to be placed under carpeted floors and to be more resistant to weight and foot traffic. Type 9 is fire resistant and is used in conduits, raised ceiling spaces, and wherever fire can spread.

Even though twisted-pair copper cable is very popular for use in networks, it does have some disadvantages. Copper makes a great antenna; therefore, it's susceptible to electromagnetic interference (EMI). Placing twisted-pair network cable next to electromagnetic forces, such as motors or fluorescent light ballasts, can interfere with the signals traveling down the wire. The effects of EMI can be reduced by placing the cable further away from the interference. Installers of network cables must follow distance specifications to reduce the effects of EMI. Because copper wire is a good antenna, this also means that it's very easy to eavesdrop on the signal electronically. In summary, the advantages of copper wire often outweigh the disadvantages.

You should be able to explain the different categories of UTP cables and their usage. In addition, be familiar with IBM's naming scheme for UTP cables.

Understanding Fiber-Optic Cable

Fiber-optic cable is increasing in popularity as a network transmission media because of its ability to carry data at much faster rates (Gbps) for longer distances than copper-based cables. In addition, because of decreased costs in recent years, more fiber-optic cable is being used for shorter, interior distances rather than just for long, outside runs.

Because fiber-optic cable uses light to transmit signals, it's immune to EMI and electronic eavesdropping. However, installation of fiber-optic cable and the connection requirements make it more difficult to install and configure. It requires care in manufacturing and handling and is generally more expensive overall than copper cables. If the fiber-optic cable or connection is compromised and the drop in signal is 11dB or more, the signal is unreliable and a poor connection results.

Fiber-optic cable is composed of a central core of extremely thin plastic or glass fibers. These fibers are surrounded by a reflective cladding material that's designed to reflect the light toward the core. This cladding is then surrounded by several coats of plastic or Teflon material designed to protect the fragile inner plastic or glass fibers. The glass fibers are made up of a special type of flexible glass (SiO_2). The quality of this glass is extremely pure. The transmitted light is generated by *light-emitting diodes* (LEDs) or *injection laser diodes* (ILDs). The role of the network board, for example, is to convert the light signals to electromagnetic signals through the use of photodiodes.

Fiber-optic cables come in different types, which are graded for various distances and types. The reflective cladding that surrounds the fibers varies in thickness, and thick fiber-optic cables have more area for the light signals to bounce around, which increases propagation delay. (Figure 6.3 shows a fiber-optic cable.)

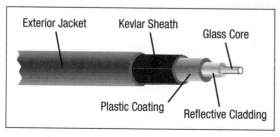

Figure 6.3 Fiber-optic cable.

Newer fibers are narrower and suffer less from signal delay. Three different types of fiber-optic cables are in use today: single mode, Multimode Graded Index, and Multimode Stepped Index. Single mode, or *monomode*, fiber is very thin, with a diameter of less than 10 microns, where 1 micron is about 1/25,000 of an inch (see Figure 6.4). These thin fibers produce very little signal bounce and therefore have the greatest bandwidth of the three fiber types.

Multimode Graded Index fiber-optic cables vary the refractive index of the cladding gradually so the signal remains more in the glass or plastic cable. The cable types range from 50 to 100 microns in diameter and can therefore be used for longer distances. The last of the three types, Multimode Stepped Index, is typically found in older installations, and the thickness ranges from 50 to 100 microns in diameter. These Multimode Stepped Index fibers do not have optimized cladding refractive indexes so the signal can bounce around more, which increases signal propagation delay. Figure 6.5 shows Multimode Graded Index and Multimode Stepped Index fiber-optic cables.

 Understand the purpose of the reflective cladding used in fiber-optic cables. Also, be able to briefly describe single mode, Multimode Graded Index, and Multimode Stepped Index cables.

Figure 6.4   Single mode fiber-optic cable.

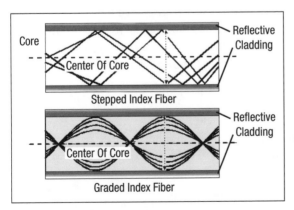

Figure 6.5   Multimode Graded Index and Multimode Stepped Index fiber-optic cables.

Understanding Coaxial Cable

Coaxial cable was the most popular form of copper network cable in the past; however, its dominance has been replaced in recent years with twisted-pair cable. Its past popularity as a network transmission media evolved from its use in other environments, and many vendors supported it. It's more resistant to physical damage, EMI, and eavesdropping than twisted-pair cable; however, it is more expensive, bulkier, and less flexible than twisted-pair cable.

Coaxial cable is still used in many networks and is often found in conjunction with other cable types. For example, many hub manufacturers include connectors to attach two or more hubs so the group acts as one logical hub. Coaxial cable is often one of the types available to attach the hubs. Coaxial cable is commonly used to connect your television to the commercial cable TV network.

The center of a coaxial cable consists of a single or stranded copper wire, which is surrounded by insulation made of plastic that's then surrounded by a wire mesh tube. This external wire tube acts as a conductor and a shield. The entire cable is then encased in a plastic tube. The term *coaxial* is derived from the cable's structure of two conductors sharing a common axis (*co* from common and *axial* from axis). Coaxial cable, when used to connect multiple devices in a bus or linear configuration, needs to have the two ends terminated. The terminators are resistors that absorb the signals at the cable ends to prevent "echoing" of the signal back down the cable. Figure 6.6 shows a typical coaxial cable.

As with twisted-pair cable, coaxial cable comes in different types, which are used for a variety of implementations. RG-58 coaxial cable is the most common form found today for networks. This type of cable requires 50-ohm resistance terminators. RG-58 is typically used on 10Base2 implementations. RG-59 coaxial cable is commonly used for cable TV connections and requires a 75-ohm terminator. RG-62 with 93-ohm resistors is used in ARCNet implementations. RG-8 and RG-11 cables are used in 10Base5 installations, and both use 50-ohm terminators. Also, as with twisted-pair cable, make sure the maximum length requirements for the different cable types are observed. If you don't, the signal attenuates and becomes weak and/or unreliable. It's very

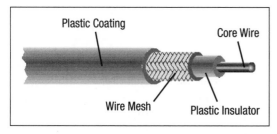

Figure 6.6   Coaxial cable.

important that you use the correct resistance terminator with the correct cable type. Terminators can be broken if handled too roughly and may not provide the required resistance. Also, because the different types of coaxial cable can look alike, make sure the correct cable type is used for the correct configuration.

 You should be able to describe the structure of coaxial cable and to identify the different types of cable and how they're used.

Building Codes And Network Cables

Network cables are often placed in areas that are out of sight to humans but not out of reach of fire. Because cables are made of materials that could be potentially harmful when they become very hot or are burned, many jurisdictions specify which types of cables are allowed in areas where fire can spread. Basically, wherever there's space between floor and ceilings and in conduits where air can pass, fire can spread easily. *Plenum* is the term used to define the space between the floor and the drop ceiling below. *Riser* is the term used to define shafts that pass vertically between floors. The material that is used to surround the outside of the cable is what determines the cable's fire rating classification. Cables that are covered with polyvinyl chloride (PVC) give off toxic fumes when burned and are not rated as fire-resistant cables. These are probably the most common types of cables produced and should not be used where codes require fire-resistant cables. Cables that are covered with Teflon fluorinated ethylene propylene (TFEP) do not release toxic fumes and are fire resistant.

 There's a standard for wiring in commercial buildings—the Electronic Industries Association/Telecommunications Industry Association (EIA/TIA) Commercial Building Wiring Standard. For more information, search for EIA/TIA with your favorite Web browser.

Ethernet Basics

Ethernet is probably the most popular standard used in most local area networks (LANs) today. Ethernet is a contention-based system, which means that devices wishing to transmit must "fight" for bandwidth. When a device wants to transmit, it "listens" to determine whether any other device is "talking." If the line is clear, the station begins transmitting data. Because of Ethernet's design, collisions between packets of data are expected. As more and more devices are added to the network, the likelihood increases that more than one device at a time will "hear" the same quiet time and therefore begin to transmit. In this situation, the packets of data from the different stations will collide and generate unusable packets. Because collisions are expected to occur in contention-based systems, the standards provide procedures for devices to help reduce the number of collisions. Ethernet standards provide Carrier Senses Multiple Access with Collision Detection (CSMA/CD) methods. In this system, the device wishing to transmit listens for the occurrence of collisions on the transmission media. If a collision is present, which is indicated by a special signal, the device will back off by a random amount of time and try to transmit later.

The packets of information moving on Ethernet networks are composed of several elements. The packets include the source and destination addresses, the type of data, and the data. Because of the amount of data a device sends and the fact that packets are not unlimited in size, most data is sent in multiple packets from source to destination. When a device receives a packet, it checks to make sure it's not damaged. If it's not, the receiver checks to make sure the packet's destination address matches its own. If the address is not the receiver's, the device does not process the packet.

Ethernet has several advantages that make it very attractive for LANs. The cables and wiring configurations have been available for some time and are relatively inexpensive. It's also easy to install and can provide communication speeds of up to 1,000Mbps. In addition, it's relatively easy to connect different systems, such as mainframes, to the LAN desktop systems.

Some disadvantages of Ethernet are related to the type of physical topology used. In a linear bus (Thin Ethernet) topology, determining the location of physical failures is usually more difficult. However, if you use concentrators or hubs to produce star physical topologies, the network is generally easier to troubleshoot.

Ethernet also follows the 5-4-3 rule, which specifies that the maximum number of hubs connected in a series is four, with a maximum of five segments. The maximum number of segments simultaneously supporting active devices is three.

There are several Institute of Electrical and Electronics Engineers (IEEE) 802.3 Ethernet standards, of which 10BaseT is probably the most popular. It uses UTP cable and is sometimes referred to as *twisted-pair Ethernet*. Each device is attached to a central device, called a *concentrator* or *hub*. The physical topology is a star, whereas the actual path the data travels (the logical topology) is a linear bus topology. This type of wiring configuration makes it very easy to reconfigure and expand a network. In addition, UTP cable, the connectors, and the hubs are all relatively inexpensive. You can use the lower grade Category 3 cable for 10BaseT, but most implementations now use Category 5 for eventual upgrades to faster specifications, such as Fast Ethernet. The specifications for the wire are 85- to 115-ohm impedance AWG 22, 24, or 26 copper. Because copper wire is susceptible to EMI, the cables should not be placed near sources of electrical power, such as fluorescent light ballasts. 10BaseT supports up to 512 active network nodes on a segment and up to 1,024 workstations per network. The 10BaseT specifications also include minimum and maximum distances. For example, the maximum distance allowed between a concentrator and a workstation, as well as between two hubs, is 100 meters (328 feet), whereas the minimum distance allowed is 0.6 meters (2 feet). Most hubs also include support for other types of connectors and cables, such as coaxial.

Another common type of cabling used for Ethernet is 10Base2, which uses RG-58A/U or RG-58C/U 50-ohm impedance coaxial cable and is often referred to as *Thin Ethernet* or *thinnet*. The maximum number of devices supported by 10Base2 is 30 per segment. Each segment can be a maximum of 185 meters (607 feet), and the entire network cannot be more than 925 meters (3,034 feet). The minimum supported distance between two devices is 0.5 meters (1.5 feet). Each device is attached to the coaxial cable with a T-connector, so the entire segment is a physical bus topology. Each end of a segment must be connected to a 50-ohm terminator, and only one terminator in a pair should be grounded.

100BaseT, or *Fast Ethernet*, is becoming more popular as the demand for faster LAN speeds increases. This specification uses the same CSMA/CD as 10BaseT, but it supports speeds up to 100Mbps. It's also configured the same as 10BaseT—physical star and logical bus topologies. There are actually three different Fast Ethernet specifications, and they're outlined in Table 6.1.

The maximum distance supported by 100BaseTX and 100BaseT4 is 100 meters (328 feet). 100BaseFX allows distances of up to 412 meters (1,351 feet).

Ethernet that supports data transfer rates of 1,000Mbps is called *Gigabit Ethernet*, *1000BaseT*, or *1000BaseX*. Gigabit Ethernet uses either copper or fiber-optic cables wired in a physical star. The maximum distance for the copper-based 1000BaseT is 100 meters.

Another type of Ethernet cable that was popular in the past but is not often found in newer installations is 10Base5. This 50-ohm impedance RG-11 coaxial cable is very thick, not easy to work with, and difficult to install. It's often referred to as *Thick Ethernet* or *thicknet* and supports longer segments than 10Base2. It's wired as a physical linear bus similar to 10Base2. Because the

Table 6.1	Fast Ethernet specifications.	
Type	**Cable Specifications**	**Notes**
100BaseTX	Two pairs of Category 5 UTP or Type 1 shielded cable	One pair for transmission and the other pair for receiving. High-quality cables, connectors, and hubs are required to be compliant with Category 5 specifications.
100BaseT4	Four pairs of Category 3, 4, or 5 UTP cable	When used with Category 3 and 4 cables and poorer quality Category 5, the extra pairs of wires are needed to divide the signal among the wires.
100BaseFX	Two strands of Multimode	One strand for transmitting, one strand for receiving.

cable is relatively inflexible, connectors are not used to attach the cable to the network board. Instead, the cable is pierced with a clamp that passes through the insulation and comes in contact with the inner conductor. This clamp usually contains the transceiver and is called a *vampire tap*, because it has two teeth. The network board is attached to a drop cable with a four-pair Attachment Unit Interface (AUI) connector. The other end of the drop cable is then attached to the clamp. Figure 6.7 shows a 10Base5 cable and the vampire taps.

Note: AUI is also sometimes expanded as Autonomous Unit Interface.

Similar to 10Base2, each end of a 10Base5 segment must be terminated with a 50-ohm resistor, and one end of each segment should be grounded. The minimum

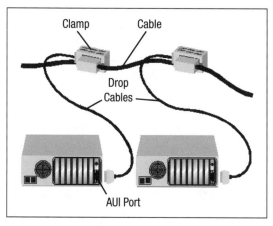

Figure 6.7 10Base5 cable and vampire taps.

distance supported between vampire taps is 2.5 meters (8 feet), and the maximum distance is 500 meters (1,640 feet). The total maximum length of a 10Base5 network is 2.5 kilometers (1.55 miles), where any one segment cannot be greater than 500 meters (1,640 feet). The maximum number of active devices supported per segment is 100. The maximum length of a drop cable is 50 meters (164 feet), with no minimum length specified.

 Be able to explain how Ethernet works. Also, be aware of minimum and maximum distances for cables and the number of nodes supported.

Token Ring Basics

A token ring network is not a contention-based system like Ethernet. A device can only transmit on the communication media when it's in possession of a token. The *token* is a special type of packet that consists of a 3-byte Media Access Control (MAC) frame. The token is like a permission slip that allows a device to transmit when it has the permission. Because devices on a token ring network do not contend for the transmission media, collisions do not occur and throughput is very good on large, busy networks.

When devices are not transmitting, the token travels freely around the ring and can be picked up by any device. When a device is ready to transmit, it must first wait for the free token; when it grabs the token, it changes the token's data to reflect that it's busy. The busy token is then sent out on the ring by the transmitting (or *source*) device and is passed from each device to the next. When the destination device receives the busy token, it copies the data from the frame so it can be used. The destination device alters the token's information to indicate that the destination device has received it. The alteration is performed by reversing two bits in the token's frame to acknowledge receipt. The destination device then sends the altered information back onto the transmission media where the source device receives it. When the source device analyzes the frame, it knows the data was received successfully by the destination device. When the source device has finished its conversation with the destination device, the source device generates a free token and releases it onto the ring so another device can transmit. Token ring is referred to as a *deterministic protocol* because the time it takes for the free token to go around the ring and the transmissions times can be calculated.

Note: This process is the same for 4Mbps and 16Mbps implementations of token ring, except for one major difference: On a 16Mbps ring, the transmitting device does not wait for the token frame to come back from the destination device. Instead, as soon as it finishes sending the data, it sends out a free token. This feature is called early token release and is only supported on 16Mbps implementations.

The data is passed around the network from device to device in a logical ring. The IEEE 802.5 specifications do not require a physical star-logical ring configuration, but it is the most popular implementation of token ring.

Token ring network boards need to have the speed specified, and all speeds should be set the same in a ring. The ring speed value can be set with either dual in-line package (DIP) switches, jumpers, or software, depending on the type and manufacturer of the board.

The first device in the ring that's powered on becomes the *active monitor*. Only one active monitor is allowed per ring. The role of the active monitor is to handle lost tokens and those that have gone around the ring more than once. It also maintains the master clock and checks to make sure the ring does not have more than one active monitor. The active monitor also makes sure that the transmitting device can hold onto the token in small rings. The other devices in the ring operate as *standby monitors*. Any device operating as a standby monitor can assume the role of the active monitor if the current active monitor is no longer available.

The active monitor sends out a special packet every seven seconds, which is sent to the next device in the network. The information in the packet lets the device know which device is the active monitor. In addition, the packet informs the active device to contact the next device in the ring. This continues around the ring for all devices so each device knows who its neighbor is. This information is also used to determine the ring's fault domain.

The devices in a token ring network are physically connected as a star topology with Multistation Access Units (MSAUs, or MAUs) or Controlled Access Units (CAUs) providing the central hub of the star. *CAUs* are powered devices and can participate in network management functions. *MSAUs* do not have power and are passive concentrators, and they have no network manageability features. IBM 8228 is an MSAU that allows a maximum of eight attached active devices. The devices are attached to the hub with adapter cables. These adapter cables were originally IBM Type 6 cables with an IBM connector on one end and a connector for the network board at the other end. More current implementations support other cable and connector types. Probably the most common implementation today is Category 5 UTP with RJ-45 connectors. The active device can also be connected directly to the MSAU or to a wall jack. The other side of the wall jack supports a cable that connects to the MSAU. IBM Type 1 cables are still used in environments that produce a lot of EMI.

Multiple 8228s can be connected with patch cables to produce a larger ring. On each MSAU there's a RI (ring in) and a RO (ring out) connector. To attach two hubs, a patch cable is connected from the RO of one MSAU to the RI of the other MSAU. The original patch cables were IBM Type 6 cables, but current implementations allow other cable types. In addition, original implementations used IBM connectors, but again, current implementations support other connector types.

Type 1 and Type 2 cables provide the greatest cable lengths, varying from 100-meter (328-foot) adapter cables to 200-meter (656-foot) patch cables. Type 6 and Type 9 cables have shorter distances of 45 meters (148 feet) for patch cables and 66 meters (216.5 feet) for adapter cables. Each of these four types of cables can support from 250 to 260 active devices. The IBM Type 3 cables allow adapter cables up to 45 meters (147.6 feet) and patch cables up to 12 meters (39 feet). However, only 72 active devices are supported on a Type 3 segment. There are also limitations on the number of segments connected and the number of MSAUs per ring. You cannot have more than three cable segments connected in a series. There's also a maximum of 33 MSAUs allowed in one ring.

If an attached device is not active or a port is left empty, the signal continues around the ring because of relays. When a device enters the ring, a five-volt signal (phantom signal) is produced that opens the relay. This allows the new device to participate in communications. There may be times when you need to reset all the relays. This can be done with a setup aid or an initialization aid provided by the vendor.

Each transmitting device in the ring is referred to as an *active station*. They are called active stations because they also function as repeaters. When a device receives a packet that isn't intended for it, these active stations retransmit the packet to the next station in the ring.

Token ring has several advantages, such as better throughput than contention-based systems under high-load situations. Because many mainframe setups use token ring, it's easy to connect the LAN to the mainframes. Another advantage of token ring is fault tolerance. Ring wrap uses a single cable connected to two concentrators to form a complete ring. This allows the ring to reconfigure itself in the event of a failure to allow data to continue flowing.

Traditionally, token ring was more expensive than Ethernet, but with the implementation of UTP, the cost has dropped and is now more competitive. Token ring networks in the past required more expertise and understanding of the technologies than Ethernet. However, with the presence of more intelligent CAUs, troubleshooting and configuration can be easier.

IEEE 802.5 token ring networks are available from a variety of vendors, but IBM's implementation is probably the most common. However, some slight differences exist between the IEEE and IBM specifications. For example, IBM allows 260 active devices on a ring composed of STP cables, whereas the IEEE standard allows 250. Table 6.2 indicates some of the cabling requirements for token ring. Note that these values can vary depending on the ring speed, the cable types, and MSAU specifications.

 Be able to explain how token ring works. You should also be able to identify maximum and minimum cable distances and the number of active stations supported. Recognize the differences between an MSAU and a CAU and IBM's MSAU model, 8228.

FDDI Basics

Fiber Distribute Data Interface (FDDI) uses fiber-optic cable. There's also a variation for FDDI on copper wire for short distances called *Twisted Pair Physical Media Dependent* (TP-PMD).

FDDI is a timed token-passing protocol whose physical layout consists of two rings. The data travels in different directions on the two rings and is therefore called *dual counter-rotating rings*. One ring in the pair is used for the actual movement of data, whereas the other is used for a backup route and other services. FDDI also supports concentrators to bring devices together. These concentrators can attach to either one of the two rings. Furthermore, devices and other concentrators can be attached to concentrators in a tree-like structure. The maximum number of devices that can be attached is 1,000, and the maximum cable length permitted is 2 kilometers (1.2 miles). The typical transmission speed is 100Mbps, and the cost of the cables is competitive with UTP. However, the network boards and concentrators tend to be expensive. In addition, installation and physical maintenance of an FDDI network is not simple and usually requires skilled technicians.

For a device to transmit on an FDDI network, it must have possession of the token. FDDI tokens contain a Token Holding Timer (THT), which indicates how long the device can hold onto the token and therefore transmit data. This

Table 6.2 Cabling requirements for token ring.	
Connection	**Maximum Distance**
Device to MSAU	100 meters (328 feet)
Ring In to Ring Out	2.5 meters (8 feet)

value can be varied to produce high-priority and low-priority devices. When a device comes online, it negotiates for a level of service, which determines its priority of getting the token. In contrast to 16Mbps token ring, there can be only one token at a time on an FDDI network.

When a device in an FDDI network no longer passes the data to its neighbor, the two stations on either side of the offending device put the data onto the second ring, which sends the data in the opposite direction. This prevents the ring from becoming broken; this process is known as *wrapping*.

ATM Basics

Asynchronous Transfer Mode (ATM) is a newer technology that can be used on existing fiber-optic and UTP cabling. ATM uses packet-switching processes, and it supports speeds from 25 to 2,488Mbps. A circuit is set up between the destination and source devices and remains open for the entire length of the communication. ATM can be a useful alternative for LANs that move a lot of data, such as multimedia information and Computer-Aided Design (CAD) applications. The packet-switching technology also allows you to load-balance your network traffic over multiple virtual circuits.

 Be able to briefly explain how FDDI and ATM work.

Troubleshooting Network Boards And Cabling

Many items and events can lead to data transmission failure. Not all of these are avoidable, but having good troubleshooting skills and a basic knowledge of the systems involved can help you solve the problem or, at the very least, help you reduce downtime.

Many types of tools are available for troubleshooting network-connectivity problems. Protocol analyzers can be used to capture data and develop baseline network values. These tools can range from very expensive, but sophisticated, physical network analyzers and sniffers to software protocol analyzers, such as LANalyzer for Windows from Novell. Network management products, such as ManageWise, often include protocol analyzers and other tools to document and assist in network troubleshooting. There are also simpler tools and techniques that can be used to aid in troubleshooting.

Ethernet

10BaseT is usually easier than 10Base2 to troubleshoot because of the star configuration. Newer hubs are more intelligent and can shut down a port that's connected to a defective device, which allows packets to continue travelling. If the hub is Simple Network Management Protocol (SNMP) compliant, you can use management software that's supplied by the vendor or other products, such as ManageWise, to help determine the problem.

10Base2 Ethernet cabling is generally more difficult to troubleshoot because several devices can be involved. Having a good wiring diagram that includes the location of key services may help reduce the time it takes to isolate the faulty device or section.

There are also other relatively simple situations that are easy to fix but can be hard to isolate that can create significant downtime. Because Ethernet is a contention-based system, a faulty piece of hardware or corrupt network board driver can create a device that's transmitting regardless of what is on the wire. This jabbering, or chattering, device may actually stop throughput on the network because the transmission media is being flooded with bad packets. Fortunately, on a 10BaseT configuration, the newer hubs will shut down a port connected to a jabbering connection. However, on a 10Base2 network, these may be harder to find. You may need to divide the network into smaller pieces and bring those devices online and watch the types of packets being generated. Other items such as bad terminators and T-connectors can also cause network problems.

Many network vendors supply diagnostic software to test their network boards. If you suspect the network board may be at fault, you should run these tests to determine whether the board is a problem. If you've replaced or added boards and problems arise, check to make sure there are no conflicts, such as interrupts, with other devices in the system. Vendors often ship their network boards with factory settings, such as IRQ 3, which usually conflicts with the system's COM2 port. Sometimes it's helpful to remove boards and then add them back one at a time to determine which ones are in conflict.

If a workstation is unable to find a server, for example, you can observe the workstation's attempt on a NetWare server console. Typing "TRACK ON", for example, allows you to watch for service requests and/or fulfillments. A protocol analyzer is also an excellent tool for capturing the packets sent and delivered to a workstation as the client software is loaded.

The TOKEN-DOS-207: Installion Error = 27 Ring Beaconing error indicates that the adapters are not running at the same speed.

Token Ring

Token ring implementations include mechanisms to assist in troubleshooting. One of these processes is called *beaconing*. When a station does not receive a packet from its neighbor during an expected time frame, the station will announce this lack of packet delivery by beaconing. A *beacon* is a type of message that indicates to the other devices that a device has not heard from its neighbor for more than seven seconds.

The second process is referred to as *autoreconfiguration*. When an active station is brought online, it will attempt to enter the ring. If a problem occurs, such as a different device ring speed than the speed of the ring, the station tries to reconfigure itself and attempts to join the ring again. If the problem cannot be resolved by automatic configuration, you'll need to intervene and correct the network board settings.

Several troubleshooting tips can help you discover and solve problems with a token ring network. Because token ring has been in use for several years, the items mentioned are derived from these implementations:

➤ Make sure all devices on the ring are set to communicate at the same speed. When a device with a mismatched ring speed attempts to enter the ring, the other devices may begin reporting problems and throughput will be affected.

➤ Verify that the hardware settings on the board do not conflict with any other device in the system. These may include interrupt, I/O addresses, Direct Memory Access (DMA) channels, network board addresses, and support for early token release.

➤ The network should have a physical and logical map of its devices and connections. Sometimes, different vendor products may not work well together and different cable types may lead to problems.

➤ If the devices on the network are SNMP-compliant, you may be able to use a tool such as ManageWise to assist in documentation and troubleshooting.

➤ Novell produces a simple communication-check tool called COMCHECK that can be used to check simple connectivity based on the Internetwork Packet Exchange (IPX) protocol.

FDDI

Make sure the correct type of fiber-optic cable is being used for the transmission lengths you need. Single-mode fiber can go beyond 2 kilometers (1.2 miles), but multimode fiber can only go up to 2 kilometers (1.2 miles). If the strength of the signal drops by more than 11 decibels, the data is essentially useless. You can use an Optical Time Domain Reflectometer (OTDR) to test the strength of the signal and the integrity of the cables. It's very important to make sure that all connections are clean and "light tight." A dirty connection can reduce the strength of the signal, thus reducing the effective distance.

Be able to apply the various troubleshooting tips to different scenarios.

Practice Questions

Question 1

What's the purpose of twisting pairs of copper wires around each other?

- O a. To maintain a compact cable structure that's easier to work with
- O b. To enhance the effects of crosstalk, which allows cable distances to be longer
- O c. To reduce the effects of attenuation, which reduces the effective cable distances
- O d. To reduce the effects of crosstalk, which reduces the effective cable distances
- O e. To allow more copper wires to fit inside the same plastic sheathing

The correct answer is d. Twisting pairs of copper wire reduces the effects of crosstalk, which reduces the effective cable distances. Twisting copper wire does not reduce the mass of the wires. Therefore, answers a and e are incorrect. Because answer d is correct, answer b is incorrect. Attenuation is a property of copper wire whether it's twisted or not. Therefore, answer c is incorrect.

Question 2

Ethernet is described as a contention-based system. Because of this, several devices may transmit simultaneously, which causes which of the following to be generated?

- O a. Collisions
- O b. Packet bursts
- O c. Large Internet Packets (LIPs)
- O d. Crosstalk
- O e. Merging of data packets with the same destination address

The correct answer is a. Several devices transmitting simultaneously causes collisions. Packet Burst is another protocol that allows several packets to be sent to the same destination in a burst. Therefore, answer b is incorrect. LIPs are designed for travel across routers. Therefore, answer c is incorrect. Crosstalk occurs when copper wires placed in parallel are used to transmit electrical energy. Therefore, answer d is incorrect. Because answer a is correct, there cannot be merging of data. Therefore, answer e is incorrect.

Question 3

What is meant by *early token release*?

○ a. On a 4Mbps token ring network, the transmitting device sends out a free token as soon as it's finished sending the data.

○ b. When a transmitting device has used up the time specified on the token, it must release the token even if it has not finished sending the data.

○ c. On a 16Mbps token ring network, the transmitting device sends out a free token as soon as it's finished sending the data.

○ d. If the token ring segment has over 260 devices, the devices furthest from each other can release additional tokens to help reduce the propagation delay.

○ e. This is used by FDDI to permit data to be sent on the second ring in the event the first ring has a failure.

The correct answer is c. Early token release occurs on 16Mbps token ring networks when the transmitting device sends out a free token as soon as it's finished sending the data. Early token release is only supported on 16Mbps networks. Therefore, answer a is incorrect. Answer b refers to timed tokens, which are used in FDDI networks. Therefore, answer b is incorrect. The maximum number of devices supported on a token ring network is either 250 or 260. Therefore, answer d is incorrect. Early token release has no involvement with switching data to the second ring on an FDDI network. Therefore, answer e is incorrect.

Question 4

What's the role of the reflective cladding in a fiber-optic cable?

- ○ a.   Cladding is used to increase the stiffness of the cable so it handles more bends.
- ○ b.   Because light can bounce around inside the cable, the cladding helps redirect the light to the center of the core.
- ○ c.   The cladding shields the cable from external light sources, which would add noise to the signal.
- ○ d.   Cladding is used around fiber-optic connectors to ensure they're "light tight."
- ○ e.   Cladding acts as a center core around which the fiber-optic strands are attached.

The correct answer is b. Because light can bounce around inside the cable, the reflective cladding is used to help redirect the light to the center of the core. Because answer b is correct, all the other choices are invalid and incorrect.

Question 5

Which of the following are the correct cable types for Ethernet on coaxial cable? [Choose the two best answers]

- ❑ a.   RJ-59
- ❑ b.   RG-59
- ❑ c.   RG-11
- ❑ d.   RG-45
- ❑ e.   RG-58

The correct answers are c and e. The correct cable types for Ethernet on co-axial cable are RG-11 and RG-58 ; however, RG-11 coaxial cable is thick and difficult to work with. RJ-59 and RG-45 do not exist. Therefore, answers a and d are incorrect. RG-59 is commonly used for cable TV. Therefore, answer b is incorrect.

Question 6

What's the maximum number of devices supported on a 10Base2 segment?

○ a. 300

○ b. 250

○ c. 30

○ d. 120

○ e. 130

The correct answer is c. The maximum number of devices supported on a 10Base2 segment is 30. Because answer c is correct, the other choices are incorrect.

Question 7

What's an MSAU?

○ a. MSAUs are powered concentrators used in token ring networks.

○ b. MSAUs are nonpowered concentrators used in token ring networks.

○ c. MSAUs are powered concentrators used in FDDI networks.

○ d. MSAUs are powered concentrators used in IBM Ethernet networks.

○ e. MSAUs are nonpowered concentrators used in IBM Ethernet networks.

The correct answer is b. MSAUs are nonpowered concentrators used in token ring networks. Because answer b is correct, the other choices are incorrect.

Question 8

> What are some of the roles of the active monitor in a token ring network? [Choose the three best answers]
>
> ❏ a. Maintains the master clock.
>
> ❏ b. Checks to make sure the ring does not have more than one standby monitor.
>
> ❏ c. Handles lost tokens.
>
> ❏ d. Sends out special "hello" packets every seven seconds.
>
> ❏ e. It's the last device that joins the ring.

The correct answers are a, c, and d. In a token ring network, the active monitor maintains the master clock, handles lost tokens, and sends out special "hello" packets every seven seconds. The active monitor checks to make sure the ring does not have more than one *active* monitor; all other stations are standby monitors. Therefore, answer b is incorrect. The active monitor is the first device that enters the ring. Therefore, answer e is incorrect.

Question 9

> Which type of communication protocol does FDDI support?
>
> ○ a. Early token release
>
> ○ b. Timed token passing
>
> ○ c. CSMA/CD
>
> ○ d. Dual counter-rotating rings
>
> ○ e. Fiber optic

The correct answer is b. FDDI is a timed token-passing protocol. Early token release is not a communication protocol. Therefore, answer a is incorrect. CSMA/CD is a process used by Ethernet to reduce the number of collisions. Therefore, answer c is incorrect. FDDI supports dual counter-rotating rings in the event of a ring fault. Therefore, answer d is incorrect. Fiber optic is not a communication protocol. Therefore, answer e is incorrect.

Question 10

> Why does an active device in a token ring network beacon?
>
> ○ a. When the active device first joins the ring, it sends out a special beacon packet to indicate its presence.
>
> ○ b. The active monitor station sends out a special "hello" or beacon packet every seven seconds. This is passed from device to device so devices know who their neighbors are.
>
> ○ c. When an active device has not heard from its neighbor within a seven-second window, it will begin to beacon, which lets other devices know about a nontransmitting device in the ring.
>
> ○ d. When the active device is attempting to enter the ring and a problem arises, the device will send out a beacon and then attempt to reconfigure its settings.
>
> ○ e. Beacons are sent around the network to let devices know that they can transmit when the beacon arrives at their location.

The correct answer is c. An active device beacons when it has not heard from its neighbor within a seven-second window, which lets other devices know about a nontransmitting device in the ring. Because answer c is correct, the other choices are invalid and are therefore incorrect.

Question 11

> What is happening when a network board on an Ethernet network is jabbering or chattering?
>
> ○ a. The device is sending packets in bursts to improve throughput.
>
> ○ b. The network board is experiencing troubles gaining access to the transmission media and is attempting to reconfigure itself.
>
> ○ c. This is a normal effect of supporting SAP on an Ethernet network.
>
> ○ d. The network board or driver is faulty and the device is sending out random data, which is taking up bandwidth; therefore, other devices cannot communicate properly.
>
> ○ e. The network board or driver is faulty, and the device is sending out special packets to indicate there's a problem.

The correct answer is d. When a network board on an Ethernet network is jabbering or chattering, the network board or driver is faulty and the device is sending out random data, which is taking up the bandwidth; therefore, other devices cannot communicate properly. Packet Burst and SAP have nothing to do with faulty Ethernet components. Therefore, answers a and c are incorrect. Answer b describes autoreconfiguration, which occurs on token ring networks. Therefore, answer b is incorrect. Because answer d is correct, answer e is incorrect.

Question 12

You've recently installed a token ring network for a small branch office. The new NetWare 5 server is up and running, and four of the five workstations can log in to the NDS tree with no problem. However, station 5 appears to be experiencing difficulties. You've checked all cables and CAUs and have switched those items around and verified that the physical network is functioning properly. When you run LANalyzer to observe the packets sent out by station 5, you notice the station is not sending out any packets. On further observation, you notice the carrier sense light associated with station 5's port on the CAU cycles off and on when you bring the station up and load the Novell client. Which of the following best describes what is occurring?

- ○ a. Station 5 is beaconing when it's turned on, and the hub's lights are flashing to indicate a faulty device.
- ○ b. Station 5 is attempting autoreconfiguration to fix its configuration problem.
- ○ c. Station 5 is unable to join the ring because the port on the CAU has been deactivated.
- ○ d. The port connected to station 5 has enabled ring wrap to redirect the data on the other ring.
- ○ e. There's nothing wrong with station's 5 configuration. Check to make sure the proper storage device driver is in use along with the proper frame type.

The correct answer is b. One of the symptoms of a device performing autoreconfiguration is its repeated attempts to join the ring. This is often witnessed as a pattern to the port's associated lights and/or an audible click as the relay is opened and then immediately shut. This question is tricky because you may not be aware of what an actual hub does when a station reconfigures; however, the pattern of activity and the lack of data packets are good clues that the station is not able to join the ring. In addition, reconfiguration is a troubleshooting process supported by token ring. Beaconing does not occur when a device attempts to join the ring. Therefore, answer a is incorrect. If the port has been deactivated, the device has no need to reconfigure because it's not at fault. Therefore, answer c is incorrect. Ring Wrap is supported by FDDI. Therefore, answer d is incorrect. Autoreconfiguration has nothing to do with storage device drivers. Therefore, answer e is incorrect.

Need To Know More?

 Theakston, Ian. *NetWare LANs: Performance and Troubleshooting*. Addison Wesley, Redding, MA, 1995. ISBN 0-201-63175-X. Chapters 3 and 4 cover Ethernet and Chapters 5 and 6 cover token ring in detail.

 The SupportSource CD product by Micro House is an excellent resource for information about network cabling and boards.

 http://support.novell.com/servlet/Knowledgebase is Novell's knowledgebase. Perform a search on any of the topics covered in this chapter (such as token ring, Ethernet, FDDI, and so on) to obtain lots of related information.

Setting Up
A Server

Terms you'll need to understand:

√ Kernel

√ SERVER.EXE

√ Server console

√ AUTOEXEC.NCF

√ STARTUP.NCF

√ Disk drivers

√ The INSTALL program

√ NetWare partition

√ Parity

√ Host Bus Adapter (HBA)

√ Novell Storage Services (NSS)

√ Disk mirroring

√ Disk duplexing

Techniques you'll need to master:

√ Learning the computer requirements for server installation

√ Understanding server-related terms

√ Understanding how to install a server

√ Learning how parity is calculated

√ Accessing a CD-ROM as a NetWare volume

√ Setting up disk mirroring and disk duplexing

As a network administrator, you'll have to set up Novell NetWare 5 servers so users can utilize the resources on the network. If a server ever experiences a disk failure, you'll have to reinstall the software and attempt to recover the data. In this chapter, you'll learn how to install the NetWare server software and how to use the various levels of Redundant Array of Inexpensive Disks (RAID) to protect your data. In addition, you'll learn how to mount a CD-ROM as a NetWare volume.

NetWare 5 Server Installation

The installation of a NetWare 5 server is relatively simple. But before you can install Novell NetWare 5 on a server, there are certain requirements the computer must have and some general NetWare terminology with which you must be familiar.

Requirements

The computer on which you'll install NetWare 5 must meet the following minimum hardware requirements:

➤ Pentium class CPU.

➤ 64MB of RAM. (Novell recommends 128MB because of the Java applications such as ConsoleOne.)

➤ At least 550MB available on your hard disk, broken down as follows:

  ➤ 50MB for the DOS boot partition.

  ➤ 500MB for the NetWare partition that will contain server files. (Note that technically, the absolute minimum is 350MB for a basic install.)

➤ Video Graphics Adapter (VGA). (Novell suggests a Super VGA, or *SVGA*.)

➤ At least one network board. There can be more network boards if your server will be servicing multiple segments and/or if your server will act as a router.

➤ An ISO 9960-compatible CD-ROM.

 These hardware requirements are just a minimum. If you add more RAM and faster hardware, your server will perform better. Novell utilizes all available RAM on the server for caching of user files after the server program and other NetWare Loadable Modules (NLMs) load.

You'll also need DOS version 3.3, or higher, installed for the DOS boot partition. It's not recommended that you use the version of DOS that comes with Windows 95/98 and Windows NT. The NetWare 5 License disk comes with DR DOS version 7, which can be installed on the boot partition. You should also have the following items handy before you begin the installation:

➤ The NetWare 5 operating system CD-ROM.

➤ The DOS CD-ROM drivers, so the computer will see the CD-ROM. (Most new CD-ROM drives support bootable CDs, which relaxes this requirement.)

➤ The NetWare 5 License disk.

➤ The interrupt requests (IRQs), port addresses, base memory addresses, and Peripheral Component Interconnect (PCI)/Extended Industry Standard Architecture (EISA) slots for your disk drives and network boards.

➤ A registered Internet Protocol (IP) address, if you're going to run Transmission Control Protocol/Internet Protocol (TCP/IP) on the server.

Server-Related Terms

As mentioned, there are some terms with which you must be familiar before you can install a NetWare server. We'll briefly define these terms in this section, but for more detailed information, we suggest you search for them in the online documentation that ships with the NetWare 5 CD-ROM. These terms and their definitions are as follows:

➤ **Kernel** The kernel is the core module that must be loaded on a NetWare server. The kernel is responsible for handling server RAM, processes, and the server's disks. The kernel is called SERVER.EXE on a Novell server.

➤ **Server console** The server console is where you manage the server. The server console provides you with a console prompt, which defaults to the name of the server. You enter commands at the prompt to either monitor or interact with the server. Here's a list of some activities that you can do at the server console:

    ➤ Down the server and start the server.

    ➤ Modify server swap space.

    ➤ Modify the server's configuration files (STARTUP.NCF and AUTOEXEC.NCF).

➤ Add and remove name space to store other operating systems files' on a NetWare server.

➤ Tune your server using the **SET** commands.

➤ Monitor server CPU, disk, memory, volume, and user-connection activity.

➤ Broadcast messages to users.

➤ Mount, dismount, and repair volumes.

➤ Manage Novell Directory Services (NDS).

➤ **Novell Directory Services (NDS)** This is Novell's directory service that stores information on the network resources and regulates their access. NDS is a hierarchical distributed database that's X.50x-compliant. The NDS database is stored on the SYS volume in a hidden directory named _NETWARE.

➤ **NetWare Loadable Modules (NLMs)** An NLM can be thought of as a NetWare executable. NLMs are modular and can be loaded and un-loaded without bringing down the server. This also means that a third-party company can write an NLM to Novell specifications and it will fit in with the server. An NLM can have one of the following extensions:

 Think of NLMs as components that surround the kernel (SERVER.EXE).

➤ **.NLM** Utilities that end in the NLM extension are often server utilities, such as VREPAIR.NLM, DSREPAIR.NLM, NWCONFIG.NLM, and MONITOR.NLM.

➤ **.LAN** These are drivers that control access to the server's network boards. Each network adapter has a separate LAN driver. Many LAN drivers come with the NetWare 5 installation CD.

➤ **.NAM** These are name space modules that allow users to store files on a NetWare volume that exceed the DOS 8.3 file name length or are of a different file structure.

➤ **.HAM and .CDM** Disk drivers are modules that allow the server to communicate with the disk and other storage devices installed on the server computer.

➤ **.DLL** Dynamic link library (DLL) files are available with NetWare 5. However, these DLLs are not Windows-compatible, despite having the same extension. These files are libraries of executable code linked to applications when the applications are run, rather than being compiled with a program's executable. These files may be shared by several applications because they're linked dynamically and exist as independent files on the hard drive.

Note: The NetWare network operating system does not become available until SERVER.EXE and the necessary NLMs are loaded on the server computer.

Installing A Server

Now that you understand the requirements that must be met before you can install a NetWare server as well as some important server terms, it's time for you to learn how to install a NetWare 5 server. Before you can run the NetWare installation, you must create a DOS partition. Follow these steps to create a DOS partition:

1. Make sure the hard disk has no valuable data on it or that the data has been backed up.

2. Use the DOS **FDISK** command to create a DOS partition that's at least 50MB. (FDISK erases any data currently on the hard disk.) Novell recommends that the size of the DOS partition be large enough for the server components and to hold a core dump. (A *core dump* is a file that consists of the contents of the server's memory when the dump is initiated.) Sometimes, core dumps are needed for troubleshooting (Chapter 12 covers how to create one). For example, a server with 256KB RAM should have a DOS partition of at least 300MB.

3. Set the newly created DOS partition as the active partition in FDISK.

4. Reboot the computer with a bootable floppy disk.

5. At the floppy prompt, type "FORMAT C: /S".

6. Copy any DOS files you want from the floppy disk to the DOS partition and reboot the computer.

7. Install the CD-ROM drivers for your appropriate CD-ROM drive.

8. In the CONFIG.SYS file, set the following:

   ➤ **FILES=40** This allows up to 40 concurrent open files.

   ➤ **BUFFERS=30** This allows up to 30 buffers of 512KB each for caching.

9. Reboot your computer.

Note: As mentioned previously, the installation disk is bootable and contains a limited copy of DR DOS 7. If your CD-ROM drive supports boot disks, an alternate method is to boot from the CD-ROM. The steps will be virtually identical to those in the previous list.

After you've completed this part, you're ready to move on to the Novell portion of the installation. You can perform the installation using the installation CD-ROM that ships with NetWare 5, or you can install over the network using a mapped drive that points to the installation files. Change to the appropriate drive (either the CD-ROM drive or the mapped drive) and type "INSTALL". (The full name of the file loaded is INSTALL.BAT.)

 Type "INSTALL" to begin the installation. (The actual name of the file loaded is INSTALL.BAT.)

There are two phases to the installation process: the text-based installation and the graphical user interface (GUI) installation.

Text-Based Installation

After the installation program starts, you're presented with a graphical splash screen. (You can toggle to the console screen behind the graphic by pressing Alt+Esc.) Then, you're presented with some text-based screens. Follow these steps:

1. Read and understand the license agreement. Press F10 to accept the license agreement.

2. Next, you need to determine whether the server is a new server or a server upgrade. You can also change the default destination directory from C:\NWSERVER to whatever you want.

Note: If you select a new server and a NetWare partition exists on the server, the installation program will detect this and delete the partition if you decide to continue. You must select the upgrade to preserve a previously installed NetWare 4.x or NetWare 3.x server. It must be unique among all IPX network numbers accessible to this server.

3. Press F2 to get the advanced settings, which allow you to choose a server ID number. A server ID number is a hexadecimal number that uniquely identifies the server on the network. Its maximum length is eight digits, and it's automatically generated unless you customize it. You can also change an option to modify the computer's AUTOEXEC.BAT file to automatically start the server on computer boot up. Select Continue when you've made the necessary changes.

   Note: Servers will sometimes use this hexadecimal number to communicate with each other. All NetWare servers of any version that are on the same network must have different server ID numbers. In NetWare 4.x and NetWare 3.x, this is referred to as the internal IPX number.

4. Next, you need to select from the following regional settings:

   ➤ **Country name** The default is 001 for USA.

   ➤ **Code Page** The default is 437 for United States, English.

   ➤ **Keyboard** The default is United States.

   Select Continue.

5. Select the mouse type and video type for the server. There are two mouse choices: PS2 and serial. Select Continue.

 Although a mouse is not required, it comes in handy with the GUI-based installation steps. For the video type, choose Standard VGA only if your video card cannot handle 256 colors.

6. NetWare 5 automatically detects network boards and storage devices. If NetWare cannot find the hard disk, you need to select it from the list of devices, or you may have to copy it from a floppy disk. After it finds the devices and matching drivers, the installation process displays the detected devices and drivers. Choose Continue.

7. The installation then attempts to detect the network boards and their settings. If the installation process does not detect the network boards, you need to install the appropriate drivers. Choose Modify to make the

necessary changes. You need to either load the network board drivers from the installation program or insert the floppy that came with the network board. You may also have to change such properties as interrupt, port value, and slot number (for PCI network adapters).

8. Other NLMs can also be loaded here. For example, you could load ROUTE.NLM for a token ring network. Select Continue.

9. Now, you need to create a NetWare partition and specify the SYS volume size. During this phase of the installation, the SYS volume is created and the Java-based programs that are needed for the GUI portion of the installation are copied to the SYS volume. You can change the following SYS volume information:

➤ **Block size** Depending on the size of the volume, this value will vary. Novell recommends you use the suggested block size for the volume sizes you create.

➤ **File Compression** This indicates that the volume supports NetWare file compression. Files stored on the volume will be compressed according to the values specified in the compression **SET** parameters.

➤ **Data Migration** NetWare provides the ability to migrate files from the server's faster devices to slower devices when certain conditions are met. For example, you could indicate that files that have not been accessed for six months are migrated to an optical storage device. The user does not notice a difference in the location of the files, and this allows files that aren't used often to remain actively available without the need to restore from a backup system. To use NetWare migration, the hardware devices need to be certified to work with NetWare's High Capacity Storage System (HCSS).

➤ **Hot Fix** This is a percentage of the disk that's reserved for storing data that has been redirected from bad disk blocks.

After you've made any necessary changes, select Continue.

Now, you're ready for the GUI portion of the installation.

Graphical User Interface (GUI) Installation

The rest of the installation is done via the Windows-based GUI screens. The initial GUI installation screen is shown in Figure 7.1.

The server name should be different from the name of the NDS tree. Also, the server name must be unique from any other server names on the network. The

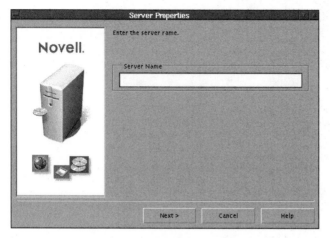

Figure 7.1   The Server Properties installation screen.

name of the server can be from 2 to 47 alphanumeric characters, including any underscore characters, but it cannot contain spaces. The first character must not be a period because periods are used by NDS as part of its object- and context-naming conventions. To continue with the installation, follow these steps:

1. Name your server and click on Next.

2. In the next dialog box, you can choose to modify existing NetWare volumes or create additional volumes from available free space. Volume names can be from 2 to 15 characters. The characters can include letters A through Z, numbers 0 through 9, and some other special symbols. Click on Next after you've made any necessary changes.

It's recommended that the SYS volume be used only for the operating system and its necessary files and directories. Consider placing applications, data, print queues, and home directories on volumes other than SYS. This helps reduce the risk of running out of disk space on SYS and makes the environment much easier to manage and secure.

3. If you've made changes to the volumes, the next screen asks if you would like the volumes to be automatically mounted when the server starts. Make your selection and click on Next.

4. The next screen gives you the ability to bind a protocol to the network board (see Figure 7.2). You can choose IP, Internetwork Packet Exchange

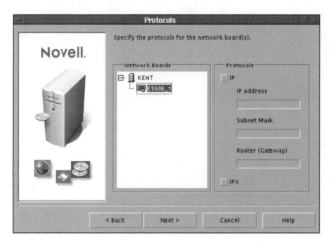

Figure 7.2 The Protocols selection screen.

(IPX), or both. For IP, the default frame type is Ethernet II. If you choose the IPX protocol, NetWare will install the Ethernet 802.2 frame type by default.

If you pick the IP protocol, you need to determine the following:

➤ **IP Address** A dotted decimal number that uniquely identifies the server—for example, 160.100.100.1.

➤ **Subnet Mask** A dotted decimal number that masks the host ID portion of the IP address—for example, 255.255.0.0.

➤ **Default Gateway (Router)** The default gateway is the computer that will route the packets of data from one subnetwork to another.

Additionally, if you choose only IP, the system automatically loads the Compatibility Mode Driver SCMD.NLM. Click on Next.

5. Now, you need to set the time zone and daylight saving time (DST) options for the server. Make the appropriate selections for your server and click on Next.

6. Next, select the NDS installation type. You can choose from the following selections:

➤ Install This Server Into An Existing NDS Tree

➤ Create A New NDS Tree

If you choose to create a new tree, the dialog box in Figure 7.3 appears. Enter the appropriate information and click on Next.

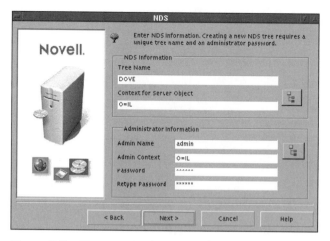

Figure 7.3   The new NDS tree configuration screen.

7. An NDS summary dialog box appears. Confirm the information presented and click on Next.

8. The license window appears and prompts you to put in the server license disk. You can install without a license, but the server will not be able to provide services until the server base license and connection licenses are installed. Click on Next.

Do not install the three-user demo license if you plan on having the server operate as a non-test production server. Refer to TID 2944702, which is available on Novell's support Web site at **http://support.novell.com**.

9. You can now choose to install additional products by selecting from the list of product options, as shown in Figure 7.4. Make your choices and click on Next. If you select to install additional products, the summary screen appears, which allows you to customize the products. When you're done, click on Finish.

10. Finally, the installation program uses all the previous selections and copies files to the SYS volume on the server. An Installation Complete dialog box appears, and you can choose to restart your computer, not restart your computer, or view the Readme file. Make your selection and you're done.

Now, you've completed a server install.

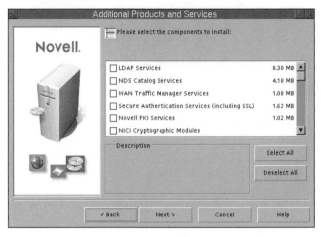

Figure 7.4 The Additional Products And Services screen.

Accessing A CD-ROM As A NetWare Volume

You can access a CD in a NetWare volume, but first you must make your CD accessible by mounting it. To mount a CD on a CD-ROM drive as a NetWare volume, you need to perform the steps outlined in this section. The steps are broken into two major categories: physically installing the CD-ROM drive and mounting the CD-ROM. These steps assume an Integrated Drive Electronics (IDE) disk is being used.

Physically Installing A CD-ROM Drive

The first portion of installing a CD-ROM drive as a NetWare volume involves physically installing the drive into the server. Follow these steps:

1. Shut down the server.

2. Power off the server.

3. Unplug the power cable from the wall.

4. Make sure you're using an anti-static wrist strap and mat while you're working with the internal components of your computer. You don't want to short any circuitry, and you want to ground yourself.

Don't use wrist straps when working with a monitor. They carry a potentially lethal voltage that can reach you through the strap.

5. Open the computer.

6. Insert the CD-ROM drive and secure it to mounting brackets.

7. Verify that the Host Bus Adapter (HBA) to which the CD-ROM is attached has the following parameters correctly configured:

   ➤ **Input/output (I/O) Address** This is a range of memory addresses reserved where the device and the CPU exchange data.

   ➤ **Interrupt request (IRQ)** This is a signal that can be generated by either software or hardware. Devices use this to signal or interrupt the CPU to tell the CPU that its attention is needed. IRQs range from 0 to 15 and are unique for each device.

   ➤ **Direct Memory Access (DMA)** Devices that take advantage of DMA can access memory directly without having to go through the CPU. This is faster than if the device had to communicate with the CPU.

   Note: Refer back to Chapter 4 for the details on I/O addresses, IRQs, and DMAs.

   ➤ **Master/Slave** For each IDE controller, there can be two devices. One is a master and the other is a slave. (For a Small Computer System Interface—SCSI—CD-ROM, make sure the proper SCSI ID and termination settings are selected.)

8. Physically attach the data and power cables for the CD-ROM.

9. Place the cover back on the computer.

10. Plug the power back in and bring the server up by running SERVER.EXE.

   Note: If you've set up the AUTOEXEC.BAT file on your server to automatically run the server executable (SERVER.EXE), you don't have to manually execute SERVER.EXE.

Mounting A CD-ROM As A NetWare Volume

After performing the physical installation of the CD-ROM drive, you would follow these steps:

1. Load the Host Bus Adapter (HBA) driver for the CD-ROM.

 An *HBA* is an adapter board or disk controller that adds a bus where peripheral devices can connect to the CPU. Many peripherals have embedded HBAs. The driver is called a *Host Adapter Module* and has a .HAM extension. NetWare 5 does not support drivers with the .DSK extension. You load a HAM for the one adapter. Because the adapter can control a tape drive, disk drive, or a CD-ROM drive, you'd load a Custom Device Module (CDM) for each of these devices.

2. In NetWare 5, CD-ROMs are accessed as Novell Storage Services (NSS) volumes. With NetWare 3.x and NetWare 4.x, CDROM.NLM is used. If you use CDROM.NLM in NetWare 5, it automatically loads three support components (if they're not already loaded): NSS.NLM, CD9660.NSS, and CDHFS.NSS. These components are explained later in this chapter.

   *Note: In pre–NetWare 5 versions, you would issue the **CD MOUNT Volume_Name** command to mount a CD-ROM as a NetWare volume. Then, you'd issue the **CD DEVICE LIST** command to identify the volume name.*

3. Insert the CD-ROM in the drive. Within a few moments, the CD-ROM will be automatically mounted.

   If the CD-ROM has a volume name, it will appear when it mounts. If it doesn't, one will be generated for it. The name will be in the format of CD*nnnnnn*, where *n* is a numeric value.

 If your CD-ROM doesn't mount, try physically ejecting and inserting it again. After this, if it doesn't show up in the list, the CD may not be mountable as a NetWare volume. There are some vendors who don't comply 100 percent with the ISO 9660 standard.

4. Optionally, you may need to reserve memory for your CD-ROM driver. If the CD-ROM storage device driver needs RAM below the 16MB boundary and your server has more than 16MB, you'll need to add a SET command to your STARTUP.NCF file so that when the server boots, the command will execute. Alternatively, to make the change occur right away, you could just run it at the server prompt, as follows:

```
SET RESERVED BUFFERS BELOW 16 MEG=250
```

Note: *The variable after "MEG" can range from 8 to 300—the default is 200.*

Now that your volume is mounted and you have the name of your volume, you could map a network drive to it from a Windows 95/98 or Windows NT client. After this mapping, a user can access the information on the drive. Also, the user could just browse Network Neighborhood to find information on the volume. In addition, you can create an NDS Volume object for the CD-ROM, a Directory Map object, or Application objects that refer to applications on the CD-ROM.

You cannot use a CD-ROM in a server's CD-ROM drive if it's not mounted.

Now, let's look at the modules that are loaded when CDROM.NLM is loaded on the server—NSS.NLM, CD9660.NSS, and CDHFS.NSS. These NLMs can also be loaded and unloaded manually.

Novell Storage Services (NSS)

NSS is a new file system architecture that runs on NetWare 5. As its name implies, NSS is a storage service. NSS can manage unused disk space from the hard drives on your server as well as unused space from NetWare volumes. You can use the traditional NetWare file system and NSS simultaneously. NSS provides the following benefits:

➤ NSS allows for an 8TB (terabyte) file size.

➤ NSS can store up to 8 trillion files on a single NSS volume.

➤ NSS allows you to create and mount an unlimited number of NSS volumes on a single server.

➤ You can mount an NSS volume with only 32MB of RAM on the server.

➤ NSS mounts much faster than a traditional NetWare volume.

➤ Repair of NSS volumes is much faster than traditional NetWare volumes.

➤ NSS is the default method for mounting CD-ROMs as volumes.

The CD9660.NSS Module

The CD9600.NSS software allows for ISO 9660-compatible file formats. The International Organization for Standardization (ISO) is an entity that creates many standards. The ISO 9660 file format for reading CD-ROMs is one of them. There's also a subset of the ISO 9660 standard that's called the High Sierra format. The CD9660.NSS makes the CD-ROM a read-only volume. As long as the CD is in the actual drive when the module loads, it will mount the volume automatically. There are no indexes created as in the NetWare 4.x and NetWare 3.x versions of CDROM.NLM. Also, you can load just CD9660.NSS instead of CDROM.NLM. To load CD9660.NSS, you enter the following at the server's console:

```
CD9660.NSS
```

The CDHFS.NSS Module

The CDHFS.NSS module is the compatible file format for the Apple Macintosh Hierarchical File System (HFS). You can map a drive letter to both a CDHFS mounted CD and a CD9660 mounted CD from one client. You can also load just CDHFS.NLM instead of running CDROM.NLM. To load this on a server, enter the following:

```
CDHFS.NSS
```

Disk Mirroring And Disk Duplexing

The NetWare operating system provides and manages two fault-tolerant mechanisms for storage devices: disk mirroring and disk duplexing. With *disk mirroring*, the entire disk's NetWare partition data is duplicated, or *mirrored*, on another disk. Both of the disks are physically connected to the same disk channel, and NetWare maintains synchronization of the data across the disks. Novell defines a *disk channel* as all the hardware components that allow data to be stored and retrieved from the storage device. This includes the storage device, the controller, the HBA, and the cabling.

When you set up disk mirroring, you want to make sure the NetWare partition sizes on both disks are identical. If the sizes are different, you may have to modify the Hot Fix Redirection size to make the two partitions compatible. If the partition sizes are different, the effective partition size is the smaller of the two partitions. You can view the status of the mirrored partitions with NWCONFIG.NLM for NetWare 5 and INSTALL.NLM for NetWare 4.x and 3.x. In addition to the NetWare operating system maintaining disk mirroring, NetWare also supports hardware mirroring. However, only one of the two mirroring systems can be supported at a time—software or hardware, not both.

After disk mirroring is set up and running, the user doesn't see a difference in the storage system. When data is saved to the initial disk, it's written to the mirrored disk. If either of the two disks fails, the other disk takes up all the work and the user may never know there was a failure. However, if any other element of the disk channel fails—for example, the HBA—neither disk is available.

Disk duplexing is the same as disk mirroring except there are different disk channels for each of the storage devices. The data is mirrored between the two disks, but they're on different channels. In this configuration, if any component in one of the disk channels fails, the other channel can maintain services for the user. Therefore, if either the disk fails or the controller, the cables, or the HBA fails, the other channel provides hardware fault tolerance for these elements. Disk duplexing and disk mirroring are configured the same way within NWCONFIG.NLM for NetWare 5 (or INSTALL.NLM for NetWare 3.x and NetWare 4.x). The only difference is the hardware configuration.

In Chapter 5, we covered the basics of storage devices, including a discussion of SCSI and IDE. For either disk mirroring or disk duplexing, SCSI is the preferred architecture to use. One of the primary reasons for not using IDE drives, especially for disk mirroring, is that the master drive's controller also controls the slave disk. Therefore, if the master disk controller fails, the slave disk cannot continue to provide services. Also, it's recommended that you use components of the same model and brand for the mirrored or duplexed devices.

It's also very important (in both disk duplexing and disk mirroring) that the device codes for the storage devices are documented. On a SCSI system, these device codes are hexadecimal values made up of several elements, which are shown in Table 7.1.

In the event of a failure, you'll know which device has failed because the device codes are included in the information reported by the system. Because these device codes identify which device is which, it's very important that the storage device drivers are always loaded in the same order. Also, periodically check the synchronization status of the duplexed or mirrored devices. This is accessible in NWCONFIG.NLM for NetWare 5 and INSTALL.NLM for NetWare

Table 7.1 SCSI device codes.	
Item	**Digit Position**
Manufacturer's device driver ID number	1 and 2
Instance of device driver on the system	3 and 4
Logical unit number	5 and 6
SCSI ID number	7 and 8

4.x and NetWare 3.x. Make sure you check the physical status of the drives, not just the logical status. Remember that disk duplexing and disk mirroring provide dynamic fault tolerance in the event of a storage-device failure and are not designed as replacements for daily data backups.

In recent years, disk mirroring and disk duplexing for fault tolerance have been replaced with the usage of RAID 5 systems. When configured and set up properly, they provide the best mechanisms to handle failure of midsize storage systems. RAID 5 and the other RAID levels are discussed in Chapter 5.

For several years, Novell has provided System Fault Tolerance (SFT) III, which is complete redundancy of servers. Because the entire server is duplicated on another SFT III server, if any item in the server fails, the SFT III server continues with no interruption of service. (SFT III is being replaced with alternate methods in NetWare 5 and is currently only available for NetWare 4.11/4.2.)

Setting Up Disk Mirroring And Duplexing On A NetWare 5 Server

Before configuring the system for mirroring or duplexing, install the second storage device or disk channel. Document the device codes for each storage device installed so you know which device is which. The process for configuring NetWare operating system disk mirroring or duplexing is the same for both configurations. Follow these steps:

1. At the server console, enter "NWCONFIG" to launch the NetWare Configuration utility, which is where you set up mirroring or duplexing.

2. Choose Standard Disk Options from the options listed.

3. Select Modify Disk Partitions And Hot Fix. Notice the different storage devices listed at the top of the screen.

4. Select the device in the list that corresponds to the additional storage device you've added for mirroring or duplexing. This will probably be the highest value in the list, but it might not be.

5. Choose Create NetWare (Disk) Partition, and the resultant screen indicates the detected space found on the storage device.

6. If necessary, adjust the partition size to match the size of the partition you'll be mirroring or duplexing. Press Esc. Then, at the Create Partition? prompt, choose Yes.

7. Press the Esc key twice to return to the Disk Options selection box.

8. Choose Mirror/Unmirror Disk Partitions and notice that all the partitions and their statuses are listed. The various status definitions are as follows:

   ➤ **Not Mirrored** This is a normal message for a partition that's not mirrored and is functioning normally.

   ➤ **Mirrored** This message indicates the partition is part of a mirrored set and the data is synchronized between the two partitions.

   ➤ **Out Of Sync** This message indicates that the information on the partition is not consistent. You're not able to perform any actions on this partition until the data is synchronized. Press F3 to attempt synchronization of the information.

9. Select the partition that contains the data you want to mirror or duplex onto another partition and press Enter. The resultant display indicates the partition is in synchronization with itself because you haven't made the mirror/duplex set yet.

10. Press the Insert key to display a list of available partitions and select the partition on which you want to mirror the data. If the size of the selected partition is larger than the other partition, you're prompted to resize the selected partition as necessary.

11. As soon as the second partition is selected, the information will begin to synchronize. Depending on the size of the partition, it may take some time for the data to become synchronized. When the two disks are synchronized, a message will appear on the console screen stating "All mirrored objects on this system are synchronized." You can also check the status in NWCONFIG if you exit the Mirrored NetWare Partitions area and return to it after the disks are mirrored.

Practice Questions

Question 1

> What's the name of the CD-ROM support file for accessing Apple Macintosh CDs?
>
> ○ a. CDHFS.NAM
>
> ○ b. CDHFS.NSS
>
> ○ c. CDAPPLE.NSS
>
> ○ d. CD9660.NSS

The correct answer is b. The CDHFS.NSS is the NSS component for accessing Apple Macintosh CD-ROMs. Apple uses the Hierarchical File System (HFS) file format for its CD-ROM drives, and you must load that module on the server to access a Macintosh CD-ROM. Answer a is incorrect because it has the wrong extension. Answer c is incorrect because it's a fictitious file name. Answer d is incorrect because CD9660.NSS allows for ISO 9660-compatible file formats.

Question 2

> Zac is a network engineer who works for a small international firm. He has two NetWare servers connected to the Internet running the TCP/IP protocol. Both servers have 256MB of RAM. The NetWare servers run with a RAID 1 configuration for the disk drives. About 250 users access this server daily. One server, MEADORS-A, is using the ISO 9660 file format, and the other server, MEADORS-B, is also ISO 9660-compatible and has a CD-ROM drive that needs to use memory below 16MB. Both servers have CDROM.NLM loaded. Zac is trying to access the CD-ROM on MEADORS-B and it's not working. What does Zac need to do to make his CD-ROM accessible from a NetWare Client so a user can access the CD-ROM by drive letter? [Choose the two best answers]
>
> ❑ a. Zac needs to install CD9660.NSS on MEADORS-B.
>
> ❑ b. Zac needs to install CDHFS.NSS on MEADORS-B.
>
> ❑ c. Zac needs to change the STARTUP.NCF file with the following entry:
>
>   MEADORS-B: SET RESERVED BUFFERS BELOW 16 MEG=200
>
> ❑ d. Zac needs to map a drive from the client machine to the CD-ROM volume name on the NetWare server.

The correct answers are c and d. Because MEADORS-B has a CD-ROM drive that needs to access RAM below 16MB, Zac needs to place a **SET** command in the STARTUP.NCF file. He also needs to map a drive on the client computer for the user to access this CD-ROM by using a drive letter. Zac doesn't need to load CD9660.NSS or CDHFS.NSS on MEADORS-B because the CDROM.NLM module is loaded; it autoloads CD9660.NSS and CDHFS.NSS. Therefore, answers a and b are incorrect, and this is why this is a trick question.

Question 3

> Jessie is a LAN engineer who works for a large domestic firm. The company has five NetWare servers connected to the Internet running the TCP/IP protocol. All servers have 128MB of RAM. She is trying to set up a disk mirror for a volume, called APPS, on one of the servers. There are three disk drives in this server and they're 2GB each. This server also has an ISO 9660-compatible CD-ROM drive and a tape backup system. If Jessie mirrors two entire disks, how much space can be employed for storage of the company's data on that volume?
>
> ○ a. 2GB
>
> ○ b. 6MB
>
> ○ c. 4GB
>
> ○ d. 1GB

The correct answer is a. When you're implementing disk mirroring, the total amount of disk space that can be used for data storage will be half of the total size of the two volumes or disks. Therefore, if one disk has 2GB and the other disk has 2GB, when Jessie goes to mirror these as volumes, she'll end up with only 2GB of data storage. Why not 4GB? Well, the data is written to one 2GB area, and an exact copy is written to the other. Because it's a copy, you cannot store other data on it. All other answers represent incorrect values and are therefore incorrect.

Question 4

Novell NetWare 5 requires the use of drivers with a _____ extension for
the HBA module.

○ a. .DSK

○ b. .HAM

○ c. .DRV

○ d. .COM

○ e. .NSS

The correct answer is b. NetWare 5 no longer supports modules with a .DSK
extension. Instead, the more modular HAM drivers are used. Therefore, answer a is incorrect. The .DRV and .COM extensions are typical for drivers
used on a DOS- or Windows-based machine. Therefore, answers c and d are
incorrect The .NSS extension is for the different NSS support modules, such
as CD9660.NSS. Therefore, answer e is incorrect.

Question 5

What's the name of the device driver for a CD-ROM drive that provides for ISO
9660 compatibility?

○ a. CD-IS9660.NAM

○ b. CDHFS.NSS

○ c. CD9660.NSS

○ d. CD9660.NAM

The correct answer is c. The CD9660.NSS module is loaded to provide for
ISO 9660 compatibility. CD-IS9660.NAM and CD9660.NAM are made-up
modules, and the extension .NAM is used for name spaces, not CD-ROM
drivers. Therefore, answers a and d are incorrect. The CDHFS.NSS module is
loaded for Macintosh's HFS. Therefore, answer b is incorrect.

Question 6

Todd, a network administrator, is trying to install NetWare 5 on a computer. This computer has two 1.2GB disks, a High Sierra CD-ROM drive, 32MB of RAM, and an SVGA video card. He's running into trouble installing NetWare 5. What could be the problem?

○ a. There's not enough disk space.

○ b. He cannot have a High Sierra CD-ROM drive.

○ c. He doesn't have enough RAM on this computer.

○ d. The video card is incompatible.

The correct answer is c. A NetWare 5 server requires at least 64MB of RAM. There's enough disk space on this computer. Therefore, answer a is incorrect. The High Sierra CD-ROM drive is a version of ISO 9660 and is compatible. Therefore, answer b is incorrect. The video card is suitable. Therefore, answer d is incorrect.

Question 7

Part of your company's plan for handling failures is to implement disk duplexing on the servers that provide storage for users' home directories. Which of the following describes the hardware configuration for NetWare disk duplexing?

○ a. The second drive in each server is installed with a SCSI number different from the first drive. Because it's the end of the chain, the terminator is moved from the first disk to the newly installed second disk.

○ b. The second drive in each server is installed with the same SCSI number as the first drive. Because it's the end of the chain, the terminator is moved from the first disk to the newly installed second disk.

○ c. The second drive in each server is installed with the same SCSI number as the first drive. The second HBA is configured with different settings from the first HBA, and the second drive is attached to the second HBA.

○ d. The second drive in each server is installed with the same SCSI number as the first drive. The second HBA is configured with the same settings as the first HBA, and the second drive is attached to the second HBA.

○ e. The second drive in each server is installed as an HCSS device and given a different SCSI number from the first drive.

The correct answer is c. Answer a describes disk mirroring and is therefore incorrect. Answer b is incorrect because it's not the correct description for disk duplexing or SCSI configuration. Two devices on the same SCSI channel must have unique SCSI ID numbers. Answer d is incorrect because two HBAs in the same machine cannot have the same settings. Answer e refers to data migration and is therefore incorrect.

Question 8

Micki is running a Novell NetWare 5 server with a Pentium II 400MHz CPU and 64MB of RAM in a RAID 1 configuration. This server also happens to have multiple network adapters, so it's also acting as a router. It's running both the IPX and IP protocols. She is running ConsoleOne at the server, and it's running very slowly. What would you suggest she do to improve the performance of ConsoleOne?

○ a. She should unplug one of the network adapters.

○ b. She should add more memory to all her client computers.

○ c. She should add more memory on the server.

○ d. She should stop running both IPX and IP and only choose one protocol.

The correct answer is c. ConsoleOne runs at the server and the workstation. Micki is running it from the server, and ConsoleOne is Java-based. Java-based programs take up more memory on the computer. If she unplugs one of the network adapters, that will not improve ConsoleOne performance. ConsoleOne runs on the local server's CPU. Actually, if she unplugs one of the network adapters, she may cause other network-related problems. Therefore, answer a is incorrect. She can run ConsoleOne at a client machine; it's in the PUBLIC folder. However, she isn't running it on a client at this time. Therefore, answer b is incorrect. She could stop running both the IPX and IP protocols, and that would speed up the LAN. However, doing this would not improve the performance of ConsoleOne. Therefore, answer d is incorrect.

Need To Know More?

 www.novell.com/documentation is the NetWare 5 online documentation. In the initial screen, click on Procedures, then click on Setting Up, Installing for detailed information on setting up a NetWare 5 server.

 www.novell.com/documentation is the NetWare online documentation. It contains additional information on setting up a server, disk mirroring and duplexing, and CD-ROMS. Use keywords such as "Mirror" and "CD".

8

NDPS Printing

. . . .

Terms you'll need to understand:

√ Novell Distributed Print Services (NDPS)

√ Printer Agent

√ NDPS Manager

√ NDPS Broker

√ Gateway

√ Public access printer

√ Controlled access printer

Techniques you'll need to master:

√ Understanding the improvements in network printing with NDPS

√ Explaining the process for installing and configuring NDPS

√ Managing multiple Printer Agents from a single location

√ Creating Printer Agents using the NDPS Printer Manager

√ Creating and managing the three types of NDPS gateways

√ Creating public access and controlled access printers

√ Configuring workstations for NDPS printing

√ Tracking problems in the printing subsystems

Printing is the most critical network function for many users, especially those who don't believe something is real until it's printed on paper. Printing problems regularly rate near or at the top of complaints that require network administrator action. To better serve users and their network printing needs, which have become more complicated over time, Novell created Novell Distributed Print Services (NDPS) to replace queue-based printing.

The software that's required on the network to handle the increased functions of NDPS is more advanced than the software required for queue-based printing. NDPS simplifies the printing process for the users, because NDPS takes care of many more details than queue-based printing did. The workload on administrators will decrease too, because NDPS also addresses many of the customer complaints about printing. However, new software for printer control and printer management means new utilities for you, as an administrator, to learn.

In this chapter, we cover the basics of NDPS printing, including its installation and configuration. Additionally, you'll learn some helpful NDPS troubleshooting techniques.

NDPS Overview

As mentioned, NDPS is not an upgrade of queue-based printing but rather its replacement. The effect is similar to an upgrade, because NetWare users have better printing support, but NDPS has a completely different philosophy than queue-based printing. Because millions of queue-based printers are in use, however, Novell made sure that NDPS is completely backward compatible. Mixed queue-based and NDPS printing environments are no problem to install and/or manage.

All the functions of queue-based printing are included in NDPS, and there are lots of new features. Novell's partners in NDPS development were Hewlett Packard and Xerox—two companies that know printing and document management as well as any company. NDPS is the default print environment for NetWare 5, but queue-based printing is supported for an easy transition from the old to the new.

Important Points About NDPS

NDPS was an option for NetWare 4, but because printing is critical to most users and there are literally thousands of variables to deal with (such as the different printers and drivers), NDPS is the default for NetWare 5. It's the default print service because the bugs are worked out and the advantages are clear. The following list describes some advantages of NDPS:

➤ **NDS integration** This may be the best advantage of NDPS. The intelligence of Novell Directory Services (NDS) is harnessed for printer control and administration. User access to print resources is controlled by NDS, as is administration.

➤ **Single point administration** Because NDPS is integrated with NDS, NDPS can be controlled via NetWare Administrator. NDPS Manager snaps into NetWare Administrator, putting critical print resources under the same control as all other NetWare resources.

➤ **Plug and print** Adding a public access printer no longer requires loading new drivers to all workstations. (We discuss public access printers later in this chapter.)

➤ **Printers and clients communicate** Technically, this is bidirectional feedback and control, but it means users and administrators get realtime, printer-specific information (such as the status of toner, paper, and the printer), and details about the job properties (such as number of copies and notification when finished). These details are only limited by the intelligence of the printer.

➤ **Better notification options** New notification options for print operators include pop-up screen messages, email (with GroupWise for Internetwork Packet Exchange, or *IPX*, networks and Simple Mail Transfer Protocol, or *SMTP*, for IP networks), and third-party options, such as beeper gateways. User notifications can be routed to someone besides the print job submitter, such as the head of a committee.

➤ **Print drivers download automatically** NDPS includes a database of common print drivers, and these drivers can be automatically down-loaded to clients when necessary. If a client picks a printer he or she has never used, such as a new color printer, the driver will be supplied automatically. This requires the NetWare 5 Client, however.

➤ **Administrative push of new printers** NDPS printers can be pushed out to NDPS clients using NetWare Administrator. This long-awaited feature finally returns real management capabilities to the client's printing environment.

➤ **Print job scheduling** Print jobs may be scheduled according to size of the job, media availability, or the time of day.

➤ **Compatibility across clients, applications, and operating systems** Windows 95/98/NT and Windows 3.1 clients are supported by all NDPS functions (when used with the latest NetWare Client software). Additional clients will be supported soon.

➤ **Backward compatibility** All NDPS clients can send jobs to legacy (queue-based) printers, and existing clients can route jobs through special queues to NDPS printers. New printers (first from HP and Xerox) will include the new NDPS features, but existing clients will not have access to the advanced features unless they have NDPS software loaded through the NetWare 5 Client.

➤ **Reduced traffic** Traditional print services require a print stream to be sent from the workstation to the print queue on a server. From there, a print server picks up the data and sends it, as requested, to the remote printer, or RPRINTER (these functions may be collapsed). Fully intelligent NDPS printers, on the other hand, require no direct server intervention. A possible configuration includes a printer hard drive, which is used to spool files directly from the workstation; this reduces the network traffic caused by printing by at least half.

Another important advantage of NDPS printing is that you can configure two types of printers: public access and controlled access.

A *public access printer* is available to any network user without restrictions or any type of security. Public access printers don't have the full range of features seen with other NDPS printers because they're not tied to NDS. Important points about public access printers include the following:

➤ No NDS Printer objects

➤ Immediately available to everyone

➤ Minimal administrative controls

➤ No security (no NDS)

➤ Basic job-notification features, similar to queue-based printers

The opposite of public access is *controlled access*. Controlled access printers provide a much higher level of security. Important points about controlled access printers include the following:

➤ Tied to an NDS Printer object

➤ Available only to users with access to the printer through NDS

➤ Full control through NetWare Administrator as a regular NDS object

➤ Complete NDS security options

➤ Increased range of notification options and information to be conveyed, limited only by the intelligence of the printer

Any NDPS printer can be either public access or controlled access. It doesn't matter whether the printer is connected to a NetWare file server, to a remote printer application, or through a printer gateway.

NDPS Building Blocks

A system with as many features as NDPS requires multiple pieces, and NDPS is no exception. There are four main NDPS components—NDPS Manager, Printer Agent, brokers, and gateways—but not all of them are necessary to support NDPS on a network. Gateways, for example, will gradually fade away as NDPS-aware printers are added and the clients are migrated away from queue-based printing to NDPS.

Designed to handle larger and more complex networks and printing situations, NDPS has a variety of components that can reside in multiple places. Distributed networking is upon us, as you'll see as we discuss the components of NDPS.

NDPS Manager

Before you can have Printer Agents, gateways, and the like, you must have management control. That's the domain of the NDPS Manager—a logical software utility component that resides on a server and is used to create and control Printer Agents. The NDPS Manager can be on any server, unless a server has a locally attached printer that must be managed. In this case, the NDPS Manager must run on the server hosting the NDPS printer.

 The NDPS Manager manages the connection between Printer Agents and printers.

The NDPS Manager NetWare Loadable Module (NDPSM.NLM) program loads on the host server. It can be controlled through the server console (or RCONSOLE) or through a workstation running NetWare Administrator. Controlling it through NetWare Administrator is the best option.

There's no practical limit to the number of Printer Agents that can be controlled by an NDPS Manager. The NDPS Manager must be created in NDS before creating the first Printer Agent.

Printer Agent

The Printer Agent is a versatile piece of code that actually replaces the functions performed by the print queue, print server, and spooler, as well as the printer in queue-based printing. Unlike print queues and print servers, there must be a specific Printer Agent for each and every NDPS printer.

 The Printer Agent represents a physical printer.

The Printer Agent is key to NDPS. Novell goes as far as saying it "lies at the heart" of NDPS. A Printer Agent is described as follows:

➤ An entity running on a network-attached printer. (This is a software entity, but it may be hard-wired in ROM in the printer, so it will not be software in the traditional sense.)

➤ A complete software module (entity) running on the server or workstation hosting a printer.

➤ A complete software module (entity) running on a server that represents a network-attached printer.

A Printer Agent is multitalented, handling the following chores:

➤ Processing the print jobs and other operations of the printer

➤ Answering queries about the print job or the attributes of the printer itself, when queried by NDPS clients

➤ Generating the event notifications, such as completion, problems, errors, or changes on the part of the job or the printer

Now, you should understand how Printer Agents are able to replace the printers, print queues, and print servers from queue-based printing systems.

NDPS Broker

Queue-based printers advertise their availability using Novell's Service Advertising Protocol (SAP) announcement routines, which use bandwidth and are especially noticeable over wide area network (WAN) links. NetWare 5 has moved completely away from SAP broadcasts, especially with the use of TCP/IP as the primary client-to-server protocol. However, some method must replace the advertisement of services to all clients. For NDPS, that replacement is the broker.

The NDPS Broker object is installed automatically during NDPS installation. New brokers are created whenever there's no other broker within three hops of the current server. Three new services are provided by the NDPS Broker in NetWare 5:

➤ **Service Registry Service (SRS)** Although redundantly named, the SRS provides details about all the public access printers on the network. This service allows a public access printer to advertise information about itself, including its type, name, address, and other details, such as its model number and manufacturer. The SRS also tracks the list of other services available, such as the next two items. With IPX networks, SRS uses SAP. For IP networks, SRS uses multicast.

➤ **Resource Management Services (RMS)** RMS is the central repository of all resources to be installed and accessed by NDPS devices. Keeping all these details in one basket makes management simpler and takes advantage of a reliable, fast network for delivery. RMS tracks, downloads, and installs banner pages, fonts, printer drivers for Windows 3.x, Windows 95/98, and Windows NT, and Novell printer definition files (PDF).

➤ **Event Notification Services (ENS)** ENS handles all the upgraded communications capabilities among printers, clients, and operators. New types of information, when provided by the printer, can be transmitted by the ENS. Message recipients can be the print job owner or another person.

The added intelligence of NDS is apparent when looking at the expanded notification options provided by ENS. Unlike pre-NDS printing, where job information was severely limited and sent to the job owner, ENS provides more printer details than ever before. Even more indicative of the power of NetWare 5's communication capabilities, ENS uses the following notification methods:

➤ **Pop-up notification** This is enabled when ENS is enabled; messages pop up on the screen of the individuals designated as message recipients. These recipients can include anyone on the network, not just the print job owner.

➤ **GroupWise** ENS integrates easily with GroupWise to route messages through anyone in the GroupWise system.

➤ **Message Handling System (MHS)** Anyone still using the Novell Message Handling System can tie the older message architecture to ENS as well.

➤ **SMTP** IP-based networks have the option of using SMTP for message delivery.

➤ **Log file entries** Special logs can hold messages, allowing those users or administrators with the appropriate access rights to see the log.

➤ **Programmatic options** NDPS includes two programmatic options. Both Sequenced Packet Exchange (SPX) and Remote Procedure Call (RPC) functions are available to tie into ENS for truly creative and custom messaging options.

➤ **Open architecture for the future** NDPS is designed to be extended by end users and developers. There are no limits on notification types for those companies or vendors willing to develop new processes on the open foundation of NDPS.

As networks expand and go global, an on-screen pop-up "Send" message is no longer enough to manage and control a network. This enterprise scope for notification services alone shows the increase in system intelligence for NDPS and NetWare 5.

NDPS Gateways

NDPS is a new service; therefore, your legacy printers are not NDPS-aware. Unless you can afford to replace all existing printers with new, NDPS-enabled printers, you must have some way to integrate NDPS and queue-based printing: the NDPS gateways.

NDPS gateways from HP and Xerox are included with NetWare 5, but only because they helped develop NDPS. Third-party gateways are in development and will appear as needed. Novell adds a generic gateway, simply called the Novell gateway, to handle legacy printers.

The HP and Xerox gateways provide almost as much information as NDPS printers themselves, because the HP and Xerox gateways can pull their proprietary information out of their printers and pass it along. Novell's default gateway is more limited, because Novell has no idea which printers will be connected and need to be managed. The included Novell gateway uses a print device subsystem (PDS) and a port handler for communications.

Functions possible with the Novell gateway include the following:

➤ Accessing systems that require jobs to be placed in queues

➤ Managing the printer to limit the support by the non-NDPS printer

➤ Querying the printer for status and attributes

➤ Sending print jobs to non-NDPS printers

➤ Sending print jobs to non-NDPS printers not controlled by NetWare, such as to Macintosh, Unix, and mainframe printers

At a minimum, NDPS provides the highest level of printer system control available with NetWare pre-NDPS utilities. As more NDPS-aware printers are sold and more gateways are developed by third parties for legacy printers, the control of the printing process on NetWare will increase.

NDPS Installation And Configuration

Installing NDPS does not change, modify, or disable the network's existing queue-based printing configuration. NDPS may be added gradually, one printer at a time, and the migration may take as long as necessary.

These instructions assume you have a working NetWare 5 server and that NDPS was added during installation. If NDPS is installed after NetWare 5 installation, the person doing the installation must have the rights to create NDS objects and modify the NDS schema.

The basic steps for activating NDPS are as follows:

1. Create an NDPS Manager object.

2. Create the necessary Printer Agents.

3. Verify clients are using NDPS-aware NetWare client software.

4. Install any printers hosted by remote workstations.

These steps make the process seem harder than it really is, so let's uncover the mystery.

NDPS Manager Creation

Although creating a manager of any type sounds a bit "Frankensteinish," the NDPS Manager is actually a software component that resides in NDS. The NDPS Manager acts as a platform for Printer Agents that run on the server. You must have the NDPS Manager in place before you can add any Printer Agents. A single NDPS Manager handles all the Printer Agents you want to manage.

You create an NDPS Manager from NetWare Administrator. You must be logged in as Admin or equivalent. (The user creating the NDPS Manager must have at least Read, Write, Modify, and Create rights for the container in which the NDPS Manager will reside.) After you're logged in, do the following to create an NDPS Manager:

1. In NetWare Administrator, choose the container in which you want to create the NDPS Manager.

2. From the Object menu, choose Create. (Alternatively, you can right-click on the container and choose Create, or click on the Create A New Object button on the toolbar.) Select NDPS Manager from the resulting dialog box and click on OK.

3. Enter the name for the NDPS Manager (such as NDPSMGR).

4. In the next field, Resident Server, click on the browse button and select the server to which you want to assign the NDPS Manager. Click on OK. Any Printer Agent controlling a locally attached printer under control of this NDPS Manager must be on the server hosting the Manager.

5. Click on the browse button next to the Database Volume field and choose a volume on the host server on which to place the NDPS Manager database. Managers controlling a large number of Printer Agents will need at least 5MB worth of disk space. SYS is usable, but if disk space is anywhere near tight, put the NDPS Manager database on another volume. Click on OK.

6. Check the Define Additional Properties box if you want to add additional information for this NDPS Manager, such as description and location. You can also set security access to the NDPS Manager via Access Control rules, and you can control existing Printer Agents via this object.

   Note: If this is the first NDPS Manager, you'll have to wait to create Printer Agents until at least one NDPS Manager is up and running.

7. Click on Create and enter any additional information if you checked the Define Additional Properties check box. Then, click on OK.

8. At the server console of the server on which you created the NDPS object, type "NDPSM *NDPS Manager Name*" (in this example, you would type "NDPSM NDPSMGR").

9. To auto load the NDPS Manager, add the following command at the end of the server's AUTOEXEC.NCF file:

```
NDPSM NDPS Manager Name
```

All this looks like a lot, but it's not much more than using the Quick Setup in queue-based printing. You would expect to name and locate any object you create. Adding the load statement in the AUTOEXEC.NCF file is extra work, but NetWare Administrator will probably be smart enough to do this in another version or two.

Creating Public Access Printer Agents And Printers

After you have an NDPS Manager object, you need to create printers to manage. As mentioned previously, there are two types of NDPS printers—public access and controlled access. Let's create a public access printer now by creating the necessary Printer Agent.

You must have an NDPS Manager before you can create a Printer Agent for several obscure system reasons, but also because the first step in creating a Printer Agent of any type is that you create Printer Agents via NDPS Manager. Let's create a public access Xerox printer directly connected to the network, rather than being locally attached to the server. Follow these steps:

1. In NetWare Administrator, double-click on the NDPS Manager object (NDPSMGR in the previous example).

2. Click on the Printer Agent List tab, select the appropriate NDPS Manager, and click on New.

3. In the Create Printer Agent dialog box, shown in Figure 8.1, type a name for the new Printer Agent in the Printer Agent (PA) Name field.

4. Select the printer gateway to use. For example, select Novell Printer Gateway and click on OK.

5. To configure the Novell printer gateway, select the appropriate printer type and printer.

6. Click on OK and configure the necessary information for the type of printer you selected. Then, click on OK, and the Printer Agent starts and loads the printer gateway automatically.

7. The Select Printer Drivers dialog box appears (as shown in Figure 8.2). Pick the appropriate printer drivers for this printer and the various Windows systems you need to support. These drivers will download automatically to the clients that need them.

8. Click OK and you're done.

You can force your users to find and load the appropriate printer driver on their own by choosing None as the printer driver. This is highly discouraged. After all, you're trying to make things easier for your network users, not more difficult. You can add new printer drivers to the Resource Management Service (RMS) through NetWare Administrator as drivers are added or updated.

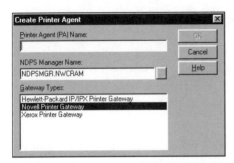

Figure 8.1 The Create Printer Agent dialog box.

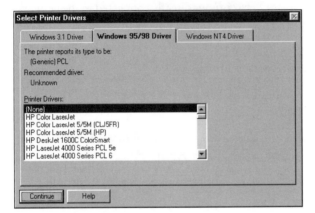

Figure 8.2 The Select Printer Drivers dialog box, with the Windows 95/98 tab selected.

Remember that public access printers have no security and little manageability. They are not part of NDS; therefore, there are no access controls on these printers.

The process for creating a public access printer that's locally attached to the server is almost the same as the previous steps. The difference comes when you must configure the Printer Gateway used to reach the printer. Pick Novell Port Handler and then pick Local (as in a physical connection to the server) rather than Xerox or HP. Naming the printer before this difference and configuring the printer drivers afterward happen exactly like the steps just listed.

Creating Controlled Access Printer Agents And Printers

The process for creating controlled access printers and the corresponding Printer Agents should be familiar. To create a controlled access printer, follow these steps:

1. In NetWare Administrator, select the container in which you want to create a controlled access printer.

2. Select Create from the Object menu. (Alternatively, you can right-click on the container and choose Create, or click on the Create A New Object button on the toolbar.) Then, select NDPS Printer. The Create NDPS Printer dialog box appears, as shown in Figure 8.3.

3. Enter a name in the NDPS Printer Name field.

4. You can choose to create a new Printer Agent or modify an existing one. Select either.

5. Check the Define Additional Properties checkbox and click on Create.

6. In the Create Printer Agent dialog box, click the browse button next to the NDPS Manager Name field to find the appropriate NDPS Manager (NDPSMGR in this example).

7. Choose the appropriate Printer Gateway and click on OK. Configure the gateway as needed.

8. After you've configured the necessary gateway and the Printer Agent has loaded, you need to set the access control for the users you want to have access to the printer. Click on Users, select the appropriate users, and then click on OK. Figure 8.4 shows the Access Control property page.

In NetWare Administrator, the new controlled access printer appears and is ready to be used by the approved users.

You may continue and tighten the access controls or modify the event notification parameters to your heart's content. By default, everyone in the container holding the NDPS Printer object can use that resource.

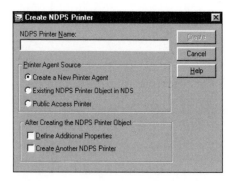

Figure 8.3   The Create NDPS Printer dialog box.

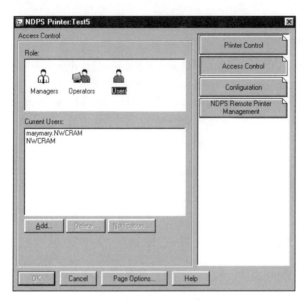

Figure 8.4 The Access Control property page.

Configuring NDPS Remote Printer Management For Clients

For workstations to use NDPS resources, two separate steps must be completed. First, you must configure NDPS Remote Printer Management through NetWare Administrator. Second, the users' workstations must be NDPS-aware.

To configure Remote Printer Management through NetWare Administrator, follow these steps:

1. Select the container holding the NDPS Manager and choose Details from the Object menu.

2. Scroll down and choose the NDPS Remote Printer Management property page (shown in Figure 8.5).

3. Check the Show The Results Window On Workstations checkbox. Then, under the Printers To Install To Workstations field, click on Add.

4. Select the appropriate printer from the Available Printers Option dialog box and click on OK.

5. Highlight the printer in the Printers To Install To Workstations field, click on Select As Default, and then click on Update Driver. Click on OK twice to exit.

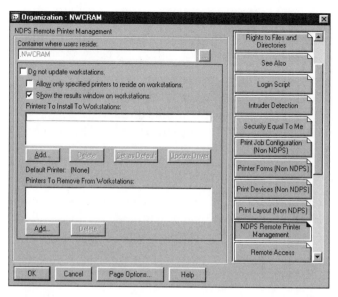

Figure 8.5   The NDPS Remote Printer Management property page.

These changes allow the NDPS printer to communicate properly with NetWare clients, assuming they're prepared to use NDPS resources.

As mentioned, the second requirement for workstations to use NDPS printing is that they must be NDPS-aware. This is not a problem for new installations with NetWare Client 3.0 and above software for NetWare 5. If your users have older client software, they may need to upgrade the client before they can access NDPS devices.

Assuming your clients are running the proper level of client software (or you have just upgraded their software since the last paragraph), your clients have the capability to utilize NDPS resources. This is the default in client software that ships with NetWare 5, and this capability will be on the client unless the installer went into the Custom screens and unchecked NDPS. To configure a Windows workstation to be NDPS-aware, follow these steps:

1. On the Windows 95/98 or Windows NT desktop, right-click on the Network Neighborhood icon and choose Properties.

2. Click on the Configuration tab (if it's not the default) and then click the Add button.

3. In the resulting Select Network Component Type dialog box, choose Service and click on Add.

4. In the Select Network Service dialog box, select Novell under Manufacturers and then select Novell Distributed Print Services in the Network Services window. Click on the Have Disk button just below the Network Services window.

5. Point the installation routine to the contents of the Novell Client CD-ROM and the \products\Win95\ibm_enu directory (assuming the language is English). If necessary, use the physical CD-ROM or the CD contents on a network path.

6. Let the install routine run and then reboot as necessary.

When the client reboots, NDPS will be enabled. Windows 3.x workstations need to have their Novell Client software completely reinstalled to add NDPS capability.

Troubleshooting NDPS Printing

There are many problems that can occur in any printing system, and NDPS is no exception. Problems with a printing system do not indicate a system failure. The secret is to troubleshoot the problem by finding the culprit and fixing it in a reasonable amount of time.

The first thing to check when troubleshooting any type of system is what has recently changed. Changes, no matter how trivial to the user and how far removed from the symptom, cause problems most of the time. However, users may not realize what they've changed, and sometimes the changes happen elsewhere. Networks are dynamic and fluctuating environments, meaning you must have some plan of attack when problems cause your phone to ring, email basket to overflow, and beeper to screech.

Starting The Search For A Resolution: Initial Steps

NDPS printing problems are fundamentally no different than any other network problem. The plan of attack should be consistent and thorough.

> *Note: Refer back to Chapter 2 for the formal troublshooting procedure.*

Find The Error Message And Fix It

Part of the intelligence added to NDPS Printing and NetWare 5 clients includes better and more descriptive error messages. Go to the source of the problem and read the error message. If the user has cleared the message, recreate the situation. If printing works, you're done; if printing doesn't work, you'll have your error message. Here are some common situations associated with various types of error messages that you should check:

➤ **Not authorized to print** Make sure the user is logged in to the network correctly.

➤ **Cannot connect to Printer Agent** Make sure NDPSM.NLM is in the AUTOEXEC.NCF file. Because this NLM is not automatically added to the AUTOEXEC.NCF file, a server restart could have eliminated this from memory. Add it if it's not there.

Verify that the NDPS Manager and NDPS Broker are up and running. If they aren't, the user may not be able to connect to the Printer Agent.

➤ **Print job was rejected** Verify that the volume has ample free space for large print jobs to stack up without causing problems. If the volume hosting the NDPS Printer Agent is full or has reached the limit set for spooling, jobs may be rejected. We recommend that you move spooling to other volumes beside SYS. Full SYS volumes wreak all sorts of havoc, including NDS problems. Set a spooling space limit if all your volumes are near the edge, so the spool size can't outgrow the disk space.

You can move spooling to a new location without destroying and having to re-create printer definitions. Spooled files will transfer themselves without resulting in a printing disaster. Perhaps a small delay occurs as the files transfer, but no break will come after moving a spooling location.

Try The Easy Fix First

When troubleshooting, there are several "easy fixes" you should try. If there's a problem with a single workstation, here are some of the things you should check:

➤ **Network cabling** Make sure the cables from the workstation to the server are connected correctly.

➤ **The printer forms** Check the settings and job configuration details.

➤ **The printer job list** Verify that the job is getting to the proper printer and is showing up in the spool area.

➤ **The printer configuration** Find out what has changed since the workstation was able to print last, and reverse any changes made to the printer configuration.

If more than one workstation is experiencing the problem, do the following:

➤ Turn the printer off and back on again, rebooting it. If the job still shows up, delete the job itself—it may be corrupt.

➤ In the Print Manager, check for extra NDPS error messages in the Printer Information area.

➤ Check the printer for error codes, flashing lights, printed error messages, or burning parts.

➤ Check any cables associated with the printer and the network.

➤ Check your NDPS software version; there may have been an upgrade.

➤ Verify that the job is reaching the spooling area by checking the printer's job list.

➤ Check Novell Support Connection Web site for reports of similar problems and possible fixes.

Is There A Problem With The Printing Environment?

Check your printing environment. NDPS does not handle DOS, Macintosh, OS/2, and Unix clients. Currently, only queue-based printers will support these NetWare clients. However, this may change.

Just because you've enabled NDPS doesn't mean there aren't still some queue-based systems in use. Check your Windows 3.x, Windows 95/98, and Windows NT clients by looking in the Windows Control Panel under Printers and verifying the network setting is to an NDPS printer name. The name shown will be NDPSxx. If not, the listed printer is probably routed to a queue.

Check the server modules. NDPSM.NLM and BROKER.NLM must be running. Finding PSERVER.NLM running on the server indicates that queue-based printing is still in use or that there may be some remnant of it causing problems.

 If clients are sending any jobs to queues and PSERVER is running, you're using queue-based printing. If the clients all have NetWare Client 2.2 and above and they only reference Printer Agents, you have a pure NDPS environment.

When you have both systems, as in the transition time between completely queue-based printing and completely NDPS printing, things get more complicated. Non-NDPS clients, such as DOS, Macintosh, Unix, and OS/2, cannot send print jobs to NDPS printers without assistance. A print queue must be created and attached to the NDPS printer in NetWare Administrator to provide this backward compatibility.

NDPS clients trying to reach queue-based printers will have a similar problem and solution. Direct the Printer Agent to send jobs to the queue-based printer via the proper NetWare queue.

Tightening The Troubleshooting Parameters

You can't kill a problem until you isolate it. Sometimes, narrowing the focus of the search is an art in itself. You need to see if the workstation or the printer can be eliminated as the source of the problem. Can you determine whether the workstation or the printing system is the problem?

If the troubled workstation has printed to the problem printer before, check the following:

➤ Verify that this workstation and this printer are coordinated, rather than this workstation and a similar printer.

➤ Find out whether this combination worked in the past. If so, find out what has changed.

➤ Determine whether this is a new setup and whether these two devices have ever successfully collaborated.

If these devices haven't worked together previously, you must focus on either the workstation or the printer, depending on what you find out next. Try sending a similar print job to the same printer from other workstations. If you're successful, focus on the workstation.

Verify the initial configuration for NDPS. Refer to the NDPS installation documentation and notes made during installation and check that the tested and approved parameters are still valid.

New setups and configurations make it harder to narrow the focus, because you have no history of success. That's why determining whether the workstation can print to other printers or whether the questionable printer accepts jobs from other workstations, helps narrow the focus for continued troubleshooting.

Workstation Problems

Usually, the workstation will be the source of the problem, simply because workstations change more often than printers. After all, no one ever downloads a screensaver from the Internet for the printer.

Because this chapter focuses on NDPS printing, you may think the only clients you must consider are Windows-based clients. However, because NDPS printers handle jobs from queues as well as jobs sent directly to their Printer Agents, you must at least check non-NDPS clients.

Clients not running NDPS software may be sending print jobs to a queue serviced by an NDPS printer. DOS, Macintosh, Unix, and OS/2 clients cannot use a Printer Agent directly and therefore must route print jobs through queue-based printing. If the workstation having trouble is not NDPS-enabled, check the network printer to verify that it's queue-based or an NDPS printer is servicing the queue. If the target printer is not NDPS-enabled, skip to queue-based printer troubleshooting (which is covered in detail in Chapter 9).

If an NDPS printer is servicing a print queue, verify that connection by checking all the configuration details. Run print jobs from other workstations through the queue to that NDPS printer. Send NDPS jobs directly to that printer, bypassing the queue. If these tests work, the problem must be in the workstation.

If there are no NDPS printers in the equation, check the queue-based printing system setup.

Isolating Print Problems At One Windows Workstation

The Windows operating system has become a huge, complex mass of often contradictory software. Luckily, there aren't too many troubleshooting steps to fix printing problems after you have the problem isolated to a single Windows workstation. Windows 3.x doesn't provide as much information as Windows 95/98 or Windows NT, but it's enough that you'll have some help available.

Occasionally, Windows users will add, change, or delete software from their own systems. These users may not be willing, or able, to tell you what has changed recently. Therefore, you should follow proper procedure even when the user appears to be cooperating.

In Windows 3.1, open Control Panel|Printers, select the installed printer, and choose Connect. If this listing is LPT followed by a name, it's pointing to a queue-based printer. Change it.

Here are the first two items you should check in Windows 95/98 and Windows NT:

➤ **Check the printer in the Windows Control Panel** Verify that the printer is created properly and pointing to the proper Printer Agent. Delete any old or unused printer definitions just for safety's sake.

➤ **Check the network object listed as the target printer** Check the Printers listing (Start|Settings|Printers or Control Panel|Printers). Then, check the properties of the default printer (File|Properties) and look at Details. The Print To The Following Port entry should be the name of the NDPS Printer Agent set as the default printer.

Never forget the easy stuff. Windows 95/98 and Windows NT allow printers to work offline, meaning the print jobs are spooled locally, awaiting proper network connections. These settings are handy for laptops but a pain for desktops. Verify the workstation has not tagged a printer as offline or paused the printer for any reason.

If all is well at the workstation level, go back to NetWare Administrator and the NDPS Print Manager program. See whether the print job from the suspect workstation appears in the job list. If not, follow these steps:

1. Open Printer Manager by double-clicking on NWPMW32.EXE in the SYS:/PUBLIC/WIN32 directory. The Novell Printer Manager interface screen appears, as shown in Figure 8.6.

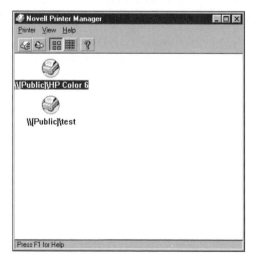

Figure 8.6 The Novell Printer Manager interface.

2. Select the suspect printer in the Printer Manager window and choose Printer|Information.

3. Look at the Status and the State Details information. Status tells you if the printer thinks there's a problem. State Details lists the problem and recommendations.

4. Check that the NDPS printer is, in fact, the one you meant to install.

5. Verify the Printer Agent and printer match.

6. Check the Printer Status details and make sure there are no errors.

7. Verify that the Printer Agent is still up and running and available.

8. Verify that the port listed is an NDPS port.

9. Verify that the context listing is the correct context for the proper Printer object.

Read every error message you can find. Check every spot for potential error messages, including the printer, the Printer Agent, the server, and the workstation (again). Fix what you can fix. Start looking for the printer manual if the printer shows an error message, and follow those troubleshooting steps when you find the manual.

If the printer is queue-based and the client thinks the printer is NDPS-enabled, you may have solved your problem. However, you should check whether the queues are routed to an NDPS Printer Agent. If so, check the print server's configuration to verify the correct printer is listed in the queue information.

If NDPS objects are defined properly, check those objects. NDPS objects must be configured to emulate a print server if they're servicing jobs from a queue.

If the NDPS object is configured to accept print jobs from a queue, verify the queue is routing print jobs correctly. Refer to Chapter 9 on queue-based printing if you suspect the queue-based systems are incorrectly configured.

If the problem is with Windows, refer to the Windows online help and extra documentation and make a backup quickly, because many troubleshooting expeditions with Windows wind up requiring a reinstallation of Windows. Get ready before the situation becomes critical.

Stalking The Print Job From The Source (Workstation)

When printing works properly, NetWare zooms the print jobs through the maze from workstation to printer so quickly you can barely see the job hit any of the stops in between. When troubleshooting, you want to put the process into slow motion so you can track the job through each step of the journey.

Pausing the NDPS printer that's the target of the workstation in question allows you to see the print job more clearly. The more places you can see the print job's progress, the more places you can verify that it's working properly.

Stopping an NDPS printer forces the print job to stay in the spool area rather than zooming into the printer's memory. This gives you time to see the job hit the spool area or not arrive (as it should). The fewer components you can test at one time, the more confident you'll feel in your troubleshooting.

You can pause a controlled access printer by performing the following steps:

1. Open NetWare Administrator and double-click on the NDPS Printer object.

2. Click the Pause Output button. The state changes to Resume Output.

To pause a public access NDPS printer, do the following:

1. Switch to the NDPSM.NLM screen on the server console, either by going to the console physically or using RCONSOLE.

2. Select Printer Agent|Status|Control.

3. Choose Pause Output and press Enter.

When these printers are paused, send a new print job to the printer. If the print job reaches the spooling area, you're in good shape.

Here's how to check the job list for a controlled access NDPS printer:

1. Open NetWare Administrator and click on the NDPS Printer object under investigation.

2. Select Jobs|Job List.

You can view the job list for a public access NDPS printer from the server console or the NDPS Print Manager. It's your choice.

To resume printing from an NDPS controlled access printer, follow these steps:

1. Open NetWare Administrator and double-click on the NDPS Printer object.

2. Click on the Resume Output button. The button will change state back to Pause Output.

To resume printing from an NDPS public access printer, follow these steps:

1. Switch to the NDPSM.NLM screen on the server console or through RCONSOLE.

2. Choose Printer Agent|Status|Control and press Enter.

3. Select Resume Output and press Enter.

If the print job succeeds after stopping and restarting the printer (and you've changed nothing else), print another job without pausing the printer this time. If printing is successful, go about your business. You probably won't be that lucky, however.

The job may print but remain listed in the job list. In this case, check for delay settings, job holds, and priority settings that may delay jobs from one user over another.

If the job does not print but disappears from the job list, NetWare thinks the job has printed. At this point, you need to do the following:

➤ Verify that you're checking the proper printer. You may see the printer in the next cubicle full of your print tests.

➤ Make sure the printer drivers are current and match the printer in question.

➤ Verify that you're sending Printer Control Language (PCL) jobs to PCL printers rather than mixing your Printer Control Languages and sending PostScript jobs to PCL printers, or vice versa.

➤ Verify that the printer doesn't have a banner page configured as PCL, but that the print jobs are PostScript.

➤ Verify that the banner settings are correct in all other configuration details.

Test Files And Printer Output

Remember that problem isolation is the key to troubleshooting. When you can skip parts of the system, you make troubleshooting the rest of the system that much easier. This is why you should try printing files by the drag-and-drop method rather than involving an application.

First, of course, verify that the printer is not paused (via NetWare Administrator) and that you have the correct printer under examination. You might try replacing any printer cables with known working cables, just to be on the safe side.

The easiest way to drag and drop a text file for a printer test is through Windows Explorer for Windows 95/98 and Windows NT or File Manager for Windows 3.x. Follow these steps to drag and drop a print job from Windows Explorer:

1. Open Windows Explorer and find an appropriate test file (such as a small text file that will print in one page or less).

2. Open the Novell Printer Manager workstation utility.

3. Click on the file name or icon, hold the left mouse button down, and position the file name or icon over the NDPS printer. Release the left mouse button to "drop" the file onto the printer.

Check the result. If this doesn't work as well as expected, make sure the test file is printer-ready. Do not use DOC or WPD files because they expect a word processor to convert the files for printing. Text files or batch files, such as AUTOEXEC.BAT, make the best test files.

Look around on all the participating devices for error messages. Check the printer, the client, and the server. If there's an error message somewhere, fix the problem reported by the error message immediately.

If the test file prints correctly but files from applications don't, check the application or the printer drivers. If some applications print properly from a workstation but other applications don't, the driver is probably not the culprit—it's the application that won't print correctly. If no applications print properly from a workstation but test files do, you need to upgrade the driver.

Jobs that get stuck in the spooler indicate a printer set on pause or delay or messed up priority levels. Check those and try again.

All Users Are Having Problems

When no one can print or all users are having problems, it's a mixed blessing. You know the printer system is the problem, but all users are affected. Novell outlines several steps to printing resuscitation.

Check the severity of the printing problem. Are all printers dead to all users? Can some users print to all printers but other users cannot print to any printers? Do some printers work but not others? Find out so you'll know where to start troubleshooting.

If no print jobs come out of any network printers, you have a universal system problem, such as one of the following:

➤ The printing system is disabled.

➤ Some printing files have been unloaded from the server.

➤ The server is having troubles, such as running out of spool space or memory.

➤ Your network is in the process of crashing.

If no print jobs come from one specific printer, you know what to fix. Either the configuration or printer itself (hardware) is having a problem.

Slow and/or corrupted print jobs are caused by various configuration problems. Examples for slow printer problems include the following:

➤ **Isolated client** The application may have a long delay set before files are spooled for the printer.

➤ **All clients using a serial printer** The baud rate (throughput) may be set too low or handshaking may have changed. Try to enable the XON/XOFF setting on your printer according to the manufacturer's directions.

➤ **All clients using any type of printer** Check your hardware. Your port, cable, or printer connection may be the problem.

Job corruption is a different story. Mangled or partial print output may mean your printer needs more memory so it can hold the entire print job. Large print jobs, especially those that require lots of application "thinking time," such as graphics renderings, are sometimes so slow the printer times out because it sees the job as spooled when it's really only partially finished. Set the timeout value higher, or print to disk and then to hard copy.

Verify the NDPS Printer status in NetWare Administrator. The Information tag shows status details about the printer, such as the fact that it exists and is online.

If jobs are getting to the job list but still not progressing to the printer, check the printer gateway. All NDPS printers need a gateway of some type unless the Printer Agent is built into the printer itself. An incorrectly configured or missing gateway will stop printing faster than a wall stops a bicycle.

A Mixed Environment Mess

Because there aren't many NDPS-enabled printers currently, you probably have a mixed environment and will for a long time. The trick with a large, mixed environment is to isolate problems to one environment or the other as quickly as possible. For example, if jobs sent through a queue are not printing, you must verify whether the queue is going only to queue-based printers or whether an NDPS Printer Agent is feeding a queue. Additionally, a non-NDPS client can feed a queue that then ties to an NDPS Printer Agent, or the NDPS client and Printer Agent could be routing through a queue to a user-based printer.

When this type of problem occurs, check the spooling configuration. It must be matched to the queue you intend, rather than some queue that's one mistyped letter away.

You can check a queue's job list by following these steps:

1. Double-click on the Queue object in NetWare Administrator.

2. Click on Job List and look for any problems.

When you determine that a job is hitting the queue, you're halfway home. Refer to the "Stalking The Print Job From The Source (Workstation)" section earlier in this chapter to handle the problem from there.

Verify that your application can print to a network printer. Some applications, although rare today, refuse to support networked printers and their network names. For these applications, capturing the LPT1 port using the **CAPTURE** command may be the only answer.

Verify that Printer Agents are configured to forward print jobs to the proper queues. Check the name of the queue and verify that the Queue object exists and is in good shape.

Troubleshooting Summary

The presentation of this information may look a bit awkward; however, the most important thing to remember is to use common sense. Here are some helpful troubleshooting suggestions:

➤ Take one step at a time.

➤ Look for easy stuff first. Is the printer on? Is there a cable? Did the user just add new software?

➤ Isolate each subsystem as much as possible.

➤ Ask the user what he or she changed.

➤ Ask the user what he or she changed a second or third time until he or she remembers what it was.

Practice Questions

Question 1

Which of the following items is *not* a feature of NDPS?

○ a. NDPS was developed by Novell, HP, and Xerox.

○ b. NDPS introduces the Printer Agent—an intelligent module that replaces many pieces of the queue-based printing puzzle.

○ c. Bidirectional communications between printer and client provide much more feedback to users.

○ d. Printer drivers are downloaded automatically when necessary.

○ e. You can't mix NDPS and queue-based printing on the same server.

The correct answer is e. You *can* mix NDPS and queue-based printing on the same server. All other statements are features of NDPS. Therefore, answers a, b, c, and d are true and incorrect.

Question 2

Which of the following statements are true concerning public access printers? [Choose the three best answers]

❑ a. Public access printers are immediately available to all network users.

❑ b. There are no security controls on public access printers.

❑ c. Public access printers provide much more feedback than queue-based printers.

❑ d. Public access printers must be physically connected to a file server.

❑ e. Public access printers do not have corresponding NDS objects.

The correct answers are a, b, and e. Public access printers provide only basic job notification features, just like queue-based printers. Therefore, answer c is incorrect. Public access printers may be located anywhere on the network—on a server or attached to a workstation. Therefore, answer d is incorrect.

Question 3

> Which of the following is *not* true about controlled access printers?
>
> ○ a. Each controlled access printer has an NDS object.
>
> ○ b. Users must have NDS access to reach the controlled access printers.
>
> ○ c. Feedback from controlled access printers is the same as from public access printers.
>
> ○ d. Controlled access printers are managed though NetWare Administrator.

The correct answer is c. Almost every statement about public access printers can be turned upside down for controlled access printers. They provide many more job notification details, limited only by the intelligence of the printer itself. Answers a, b, and d are true of controlled access printers and are therefore incorrect.

Question 4

> Which of the following accurately describe a Printer Agent? [Choose the three best answers]
>
> ❏ a. A Printer Agent is an entity that can run in a printer, server, or workstation.
>
> ❏ b. One Printer Agent can handle many printers.
>
> ❏ c. The Printer Agent replaces queue-based printers, print servers, and print queues.
>
> ❏ d. A Printer Agent generates a wide range of job notification information.
>
> ❏ e. A Printer Agent must be created before the NDPS Manager.

The correct answers are a, c, and d. Printer Agents are talented, but there's only a one-to-one relationship between printers and Printer Agents. Therefore, answer b is incorrect. Additionally, the NDPS Manager must be created before it can be used to create Printer Agents. Therefore, answer e is incorrect.

Question 5

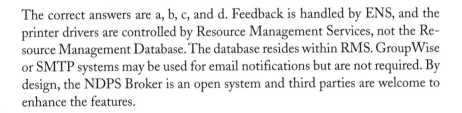

Which of the following are *not* correct about the NDPS Broker? [Choose the best answers]

- ❑ a. The NDPS Broker includes a service called the Communication Module, which handles all the feedback from NDPS printers to clients.
- ❑ b. The NDPS Broker Resource Management Database acts as the central repository for all print drivers.
- ❑ c. The NDPS Broker must have access to either GroupWise or an SMTP system for notification purposes.
- ❑ d. The NDPS Broker is a closed system that can only be extended by Novell engineering.

The correct answers are a, b, c, and d. Feedback is handled by ENS, and the printer drivers are controlled by Resource Management Services, not the Resource Management Database. The database resides within RMS. GroupWise or SMTP systems may be used for email notifications but are not required. By design, the NDPS Broker is an open system and third parties are welcome to enhance the features.

Question 6

Which of the following is *not* true about the NDPS Manager?

- ○ a. NDPS Manager is an NDS object and supports Printer Agents.
- ○ b. NDPS Manager can easily handle multiple Printer Agents.
- ○ c. When you create an NDPS Manager, the AUTOEXEC.NCF file is modified automatically.
- ○ d. Public access and controlled access Printer Agents are both managed by the NDPS Manager.
- ○ e. You must provide a name for the NDPS Manager when creating it.

The correct answer is c. The AUTOEXEC.NCF file is not modified automatically. All other statements are true and therefore incorrect.

Question 7

Which of the following are good NDPS printing troubleshooting techniques?
[Choose the three best answers]

○ a. Try to determine whether anything has recently changed in the print
system.

○ b. Determine whether the printer works with other workstations,
besides the workstation in question.

○ c. Always back up the server hard drive before attempting any type of
printer troubleshooting.

○ d. Take advantage of any error messages for hints toward solving the
problem.

The correct answers are a, b, and d. Although it's always good to back up the
server hard drive, that's not a necessary step when troubleshooting NDPS printing problems. Therefore, answer c is incorrect.

Need To Know More?

 Gaskin, James. *Mastering NetWare 5*. Sybex Network Press, Alameda, CA, 1999. ISBN 0-7821-2268-X. Chapter 8 covers printing, and Chapter 20 provides troubleshooting tips.

 Shilmover, Barry and Doug Bamlett. *Exam Cram for NetWare 5 Administration CNE/CNA*. The Coriolis Group, Scottsdale, AZ, 1999. ISBN 1-57610-350-1. Chapter 6 covers NDPS configuration as it relates to the NetWare 5 Administration exam and may contain additional helpful information regarding NDPS printing.

 http://www.novell.com/documentation/lg/nw5/docui/index.html is the NetWare 5 online documentation. Search for terms such as NDPS, Printer Agent, controlled access printer, and public access printer for information covered in this chapter.

Queue-Based Printing

Terms you'll need to understand:

√ Print queue

√ Auto load printer

√ Manual load printer

√ Print server

√ PSERVER.NLM

√ NPRINTER.EXE, NPTWIN95.EXE, and NPRINTER.NLM

√ Print queue and print server operator

√ Print queue and print server user

Techniques you'll need to master:

√ Describing the print process and path from user to network printer

√ Configuring the queue-based print objects

√ Managing the queue-based printing environment

√ Specifying users and operators of print queues and print servers

√ Identifying print queue problems and applying troubleshooting techniques to solve these problems

√ Troubleshooting and recognizing print server-related issues

√ Recognizing printer-related issues and troubleshooting them

√ Identifying and troubleshooting remote printer problems

Probably the number one reason for using a network is to share resources. These resources consist of software and hardware elements, and one of the most common types of hardware resources to share are printers. Novell has provided the ability to share printers with several versions of NetWare for quite some time. One method is referred to as *queue-based printing*, which is similar in NetWare 3.x, NetWare 4.x, and NetWare 5 networks. In this chapter, we'll cover queue-based printing—what it is and how it's configured and managed— as well as some troubleshooting tips and techniques.

> *Note: Novell Distributed Print Services (NDPS) is the other method of printing on a Novell network. NDPS printing is covered in Chapter 8.*

A Queue-Based Printing Overview

Before we discuss network printing, let's review the process that happens when a Windows 95/98 user prints to a non-network printer attached directly to the computer. When the user chooses Print from the File menu, the application and operating system create a print file that's stored locally (spooled). The operating system then sends this print file, which is stored on the user's local hard disk, to the physical printer attached to the machine. Portions of the print file contain information and instructions that are specific to a particular print language and/or printer. To obtain the correct commands to the proper printer, Windows 95/98 installs the proper software, or *print driver*, for the manufacturer and model of the printer specified in the setup. The print file constructed by the application contains a header, a body, and a tail. The header contains information about the type of printer, which is derived from the information contained in the print driver. If the incorrect print driver is used to compose the header and the resultant print file is sent to a printer that doesn't understand the commands, the output is typically unreadable. Therefore, it's very important that the correct print driver is selected for the type of printer used.

The process used to print to a network printer is very similar to that of a local printer—except some of the storage locations are on a server, and the software that handles delivery of the print file to the printer is handled by server software. With NetWare-controlled printing, you can basically think of the network as a very long printer cable.

A NetWare queue-based printing environment has three main Novell Directory Services (NDS) objects: Print Queue, Printer, and Print Server. Each of the NDS print objects represents a hardware resource or a software component. None of these items is configured automatically, and you cannot print to a NetWare-controlled printer until you configure and initialize these components.

Print Queue

The NetWare 5 and NetWare 4.x print queue is the storage location for the print files generated by the user. The queue is a directory located on a server that contains no special directory properties. When you create this queue, you specify the volume on which you want the queue to reside. The system then creates a directory on that volume titled QUEUES and creates a subdirectory below it for your queue. The name of this subdirectory is a hexadecimal value with a QDR extension. You don't usually have to concern yourself with this directory at the file level because NetWare Administrator handles the interface between the name of the queue and the associated QDR directory.

Depending on the applications in use, the size of the print queue files may be very large. In addition, there may be bursts of network printing, such as during tax seasons, quarterly and annual reports, and inventory. You should take into account the worst possible scenario to determine the required disk space necessary to support storage of the print files. You should not place the print queues on the SYS volume. If the SYS volume runs out of disk space, serious problems may occur.

Printer

The Printer objects created in NDS represent the printers that are physically attached to the network. Network-aware printers are connected directly to the network and are often configured for a specific protocol or protocols. Depending on the configuration and manufacturer, these printers may have network addresses and network names. Additionally, the vendor may provide utilities that are used to manage and configure a printer.

Another attachment point for a printer is a user's workstation. This configuration only works well in very small environments that don't perform extensive printing.

The third network connection point for a printer is the server. In this scenario, the printer is attached directly to a server, and the server does not have to be running the print services software. This configuration is used in administrative situations in which the information printed should not be accessible to the general user.

Print Server

That last of the three print objects is the Print Server object. In NetWare 4.x and 5, the print server is a NetWare 4.x or 5 server running an application to provide network printing. The application is a NetWare Loadable Module (NLM) and can be loaded and unloaded at your discretion. Once this software is loaded, the print server software (PSERVER.NLM) controls the communication between the print files stored in the queue to the printer specified in the setup.

After the printing environment is configured and tested to make sure everything is set up properly, you can place the command to launch the print server software in the server's AUTOEXEC.NCF file. This loads the print server automatically when the server is launched.

Queue-Based Printing Setup

The primary tool for configuring the print objects is NetWare Administrator. As with other NDS objects, you'll need to decide in which container (or containers) your print objects will reside. Depending on the size of the network, you may have many print objects to create and configure. The location, name, and properties of these print objects should be decided during the NetWare 4.x or 5 network design process. You do have the ability to move the objects in the NDS database later, but whenever possible, you should try to plan for current and future network needs.

The NDS print objects have several properties, some of which are critical. These critical properties, sometimes referred to as *required properties*, must have values so the objects can be created and will function properly. Also, some property values are filled in automatically as you create these objects. These values must also remain for the printing environment to function properly.

Creating An NDS Print Queue

You use NetWare Administrator to create and manage your print queues. The following steps outline the process used to create a Print Queue object:

1. Select the container in which you want the print queue to reside.

2. Choose Create from the Object menu. (Alternatively, you can right-click on the container and choose Create, click on the Create A New Object button on the toolbar, or press the Insert key.)

3. Select Print Queue from the New Object dialog box.

4. Enter the name of the queue. NDS is not case sensitive, so part of your design may use mixed case as a mechanism to make the name more readable to users (for example, ResearchQ versus researchq).

5. Use the browse button to select the volume on which you want the resultant queue directory to reside.

6. After you enter both of these properties, the Create button is enabled. Click on Create to create the Print Queue object. Figure 9.1 shows the Create Print Queue dialog box.

When the NDS Print Queue object is created, the system creates the corresponding physical subdirectory containing the QDR extension under the QUEUES directory on the volume you specified in Step 5.

Creating An NDS Printer (Non NDPS)

The Printer object you create in NDS represents the physical printer located on the network. Novell uses two terms to identify the location of the printer in respect to the print server: auto load and manual load. This is necessary so the print server software running on a server knows where to "look" for the printer; consequently, the print server can communicate with the printer. You'll also need to have this information available when you create the Printer object because this is one of the required properties. In this chapter, we'll cover the creation of an NDS Printer object that's attached to the parallel (or LPT1) port of a workstation.

If the printer is attached to the server running the print server software, it's referred to as an *auto load* printer. A printer attached to anything else is referred to as a *manual load* printer. This includes printers attached to workstations and those connected directly to the network. The word *load* in both of these terms refers to additional software that needs to be loaded—either automatically or manually. We'll discuss the additional software and its configuration later in this chapter.

The following steps outline the process used to create a non-NDPS printer:

1. Select the container in which you want the printer to reside.

2. Choose Create from the Object menu. (Alternatively, you can right-click on the container and choose Create, click on the Create A New Object button on the toolbar, or press the Insert key.)

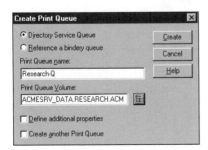

Figure 9.1 The NDS Create Print Queue dialog box.

3. Select Printer (Non NDPS) from the New Object dialog box.

4. Enter the name of the printer, check the Define Additional Properties checkbox, and click on Create.

5. Select the Configuration button displayed on the left side of the dialog box that's presented.

6. At the top of the dialog box that appears, select the printer type from the available options (see Figure 9.2). Select Parallel, because the printer in this example is attached to the LPT1 port of a workstation.

7. To specify the hardware settings of the printer, select the Communication button.

8. In the Parallel Communication dialog box, select the port to which the printer is physically attached (see Figure 9.3).

9. Indicate whether you want to use interrupts. If you do, specify the correct interrupt value. If you select Polled, the computer to which the printer is

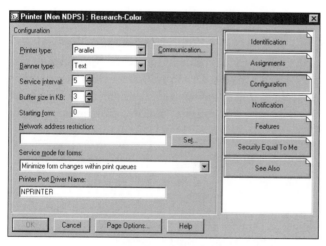

Figure 9.2   An NDS printer configuration dialog box.

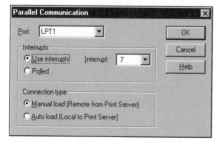

Figure 9.3   The Parallel Communication dialog box.

attached uses the computer's timer interrupt to determine signals destined for the printer. This option is useful in situations where the interrupt is unknown or may vary—as with plug-and-play configurations.

10. At the bottom of the dialog box, specify the printer connection type. If the printer is attached to the server running the print service's software, select Auto Load (Local To Print Server). If the printer is attached elsewhere on the network, choose the other option: Manual Load (Remote From Print Server). Click on OK.

11. In the Printer dialog box, click the Assignments button to view the printer's Assignments dialog box (see Figure 9.4). This allows you to indicate which print queue's print files will go to the printer you're creating.

12. Click on the Add button and navigate to the printer you want assigned to this queue. Click on OK.

The step in which you assign the print queue to the printer is very important. If this step is omitted, the user's printout will not go to the printer. The print files will "sit" in the queue until a printer is assigned to a queue. Remember to "connect your P's to your Q's!"

As you can see from the printer's Assignments dialog box, you can attach several queues to a printer. If this is done, make sure the workstations using the different queues are all using the same print driver.

In the printer's Assignments dialog box, there's also the option to indicate a priority value for the queue attached to the printer. This value ranges from 1

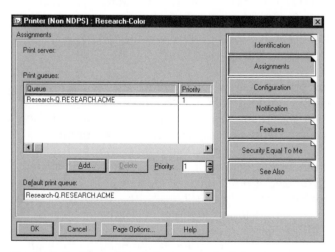

Figure 9.4 The printer's Assignments dialog box.

(the default) to 10—where 1 is the highest and 10 is the lowest. If you want to assign a higher print priority to certain users, you create a queue for each priority you want to support. Then, when you add these queues to the printer, you can specify a priority value for each of the queues. NetWare uses these priority values to indicate the processing order of the queues, and the queues with a value of 1 are serviced first.

Creating An NDS Print Server (Non NDPS)

The last object you need to create and configure for queue-based printing is the Print Server object. This NDS object represents the print server software that will run on a NetWare 4.x or 5 server. The following steps outline the process used to create a non-NDPS print server:

1. Select the container in which you want the Print Server object to reside.

2. Choose Create from the Object menu. (Alternatively, you can right-click on the container and choose Create, click on the Create A New Object button in the toolbar, or press the Insert key.)

3. Select Print Server (Non NDPS) from the New Object dialog box.

4. Enter the name of the print server, check the Define Additional Properties checkbox, and click on Create.

5. In the Print Server Identification screen, select the Assignments button to specify which printer or printers the print server will be servicing.

6. Click on the Add button and navigate to the printer you want to place on the Assignments list. Click on OK.

As with the Print Queue objects, it's very important that you assign the printer or printers to the Print Server object. If this step is omitted, the users' print files will accumulate in the print queue because there's no print server specified to service the queue attached to the printer.

The Print Server Details window contains the Print Layout (Non NDPS) button. This button presents a graphic of all the connected objects and their statuses. This is useful for making sure all components are assigned properly and for troubleshooting. In Figure 9.5, notice there's an exclamation point next to the Print Server object. This indicates that something about that object is not configured properly or that there may be a problem. Notice also the Status button, which is enabled when an object is selected. In this example, the problem is simple. All the objects have been created and assigned properly, but the print server software is not running on the server.

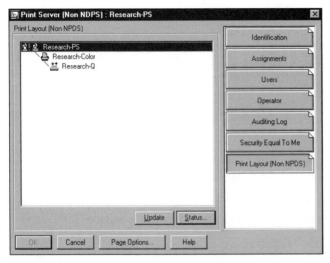

Figure 9.5   The Print Server Print Layout (Non NDPS) dialog box.

Print Services Quick Setup (Non NDPS)

There's also a quick setup option you can use, but the initial configuration of the objects is not as flexible as the methods described previously. To access this option, select Print Services Quick Setup (Non NDPS) from the Tools menu in NetWare Administrator. In the Print Services Quick Setup dialog box shown in Figure 9.6, you can either accept the default names of the print server, printer, and queue or modify these values. You must specify the queue volume before you can create the object.

You do have some restrictions when using the quick setup, and these should be considered before using this option. Here's a list of some of these limitations:

➤ All three print objects reside in the same container.

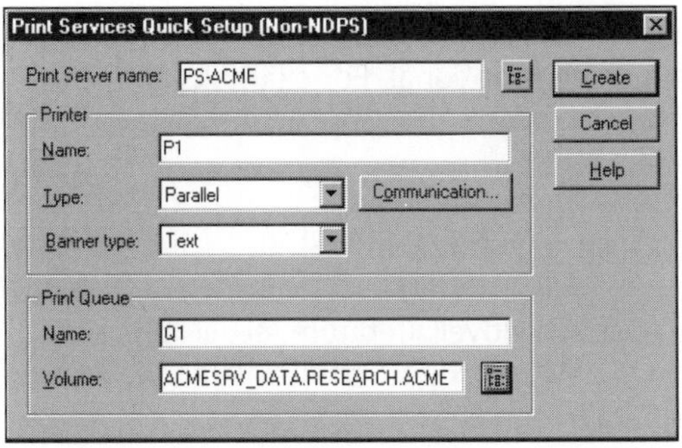

Figure 9.6   The Print Services Quick Setup (Non NDPS) dialog box.

➤ The quick setup method cannot be used to modify or edit existing print objects.

➤ You cannot modify other property values not presented in the dialog box during the creation process. However, these can be edited after the object is created.

Now that we've discussed the queue-based print objects and their creation processes, the next step is to load the print server software on a NetWare 4.x or 5 server.

 NetWare 4.x includes another utility to configure queue-based printing components. It's a text-based utility called PCONSOLE.

Starting Queue-Based Print Services

In NetWare 4.x or 5, the queue-based print server software is run on a NetWare 4.x or 5 server. The software can be loaded manually, or the appropriate command can be placed in the server's AUTOEXEC.NCF file so that when the server is booted, the print server software loads automatically.

The print server software is an NLM called PSERVER.NLM. To load the print server software, you enter "PSERVER" followed by the name of the NDS Print Server object at the server's console prompt. Here's an example:

```
PSERVER .RESEARCH-PS.RESEARCH.ACME
```

You can use either the distinguished name or relative distinguished name of the print server, and the case is not significant.

 In NetWare 5, using the **LOAD** command before the name of the NLM you're launching is optional. For example, the following command will perform the same action as the previous line of code:

```
LOAD PSERVER .RESEARCH-PS.RESEARCH.ACME
```

You may see **LOAD** used in Novell literature, especially if the NLM is the same on NetWare 4.x and/or NetWare 3.x, where the use of **LOAD** is required.

It's good practice to use the distinguished names of objects rather than the relative distinguished names, because with distinguished names, you're not dependent on the context of the server where you're loading the print services. If you do not know or are not sure of the distinguished name of the print server, type "PSERVER" without a name at the server console. This allows you to navigate to the container that contains the Print Server object and then select the object.

When the print server software is loaded and running, all the information about the configuration is stored in the server's memory. If you make changes to the print objects' configurations when the print server is running, these changes might not take effect. To enable these new changes, you need to unload and reload the print server. This causes a brief disruption in the print services and should therefore be performed at times that result in the least inconvenience to users.

You can unload the print server software in several different ways. One procedure is at the server console in the NetWare Print Server screen. Select Print Server Information and then press Enter on the Current Status field. Two options are available: Unload and Unload After Active Print Jobs. The first option unloads the print server immediately, and the second option unloads it when the files currently being printed are completed. In both cases, inactive or waiting print files remain in the queues.

Configuring Network Printers

In a NetWare-controlled printing environment, the printer may be connected to the print server, to a workstation, or directly to the network. The term *auto load* is used to define printers attached directly to the print server, and the term *manual load* is used for printers attached elsewhere. If you have a printer attached to the print server that has been defined as an auto load printer, when you load PSERVER, the server automatically loads additional software. This additional software is NPRINTER.NLM, and it loads for each printer assigned to the print server as "auto load."

For a printer attached elsewhere, there's no automatic loading of software. In the previous configuration example, we specified the printer as "manual load" because it's attached to a workstation. For the print server to find this printer and communicate with it, you need to manually load software on the workstation. This software is generically called *NPRINTER*, and there are specific versions for DOS/Windows 3.x, Windows 95/98, and Windows NT. These are all found in the SYS:\PUBLIC directory—either at the root or in a subdirectory.

NPTWIN95.EXE is the application you run on a Windows 95/98 machine that has the network printer attached to it. This is a graphical utility that can be run automatically using the Windows Startup folder, NetWare login scripts, or Z.E.N.works. When the utility is run, you select the NDS printer defined for the workstation's printer. Once this is accomplished, users on the network can use the printer.

To manually load software on DOS and Windows 3.x workstations, you use the NPRINTER.EXE application. This can be placed in the workstation's AUTOEXEC.BAT file after the Novell Client software is run and the user has logged into the network. For Windows 3.x, make sure NPRINTER is loaded before launching Windows.

There's a version of NPRINTER for Windows NT, but it wasn't shipped with the initial releases of NetWare 4.x and 5 because the NT NPRINTER product wasn't available. You can download the software and supporting documentation from Novell's Web site (**www.novell.com**) at no cost.

If you have a printer attached to another server that's not running the print server software (PSERVER) and you want this printer to be serviced by a print server, you need to load NPRINTER.NLM manually on the server that has the printer attached. Here's the syntax for this:

```
NPRINTER PrintServerName PrinterName
```

For example, in the previous command, if the printer isn't attached to the print server, you enter the following at the server's console:

```
NPRINTER .RESEARCH-PS.RESEARCH.ACME .RESEARCH-COLOR.RESEARCH.ACME
```

Again, case is not important when entering the command. This can also be placed in the server's AUTOEXEC.NCF file so the software is loaded when the server is launched.

Managing Print Services

When you create the various print objects discussed previously, you'll notice two buttons titled Users and Operator in some of the dialog boxes. In this section, you'll learn about the print object operators and their management capabilities.

The print object operator can manipulate and modify the object, whereas a user cannot. This type of role is designed for network administrators or the individuals responsible for network printing. When the Print Queue and Print

Server objects are created, the default operator of these objects is the user who created them. An operator can add other operators, and administrators with NDS supervisory rights can manipulate the operator lists.

Managing The Print Queue

The print queue operator can control the flow of print jobs entering and leaving the queue. There are three operator flags, and they're all turned on by default. These are viewed and configured in the Identification screen when you select the print queue's details. Here are descriptions of the three operator flags:

➤ **Allow Users To Submit Print Jobs** If this flag is turned off, users are not able to print from their applications to the queue. A situation in which you may have to turn off this flag is when the volume holding the print queue is running low on disk space.

➤ **Allow Service By Current Print Servers** When this flag is inactive, the print files generated by the users are submitted to the queue but remain in the queue until this flag is activated.

➤ **Allow New Print Servers To Attach** With this option, if you're creating additional Print Server objects that will be servicing this queue, when you load the other print servers, they will begin to service the queue immediately. If this is disabled, new print servers cannot service the queue. This will have no effect on the active print server that's servicing the queue.

Print queue operators can also manipulate the print jobs in the queue. In the Print Queue Details window, select the Job List button to display any print files in the queue. Each print job has a sequence number, and this can be modified by double-clicking on the job or by selecting the print job and clicking on the Job Details button. In the resultant dialog box, enter the new sequence number for the job in the Service Sequence field.

Several other options are also available in the Job Details dialog box:

➤ **User Hold and Operator Hold** The print queue operator can select either one of these options. If you choose the User Hold option, either an operator or the owner of the print job can release the print job. If you choose the Operator Hold option, only a print queue operator can release the job.

➤ **Print Banner** This checkbox allows you to turn the banner on or off. If the banner is turned on, the Name and Banner Name fields become enabled. The banner page is printed before the print file and is sometimes used to help separate printed documents for sorting purposes.

➤ **Form Feed** This checkbox allows you to turn form feed on or off. Form feed ejects an empty page at the end of the printed document.

➤ **Defer Printing** When this checkbox is enabled, you can specify a time and date for the file to be printed. This is a useful feature if you want to print a large file after hours. The owner of the print file can also set this option.

The operator can also remove a print file from the queue by selecting the print file and pressing the Delete key or clicking on the Delete button. More than one file can be removed at a time by selecting multiple entries with the aid of the Ctrl or Shift key.

Note: Users may wonder why a large file takes so long to start printing. This delay is because the entire print job must be in the print queue before the print server will begin servicing the queue.

Managing The Printer

The Printer object does not have an operator list, but there are several items that can be configured. NDS security is used to control who has the rights to modify the printer's properties. You can view the status of the printer through NetWare Administrator or at the server running PSERVER. Both interfaces provide similar management options. In NetWare Administrator, open the Details window for the printer and click on the Printer Status button. On the next screen displayed, you have several options:

➤ **Service Mode** This specifies how the print server servicing this printer handles forms. Forms are defined paper dimensions that are tied to a particular print job.

➤ **Mount Form** This button allows you to specify a predefined form to mount on the printer.

➤ **Eject Page** This option is similar to a form feed command. It tells the printer to eject the page being printed. If the printer is paused, a blank piece of paper will be ejected.

➤ **Pause** This option allows you to pause and restart the printer.

➤ **Abort Job and Mark Top Of Form** These options are self-explanatory. They can be performed from the print server's Printer Status screen on the server. (Note that the Mark Top Of Form option has been removed from the NetWare 5 print server.)

Another useful item to configure on the printer is the handling of messages. On the printer's Details screen is the Notification button, which allows you to specify who will receive messages generated by the printer—for example, the Out Of Paper message. By default, the owner of the print file currently being serviced will receive the message. If certain people are responsible for handling printer error messages, you may want to disable the Notify Print Job Owner checkbox and add the appropriate NDS object to the notification list. You can also specify the time interval for the first and repeated printer messages.

Managing The Print Server

In contrast to the Print Queue and Printer objects, the Print Server object has a few management tasks for the print server, including unloading the print server, specifying operators and users, and viewing the printer status.

On the print server's Identification page is the advertising name of the print server. This is the name that the print server uses to communicate on the network. By default, it's the same name as the NDS object's name, but you can change the name if you like. The Unload button deactivates the print server and unloads PSERVER on the server. Also, the Auditing Log button allows you to enable auditing of the print server, which generates a log of all print jobs handled by the print server.

Configuring Usage Privileges For The User

For users to print to queue-based printers, they must be defined as users of the print queue or queues and associated print servers. Default user assignments are specified when the objects are created. Depending on your network design, these defaults may be quite sufficient. The object's operators, as well as network administrators with NDS supervisory rights, can manipulate the user lists.

The default print queue user is the container in which the Print Queue object was created and the User object that created the Print Queue object. The default print server user is the container in which the Print Server object was created.

Troubleshooting Queue-Based Printing

From the review of queue-based printing services, you can see that there are several areas of the printing process that can develop problems. One of the most important steps in troubleshooting queue-based printing is determining whether the problem resides on the workstation or network side. Also, you need to know whether the problem exists for a single user and/or application or for multiple users and/or multiple applications. In addition, if the printing environment has just been set up and configured, there may be different issues than there are with existing network printing.

One item that can help reduce problems is to make sure the environment is using the most current versions of the various printing software components. Problems typically appear with older NetWare printing components and newer desktop operating systems. At the time the printing software components were created, the new desktop operating systems did not even exist. It's impractical to assume that software written prior to the desktop operating system will operate flawlessly. You can check out the most current versions of the printing environment for NetWare 4.x or 5 on Novell's Support Services Web site (**http://support.novell.com**).

If the printing environment has just been set up, check to make sure all the components are configured properly. Something as simple as forgetting to assign a print queue to a printer or forgetting to assign the printer to the print server may lead to many hours of troubleshooting. Also, if you're supporting bindery-based print services, make sure to keep the names of the Print Queue, Printer, and/or Print Server objects short and simple. This may also be necessary for third-party network printing configurations. Finally, check to make sure the workstation is capturing to the same port the user or application is using. Users may not be aware of the concept of "capturing" or that they can print to more than one printer on the network. In the latter case, the users may need to be trained on the proper procedure for switching printers.

Some problems will appear all of a sudden after months of flawless printing. For example, if the print jobs are large, there must be enough storage space on both the user's workstation and the volume on which the print queue resides. If the workstation runs out of disk space, the user may receive a message stating that the system is unable to write to a particular device. In addition, the partially spooled file may become stuck in the workstation and take up valuable disk space. The message the user receives in this situation typically does not make sense to users, and they may not be able to define the problems or symptoms properly.

Quite often in situations where the previous situations don't apply, network administrators will use some quick-fix techniques. These are designed to reduce the impact of troubleshooting downtime, with the hope that problem will be fixed—at least for the immediate printing crisis. These quick fixes typically include the following:

➤ Verify that the printer is online, has paper, and is not waiting for a manual feed.

➤ Check the printer for any error messages or codes on its panel.

➤ Verify that all physical connections are intact and reliable.

➤ Check the configuration on the user's workstation to make sure the proper printer port is being redirected to the desired queue.

➤ Determine whether only one user cannot print or several users are experiencing the same problem. If more than one user is affected, check to see whether they're all on one network segment or on several.

➤ Check to see whether the user can print with other applications. If the user can print from another application, the problem may reside in the application or in how printing is configured for the application.

➤ Shut down and restart the workstation. This is a common fix when only one user's workstation is affected.

➤ Reset the printer or power it off and then on again. This may be necessary if all users are experiencing similar problems. However, if any print jobs are being processed, they will be halted and may not resume when the printer is brought back online.

➤ Physically attach a printer to the problem workstation and see whether you can print to a local parallel (LPT) port without using the network.

Another important troubleshooting tip is to determine whether the problem occurs before the print job reaches the queue or after it appears in the queue. If the print job is not arriving in the queue, the problem may be workstation-based or at the location of the print queue. If the job appears in the queue, the problem may not be the workstation but the print server, print queue, or perhaps the printer itself. This separation of potential problems does not eliminate other causes but may help you focus on likely problem areas.

Make sure you're able to apply the correct techniques to determine whether the problem is at the workstation or with one of the print components.

Workstation Issues

You can verify the arrival of a user's print job in the queue using a variety of mechanisms. You can use the Windows 95/98 and Windows NT Printers folder to observe the contents of the print queue. In NetWare, the Details windows of the Print Queue object in NetWare Administrator include a button for the Job List page, which allows you to view and manage the contents of the print queue. You can freeze a print job in the queue by going to the Identification page of the Print Queue object. Under the Operator Flags choices, deselect the item titled Allow Service By Current Print Servers. When this is not selected, print jobs arrive in the queue and are not processed by the print server until the option is reversed. Pausing the items in the queue allows you to observe the status of the print job. You may need to unload and reload PSERVER.NLM for these changes to become effective.

Applications are often categorized as *network aware* and *network unaware*. Most current Windows-based applications are network aware and can be set to print to a NetWare print queue or printer using the Windows-based Add Printers Wizard. However, applications that are not network aware, such as DOS-based applications or applications in which the vendor has veered off standard development guidelines, may not be able to print to Netware printers. In these cases, you may need to configure printing using **CAPTURE** commands. If more than one printer is involved, the user may need to be instructed on the procedure to change the different LPT ports that are captured to different queues. Also, this may involve the careful selection of the print driver or drivers for the particular captured workstation printer port or ports.

When a print job is first sent to the queue, it's in an Adding state. After the entire print file is in the queue, the status changes to Ready. In this state, the print server begins servicing the job, and the status changes to Active. If the print job arrives in the queue but is not being printed, look at the status of the print job in the queue. If the print job is not listed as Ready, it will not print. If the file is large, it may take some time for the status to move from Adding to Ready. If this does not occur in a timely fashion, look at the workstation. The problem most likely resides there, and it may be a **CAPTURE** configuration error that's not releasing the print file or the port properly. Also, check to make sure the user or a print queue operator has not put the print job in question on hold or set a deferred time to print.

Current applications contain the capability to include graphics and other file types that may produce large print files. Users need to be aware that some graphic-intensive applications may take a while to print and they should not keep resending the same print files. If users are experiencing incomplete document printouts with graphic-intensive machines, verify that the timeout parameter is long enough. A slow printer and/or a slow connection between the print server and the printer may produce output that contains only a portion of the document. Normally, the print server sends pieces of the print job to the printer in chunks the printer can handle. If there's a communication delay between the printer and print server, the print server may stop sending the job because it assumes the job is finished. You can increase this wait time value in a **CAPTURE** command using the **TI** (timeout) option. This can also be changed in the Novell Client properties in the Default Capture area. This change will then apply to any new printers you create. If the problem still occurs, you may need to disable the timeout option.

Applications and printers created over the last few years can properly handle tab characters. However, in the past, it was sometimes necessary to substitute a set number of space characters whenever the tab character was encountered. Even with current applications, the printed document may not look like you expected it to. If the **CAPTURE** command is using the tab (**T**) substitution switch, consider changing the **CAPTURE** command to either remove this option or to use the **NT** (no tab) switch. This will allow the printer to handle the tab characters, and no modification or substitution is performed by the client. For example, the following **CAPTURE** statement states that each tab character is substituted with 10 spaces:

```
CAPTURE L=2 Q=.Research-Q.Research.Acme NFF NB T=10
```

You may want to change the command to the following, which doesn't contain a **T** switch:

```
CAPTURE L=2 Q=.Research-Q.Research.Acme NFF NB NT
```

There are also some special considerations for applications that send information to the communication ports (COM) and not to the parallel ports (LPT). One way to address this problem is to save the print output to a file and then send this file to a print queue with the **NPRINT** command. A similar method is to set up to print to file, then name the file for the captured printer port, such as LPT1. You might be able to use the Add Printers Wizard in Windows to redirect the output to a printer that has been defined as a serial printer in NetWare Administrator. For example, applications that print to the serial ports are specialized drawing packages designed to be used with plotters.

Finally, be aware of conditions where the **CAPTURE** command is used to send large print files to the print queue and the client's server connection is cleared or disrupted. In these cases, the portion of the print file in the queue is not complete and will not be printed. You do have the option in the **CAPTURE** command to keep the portion of the file in the queue and to print that segment. This involves the **KEEP** switch. Here's an example of it:

```
CAPTURE L=2 Q=.Research-Q.Research.Acme NFF NB NT K
```

Print Queue Issues

Sometimes, the print file arrives in the print queue just fine, but before it's picked up by the print server to be sent to the printer, the print file is damaged because the print queue is corrupt. A corrupt print queue can cause problems that range from minor to severe, such as causing the server running PSERVER to abend (abnormal end). A reason a print queue may become corrupted is that the volume holding the queue ran out of disk space while a print file was being sent to the queue. Also, NDS print queue names that contain nonalphanumeric characters may have troubles, particularly when being accessed as bindery print queues. Refrain from using the following characters in print queues (or for most NDS objects in general):

➤ Spaces

➤ Ampersands (&)

➤ Exclamation points (!)

Periods are not allowed in NDS object names, but some bindery-based print utilities may allow them.

Print Server Issues

Another area that can produce problems is the print server. Symptoms of print server errors include when a print file is no longer in the print queue, but nothing has printed. Another print server error is when the status of the print file in the queue has moved from Ready to Active, but nothing has printed.

A quick troubleshooting tip is to reinitialize the print server and see whether the problem appears again. Although this may clear the problem, it may not help you determine what the actual problem was. However, sometimes the need to get the users back to normal network usage is more important than trying to determine the exact cause of the problem at that time.

Whenever there's a change made to the queue-based printing environment, the print services software needs to be reloaded. If this is not performed after a change, the change will not take effect. For example, suppose that you, as a container administrator, create new Print Queue and Printer objects for a new printer installed at your location, and you specify an existing print server to service these new objects. If the print server associated with the new objects is not reinitialized, users won't be able to print to the new printer. You can reinitialize the print server at the server console using the options in the print server screen and reloading PSERVER. Note, however, that any files in the middle of being printed might not finish successfully. You can also use the option Unload After Active Print Jobs, so currently printing documents will finish properly. This way, any print files in the queue in a Ready or Hold state will be printed according to their schedules when the print server comes back online.

Running PSERVER on a server does use server RAM and resources such as the processor. (Even worse is the load NPRINTER places on a server while printing to a directly attached printer.) If the server is already tasked with several activities and is relatively busy, it might not be a good idea to use that server as the print server. Also, if you're pushing the envelope for sufficient RAM, do not use the server. If you receive messages such as Unable To Create Display Portal or Not Enough Free Buffers, you need to add more memory. Adding more memory may improve the performance of a print server that prints very large files.

Another common problem is when an administrator is prompted for a password when attempting to load PSERVER for a print server but doesn't have a password. Typically, this is the result of a misspelled print server name. Check to make sure the name is correct, and it's a good idea to use distinguished names. Also, loading PSERVER without a print server name will display a screen that allows you to "walk" the tree and select the print server. Whereas this is not useful for AUTOEXEC.NCF files, it can help you determine the distinguished name of the print server and to verify whether the print server can load properly.

If you're relying on messages sent from the printer to the operators or users, make sure you are using a bidirectional printer cable for printers that support this feature. Also, if you're using third-party print servers, make sure they're NetWare aware and that there are no outstanding issues with the products. Checking for the product on Novell's Support Web pages and/or the vendors' Web pages is a good starting point for tracking down issues with a third-party product. In addition, plotters may get confused with a print queue environment and they may need special consideration and configuration.

Printer Issues

Troubleshooting printer-related problems should include checking and verifying the physical connections. Suppose that a printer has had no problems, but then starts experiencing problems on the day following office carpet cleaning. This problem may be because of something as simple as a loose connection. Also, verify the printer is online and the paper source and toner cartridge are in working order. Users may not be aware of an offline/online status or may not know which "light" or status code indicates whether the printer is online or offline.

When using PostScript printers, make sure the users have access to the appropriate versions of the proper print drivers. Sending a PostScript file to a non-PostScript printer often results in pages of code, which is not what the users want.

If the printer is printing documents erratically or the Windows 95/98 System control panel Device Manager or Windows NT System Diagnostics indicates port or interrupt conflicts, you may want to try redefining a parallel printer's interrupt as "polled."

Generally, it's a good idea to avoid serial printers, and direct network attached printers are preferred over parallel port attached printers. There's certainly a speed issue—direct network attachments are much faster—but there are also communications issues involved. Sorting the correct pinout for a serial cable is hardly worth the time involved, and with the choices presented with enhanced parallel ports, it's possible to find incompatibilities between printers and server parallel ports. Finally, there's the disproportionate load placed on the server by serial and parallel ports. These are (unless replaced with expensive intelligent ports) driven by the CPU, and even trivial printing chores place a heavy load on the server.

Configuration Issues

A relatively common cause of print job output problems occurs when the printer is not attached to a queue. Although this is not a problem with the print server, you can use the Print Server object in NDS to assist in troubleshooting. Clicking on the Print Layout button in the Print Server Details window displays the print objects and their relationships to each other. For example, a properly configured printing environment is shown in Figure 9.7.

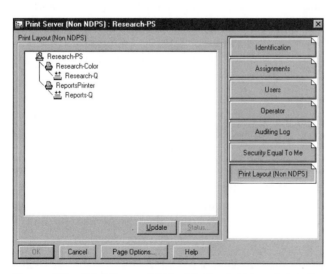

Figure 9.7 Print Server NDS object print layout details.

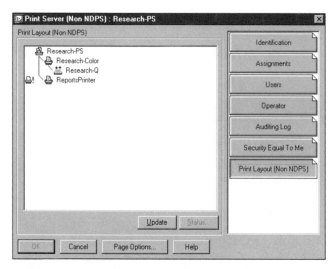

Figure 9.8   Print Server NDS object print layout details with a missing print queue assignment.

Now look at Figure 9.8, where the same print objects exist, but the Reports-Printer is not connected to a print queue.

In Figure 9.8, notice the exclamation point to the right of the ReportsPrinter. Selecting the item with the exclamation mark and then clicking on the Status button displays a dialog box with more details about the selected item. You may be able to use this information to assist you with your troubleshooting tasks.

Remote Printer Issues

In some small networks, the administrator may choose to configure queue-based printing to enable a printer on a user's workstation to be accessible to other network users. The workstation runs the appropriate version of NPRINTER, which enables the print server to see the printer. For this to function properly, the workstation and the printer both need to be on, and the workstation needs to have the Novell Client installed and running. The workstation does not need to be logged into the network, but it must have a connection to the NetWare network. If any one of these items is not in place, the printer will not be accessible to users. A typical error message when NPRINTER is not running on the workstation is shown in Figure 9.9. This occurs in either the Print Server object Print Layout screen or at the Print Server screen on the server console.

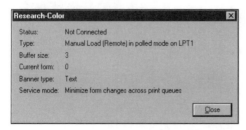

Figure 9.9   Print Server NDS object print layout details results when NPRINTER is not running on a workstation that has a network printer attached.

 You can place the appropriate operating system version of NPRINTER and all associated files on the workstation's local disk. These files can also be placed in the LOGIN directory of the server to which the workstation connects. Either one of these combinations does not require an account to be logged in at the workstation to make the printer available.

The user at the workstation with the network printer attached needs to print to his or her printer as a network printer—not a local printer. If the user prints to the printer as a local device, the printer will then become inaccessible to other network users.

If the user running NPRINTER reboots his or her workstation without logging out first, the user may receive an error message when attempting to run NPRINTER. In this case, the server has not cleared the previous session, and it will not automatically clear the earlier connection for at least 30 seconds. You either clear the previous connection manually or wait until the connection is automatically cleared. This type of problem typically appears when a workstation has hung and the user has not had the opportunity to log off the network. To make sure the fault is not with the printer itself, you can send a print file directly to the printer as a local device and avoid the network all together. If the document prints just fine, the problem could be corrupted NPRINTER software or an improper configuration of the print objects.

Practice Questions

Question 1

What are some of the roles the NDS Printer object plays in queue-based printing? [Choose the four best answers]

❑ a. The NDS Printer object is used to configure who receives printer messages.

❑ b. The NDS Printer object is used to specify the connection type of the printer.

❑ c. The NDS Printer object is used to prioritize printer usage.

❑ d. The NDS Printer object is used to specify operators and users of the printer.

❑ e. The NDS Printer object can be used to monitor the status of the printer.

The correct answers are a, b, c, and e. The NDS Printer object does not have operator or users lists. Users of the printer are specified in the print queue assigned to the printer. Therefore, answer d is incorrect.

Question 2

The following is a list of the steps necessary to set up a NetWare 5 queue-based printing environment:

1. Create the print server and assign the printers.

2. Create the print queue.

3. Specify the volume on which the print queue will reside.

4. Assign the print queue to the printer.

5. Create the Printer object.

6. Load the print server software at the server console.

Which of the following choices presents the correct order of these steps?

○ a. 2, 3, 5, 4, 1, 6

○ b. 2, 5, 4, 1, 3, 6

○ c. 5, 1, 3, 2, 4, 6

○ d. 6, 2, 3, 5, 4, 1

○ e. 2, 5, 3, 4, 1, 6

The correct answer is a. You create the print queue, specify the volume on which the print queue will reside, create the Printer object, assign the print queue to the printer, create the print server and assign the printers, and then load the print server software at the server console. All other options present incorrect orders. Therefore, answers b, c, d, and e are incorrect.

Question 3

Which of the following statements defines a NetWare 5 print queue?

○ a. A NetWare 5 print queue is a directory created on the user's workstation that holds the print files before printing.

○ b. A NetWare 5 print queue is a directory created on the server that holds the print files before printing.

○ c. A NetWare 5 print queue is a mapped drive letter created on the user's workstation that points to the queue on the server.

○ d. A NetWare 5 print queue is a specialized volume created to hold the print files so there's no risk of running out of space on the SYS volume.

○ e. A NetWare 5 print queue is defined as a bindery-based object; therefore, it's compatible with NetWare 4.x.

The correct answer is b. A NetWare 5 print queue is a directory created on the server that holds the print files before printing. Because answer b is correct, answer a is incorrect. The print queue has no interaction with mapped drive letters. Therefore, answer c is incorrect. The print queue is not a volume but rather a directory that's stored on the volume you specified in the creation process. Therefore, answer d is incorrect. The NetWare 5 print queue can be a bindery-based queue but not for compatibility reasons with NetWare 4.x. This may be necessary for compatibility with legacy third-party print servers. Therefore, answer e is incorrect.

Question 4

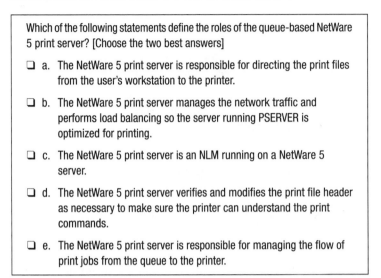

Which of the following statements define the roles of the queue-based NetWare 5 print server? [Choose the two best answers]

❑ a. The NetWare 5 print server is responsible for directing the print files from the user's workstation to the printer.

❑ b. The NetWare 5 print server manages the network traffic and performs load balancing so the server running PSERVER is optimized for printing.

❑ c. The NetWare 5 print server is an NLM running on a NetWare 5 server.

❑ d. The NetWare 5 print server verifies and modifies the print file header as necessary to make sure the printer can understand the print commands.

❑ e. The NetWare 5 print server is responsible for managing the flow of print jobs from the queue to the printer.

The correct answers are c and e. The NetWare 5 print server is an NLM running on a NetWare 5 server, and it's responsible for managing the flow of print jobs from the queue to the printer. Because answer e is correct, answer a is incorrect. The print server does not monitor network traffic or perform load balancing. Those actions are performed by either NLMs or other workstation-based products. Therefore, answer b is incorrect. The print server does not modify the print file header to adjust for incorrect print drivers selected at the workstation. The composition of the print file header that contains printer language information and printer information is performed at the workstation when the user selects Print. Therefore, answer d is incorrect.

Question 5

One of the users in the graphics department is experiencing trouble with printing. About an hour after she logged in this morning, she wasn't able to print from her graphics program to the color printer. She has been printing her documents from a coworker's workstation. Which of the following would be a good troubleshooting tactic?

○ a. Go into the Print Queue object and turn off the operator flag for Allow Service By Current Print Servers.

○ b. Unload and reload the print server.

○ c. Log the user out of her workstation and reboot it.

○ d. Edit the **CAPTURE** commands and use the **KEEP** parameter.

○ e. Determine whether the print files from the workstation are arriving at the print queue.

The correct answer is e. The best action in this situation is to determine whether the print files from the workstation are arriving at the print queue. Performing the action in answer a would not print any documents from users who are using the print queue. Therefore, answer a is incorrect. In this scenario, the problem most likely resides in the user's workstation because only one workstation is affected. You would unload and reload the print server if several users were experiencing the same problem. Therefore, answer b is incorrect. Answer c may correct the problem, but it's not a troubleshooting aid. Therefore, answer c is incorrect. The **KEEP** parameter is often used in cases where the print file is being sent to the print queue and the connection is severed. Therefore, answer d is incorrect.

Question 6

You've received an email from one of the container administrators who's having trouble loading PSERVER on one of his servers. He's using the following command:

```
PSERVER .SALES=PS.SALES.ACME
```

After he enters the command, he's prompted for a password. Which of the following best describes his problem?

○ a. He's not authenticated to NDS with the proper supervisor rights to the server on which he's trying to run PSERVER.

○ b. The Print Server object has not been created in NDS.

○ c. He has probably misspelled the name of the Print Server object. For example, perhaps SALES=PS should be SALES-PS.

○ d. A print queue is not connected to the printer.

○ e. There is no problem because, by default, each print server has a password.

The correct answer is c. He has probably misspelled the name of the Print Server object. You do not need NDS rights to load PSERVER on a server; you need either physical access to the server or a remote console session. Therefore, answer a is incorrect. If the Print Server object has not been created in NDS, you'd receive a different error message—such as "...cannot be found." Therefore, answer b is incorrect. Even if the print queue were not attached to the printer, you would still be able to load the associated print server. Therefore, answer d is incorrect. A print server does not have a password by default. Therefore, answer e is incorrect.

Question 7

The administrator for your company's remote office in Hutto, TX has set up all the print objects in NDS needed to correctly print to a printer attached to one of the workstations and can load the print server with no problems. She has also modified login scripts to make sure all is correct for accessing the printer. However, when she views the status of the printer in the Print Server object, the message states the printer is not connected. What problem is this administrator experiencing?

○ a. The workstation to which the printer is attached is not running NPRINTER.

○ b. The print queue is not connected to the print server.

○ c. The container in which the print objects reside needs to be made the print queue and print server operator.

○ d. This is a normal message whenever printing is idle.

○ e. The administrator did not have the proper rights when setting up the objects.

The correct answer is a. The workstation to which the printer is attached is not running NPRINTER. Print queues are connected to printers not print servers. Therefore, answer b is incorrect and the reason this is a trick question. No object needs to be an operator of the Print Queue or Print Server objects to make this message disappear. Therefore, answer c is incorrect. This is not a normal message. Therefore, answer d is incorrect. If the administrator did not have the proper rights, she would probably not be able to get as far as she did in creating the objects. Therefore, answer e is incorrect.

Question 8

You've just set up all the proper NDS queue-based print objects and are ready to load the print server software on the server. The name of the print server is Office-PS, and it's located in the Austin Organizational Unit. Above the Austin container lies the ACME Organization object. Which of the following represents the proper way of loading this print server on the Advertising server located in the Sales container?

- ○ a. **PSERVER .OFFICE-PS.SALES.ACME**
- ○ b. **PSERVER OFFICE-PS**
- ○ c. **PSERVER .OFFICE-PS.ACME.AUSTIN**
- ○ d. **PSERVER .OFFICE-PS.AUSTIN.ACME**
- ○ e. **LOAD PSERVER .OFFICE-PS.AUSTIN.ACME.ROOT**

The correct answer is d. **PSERVER .OFFICE-PS.AUSTIN.ACME** is the correct code used to load this print server. The first answer uses a distinguished name, but the SALES container should not be listed. It should be the Austin container. Therefore, answer a is incorrect. The second choice would work if the server were located in the same container as the print objects, the Austin container, but it's not. Therefore, answer b is incorrect. Because answer d is correct, answer c is incorrect. The last choice uses **LOAD**, which is correct, but the name of the print server is incorrect. ROOT is not part of a distinguished name. Therefore, answer e is incorrect. This question is a bit tricky because you need to be comfortable with distinguished object names, whether they're print objects or not.

Need To Know More?

 http://support.novell.com contains TIDs that cover related topics that may be of interest. At Novell's support Web site, go to the Knowledgebase and perform a search using the following TID numbers:

➤ **TID 2928524** Troubleshooting Nprinter95 Summary

➤ **TID 2943863** Print Problems After 3.12 To 5.0 Upgrade

 www.novell.com/documentation/lg/nw4/iw2sys/printenu/ data/he8klys1.html contains a document titled "Troubleshooting Printers."

 www.novell.com/documentation/lg/nw4/iw2sys/printenu/ data/h5402ovm.html contains a document titled "Troubleshooting Printing Problems."

 www.novell.com/documentation/lg/nw4/iw2sys/printenu/ data/hgvmczpc.html contains a document titled "Troubleshooting Print Server Problems."

 www.novell.com/documentation/lg/nw5/usprint/ndps_enu/ data/hy7c2qj9.html contains a document titled "Tracking Jobs From A Workstation."

10

Novell Client

. . . .

Terms you'll need to understand:

√ NIOS.VXD

√ Local area network (LAN) drivers

√ Internetwork Packet Exchange (IPX)

√ Transmission Control Protocol/Internet Protocol (TCP/IP)

√ NetWare Client Requester

√ Network Driver Interface Specification (NDIS)

√ Open Data-Link Interface (ODI)

√ ODI NDIS support (ODINSUP)

√ CLIENT32.NLM

√ NWFS.SYS

√ NetWare Graphical Identification and Authentication (NWGINA)

Techniques you'll need to master:

√ Describing the architecture and functions of the main components of the Novell Client for Windows 95/98

√ Describing the architecture and functions of the main components of the Novell Client for Windows NT

√ Using various Novell Client-related tools and features for troubleshooting

√ Understanding the role of a protocol analyzer in troubleshooting client-related issues

For many years, different desktop operating systems have been able to access Novell NetWare networks and services. These include Unix, OS/2, Macintosh, DOS, and the various versions and types of Windows architectures, including 3.x, 95/98, and NT. Often, the vendor of each operating system supplies the client software necessary to access NetWare networks, but sometimes this software does not include support for all NetWare services. For example, some of the new features of NetWare 5, such as Novell Distributed Print Services (NDPS), are not available with some vendors' client software. Novell provides client software that allows access to NetWare services and includes full support for Novell Directory Services (NDS). In addition, Novell clients are provided free of charge and can be downloaded from Novell's Web site, at **www.novell.com**.

In this chapter, we'll concentrate on the Novell Client for Windows 95/98 and the Novell Client for Windows NT. More details about the Windows 95/98 and Windows NT architectures can be found in Appendix D of this book.

Novell Client For Windows 95/98 Architecture

The Novell Client for Windows 95/98 provides access to NetWare services and can coexist with other client software for accessing other non-NetWare services. The Novell Client for Windows 95/98 has three main architectural components: the NetWare Input/Output Subsystem (NIOS), local area network (LAN) drivers and communication protocols, and the NetWare Client Requester.

NIOS provides the interface between the local Windows 95/98 operating system and the Novell Client and Novell services. The NIOS.VXD file provides this functionality (it is located in the C:\WINDOWS\SYSTEM directory). NIOS uses the Windows 95/98 extended memory manager and can dynamically adjust memory needs for the different client settings and changes. NIOS contains loader software and loads the other client modules using information in the Windows 95/98 Registry. The NIOS architecture and functionality is based on the Novell server architecture. SERVER.EXE and NIOS.VXD provide the same types of functions, except SERVER.EXE uses its own memory manager and NIOS.VXD uses the Windows memory manager.

LAN drivers, or network board drivers, provide the interface between the network board and the other Novell Client components. The drivers for the Novell Client support the Network Driver Interface Specification (NDIS) and Open Data-Link Interface (ODI) driver specifications. ODI and NDIS both provide the ability to use multiple protocols on the same software and hardware.

As long as your network board is ODI- or NDIS-compliant, you can have several protocols in your workstation, all using the same components. The Novell Client uses the ODINSUP component, which is a 32-bit ODI LAN driver that uses the ODI NDIS interface. This also allows you to run Microsoft network services and components on the same LAN driver interface.

A communication protocol specifies how data is transmitted across the network and is not concerned with the underlying physical network architecture. The communication protocol accepts data passed down from higher level protocols and converts it to a form that's acceptable to the protocols below it. When network packets are received by the network board, the data is passed to the LAN driver, which then passes it to the communication protocol (or protocols). The data then continues through the upper-level protocols until it reaches its destination service or process.

Many communication "languages" can be used for workstations to access network services. Perhaps the most common communication protocol used in today's networks is the *Internet Protocol* (IP), which is often referred to as the *Transmission Control Protocol/Internet Protocol* (TCP/IP). The IP protocol suite has been used on computer systems and networks for many years. It's often considered the standard for Unix systems and is also used on mainframe and minicomputer systems. TCP/IP has increased in popularity on local and wide area networks in the past few years—primarily for access to the Internet. In comparison to previous versions of NetWare, NetWare 5 provides native support for IP. This means you can create a pure IP NetWare network without any other protocols.

When TCP/IP is loaded on a workstation, different components, such as Winsock, NetBIOS applications, and the Novell Client, can use IP to communicate with other devices and services on the network. On a NetWare server, when IP is loaded and bound to the network interfaces, the server can use IP to communicate with other servers and workstations on the network.

Another common protocol used on Novell networks is *Internetwork Packet Exchange* (IPX), which is a Novell proprietary protocol. Until the release of NetWare 5, IPX was installed automatically when a NetWare server was set up. Now, you have the option to decide whether to install IPX, IP, or both. Each of the services that are accessible with IPX uses unique socket IDs. When a packet is received by a workstation, the IPX protocol helps determine for which socket the packet is designed. The packet also includes the address of the network segment on which the workstation is communicating. To provide support for IPX, Windows 95/98 includes an IPX/SPX-compatible protocol called *NWLink*. This protocol also allows other services that use Winsock and NetBIOS to run on IPX.

The last major component of the Novell Client for Windows 95/98 is the *NetWare Client Requester*. Most of the activities of the Requester are provided by CLIENT32.NLM, which is located in the C:\NOVELL\CLIENT32 directory. The Requester, which is also referred to as the *NetWare DOS Requester*, provides services such as adjusting automatic reconnection levels, caching files, and tracking the different network resources used. In addition, there's full backward compatibility with earlier NetWare DOS Requesters and the NETX shell.

 Make sure you can identify and describe the major components of the Novell Client for Windows 95/98. You should be able to recognize the names of the associated files as well as their roles.

Some of the features and benefits of the Novell Client for Windows 95/98 are listed in Table 10.1.

Table 10.1	Features and benefits of the Novell Client for Windows 95/98.
Feature/Benefit	**Description**
Installation	Supports an unattended installation of Windows 95/98 and the Novell Client.
	Supports Automatic Client Upgrade (ACU).
	Coexists with the Microsoft Client for Microsoft Networks.
Windows 95/98 integration	Novell Client is initiated when Windows is started.
	You can use Windows Explorer and Network Neighborhood to access Novell services.
	Supports Windows long file names.
	Supports the management of Novell Client settings using the Windows System Policy Editor.
	Can be specified to be the primary network logon.
Novell services	TCP/IP, IPX/SPX, Simple Network Mail Protocol (SNMP), Winsock, NetBIOS, and Named Pipes are supported.
	Supports running (or not running) Novell NDS and bindery scripts.
	Supports automatic reconnection to network resources.
	Provides simultaneous authentication and access to several NDS trees and/or NetWare binderies.

Novell Client For Windows NT Architecture

The Novell Client for Windows NT provides access to Novell services, and it can coexist with other client software for accessing other non-Novell services. The Novell Client for Windows NT has four main architectural components: NWFS.SYS, LAN drivers and communication protocols, the NetWare Client Requester, and the Graphical Identification and Authentication (GINA) module.

Implementation of the Novell Client on Windows NT is different than on Windows 95/98. In Windows NT, the Novell Client operates as a redirector and file system driver. It's also designed to be backward compatible with earlier Novell clients; therefore, applications that communicate directly with earlier application programming interfaces (APIs) can operate with no changes under the newer Novell Client software. The NWFS.SYS component provides the interface between the local Windows NT operating system and the Novell Client and Novell services. NWFS.SYS is located in the C:\WINNT\SYSTEM32 directory.

The drivers for the Windows NT Novell Client support the NDIS and ODI drivers. The Novell Client uses the ODINSUP component, which is a 32-bit ODI LAN driver that uses the ODI NDIS interface. This also allows you to run Microsoft network services and components on the same LAN driver interface.

The Novell Client for Windows NT supports both the TCP/IP and IPX/SPX protocols. You either use the two protocols simultaneously or just use one of the protocols. Because many Windows NT networks and clients use TCP/IP, it's now easier with NetWare 5 to standardize on one protocol in a mixed operating system network.

The third major component of the Novell Client for Windows NT is the NetWare Client Requester. Most of the activities of the Requester are provided by CLIENT32.NLM, which is located in the C:\NOVELL\CLIENT32 directory. The Requester, which is also referred to as the *NetWare DOS Requester*, provides services such as adjusting automatic reconnection levels, caching files, and tracking the different network resources used. In addition, there's full backward compatibility with earlier NetWare DOS Requesters and the NETX shell.

Windows NT requires a mandatory login to access its services and functions. Part of this process presents a graphical login screen (WinLogon) for users to enter their Windows NT account and password information. Because other vendors, such as Novell, use different authentication processes to access their information, Microsoft provides the ability for developers to replace pieces of the login process with their own. This replaceable piece is called the GINA module. The Novell Client for Windows NT replaces the Microsoft GINA (MSGINA.DLL) with a Novell version (NWGINA.DLL). In addition, the appropriate area of the Windows NT Registry is changed to reflect the use of the NWGINA module instead of the MSGINA module. When a user logs in, the NWGINA module sends all the appropriate information to the NetWare network to allow the user to access the Novell resources.

 Make sure you can identify and describe the major components of the Novell Client for Windows NT. You should be able to recognize the names of the associated files as well as their roles.

Some of the features and benefits of the Novell Client for Windows NT are listed in Table 10.2.

Table 10.2 Features and benefits of the Novell Client for Windows NT.	
Feature/Benefit	**Description**
Installation	Supports an unattended installation of Windows NT and the Novell Client.
	Supports Automatic Client Upgrade (ACU).
	Coexists with the Microsoft Client for Microsoft Networks.
Windows NT integration	Novell Client is initiated when Windows is started.
	You can use Windows Explorer and Network Neighborhood to access Novell services.
	Supports Windows long file names.
	Supports the management of Novell Client settings using Windows NT System Policy Editor.
	Can be specified to be the primary network logon.
Novell services	TCP/IP, IPX/SPS, SNMP, Winsock, NetBIOS, and Named Pipes are supported.
	Supports running (or not running) Novell NDS and bindery scripts.
	Supports automatic reconnection to network resources.
	Provides simultaneous authentication and access to several NDS trees and/or NetWare binderies.

Troubleshooting Network Clients

Before applying tools to the problem at hand, it's probably a good idea to document the situation and the symptoms that are present. You should also go through a basic checklist of hardware and software items before setting up and configuring any additional tools. Checklist entries include items such as the following:

➤ Determine whether the problem is occurring on just one workstation, on all workstations in a segment (physical and/or logical), or across multiple segments/locations.

➤ Check to make sure all physical connections are intact and secure. You can often use the status lights on network boards and hubs to help you with this task. (However, a connection light does not necessarily mean communication is occurring.)

➤ Determine whether there have been changes of any type to the workstation's hardware—regardless of how minor the change. Also, find out if there have been any software changes (either application- or client-related software) performed on the workstation.

➤ Determine whether the latest version of the Novell Client software is installed. You can obtain the latest client software from Novell's support Web site at **http://support.novell.com**.

Both the Novell Clients for Windows 95/98 and Windows NT include several features that may assist in troubleshooting client software issues. You can also use other tools besides the client software. We cover these in the following sections.

Windows 95/98

One of the troubleshooting tools that can be used on a Windows 95/98 workstation is not a Novell product; it's Microsoft's REGEDIT. You can use REGEDIT to view and modify the values for the Novell Client in the local machine's Registry. In contrast to previous versions of Windows and DOS, in which settings for hardware and software were stored in several local files, the Registry in Windows 95/98 is a local database that stores most of this same information in one location. When Windows 95/98 starts, the Registry values are used to supply the information needed for the local hardware and software. In addition, whenever you use the different control panels (such as the Network control panel) to change settings, these new values are entered into the appropriate areas in the Registry. Many of the settings that pertain to the Novell Client can be found in the following location in the Registry:

```
HKEY_LOCAL_MACHINE\Network\Novell\System Config
```

You should be very careful when directly editing the Registry with REGEDIT. (REGEDIT.EXE is located in the C:\WINDOWS directory and can be opened using the Run menu.) It's a good idea to back up the Registry before applying any changes in case there's a problem. Microsoft provides a tool on the Windows 95 Installation CD titled ERU.EXE (Emergency Recovery Utility) that you can use to back up the Registry. It's located in the \OTHER\MISC\ERU directory.

Another feature of the Novell Client is the ability to see which components are running at any point in time. Open an MS-DOS prompt window, type "MODULES", and press Enter. Each of the running Novell Client modules is listed along with its version number and file name. You can pause the listing by entering the following command:

```
MODULES | MORE
```

The listing of the loaded modules can also be redirected to a text file. To send, for example, the listing to a file titled NOVCLI.TXT located at the root of the local hard drive, enter the following command in the MS-DOS prompt window:

```
MODULES > C:\NOVCLI.TXT
```

The Novell Client also has the ability to create a log file when the client components are loaded. You basically have to configure two items to create the log file and to specify its location. Open the SYSTEM.INI file located in the C:\WINDOWS directory with any text editor, such as Notepad. Under the [386Enh] heading, add the following on a separate line:

```
NWEnablelogging=True
```

The next step is to set the location of the log file in the Novell Client settings. Follow these steps:

1. Open the Network applet and then open the properties of the Novell NetWare Client.

2. Click on the Advanced Settings tab and choose Troubleshooting from the Parameter Groups drop-down list. This reduces the number of items displayed and makes it easier to locate the appropriate settings.

3. Click on the Log File entry. Then, in the text field displayed to the right, enter in the path for the log file (for example C:\NOVLOG.TXT). You can also specify the maximum size of the log file by choosing the Log File Size entry.

4. Click on OK. Then, restart Windows 95/98 to make these changes effective.

The resulting log file contains a lot of detail and can be used to diagnose a number of problems. Listings 10.1 and 10.2 are excerpts of sample log files that indicate different problems.

Listing 10.1 Unable to bind IPX.

```
NetWare 5 Service Location Protocol for DOS/Win3.x/Win9x  v1.17
(980723)
Copyright 1997-1998 Novell, Inc.  All Rights Reserved.

Module C:\NOVELL\CLIENT32\SRVLOC.NLM initialized successfully.
CONFIG: read 'PRIMARY'
CONFIG: read 'NET BIND ETHERNET_802.2 * *'

[04-26-1999, 04:17:47 pm]
IPX was not able to bind to any board.
[04-26-1999, 04:17:47 pm]
```

Listing 10.2 Unable to locate a Novell server.

```
[04-26-1999, 04:44:34 pm]
NAME CONTEXT = .ACME
CONFIG: read 'PREFERRED SERVER ACME-SRV'

[04-26-1999, 04:44:35 pm]
PREFERRED SERVER = ACME-SRV
CONFIG: read 'FIRST NETWORK DRIVE F'

[04-26-1999, 04:44:41 pm]

NetWare 5 Requester CLIENT32 NLM  v3.03  (981028)
(C) Copyright 1995-1998 Novell Inc.  All Rights Reserved.
Patents Pending.

Client32: A file server could not be found.
Check the network cabling and the server's status before
continuing.

Module C:\NOVELL\CLIENT32\CLIENT32.NLM initialized successfully.

END_OF_LOG
```

As you can see from the two examples, the log file can indicate problems with protocol bindings and the inability to locate a server. Because the log file indicates all Novell Client components (NLMs) that attempt to load, you can also use the log file to locate any load failures.

Another helpful troubleshooting technique is to simply look at the current Novell Client settings in the Network control panel. By viewing these settings, you may be able to determine that a value is not appropriate for the current environment, make the appropriate change, and then observe the results. An example would be If you forgot to change the NetWare Protocol setting when a network was upgraded from NetWare 3.x to NetWare 5 or NetWare 4.x. If the value is set to BIND, the client will not be able to log in to a NetWare 5 or NetWare 4.x network with an NDS connection.

 Be able to apply these tools and techniques to problem scenarios. You may need to combine the skills and tools you learned in this chapter with skills and tools from other resources, such as Micro House Technical Library (MTL).

Windows NT

The same type of tools that are used in a Windows 95/98 environment can be used on a Windows NT Workstation. Windows NT includes two Registry editing tools: REGEDIT.EXE and REGEDT32.EXE. Both of these operate in a similar manner, with some slight differences, such as the search engines and the ability to "lock" the Registry against changes made with the editor.

You can also enable the Novell Client log file using the same process as outlined previously for Windows 95/98. In addition, the **MODULES** command is also available under Windows NT when you open a command prompt window.

Microsoft also provides a tool for backing up the Windows NT Registry. It's located on the Windows NT Installation CD and is also titled ERU.EXE.

LANalyzer

Protocol analyzers can be used to help track down client-related problems. They are available as hardware components or as software that can run on servers or workstations. The basic differences between expensive and low-cost analyzers are typically items such as the number of protocols supported, the speed of capturing and analyzing the data, and the level of detail contained in the data. Getting the most out of a protocol analyzer requires practice with the tool and a good understanding of the types of data it can analyze. Protocol analyzers are also useful for nontroubleshooting tasks. Capturing and analyzing network data over a period of time allows you to develop baseline data that you can use to predict future growth or to foresee problem areas before they become serious. Typically, you can be particular about the type of data captured over time when specific items need to be monitored. In addition to capturing the data, protocol analyzers assemble the packets of bits on the network into information that is more readable to humans. Most protocol analyzers also allow the data to be saved so it can be studied at a later time.

> Other protocol analyzers include Network Associates' (formerly Network General) NetXRay and Sniffer products, EtherPeek, and the Network Monitor utility bundled with Microsoft BackOffice.

LANalyzer is a software protocol analyzer produced by Novell that can be used to assist in troubleshooting workstation client components. It's available in two forms: as a standalone workstation application and as a component in Novell's network management software package, ManageWise.

The standalone workstation application is referred to as *LANalyzer for Windows* or *LZFW*. It's an entry-level, relatively inexpensive protocol analyzer that does not require a great deal of time to understand. When LANalyzer is installed on a workstation, it can only observe traffic on the workstation's segment. If you want to view another segment's network traffic, you need to either move the workstation or install LZFW on the other workstation on the other segment. LZFW can be used to watch and capture realtime data over a period of time so baselines and trends can be developed. LZFW is also a good troubleshooting tool and can alert you to the following types of problems:

➤ **Physical** Physical problems are any problems having to do with hardware, including the following:

  ➤ Crosstalk

  ➤ Broken twisted-pair wires

  ➤ Malfunctioning network boards

  ➤ Defective 10BaseT hubs and/or ports

  ➤ Defective repeaters and transceivers

  ➤ Incorrect terminators

  ➤ Improper bus topology groundings

  ➤ Incorrect spacing of 10Base5 clamps

  ➤ Duplicate or invalid network board addresses

▶ **Software** Problems dealing with software include defective LAN drivers and mismatched data-link protocols.

LZFW also includes the NetWare Expert, which presents some possible solutions when problems are detected. The NetWare Expert Tutorial can be accessed whether there's a problem or not; it contains information for both Ethernet and token ring networks.

The NetWare LANalyzer Agent, which is a part of ManageWise, operates in much the same manner as LZFW. However, the ManageWise Agent also can detect router configuration errors and inefficiencies. Another advantage of the ManageWise version is that the type of information collected contains more detail than LZFW. It also has the ability to monitor several network segments at one time without you needing to set up or move monitoring workstations. ManageWise LANalyzer Agents are also available for other operating systems such as Windows NT Server. Figures 10.1 and 10.2 show sample information obtained from LZFW.

You should be able to list the types of problems where LANalyzer can be a useful tool.

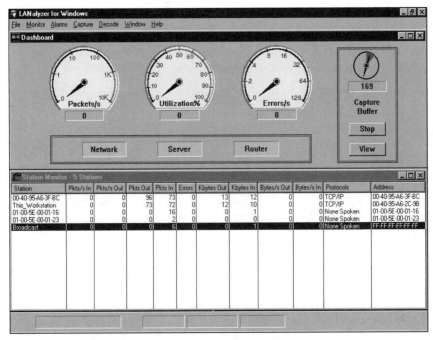

Figure 10.1 LZFW Dashboard and Station Monitor windows.

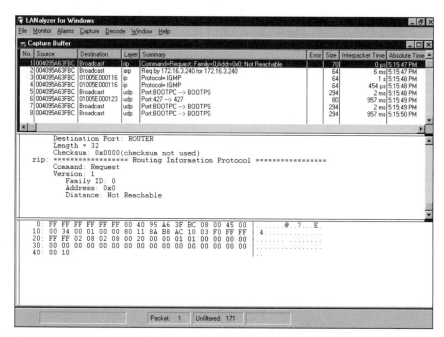

Figure 10.2 An example of the contents of an LZFW capture buffer.

Practice Questions

Question 1

What are the four main components of the Novell Client for Windows NT?
[Choose the four best answers]

❑ a. NIOS.VXD

❑ b. NWFS.SYS

❑ c. CLIENT32.NLM

❑ d. NDIS or ODI drivers

❑ e. TCP/IP and/or IPX/SPX

The correct answers are b, c, d, and e. NIOS.VXD is the companion NWFS.SYS component found on a Windows 95/98 machine running the Novell Client. Therefore, answer a is incorrect.

Question 2

What is the role of the Novell Client component NIOS.VXD?

○ a. It provides the interface between the local Windows operating system and the Novell Client and Novell services.

○ b. It provides the interface between the network board and other Novell Client components.

○ c. It provides services such as adjusting automatic reconnection levels, file caching, and tracking network resource usage.

○ d. It provides the interface between the LAN drivers and the Novell Client and Novell services.

○ e. It provides the interface between the network board and the transmission media.

The correct answer is a. Answer b describes the role of the LAN drivers and is therefore incorrect. Answer c describes the role of CLIENT32.NLM and is therefore incorrect. Answers d and e are made up and do not describe any of the Novell Client component functions. Therefore, answers d and e are incorrect.

Question 3

> What type(s) of LAN driver(s) does the Novell Client support? [Choose the best answer]
>
> ○ a. ODI
>
> ○ b. NDIS
>
> ○ c. IPX
>
> ○ d. IP
>
> ○ e. NDIS and ODI

The correct answer is e. The Novell Client supports both NDIS and ODI drivers. Because answer e is correct, answers a and b alone are incorrect. IPX and IP are communication protocols. Therefore, answers c and d are incorrect.

Question 4

> What is the role of the Novell Client component CLIENT32.NLM?
>
> ○ a. It provides the interface between the local Windows operating system and the Novell Client and Novell services.
>
> ○ b. It provides the interface between the LAN drivers and the Novell Client and Novell services.
>
> ○ c. It provides services such as adjusting automatic reconnection levels, file caching, and tracking network resource usage.
>
> ○ d. It provides the interface between the network board and other Novell Client components.
>
> ○ e. It provides the interface between the network board and the transmission media.

The correct answer is c. The CLIENT32.NLM provides services such as adjusting automatic reconnection levels, file caching, and tracking network resource use. Answer a describes either NIOS.VXD for Windows 95/98 or NWFS.SYS for Windows NT and is therefore incorrect. Answers b and e are made up answers and are therefore incorrect. Answer d describes the role of the LAN drivers and is therefore incorrect.

Question 5

> The Novell Client for Windows NT replaces which piece of the WinLogon interface with its own?
>
> ○ a. MSGINA.DLL.
>
> ○ b. NWGINA.VXD
>
> ○ c. NWGINA.EXE
>
> ○ d. MSGINA.VXD
>
> ○ e. NWGINA.DLL

The correct answer is a. The Novell Client for Windows NT replaces the Microsoftware MSGINA.DLL with the Novell NWGINA.DLL. Therefore, answer e is incorrect. Answers b, c, and d have incorrect extensions and are therefore incorrect.

Question 6

> Which command can you execute at a Windows 95/98 MS-DOS prompt or a Windows NT command prompt window to view the Novell Client loaded components?
>
> ○ a. **COMPONENTS**
>
> ○ b. **LISTNLMS**
>
> ○ c. **C32MODULES**
>
> ○ d. **MODULES**
>
> ○ e. **CONFIG**

The correct answer is d. Answers a, b, and c are made up and are therefore incorrect. **CONFIG** is used at a NetWare server console to display the protocols loaded as well as network interface bind information. Therefore, answer e is incorrect.

Question 7

> Which of the following needs to be done to create a Novell Client log file? [Choose the two best answers]
>
> ❏ a. Add the entry **NWEnableLogging=True** under the [386Enh] heading on the PROTOCOL.INI file.
>
> ❏ b. Turn on logging in the Novell Client settings.
>
> ❏ c. Add the entry **NWEnableLogging=True** under the [386Enh] heading on the SYSTEM.INI file.
>
> ❏ d. Specify the name of the log file in the Novell Client settings.
>
> ❏ e. Specify the size of the log file in the Novell Client settings.

The correct answers are c and d. PROTOCOL.INI is the wrong file name. Therefore, answer a is incorrect. Because answer c enables logging, answer b is incorrect. The size of the log file is an optional setting. Therefore, answer e is incorrect.

Question 8

> What is the role of the Novell Client component NWFS.SYS?
>
> ○ a. It provides the interface between the network board and the transmission media.
>
> ○ b. It provides the interface between the LAN drivers and the Novell Client and Novell services.
>
> ○ c. It provides services such as adjusting automatic reconnection levels, file caching, and tracking network resource usage.
>
> ○ d. It provides the interface between the network board and other Novell Client components.
>
> ○ e. It provides the interface between the local Windows operating system and the Novell Client and Novell services.

The correct answer is e. Answers a and b are made up and are therefore incorrect. Answer c describes the role of CLIENT32.NLM and is therefore incorrect. Answer d describes one of the roles of the communication protocols and is therefore incorrect.

Question 9

> What are some of the problems LZFW can detect? [Choose the three best answers]
>
> ❑ a. Improperly configured CLIENT32.NLM settings
>
> ❑ b. Cable breaks
>
> ❑ c. Malfunctioning hub
>
> ❑ d. Mismatched communication protocols
>
> ❑ e. Duplicate network board addresses

The correct answers are b, c, and e. LZFW can detect the results of improperly configured CLIENT32.NLM settings but not the actual settings themselves. Therefore, answer a is incorrect. LZFW can detect mismatched data-link protocols, not communication protocols. Therefore, answer d is incorrect.

Question 10

> IPX/SPX is supported in Windows 95/98 and Windows NT workstations through the use of which Microsoft communication protocol?
>
> ○ a. ODINSUP
>
> ○ b. NWLink
>
> ○ c. NDIS
>
> ○ d. NetBIOS
>
> ○ e. Winsock

The correct answer is b. ODINSUP provides support for ODI LAN drivers. Therefore, answer a is incorrect. NDIS is a specification for a network board driver. Therefore, answer c is incorrect. NetBIOS and Winsock are communication protocols, but they were not designed to provide IPX/SPX protocol support. Therefore, answers d and e are incorrect. This question is tricky because you need to know that NWLink is produced by Microsoft and is its implementation of Novell's proprietary protocol.

Need To Know More?

 The Novell product pages in their support area provide a lot of Novell Client information. This includes the following:

➤ What's new in the last 7, 14, and 30 days

➤ Top issues/frequently asked questions (FAQs)

➤ Search Novell Knowledgebase (an area for just client issues)

➤ Patches

➤ Download Novell software

➤ Proactive update notifications

Here are the two pages, one for each operating system:

➤ **http://support.novell.com/products/nwcl3/** for Novell Client for Windows 95/98

➤ **http://support.novell.com/products/nwcl45nt/** for Novell Client for Windows NT

 www.novell.com/documentation/lg/client/docui/index.html is the Novell Client documentation.

Network Management

Terms you'll need to understand:

√ LANalyzer for Windows (LZFW)

√ Promiscuous mode

√ Baseline

√ Trends

√ Alarms

√ NetWare Expert

√ Fragment errors

√ Cyclic redundancy check (CRC)/Alignment errors

√ Undersize and oversize errors

√ Jabber errors

√ Server overload errors

Techniques you'll need to master:

√ Outlining the importance of baseline values when determining network performance

√ Defining the four trend graphs LZFW provides

√ Identifying the different alarm thresholds that can be set

√ Describing the procedures for using LZFW to help diagnose network-related issues

The overall performance of the network impacts the performance of the users and the services they're using. If, for example, the network is not providing sufficient transmission speed, the users will begin to recognize network sluggishness and/or disconnections. There are many elements in the network that can impact performance—for example, the topology of the network, the number of active devices, the protocols used, the amount of data being transmitted, and so on. In this chapter, you learn how to use LANalyzer for Windows (LZFW) to help you diagnose and troubleshoot network-related issues.

LANalyzer

LANalyzer is a software protocol analyzer produced by Novell. It's available as a standalone Windows application, LANalyzer for Windows (LZFW), and as a component of Novell's ManageWise product to capture data from the ManageWise servers. The two are very similar in function and appearance. LANalyzer for Windows, often referred to as *LZFW*, works on both Ethernet and token ring networks. For FDDI networks, you need to use the ManageWise LANalyzer module. In this chapter, we concentrate on LZFW version 2.2 on an Ethernet network. At the end of the chapter, there's a brief section on LANalyzer and token ring networks.

 LANalyzer is only one of many protocol analyzer products. Protocol analyzers come in two categories: hardware-based analyzers and software-based analyzers, such as LANalyzer. Software-based analyzers are generally less expensive but somewhat limited. Other protocol analyzers include EtherPeek, Network Associates' Sniffer series, Digitech, and an entire range of cable/network analyzers from Fluke.

LZFW runs on Windows 3.1, 3.11, and Windows 95/98 workstations that have the Novell Client installed. LZFW can see any node on the network, regardless of its function or operating system.

Note: As of this writing, you cannot use LZFW on a Windows NT Workstation to capture data, but you can use a Windows NT Workstation to read the trace files.

The Windows 95/98 workstation does not need to be logged in to the network, but it does need to have the Novell Client running. Additionally, both the network board and driver need to be able to run in *promiscuous mode*, which is supported by most vendors. In promiscuous mode, the network board and driver can see all packets on the transmission media—not just those destined for the device. Also, if the network segment you'll be monitoring has a lot of network traffic, you can gather more information to analyze if you have a fast network card and workstation. The LZFW product can only observe one network segment at a time, which is the one to which it's attached. You can run LZFW on other workstations on other segments or connect the monitoring workstation to another segment. The LANalyzer ManageWise component has the ability to monitor different segments at the same time through the use of agents placed around the network.

> *Note: Promiscuous mode means many things to many vendors, but should not to you. Most vendors support limited promiscuous mode, but eliminate entire classes of frame and packet errors. For example, nearly all the 3Com adapters support promiscuous mode, but filter out all error packets in hardware; you'll never see an error packet when using these adapters. Other manufacturers group classes of errors or require special drivers. The last of which is becoming a major problem: Novell dropped workstation support and development of the ODI driver specification, which is both more efficient and easily provides full promiscuous-mode support. Many manufacturers provide promiscuous support in hardware but do not supply fully promiscuous drivers.*

One of the most important aspects of using a protocol analyzer to help determine network-related issues is the need for baseline values. Without baseline information for your network, you cannot realistically determine thresholds for alerts because you don't know on what to base them. LZFW allows you to capture data on your network for continuous periods of time for up to a maximum of six months. You should collect data for a time period that reflects actual usage patterns. For example, if users log in every morning during a certain time and the accounting department runs large reports once a month, then your data collection interval should include the time frame for both types of events. Knowing the types of activities and the times they occur will help you determine the best time intervals for capturing data.

 Make sure you're comfortable with the role of LANalyzer as a tool for troubleshooting network issues.

Before you learn what LZFW does, you need to become acquainted with the program. The application is installed using a typical SETUP.EXE program,

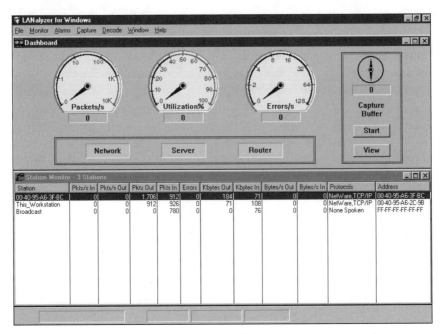

Figure 11.1 Initial information presented when LZFW is opened.

and the default installation path is C:\LZFW. When you open the program, it immediately begins to "watch" the transmission media and display information (as shown in Figure 11.1).

> *Note:* *For this chapter, LANalyzer screen images and trace files were collected on a simple network consisting of one NetWare 5 server and one Windows 95 workstation.*

The upper half of the screen contains the Dashboard window and presents information in three different dial monitors (also shown in Figure 11.1). The upper-left monitor displays the realtime number of packets per second traveling past the monitoring workstation. If you double-click on the dial monitor, the Detail - Packets/s graph window appears, as shown in Figure 11.2. This displays the number of packets per second since the application was opened. It also displays other information such as peak values and totals. When the window fills up with data, a scrollbar appears that allows you to scroll through the data. The window also contains buttons on the right for changing the graph's scale and showing and hiding grid lines.

The middle dial monitor in Figure 11.1 indicates the bandwidth usage and is referred to as *Utilization%*. The monitor displays the current realtime value,

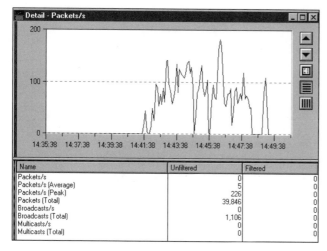

Figure 11.2   The Detail - Packets/s window.

and if you double-click on the dial monitor, the Detail - Utilization% graph window displays, as shown in Figure 11.3.

The monitor on the right displays the number of detected errors per second. Again, if you double-click on the dial monitor, the Details - Errors/s graph window is displayed, as shown in Figure 11.4.

The bottom window on the screen in Figure 11.1 is the Station Monitor portion, which displays all detected, active devices on the network segment to which the monitoring workstation is connected. You can sort the information by different indexes by double-clicking on the column header label. For example, to display the stations sending the highest number of packets, double-click on the header label titled Pkts Out.

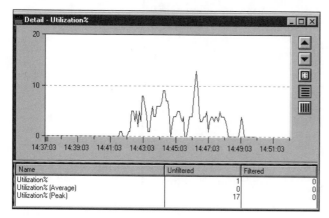

Figure 11.3   The Detail - Utilization% graph window.

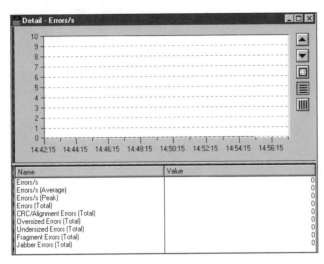

Figure 11.4 The Details - Errors/s window.

 You should be able to recognize the various portions and features of the LZFW Dashboard and Station Monitor windows.

LZFW collects four types of trend data to use to develop trend graphs. You access these by selecting Trends from the Monitor menu. The information in the Trends graphs is displayed in 15-minute intervals, and you can scroll back as far as six months. You can export the trend data to a file that can be read by other applications, such as a spreadsheet or graphing package. Figure 11.5 shows a sample trend export dialog box illustrating the export options.

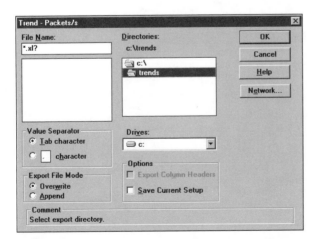

Figure 11.5 A sample Trend export dialog box, illustrating the export options.

You can also convert a binary trend file created by LZFW into a comma-separated value (CSV) format text file. This sometimes makes it easier to import into a spreadsheet or word-processing application. The binary trend file is created by the LZFW software automatically and will continue storing data until you close the application.

Here are the four types of trend data that can be collected:

➤ **Packets** This information displays the average number of packets per second for each 15-minute interval. This information is useful for determining your average network performance over time.

➤ **Errors** This value indicates the average number of errors of any type detected on the network for each 15-minute interval. This value should always be zero, because a value of one error per second or higher indicates a problem.

➤ **Utilization** This average percentage value for each 15-minute interval indicates bandwidth utilization. *Bandwidth usage* is an indicator of how much of the capacity of the transmission media is used. A steady increase in utilization over time typically reflects the growth of a network. If there are spikes or sudden, prolonged increases in utilization, faulty hardware or a device such as a router that's not configured may be a problem. When utilization is greater than 40 percent, users will begin to notice degradation in network performance. Do not confuse LZFW utilization with NetWare server utilization.

➤ **Kilobytes** The values on this trend graph show the total number of kilobytes per second transmitted for each 15-minute interval. This information is useful for determining the throughput of the network segment.

In addition to collecting the trend data, you should determine which stations are the most active most of the time and monitor any stations that demonstrate "bursty" activity. This type of activity could occur because a user generates a lot of reports and graphs once a month. You can determine who the most active user is on the Station Monitors window by observing or sorting by the number of packets per second or the number of kilobytes per second.

Be able to define the four different trend graphs and how they can help you with troubleshooting.

There are two other monitor windows in LZFW in addition to the Station Monitor. These are the Router Monitor and Server Monitor windows. You can open these windows by choosing them from the Monitor menu. To display more than one Monitor window at a time, select Tile from the Window menu.

To get details on any of the stations listed in any of the Monitor windows, just double-click on the station entry in the list. Depending on the type of device selected, there will be different informational items that you can click on for more details. Figure 11.6 shows the Station Detail window for a NetWare server.

After you have the trend data for the network, you can develop the baseline values. You use the trend data to set thresholds for alarms. LZFW allows you to set thresholds for many values, and when those numbers are exceeded, LZFW issues alarms that are viewed in LZFW. The alarm thresholds are set by choosing Alarms from the Thresholds menu. The resulting dialog box is shown in Figure 11.7.

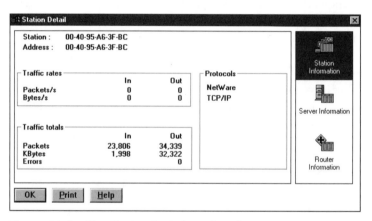

Figure 11.6   The Station Detail window for a NetWare server.

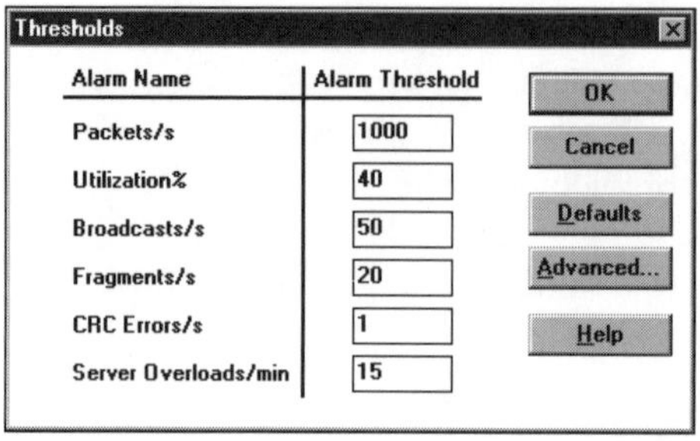

Figure 11.7   The Thresholds dialog box.

We described the Packets and Utilization selections previously in this chapter; the remaining selections in the Thresholds dialog box are described in the following list:

➤ **Broadcasts per second** This refers to the number of packets sent per second to the Internetwork Packet Exchange (IPX) network address FF-FF-FF-FF-FF-FF.

➤ **Fragments per second** *Fragments* are incomplete packets that result from collisions and are less than 64 bytes in size. Fragment errors can also occur from packets that have an invalid Frame Check Sequence (FCS) value. The FCS value is part of the error-checking process of packets using cyclic redundancy check (CRC) algorithms.

➤ **CRC errors per second** *CRC errors*, also called *CRC/alignment errors*, refer to packets that are the proper length but have bad FCS values. These also refer to packets that are not evenly divisible by eight, which is the number of bits in a byte.

➤ **Server Overloads per minute** This refers to the number of "Request Being Processed" or "Server Busy" packets sent by a busy server to clients requesting its services. These messages are a result of NetWare's congestion-control processes that are part of the server and Novell Client software. Server overloads will occasionally occur, but if the server is constantly too busy, the number of these packets will begin to increase.

The default settings may not be applicable to your network, and Novell suggests they should be adjusted according to the settings shown in Table 11.1.

As the network grows, the alarm thresholds may need to be adjusted to reflect new baseline data.

Vital Table 11.1	The default threshold settings recommended by Novell.
Alarm Name	**Suggested Setting**
Packets/s	5 to 10 percent above peak baseline value
Utilization%	5 percent above peak baseline value
Broadcasts/s	10
Fragments/s	15
CRC Errors/s	5
Server Overloads/min	5

Be able to specify the suggested alarm threshold settings for each alarm listed in the table.

LZFW also includes alarms that do not have any alarm threshold settings. The reason why there are no thresholds for these alarms is that Novell considers these to be errors that should never occur on a network; if they do occur, you need to know about them immediately. *Undersize errors* are packets that are less than 64 bytes but do not have any invalid CRC or FCS values. *Oversize errors* are packets that are greater than 1,518 bytes but do not have any incorrect CRC or FCS values. *Jabber errors* are packets that are greater than 1,518 bytes and also have invalid CRC and/or FCS values.

To access these advanced alarms, choose Thresholds in the Alarms menu and then click on the Advanced button. Figure 11.8 shows the Advanced Options dialog box for the alarm's setting. You do have the option of turning the individual advanced alarms on or off.

When an LZFW alarm sounds, the application has several methods of displaying the alarm and related information. One method is through an audible signal. If Sound On is enabled under the Alarms menu, the monitoring station will beep each time an alarm threshold is reached. Additionally, in the lower-left corner of the LZFW window, a red alarm clock appears with the alarm condition displayed in traveling text to the right of the clock. Depending on the alarm triggered, the green Network, Router, or Server buttons on the Dashboard window will turn red. Figure 11.9 shows a triggered LZFW alarm. In this example, the threshold for the number of packets per second has been exceeded.

If you double-click on the red Network, Server, or Router button, the Network Alarms window is displayed, as shown in Figure 11.10.

In the Network Alarms window, there's a button labeled NetWare Expert. To view information and suggestions about the alarm, click on the alarm listing in the dialog box and then click on the NetWare Expert icon. LZFW will open

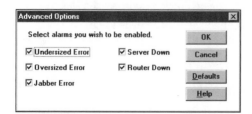

Figure 11.8   The Advanced Options dialog box.

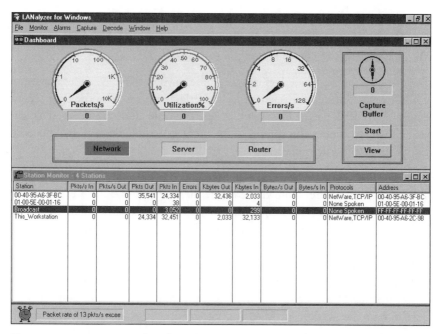

Figure 11.9   An example of a triggered LZFW alarm.

to the appropriate area in the Help file. The NetWare Expert contains information about all the alarms supported by LZFW.

The selected alarms in the Network Alarms window can be exported to a file by choosing the Export button in the Network Alarms window.

Another feature of LZFW is the capability to capture packets from the network or a specific device. This information may help you narrow down the problem and determine your course of action. To capture all network traffic, click on the Start button in the Capture Buffer area of the Dashboard window.

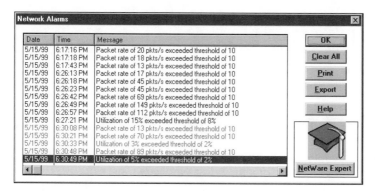

Figure 11.10   Example of the Network Alarms window.

If you want to watch a specific event, you need to initiate the event while LZFW is capturing. Figure 11.11 shows a sample capture buffer displaying a Windows 95 Novell Client logging in to a NetWare 5 network.

You can save the captured data in a trend file so you can analyze it at any time. Choose Save Unfiltered Packets from the File menu and save the file with an extension of .TR1. This allows you to open the file later in LZFW. You can also choose to export the capture buffer to a different file type by choosing Export from the File menu.

LZFW also supports the option to capture data from one station. This is available by choosing Filter from the Capture menu. In the Capture Filter dialog box, shown in Figure 11.12, you can specify the station you want to watch, whether to capture incoming or outgoing data or both, the protocol or protocols to capture, and whether to capture all packets or just good or bad packets. Once a filter is applied, the Dashboard window displays packets per seconds and utilization for both the entire segment (Global) and for the selected station (Filtered). With the filter active, you start capturing packets. You will only get those for the station specified and for any other options you configured in the Capture Filter settings.

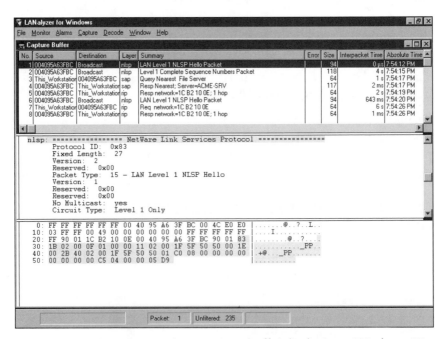

Figure 11.11 Sample LANalyzer capture buffer displaying a Windows 95 Novell Client logging in to a NetWare 5 network.

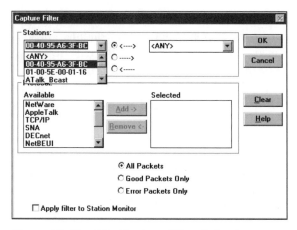

Figure 11.12   The Capture Filter dialog box.

The Capture Buffer window (refer to Figure 11.11) displays the captured packets at the top and details about the packets on the bottom. The middle of the window displays the Decode pane, which shows detailed information about the selected packet.

If you double-click on a field in the Decode area, the Display Filter dialog box is opened. The bottom area of this dialog box displays information about the selected data in the Decode pane.

Below the Decode pane is the Hexadecimal pane, which displays the hexadecimal information and the ASCII data for the selected packet. If you select a field in the Decode pane, the corresponding hexadecimal/ASCII information is highlighted in the Hexadecimal pane.

When you open a saved trace file, the information is presented in the same fashion as the Capture Buffer window. This detailed captured packets information can help you a great deal in tracking down many network problems.

 Be able to recognize the three major portions of the Capture Buffer window and what type of information is displayed.

Troubleshooting Network-Related Items

An overloaded network is usually easy to detect when the alarm thresholds are based on the network's normal activities. Often, the first sign comes from users who complain that the network is slow and/or they're experiencing Novell Client messages indicating that a server or service is not responding. The user can either try to reconnect in the background or cancel the request. Under high network load conditions, utilization will be higher and there will probably also be an increase in the number of fragment errors. You can also sort by the most active stations in the Station Monitor window to determine which devices are generating the most traffic.

A rule frequently overused is the 30-percent maximum utilization on Ethernet networks rule. Be wary of these blanket rules. Certainly, a 30-percent average is high, but a 30-percent peak is not. Utilization peaks of 60-percent or more are not uncommon; they simply mean that the servers and workstations can fill the network. If utilization stays high, it becomes difficult to fit additional traffic on the network and it may be time to restructure the network.

Broadcasts can also impact network performance. *Broadcasts* are packets that are sent to all devices on the network. You can sort the stations in the Station Monitor window by the number of packets per second. Then, you can perform a packet capture on those stations and see if they're producing a lot of broadcasts. Check the software configuration on the device to determine whether there's a reason why more than the usual number of broadcasts is being generated. If the problem is not from the station's software or the network board driver, check the network board.

Broadcasts are required by all network protocols, if, for nothing else, to find resources. IPX has received a bad name in networking circles because of excessive broadcasts, almost entirely Routing Information Protocol (RIP) and Service Advertising Protocol (SAP) packets. The intelligent use of NetWare Link Services Protocol (NLSP)- and Novell Directory Services (NDS)-aware hardware and software can help reduce these broadcast packets on your network.

More important, you should manage Microsoft networking in general and eliminate its use on IPX. All Windows NT workstations and servers have the server service turned on, by default; and many users share their Windows 95/98 workstations. Therefore, if IPX is bound to Microsoft networking, each workstation will broadcast its existence every 30 seconds. A thousand workstations broadcasting across the network will rapidly swamp it—even if switches are used. You should turn off sharing or unbind IPX from Microsoft networking and use TCP/IP.

You should be concerned about broadcasts for three reasons:

➤ A broadcast packet is designed to be sent to all devices on the network.

➤ Segmentation. A switch delivers packets based on the hardware address—each port only sends packets for machines that are attached. Unless, of course, it's a broadcast—all ports send these.

➤ Broadcasts take up precious bandwidth on WAN links.

Note: At the third layer of the OSI model (the Network layer), TCP/IP is fairly immune to broadcasts because the default is to not forward broadcast traffic. However, the default for IPX routers is to forward broadcasts. Filters must be configured to keep unnecessary traffic off the WAN link and leave room for important data.

Collisions are a normal occurrence on Ethernet networks because access to the transmission media is contention-based. As the number of devices on an Ethernet network increases, the number of collisions will also rise. Collisions cause packet fragments, which are detected by LZFW as fragment errors. If the number of fragment errors are reported as 2 to 3 percent of the total number of packets sent when the network load is high, you may need to analyze the network to determine whether additional routers/switches would help reduce the load. If the fragment errors are being reported while the network usage is low, this may indicate that a network board or interface needs to be replaced.

CRC/alignment errors are commonly seen on networks that have cable problems. Cables that are exposed to electrical noise, such as fluorescent-light ballasts, have CRC errors. If electrical interference is not the culprit, make sure all connections are tight at all contact points. You can use a time-domain reflectometer (TDR) or cable tester to check the integrity of the cables. If these actions still do not help solve the problem, try changing the network board.

Undersize and oversize packet errors may occur as a result of a device using a bad network board driver. These errors are not commonly seen on networks and are often caused by network drivers that have errors in coding to the Data Link layer protocol procedures.

Jabber errors often occur as a result of a device with a bad network board or interface. These malfunctioning devices begin to put packets on the wire that may have nothing to do with what the station is doing. These jabber packets might not contain valid IP or IPX headers, and they typically do not contain any worthwhile data. Fortunately, these are not commonly seen on healthy networks. If they are, however, the board must be replaced. Often, the challenge is finding the culprit. Look for a high transmission rate from a particular station that isn't doing anything. Occasionally, you'll have to manually segment and test to find a jabbering workstation. Fully intelligent hubs and switches with management software can also be used—the software will recognize and report the jabber, and may offer to shut down the affected port.

Mismatched frame types can prevent users from accessing the resources they need. You can use LZFW to capture packets sent by the client and by the resource to determine whether they're both communicating with the same frame type.

If the network segment you're monitoring contains Macintosh systems running System 7 or later and they're sharing their drives or printers, they advertise themselves to the network as servers. LZFW also sees these devices as servers, and when the Macintosh is shut down, LZFW generates a Server Down alarm.

 Be able to recognize the network problems covered in this section and which aspects of LZFW can help you troubleshoot these problems.

LANalyzer And Token Ring

LZFW can be used to help troubleshoot several problems that occur on token ring networks. One area is to help find a fault domain within the network that's experiencing difficulties. On a token ring network, the fault domain includes all network elements between any two stations that have a problem. This includes the hubs, or Multistation Access Units (MSAUs), network transmission media, the network boards, and the network drivers. For example, a station may begin beaconing, which triggers the beacon alarm in LZFW. The information in the beacon packet identifies the station's upstream neighbor, which is the one producing the fault.

Another performance problem that LZFW can help to reveal is a congestion error. LZFW displays an alarm when a station reports network congestion. On a token ring network, congestion errors are typically problems with a station receiving data that has insufficient buffer space to hold the incoming data.

Practice Questions

Question 1

Which software-based protocol analyzers can help diagnose network-related problems? [Choose the three best answers]

- ❑ a. Novell Monitor
- ❑ b. LZFW running on Windows 95/98
- ❑ c. ManageWise
- ❑ d. LZFW running on Windows NT
- ❑ e. NetMonitor

The correct answers are b, c, and d. Novell Monitor is used to refer to the MONITOR.NLM running on the server. Therefore, answer a is incorrect. NetMonitor is a made-up name. Therefore, answer e is incorrect. This is a trick question because even though Windows NT cannot be used to collect data, it can be used to run LANalyzer and open saved data.

Question 2

LZFW is capable of observing all traffic that passes the monitor station. Which of the following statements indicates a specification that allows the station to see all packets?

- ○ a. The network board must be able to support promiscuous mode, but the driver does not have to.
- ○ b. The network board driver must be able to support promiscuous mode, but the network board does not have to.
- ○ c. Both the transmitting device and the monitoring station must support promiscuous mode in their connection software.
- ○ d. The network board and driver must be able to support promiscuous mode.
- ○ e. Any ODI driver will work because they all support promiscuous mode with the newer client software.

The correct answer is d. Because answer d is correct, answers a and b are incorrect. Promiscuous mode has nothing to do with the connection software as a whole. Therefore, answer c is incorrect. Not all ODI drivers support promiscuous mode. Therefore, answer e is incorrect.

Question 3

What's the main purpose of initially capturing network traffic for several weeks?

O a. The captured data can be used to develop trend graphs, which show trouble spots on the network.

O b. The information can be used to develop baselines.

O c. The information can be used to diagnose problems on the network.

O d. By watching all the alarms that occur, you can develop the network's baseline values.

O e. The captured data is used to set the low values for the different alarm thresholds.

The correct answer is b. Trend graphs are used to create the baselines. Therefore, answer a is incorrect. Capturing data can be used to diagnose problems, but it's not very valuable until you have your baselines first. Therefore, answer c is incorrect. You set your alarm thresholds on your baselines, not the other way around. Therefore, answer d is incorrect. The alarm thresholds are typically set according to peak values collected from the trend information. Therefore, answer e is incorrect.

Question 4

Based on the following description of a trend graph, choose which item it's describing?

The information displayed is the average number of _____ on the network. This value should be zero, and a value of one _____ per second is a problem.

O a. Kilobytes, kilobyte

O b. Errors, error

O c. Packets, packet

O d. Utilizations, utilization

O e. Broadcasts, broadcast

The correct answer is b. The information displayed is the average number of *errors* on the network. This value should be zero, and a value of one *error* per second is a problem. Because this is a definition question, all the other choices are incorrect.

Question 5

What's the suggested value for the setting of the Packets per second alarm threshold?

○ a. 10

○ b. 15

○ c. 5

○ d. 5 to 10 percent above peak

○ e. 5 to 10 percent below peak

The correct answer is d. The suggested value for the setting of the Packets per second alarm threshold is 5 to 10 percent above peak. All the other answers represent incorrect values and are therefore incorrect.

Question 6

Based on the following description of a trend graph, choose which item it's describing.

The values on the trend graph show the total number of _____ per second transmitted for each 15-minute interval. This information is useful for determining the throughput of the network segment.

○ a. Broadcasts

○ b. Packets

○ c. Errors

○ d. Utilizations

○ e. Kilobytes

The correct answer is e. The values on the trend graph show the total number of *kilobytes* per second transmitted for each 15-minute interval. This information is useful for determining the throughput of the network segment. Because this is a definition question, all the other choices are incorrect.

Question 7

> What types of information are displayed in LZFW's Capture Buffer window? [Choose the two best answers]
>
> ❏ a. Protocol information of each captured packet
>
> ❏ b. Hexadecimal data for the selected item
>
> ❏ c. The path the packet traveled
>
> ❏ d. The total number of packets transmitted
>
> ❏ e. The average number of packets transmitted

The correct answers are a and b. The capture packets do not specify the entire path in each packet. However, you could probably determine the path with the appropriate number and types of packets analyzed. Therefore, answer c is incorrect. The capture buffer does not display summary statistics. Therefore, answers d and e are incorrect.

Question 8

> What's the suggested value for the alarm threshold value for CRC errors per second?
>
> ○ a. 5 percent above peak
>
> ○ b. 5 percent below peak
>
> ○ c. 5
>
> ○ d. 15
>
> ○ e. 10

The correct answer is c. The suggested value for the alarm threshold value for CRC errors per second is 5. All the other answers represent incorrect values and are therefore incorrect.

Question 9

You've been hired as a consultant for a company with a large Ethernet network to fix some of its network-related problems. The company has identified one segment it would like you to fix first. The brief history you're given indicates that the problem just started this week but does not happen all the time. However, when it does happen, all active devices eventually lose connections, and the server utilization also goes up. When they shut down all the workstations, the problem disappears. You begin by running LANalyzer to capture the data on the network segment in question. You start capturing the data and then, one by one, turn each device on. When all devices are turned on, you notice that the number of errors per second is rising and that some of the captured packets are different lengths and contain unknown data. Based on your observations, what's causing the problem?

- ○ a. High bandwidth utilization
- ○ b. Excessive number of broadcasts
- ○ c. Overloaded network
- ○ d. Congestion
- ○ e. Jabber errors

The correct answer is e. Jabber errors are most likely the cause of this problem. High bandwidth utilization, excessive broadcasts, and overloaded networks do not typically include an increasing number of packets of varying lengths with errors. Therefore, answers a, b, and c are incorrect. Congestion is a potential problem area on token ring networks. Therefore, answer d is incorrect. This question is "tricky" because you need to understand what type of situation causes jabber errors and what you would detect in LZFW.

Need To Know More?

 One of the first places to look for descriptions and information about network-related issues is the Help file that comes with LANalyzer. This includes the NetWare Expert information and other information.

 http://support.novell.com is where you can find the following TIDs, which contain related topics that may be of interest. At Novell's support Web site, go to the Knowledgebase and perform a search using the following TID numbers:

➤ **TID 2933450** Using LANalyzer And MW To Detect Jabber NICs

➤ **TID 2924660** Packet Trace Guidelines

➤ **TID 2942544** How To Take A Trace, LANalyzer For Windows

 www.netanalysis.org is the Network Analysis Institute, LCC Web site, which contains a wealth of information about network analysis for both Novell and non-Novell networks.

Server
Management

Terms you'll need to understand:

√ Server bottlenecks

√ Support packs

√ NetWare Peripheral Architecture (NWPA)

√ Host Adapter Module (HAM)

√ Custom Device Module (CDM)

√ CONFIG.NLM

√ Abnormal end (abend)

√ Nonmaskable interrupt (NMI)

√ Preemptive

Techniques you'll need to master:

√ Using MONITOR.NLM to help identify possible server bottlenecks

√ Identifying some causes of server bottlenecks

√ Applying and identifying NetWare patches and support packs

√ Troubleshooting server problems

√ Defining the types of server abends

Servers are a very vital element of networks, and when they're out of commission or performing below their capabilities, users are not able to perform activities that are dependent on servers. In Novell networks, and networks in general, it's important to maintain the servers and to make sure the hardware and software are current and have sufficient horsepower to provide the services for now and the future. In this section, we'll address some of the issues that adversely affect servers and either render them inoperable or cause slow performance. These topics include common server bottleneck areas, maintaining current operating systems and components, troubleshooting server problems, and server lockups and abnormal ends (abends).

 We cannot cover all potential problems in this book; therefore, you'll need to access additional resources. One of the best initial resources in which to look for suggestions and/or solutions is Novell's Support Services, which is accessible on the Web at **http://support.novell.com.** Novell's Knowledgebase contains incident reports and solutions in addition to other material. It's possible that you can find your exact problem and solution and/or related issues on this site.

If you're having problems with hardware or software from a third-party product, you should check the vendor's Web site and its knowledge bases. Also, don't forget that asking a fellow administrator and/or coworker may also provide useful assistance.

Performance Bottlenecks

Server bottlenecks refer to some system on the server that's slowing operations because a particular task or activity is using too many resources and/or the hardware or software is not capable of meeting the demand. Because a NetWare server has so many components, there's the potential for bottlenecks to develop in specific areas, including these:

➤ CPU

➤ Bus architecture

➤ Storage system

➤ Network board

CPU Bottlenecks

Depending on the age and architecture of the server, the speed of the processor may be contributing to the server's "sluggishness." If the server is several years old, the processor, although considered fast five years ago, is probably now considered "pokey" by current standards. Making sure the server's CPU keeps up with network demands can help reduce poor performance of the server for many activities. You can observe the amount of the CPU that's used with the MONITOR.NLM utility. The Utilization value on the main screen displays the average CPU usage for each measurement cycle, which is one second by default. If the Utilization value stays high for extended periods of time, this may indicate a bottleneck. However, you need to be aware of the types of tasks and the activities the server is performing before you can determine whether a bottleneck is present. For example, when the server is compressing files during its compression time slice, utilization is typically quite high, and this is normal. However, if the server's utilization is constantly over 80 percent during normal working hours, this may indicate some type of CPU bottleneck or other problem.

> *Note: Be wary of assuming that high utilization is caused by a CPU bottleneck. The efficient use of CPU cycles by NetWare means that, with proper system design, high system loads can be handled by servers most would deem antiquated (or at least insufficient). Check for I/O channel bottlenecks and non-busmaster adapters before assuming that a faster processor is the solution to high utilization.*

Current CPUs are usually quite sufficient and are typically not the cause of a bottleneck. Also, multiple processors can be used to "divide" processing of the server's tasks or threads. The NetWare 5 operating system transparently handles the division of labor among the processors so the software developers don't need to concern themselves with the number of processors available.

 With NetWare 4.11, it was the responsibility of the software developer to address multiple processors. As a result, many NetWare 4.11 applications do not take advantage of additional processors or can run into problems with multiple processors. For these situations, upgrading to NetWare 5, where multiprocessor support has been reengineered, may be a viable solution.

Bus Architecture Bottlenecks

The type and age of a server's bus architecture can have a great impact on the server's performance. For example, a company that has been upgrading and replacing its disk storage system with newer and faster disk architectures may run into a bottleneck at the server's bus. If the server is still Industry Standard Architecture (ISA)-based, there's a fixed speed at which data can go across the motherboard, and it will not increase as the peripheral boards increase in speed. For these situations, the underlying architecture of the server needs to be updated or a new system put into place. Also, if peripheral boards contain their own processors and perform some tasks themselves, such as data transfer in bus-mastering boards, the server's processor doesn't need to be involved in the task.

Storage System Bottlenecks

Imagine that a NetWare server contains the information for a company's database, including all client records—past and present. Over the last five years, the company has expanded, and its database has grown to accommodate its new clients. Now, users are complaining that it takes forever to open a record, printing is too slow, and they sometimes can't access the information they need to do their work. If the hardware has not been upgraded during that time, the database has grown, and more employees are accessing the database, what is happening is probably not a failure in the database software.

Chances are the bottleneck is occurring in the storage system. In this database example, the server hosting the database is probably experiencing a lot of disk activity. When an employee accesses the information in the database and/or changes are made, the information needs to be read and written to the server's hard drives. Because the hardware is now five years old and the database is getting bigger, a disk input/output (I/O) bottleneck exists. Some techniques and tools are available that can be used to point out this potential bottleneck.

Run the MONITOR.NLM utility at the server console and observe the following items:

➤ **Dirty Cache Buffers** These are the number of buffers that contain data that has not been written to disk within the value specified by the Dirty Disk Cache Delay Time parameter. The default for this parameter is 3.3 seconds.

➤ **Current Disk Requests** These are the number of disk system I/O requests that are waiting to be processed.

If the number of Dirty Cache Buffers value is approaching 50 percent of the Total Cache Buffers for extended periods of time, this usually indicates a disk I/O bottleneck, as shown in Figure 12.1. Also, if the number of current disk requests is high and stays high, this can also indicate a disk I/O bottleneck. Simple observation of the server itself as well as the amount of time the disk activity light is on can also indicate a heavily used disk.

There are various actions you can take to reduce a disk I/O bottleneck. First, make sure the hardware is current and is designed for intensive disk activity. In the server example, the Small Computer System Interface (SCSI) system that

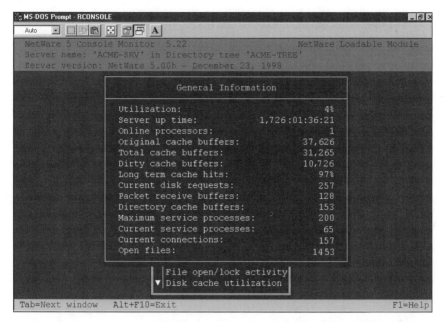

Figure 12.1   A sample MONITOR screen illustrating a disk I/O bottleneck.

was quite sufficient and peppy five years ago is now slow compared to the newer Ultra Wide SCSI, Fast/Wide SCSI, and Fast SCSI II systems available today. Take a look at the Host Bus Adapter (HBA) and check whether it supports its own processor chip. Interface adapters with their own processors can help reduce the demand on the server's processor and allow simultaneous transactions that improve performance.

Another factor to look at is the size of the server's hard drives. Sometimes, it's more efficient to have several smaller drives than one large one. Multiple smaller drives allow simultaneous read/writes to occur because several different hard drive read/writes heads are involved rather than having one read/write head do all the work.

Finally, adjusting **SET** parameters can have a profound effect on system input and output, improving throughput at the price of a small increase in latency or RAM requirements. The most useful parameter changes are generally the Concurrent Disk Cache Writes and Directory Cache Buffers setting, but it's difficult and dangerous to generalize for all servers. Performance tuning of **SET** parameters needs to be approached on an individual basis and is the subject of another book entirely.

*Note: For more information on the various **SET** parameters, search the NetWare online documentation using the keywords "SET paramenters".*

Network Board Bottlenecks

Another area where bottlenecks can develop is with the network board and/or its software drivers. In this situation, a symptom often includes users experiencing sluggishness on the server. If the server is performing some type of active network I/O, such as what would occur on a Web or imaging server, it may not be able to keep up with the demand. Again, MONITOR.NLM can be used as a tool to note any inefficiency with the network board and/or driver. In the Available Options selection list, choose the entry titled LAN/WAN Drivers. Then, select the appropriate network interface card (NIC) driver for the card and the desired frame type. Once an item is selected, you're presented with a scrolling list of information and statistics about that item. There are usually three main divisions of the displayed NIC driver information:

➤ **Generic Counters** This category and its subitems display statistics that are supported by most network card driver manufacturers, as shown in Figure 12.2. Some of the statistics you should view to help you determine whether a network I/O bottleneck is present include the following:

   ➤ Receive Discarded, No Available Buffers

   ➤ Transmit Failed, Packet Too Big

   ➤ Receive Failed, Adapter Overflow Condition

Figure 12.2 A sample MONITOR screen illustrating the generic counters.

➤ Receive Failed, Packet Too Big

➤ Transmit Failed, Miscellaneous Error

➤ Receive Failed, Miscellaneous error

When there are no bottlenecks on the network card and driver, these values should be zero or low numbers. If these values increase over the time you're monitoring the server, there might be a network I/O bottleneck.

➤ **Topology-Specific Counters** This category includes statistics supported by the majority of the vendors for a specific type of topology or media access methodology. For example, if you have an Ethernet card installed on your server, this counter would read Ethernet Counters, as shown in Figure 12.3.

➤ **Custom Counters** This category contains statistics that apply to a specific type of network board and/or driver.

To reduce network I/O bottlenecks on the server, you should make sure the network card(s) are current and take advantage of the underlying bus architecture. For example, ISA-based cards cannot handle high levels of network I/O, but Peripheral Component Interconnect (PCI) cards perform much better in this situation. Therefore, replacing the five-year old, 16-bit, ISA-based card

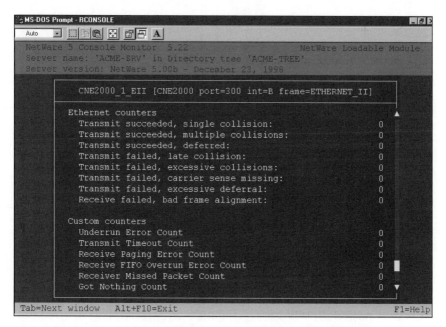

Figure 12.3   A sample MONITOR screen illustrating the Ethernet and custom counters.

with a newer PCI card can solve the bottleneck, and no other modifications are necessary. Also, you can place additional network cards in the server so the network I/O tasks can be processed by more than one hardware interface. Note, however, that as you increase the number of network cards in the system, this may impact the CPU performance of the server, and noticeable improvements may not result.

Another item that may help improve performance is the usage of multiport cards. These network cards support more than one physical connection to the transmission media and typically contain a lot of onboard intelligence, which results in lower demands on the server's CPU. These cards, although expensive, may be a good solution for servers that perform a lot of network I/O for extended periods of time.

Also, 64-bit and 66Mhz PCI adapters can be used if the server supports these extensions to the standard PCI bus. Another related solution is to use the new I2O specification cards. These fully intelligent adapters use sophisticated communications techniques to eliminate CPU interrupts, which have a serious impact on performance. I2O adapters can also perform direct data transfers, bypassing system memory and reducing load on the PCI bus. Throughput can be increased as much as 20 percent and CPU utilization dropped by 50 percent as compared to similar, non I2O adapters.

> *Note:* *The name of the statistics and the number of statistics available are slightly different when viewed on a NetWare 4.x or NetWare 3.x server. For example, "Receive Discarded, No Available Buffers" is labeled "No ECB Available Count" on NetWare 4.x and NetWare 3.x servers.*

Also note that transmission media, router, and physical connectivity problems can also create network bottlenecks. Utilities such as ManageWise can be used to monitor and alert you when connectivity or router problems arise.

 When presented with a troubleshooting scenario, you should be able to determine the type of bottleneck and some possible solutions.

Updates And Patches

One of the first items to check when you suspect a server-related problem is to determine whether the most recent applicable patches are applied. If you contact Novell Technical Support to request assistance with a server problem, one of the first questions you'll be asked is whether your server is patched with the most current support pack version. If your answer is no, typically the first thing they'll suggest is that you apply the most recent support pack.

Novell tends to categorize its support packs by operating system patches, device driver updates, and NetWare Loadable Module (NLM) updates. Patches are also available for specific products, such as GroupWise and BorderManager. The patches may exist as one of three possible types, as listed in Table 12.1—the type is determined by how the changes are applied to your system.

The name of the service packs is usually reflective of the category of patch and follows a naming convention. For example, one of the first support packs for NetWare 5 is titled NW5SP1A for NetWare 5 Support Pack 1a. For NetWare 4.11, the current operating system patch at the time of this writing is titled NW4SP6 for NetWare 4.11 Support Pack 6.

These patches are delivered as self-extracting files and contain all the patches of the core operating system and other services. Because of this, they tend to be quite large—NW5SP1A is just under 60MB, and NW4SP6 is approximately 24MB.

 Make sure you can interpret the naming convention of Novell's support packs and patches.

The naming for patches prior to NetWare 4.11 (intraNetWare) is slightly different. For example, an operating system patch for NetWare 3.12 might be 312PTD.EXE, which is revision D of the core operating system patch for

Table 12.1	The different types of patches and their definitions.
Type	**Definition**
Static	Causes a permanent change and modifies the SERVER.EXE file. Make sure you retain a copy of the original SERVER.EXE file before you modify it.
Dynamic	Can be loaded and unloaded at the server console without the need to restart the server. Typically, when these are unloaded, the system is back to the state it was in prior to the installation of the dynamic patch.
Semi-static	Does not permanently modify files and can be loaded at the server console. However, in comparison to dynamic patches, semi-static patches cannot be unloaded while the server is running. To unload a semi-static patch, you must restart the server.

NetWare 3.12. Additionally, *PT* signifies that the patch has "passed testing." Sometimes, you'll see a new patch with a label such as 312ITE.EXE, in which *IT* stands for "in testing." These should be applied only if you have a specific problem stated in the patch or for testing purposes.

 All the support packs have some sort of readme file, which you should always read before you apply the patch suite.

Installing support packs for NetWare 5 and NetWare 4.11 has changed a great deal and is mush easier than it was in the past. The NW5SP1A pack for NetWare 5 includes a demo version of a workstation utility for installing the patch suite for up to three servers at one time. The complete version allows you to install a patch on any number of servers you want. If you choose not to use the workstation utility, you install the support packs using NWCONFIG at the NetWare 5 server console. The steps are as follows:

1. Run NWCONFIG at the server console (or via a Remote Console or RConJ session).

2. Select Product Options and press Enter.

3. Select Install A Product Not Listed and press Enter.

4. At the prompt, press F3 to specify the path to the location of the support pack files.

5. Follow the remaining prompts and reboot the server when the installation is finished.

 You can download the support packs and patches directly from Novell's Web site (**http://support.novell.com**). Typically, the patches will be compressed in self-extracting files. The patches will need to be decompressed to a server directory before you attempt to install the patch.

Patches available for NetWare 3.x are structured a bit differently and are not installed with the INSTALL.NLM utility. (In NetWare 5, NWCONFIG is essentially the same as INSTALL.NLM, which is found in previous versions of NetWare.) These patches use a patch manager, such as PATCH312.NLM, that runs on the server and helps automate the process. If the patch is a dynamic patch, the patch manager NLM must be loaded prior to loading the patch. Typically, the installation process will verify this functional requirement. One very important item about the patch manager is that different versions exist for different operating systems; therefore, make sure the proper version is present for the appropriate operating system.

 Know the general steps for applying a patch or support pack.

In addition to operating system patches, Novell sometimes releases patches or updates to various categories of drivers, such as network card or storage device drivers. For pre-NetWare 5 operating systems, the storage device driver files typically end with a .DSK extension. These may need to be updated as the hardware evolves (most common vendor storage device drivers are contained in Novell device driver updates and patches). If your storage devices are proprietary, you may need to contact the vendor for specific device drivers.

The current architecture for storage devices is referred to as the *NetWare Peripheral Architecture* (NWPA). The NWPA drivers are preferred over the older DSK drivers and provide better performance and stability. This type of system contains two types of modules: Host Adapter Module (HAM) and Custom Device Module (CDM). The HAM is the driver for the interface between the server's bus architecture and the storage device interface. The associated driver files usually end with a .HAM extension.

The other component of NWPA is the Custom Device Module (CDM), which is specific to the type of storage device. For example, you may have one HAM module for each bus interface and several CDM modules for each device on the storage system buses. Novell or the vendor can provide the files for SCSI-based systems. Novell provides generic SCSI CDM device drivers and quite a number of HAM drivers. Here's a list of some of them:

➤ SCSIHD.CDM

➤ SCSICD.CDM

➤ AHA2740.HAM

➤ AHA2920a.HAM

➤ AHA2940.HAM

➤ SCSIDPT.HAM

➤ SCSIOSM.HAM

The server's STARTUP.NCF contains the commands to load the storage device drivers. Here's an example of these commands for an IDE-based NetWare 5 test server:

```
LOAD IDEHD.CDM
LOAD IDECD.CDM
LOAD IDEATA.HAM PORT=1F0 INT=E
LOAD IDEATA.HAM PORT=170 INT=F
```

> *Note:* *NetWare 5 does not support DSK drivers and uses the NWPA device drivers.*

Server Troubleshooting

You can use several techniques to troubleshoot server-related problems. The first and foremost technique is to maintain complete, up-to-date documentation of the server's hardware and software components. Knowing, for example, the version of an NLM, the NIC card settings, or what patches are applied and their version numbers can greatly assist in troubleshooting. There are some aids that can assist you in documentation, and the price is right—free.

CONFIG.NLM and CONFGNUT.NLM are two utilities that create a text file that contains items such as the content of the STARTUP.NCF and AUTOEXEC.NCF files, what NLMs are currently running, and more. When CONFIG.NLM is run, it creates a text file titled CONFIG.TXT in the SYS:\SYSTEM directory. CONFGNUT.NLM contains a menu that allows you to specify whether the CONFIG.TXT file is overwritten or appended to, and to specify what type of information is placed in the CONFIG.TXT file, as shown in Figure 12.4.

Novell also provides a graphical CONFIG.TXT viewer that helps present the material in a graphical user interface (GUI) that separates the information based on type. It's called Config Reader and can be downloaded from Novell's Web site.

 Another NLM, titled TECHWALK.NLM, will also document some of the server's information. It's a Novell Technical Support module that can also be used to provide documentation.

The documentation should also include a change log and past history of any problems and their resolution. If the server abends or generates error messages,

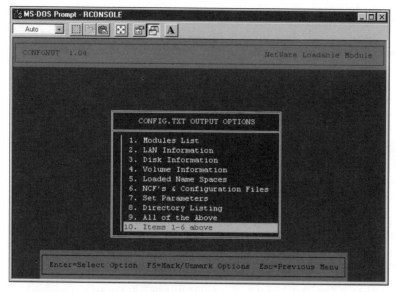

Figure 12.4   CONFGNUT.NLM, which shows the items that can be placed in the CONFIG.TXT file.

these messages should be written down in their entirety. You should also look at the server's error log files, any volume log files, and the ABEND.LOG file (to see if the server has ever abended).

After you've gathered all the information you can, look for any patterns to the errors, such as the time of day or if the problems are tied to certain activities. Also, look for problems that occur around certain changes, such as the addition of new NLMs or hardware.

Server Abends And Lockups

A NetWare server continuously monitors many events on the server to make sure the provided services are operating properly. If the operating system detects a problem that's software or hardware related, the system can become locked up or an abend will occur. In this section, we'll take a look at events that may cause a server to become locked and nonresponsive.

Server Lockups

When a NetWare server locks up, the system may be completely nonresponsive to all activities or only portions of the server may be functional. A *full server lockup* refers to a server that's not responding to anything and all connections may be dropped and all processes frozen. In this situation, the server's keyboard may also be nonresponsive, preventing you from changing screens and accessing other services running on the server. In a *partial server lockup*, some services may still be running and users may be able to access and use the server without any knowledge of a problem. A partial server lockup may clear itself up or may evolve into a full server lockup.

Outdated and/or corrupt files can cause server lockups. Servers can also lock up if an NLM or running thread has obtained control of the processor and is not relinquishing it so other services can get their processor time. Until the offending process gives up control of the processor, no other service or activity can run and the system stays frozen in time. The CPU Hog Timeout Amount SET parameter allows you to specify the maximum amount of time the operating system will wait for a process to relinquish control of the processor. If the process has not released the processor, the operating system will terminate the process. The default setting for the CPU Hog Timeout Amount parameter is one minute.

NetWare 3.x and NetWare 4.x are nonpreemptive operating systems, which means that it's up to the running NLMs to cooperate with each other and to share processor cycles. In these operating systems, the process holding onto the processor can be forcefully removed, unless it's monopolizing usage of the processor. NetWare 5, however, is a preemptive operating system, which means the operating system decides which services can use the processor and for how long. In a preemptive system, the operating system can take control of the processor and prevent all services from running. In this type of architecture, an NLM cannot hog the processor, and if it tries to, it will be kicked off so some other service can use it.

There may be times when all you do does not solve the problem you're faced with. In these circumstances, you may be instructed by Novell to send a core dump for analysis. A *core dump* is a "picture" or memory image of the server. When a server abends, you're often given the option of creating a core dump. You can also generate a core dump independent of a server abend. A core dump is created in the NetWare debugger. To create a core dump, perform the following steps:

1. Press and hold the following keys in sequence to enter the NetWare server's debugger (note that these keystrokes must be done at the server console and cannot be issued in a Remote Console session):

    ```
    right Shift + right Alt + left Shift + left Esc
    ```

2. Enter ".c" at the debugger prompt and press Enter.

3. At the prompt for the amount of information to be dumped, choose either Full, for the entire server's memory content, or Full W/O Cache, for all the memory except the file cache.

4. The next option allows you to choose whether to compress the core dump. Choose the option you want or have been instructed to use.

5. The final set of options is the path and name of the core dump file. The default is to the server's DOS partition. Here's an example:

```
C:\COREDUMP.IMG
```

After you specify the last option, the memory core dump begins. When the memory dump is complete, exit the debugger by pressing G at the prompt and then pressing Enter.

Note: *While you're in the debugger, all server processes are paused.*

Server Abends

At the beginning of this section, we mentioned that the server continually checks the integrity of its services and processes. If the checking procedure detects a condition that would potentially damage the integrity of its internal data, the system generates an abend. The primary reason the system generates an abend is to protect the data that's already stored and to reduce the risk of information corruption. When an abend occurs, the system has entered NetWare's fault handler. This is a global function that's available to all NLMs running on the server. Conditions that could violate the data include hardware problems and an NLM or process that's passing faulty information or data into a procedural call. Under these situations, the environment is unstable and an abend is generated.

Two categories of events cause abends: processor exceptions and software exceptions. *Processor exceptions*, or consistency check errors, are caused by faulty or failing hardware. The processor detects these exceptions. The second category contains exceptions that are detected by NetWare; these are called *software exceptions*. In both cases, it's a good assumption that memory has been corrupted either by a bad software process or bad hardware.

Processor exception abends are detected by the server's CPU. When this type of error is detected, the server issues an exception or interrupt. When the processor is handling a process and an error occurs, an exception is generated. These exceptions are typically categorized as traps, faults, or aborts. Depending on the type of exception generated, you may not be able to restart the running process. Events that can cause these types of problems include the following:

➤ Corrupted drivers

➤ Out-of-date NLMs

➤ Bad packets received by the server

When another device in the system needs the attention of the processor, the device sends an interrupt. Each device has an assigned interrupt; therefore, when a particular interrupt is used, the CPU knows which device needs its attention. These are called *maskable hardware interrupts*, and the system knows how to handle these. There's also a dedicated line to the processor that handles nonmaskable interrupts (NMIs). These interrupts come from some device or process, but the system cannot determine their origin. Whenever a signal is sent down the dedicated line that handles NMIs, the CPU generates an NMI error, which is then received by the NetWare operating system, which typically produces an abend. There are two types of NMI errors, and these are reported on the server's console when an NMI condition is met. One is *NMI Parity Error Generated By System Board*, which probably indicates that the problem is with the server's motherboard and/or its memory. The second type is *NMI Parity Error Generated By IO Check*, which means the problem could be anywhere in the system. Novell has created a list of hardware-related conditions that typically produce NMIs. Here are some of the most common:

➤ Low power or fluctuating power source (failing power supply)

➤ Conflicting hardware interrupts

➤ Bad memory

➤ Static electricity discharges

Whatever produces an NMI error is a hardware problem and is not related to the server's software.

When an abend is generated on a NetWare 3.x or NetWare 4.10 (4.01 and 4.02) server, the system stops responding to events. Sometimes, you're able to get into the debugger to try to shut down the bad process or to "go around" the faulty process. If you're successful, you can exit the debugger and return to the console screen so you can gracefully bring down the server. However, if you weren't successful, you can bring up the Hung Console server screen and see whether the server can be brought down. Pressing Ctrl+Alt+Esc accesses this screen. You have two options in the Hung Console Screen, as shown in Figure 12.5.

If all else fails, you may have to physically restart the server.

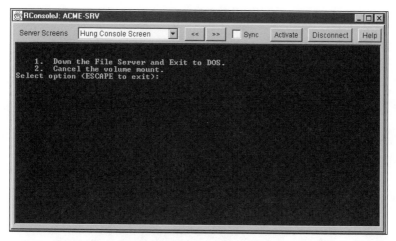

Figure 12.5   The Hung Console Screen options.

With the release of NetWare 4.11, Novell provided a different environment for the handling of abends, which included the generation of an abend log file. This file is an ASCII text file titled ABEND.LOG, and it's stored in the SYS:\SYSTEM directory by default. There are also associated **SET** parameters that specify what you should do when an abend occurs. The **SET** parameters are as follows:

➤ **Auto Restart After Abend Delay Time**   This is the amount of time the system will wait after receiving an abend before the system restarts itself. The default is two minutes, and during that two minute timeframe, the server sends out frequent broadcasts indicating the server will restart in x minutes (see Figure 12.6).

➤ **Auto Restart After Abend**   This parameter specifies what the system does when an abend is generated. The values of this parameter range from 0 to 3, and the default is 1. When this value is set to 0, the system does not attempt to recover from an abend. A value of 1 allows the system to isolate or suspend the faulty process but allows the server to continue operating (see Figure 12.7). This type of action occurs when a page fault error occurs. When an NMI or other software exception occurs, the system proceeds with the delayed restart. When this value is set to 2, the system creates a delayed restart for an abend no matter what type it is. A value of 3 causes the system to perform an immediate restart for all types of abends.

Notice that when a NetWare 4.11 or NetWare 5 server abends, the server is still functional, and a number appears in angle brackets to the right of the

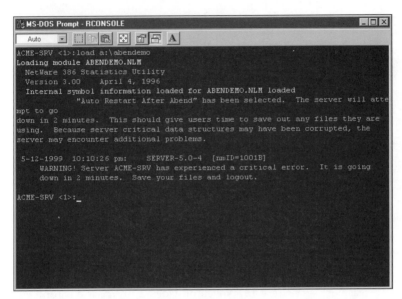

Figure 12.6 An abend message indicating a critical error has occurred, and the server will restart in two minutes.

server name on the console screen. This number indicates the number of times the server has abended since the time the server was started.

Depending on the type of abend, the system may put several lines of information on the console screen. The information in these lines is detailed in Table 12.2.

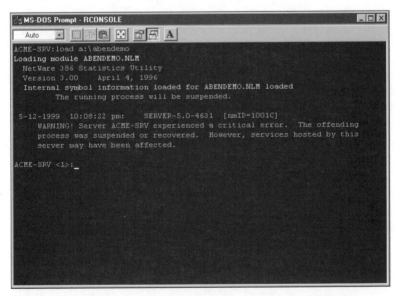

Figure 12.7 An abend message indicating that the offending process has been isolated, and the server is still functional.

Table 12.2	Server abend line descriptions.	
Line Number	**Information**	**Description**
1	Date and time	The date and time the system was halted.
2	Abend message string	This information helps determine whether the abend is hardware or software related.
3	Operating system version	The version of the operating system.
4	Running process	This information indicates the process or task that was running when the abend occurred. This does *not* imply that this process was the offending task or file.
5	Stack	The hexadecimal numbers in this line list a portion of the data on the CPU's stack for the current running process when the abend occurred.
6	Additional information	This contains the name of the NLM that was running when the abend occurred. Again, this does *not* mean that the NLM listed is the item that generated the abend.
7	Action	This line indicates the action, if any, the server is taking on the offending process.
8	Date, time, version, and status report	This line lists the date and time as well as the version of the operating system. This also includes a status report about the current state of the server.
9	Console prompt	The value to the right of the server name indicates the number of times the server has abended since it was last started.

Miscellaneous Troubleshooting Tips

In addition to the tips and techniques addressed in the previous section, there are a few more procedures that may help you while troubleshooting. The following list describes some **SERVER** commands that may be helpful:

➤ **SERVER -NS** This command bypasses the execution of the STARTUP.NCF and AUTOEXEC.NCF files.

➤ **SERVER -NA** This command bypasses the execution of the AUTOEXEC.NCF file.

➤ **SERVER -NDB** This command bypasses the opening of the Novell Directory Services (NDS) database on the server.

➤ **SERVER -NL** The NetWare 5 startup splash screen will not load so the information on the console screen is visible when the server is booting.

Here are some other procedures that may be helpful:

➤ Use CONLOG.NLM to capture the information on the console screen to a file. You can specify the location and length of the file.

➤ Load DSTRACE.NLM, which has many switches and parameters you can use for NDS troubleshooting. (See the NetWare online documentation for more information.)

➤ Unload all unnecessary NLMs and then load them manually and observe any messages.

➤ Reseat all peripheral cards, memory chips, and so on. This is often helpful in older machines that have not had any hardware maintenance for a long time.

Practice Questions

Question 1

Which informational item in MONITOR.NLM would you observe to determine if your server is experiencing a CPU bottleneck?

○ a. Dirty Cache Buffers

○ b. Utilization

○ c. Total Cache Buffers

○ d. Modules

The correct answer is b. You would observe the Utilization value to determine if your server is experiencing a CPU bottleneck. A high Dirty Cache Buffers value is an indicator of a disk I/O bottleneck. Therefore, answer a is incorrect. Total Cache Buffers indicates the number of buffers available for caching of files. Therefore, answer c is incorrect. Modules is a command that lists the currently running NLMs. Therefore, answer d is incorrect.

Question 2

Which of the following statements regarding a static patch is true?

○ a. A static patch is loaded by issuing the appropriate command at the server console and cannot be loaded automatically in either the STARTUP.NCF or AUTOEXEC.NCF file.

○ b. The static patch modifies the SERVER.EXE file, and the change is permanent.

○ c. The elements of a static patch can be loaded dynamically, but they can only be removed by restarting the server.

○ d. The elements of the patch can be loaded and unloaded at the server console.

○ e. Static patches have passed testing and will not change.

The correct answer is b. A static patch modifies the SERVER.EXE file, and the change is permanent. Answer a is incorrect because patches are usually loaded in the STARTUP.NCF and are not typically loaded on the fly. Answer c describes a semi-static patch and is therefore incorrect. Answer d describes a dynamic patch and is therefore incorrect. Answer e partially describes the naming convention of some patches and is therefore incorrect.

Question 3

> Which informational item in MONITOR.NLM would you observe to determine if your server is experiencing a disk I/O bottleneck?
>
> ○ a. Long Term Cache Hits
>
> ○ b. Original Cache Buffers
>
> ○ c. Service Processes
>
> ○ d. Dirty Cache Buffers

The correct answer is d. You would observe the Dirty Cache Buffers value to determine if your server is experiencing a disk I/O bottleneck. If the Long Term Cache Hits value is below 90 percent, that's an indicator that more memory is needed. Therefore, answer a is incorrect. Original Cache Buffers is the number of buffers available right after SERVER.EXE was executed. Therefore, answer b is incorrect. Service Processes indicates the maximum number of processes that have been used since the server was up. Therefore, answer c is incorrect.

Question 4

> A patch file titled 410PT8.EXE indicates a patch for which of the following?
>
> ○ a. A NetWare 4.10 operating system, revision 8, in preliminary testing (PT)
>
> ○ b. A NetWare 4.x operating system, revision 8, in preliminary testing (PT)
>
> ○ c. A NetWare 4.10 or 4.11 operating system, revision 8, in preliminary testing (PT)
>
> ○ d. A NetWare 4.10 operating system, revision 8, that has passed testing (PT)
>
> ○ e. A NetWare 4.10 or 4.11 operating system, revision 8, that has passed testing (PT)

The correct answer is d. 410PT8.EXE indicates a patch for a NetWare 4.10 operating system, revision 8, that has passed testing (PT). Therefore, answers a, b, c, and e are incorrect.

Question 5

Which informational item in MONITOR.NLM would you observe to determine if your server is experiencing a network card bottleneck?

○ a. Dirty Cache Buffers

○ b. Open Files

○ c. Receive Discarded, No Available Buffers

○ d. Number Of Packets Sent

○ e. Long Term Cache Hits

The correct answer is c. To determine if your server is experiencing a network card bottleneck, you would observe the Receive Discarded, No Available Buffers value. An extended high value for Dirty Cache Buffers and for Open Files indicates a potential disk I/O bottleneck. Therefore, answers a and b are incorrect. The Number Of Packets Sent is a cumulative value and will continue growing the longer the server is up. Therefore, answer d is incorrect. When the Long Term Cache Hits value is below 90 percent, this is an indicator that more memory is needed. Therefore, answer e is incorrect.

Question 6

What is NWPA?

○ a. NetWare Printer Agent

○ b. Novell Public Authentication

○ c. NetWare Public Authentication

○ d. NetWare Peripheral Architecture

○ e. NetWare Processor Architecture

The correct answer is d. NWPA stands for *NetWare Peripheral Architecture*. All other answers are made up. Therefore, answers a, b, c, and e are incorrect.

Question 7

> What is an NMI-generated abend?
>
> ○ a. An abend caused by faulty software
>
> ○ b. An abend caused by errors in NDS
>
> ○ c. An abend caused by faulty hardware
>
> ○ d. A harmless abend that's for informational purposes only
>
> ○ e. A Novell Migration Instance abend caused by faulty hardware

The correct answer is c. NMI refers to a non-maskable interrupt and is caused by some hardware event. Therefore, answers a, b, and e are incorrect. There's no such thing as a "harmless abend for information purposes." Therefore, answer d is incorrect.

Question 8

> You've just set up a NetWare 5 server and now you need to add another storage device that uses proprietary software drivers. You go to the vendor's Web site and download the drivers for DOS, Windows 95/98, Windows NT, Client32, and NWSERVER. You copy the *.DSK drivers from the downloaded NWSERVER directory to the server's NWSERVER directory on the server's DOS partition. You edit the STARTUP.NCF file and add two more lines to load the appropriate disk drivers provided by the vendor. However, after the server is restarted, the SYS volume is not mounted and you cannot mount it. What's the problem?
>
> ○ a. You need to copy the Client32 drivers to C:\NWSERVER.
>
> ○ b. You need to check the interrupt and I/O values specified in the STARTUP.NCF file.
>
> ○ c. NetWare 5 cannot use *.DSK drivers.
>
> ○ d. Make sure the new hardware drivers are loaded after the existing driver commands in the STARTUP.NCF file.
>
> ○ e. When a new storage device is added, you need to run VREPAIR on the SYS volume so all the IDs are updated.

The correct answer is c. NetWare 5 cannot use *.DSK drivers. The Client32 files are for a workstation running DOS or Windows 3.x. Therefore, answer a is incorrect. Even if the interrupt and I/O were incorrect and the load order was incorrect, the problem lies with the attempted use of *.DSK drivers on NetWare 5. Therefore, answers b and d are incorrect. There is no need to run VREPAIR on SYS just because additional hardware has been added. Therefore, answer e is incorrect.

Need To Know More?

 http://support.novell.com is Novell's support site. Here, Novell offers a toolkit called the Abend Recovery Toolkit (TABND2A .EXE). At this site, go to the Knowledgebase and search on either the file name or Abend Recovery Toolkit.

 http://developer.novell.com/research/appnotes/1995/February/02/index.htm is an AppNotes article titled "Resolving Critical Server Issues."

 http://developer.novell.com/research/appnotes/1995/June/04/index.htm is an AppNotes article titled "Abend Recovery Techniques for NetWare 3 and 4 Servers."

Sample Test

In this chapter, we provide pointers to help you develop a successful test-taking strategy, including how to choose proper answers, how to decode ambiguity, how to work within the Novell testing framework, how to decide what you need to memorize, and how to prepare for the test. At the end of the chapter, we include 79 questions on subject matter pertinent to Novell Test 050-835, "Service and Support." Good luck!

Questions, Questions, Questions

There should be no doubt in your mind that you're facing a test full of specific and pointed questions. Service and Support is a form exam that consists of 79 questions that you can take up to 120 minutes to complete. This means you must study hard so you can answer as many questions as possible correctly, without resorting to guesses.

Note: We expect Novell to change this test to an adaptive format eventually. See Chapter 1 for more information on adaptive testing.

For this exam, questions belong to one of seven basic types:

➤ Short answer

➤ Multiple-choice questions with a single answer

➤ Multiple-choice questions with multiple answers

➤ Multipart questions with a single answer

➤ Multipart questions with multiple answers

➤ Operate a simulated NetWare console or utility interface

➤ Pick one or more spots on a graphic

Always take the time to read each question at least twice before selecting an answer, and always look for an Exhibit button as you examine each question. Exhibits include graphics information related to a question. An exhibit is usually a screen capture of program output or GUI information that you must examine to analyze the question's content and formulate an answer. The Exhibit button brings up graphics and charts used to help explain a question, provide additional data, or illustrate page layout or program behavior.

Not every question has only one answer; many questions require multiple answers. Therefore, it's important to read each question carefully to determine how many answers are necessary or possible, as well as to look for additional hints or instructions when selecting answers. Such instructions often occur in brackets, immediately following the question itself (as they do for all multiple-choice, multiple-answer questions).

Simulation questions can be a mixed blessing. These task-oriented questions allow you to demonstrate your abilities to complete a certain task or to apply some analysis or management technique. Familiarity with the SupportSource Micro House Technical Library (MTL) module, NetWare, and Windows is essential because the simulations are based on troubleshooting using these utilities.

Picking Proper Answers

Obviously, the only way to pass any exam is to select enough of the right answers to obtain a passing score. However, Novell's exams are not standardized like the SAT and GRE exams, and they can sometimes be quite a bit more challenging. In some cases, questions can be hard to follow or filled with technical vocabulary, and deciphering them can be difficult. In those cases, you may need to rely on answer-elimination skills. Almost always, at least one answer out of the possible choices for a question can be eliminated immediately because it matches one of these conditions:

➤ The answer does not apply to the situation.

➤ The answer describes a nonexistent issue, an invalid option, or an imaginary state.

➤ The answer may be eliminated because of the question itself.

After you eliminate all answers that are obviously wrong, you can apply your retained knowledge to eliminate further answers. Look for items that sound correct but refer to actions, commands, or features that are not present or not available in the situation that the question describes.

If you're still faced with a blind guess among two or more potentially correct answers, reread the question. Try to picture how each of the possible remaining answers would alter the situation. Be especially sensitive to terminology; sometimes, the choice of words (*remove* instead of *disable*) can make the difference between a right answer and a wrong one.

Only when you've exhausted your ability to eliminate answers, and you're still unclear about which of the remaining possibilities is correct, should you guess at an answer (or answers). Guessing gives you at least some chance of getting a question right; just don't be too hasty when making a blind guess.

Decoding Ambiguity

Novell exams have a reputation for including straightforward questions. You won't have to worry much about deliberate ambiguity, but you will need a good grasp of the technical vocabulary involved with NetWare and related products to understand what some questions are trying to ask. In our experience with numerous Novell tests, we've learned that mastering the lexicon of Novell's technical terms pays off on every exam. The Novell tests are tough but fair, and they're deliberately made that way.

However, you need to brace yourself for one set of special cases. Novell tests are notorious for their use of double negatives and similar circumlocutions, such as

"What item is not used when creating a <insert your favorite task here>?" Our guess is that Novell includes such Byzantine language in its questions because it wants to make sure examinees can follow instructions to the letter, no matter how strangely worded those instructions might be. Although this may seem like a form of torture, it's actually good preparation for those circumstances where you have to follow instructions from technical manuals or training materials, which are themselves not quite in the same ballpark as "great literature" or even "plain English." Even though we've been coached repeatedly to be on the lookout for this kind of stuff, it still fools us anyway from time to time. Therefore, you need to be on the lookout yourself and try to learn from our mistakes.

The only way to beat Novell at this game is to be prepared. You'll discover that many exam questions test your knowledge of things that are not directly related to the issue raised by a question. This means that the answers from which you must choose, even incorrect ones, are just as much a part of the skill assessment as the question itself. If you don't know something about most aspects of troubleshooting hardware, you may not be able to eliminate obviously wrong answers. In other words, the more you know about troubleshooting NetWare, the associated workstation clients, and the associated hardware, the easier it will be for you to tell a right answer from a wrong one.

Questions often give away their answers, but you have to read them carefully to see the clues that point to those answers. Often, subtle hints appear in the question text in such a way that they seem almost irrelevant to the situation. You must realize that each question is a test unto itself and that you need to inspect and successfully navigate each question to pass the exam. Look for small clues, such as the mention of utilities, services, and configuration settings. Little things such as these can point at the right answer if properly understood; if missed, they can leave you facing a blind guess.

Because mastering the technical vocabulary is so important to testing well for Novell, be sure to brush up on the key terms presented at the beginning of each chapter. You may also want to read through the Glossary at the end of this book the day before you take the test.

Working Within The Framework

The test questions appear in random order, and many elements or issues that receive mention in one question may also crop up in other questions. It's not uncommon to find that an incorrect answer to one question is the correct answer to another question, or vice versa. Take the time to read every answer to each question, even if you recognize the correct answer to a question immediately. That extra reading may spark a memory or remind you about a networking feature, function, or piece of hardware that helps you on another question later in the exam.

Review each question carefully; test developers love to throw in a few tricky questions. Often, important clues are hidden in the wording or special instructions. Do your best to decode ambiguous questions; just be aware that some questions will be open to interpretation.

You might also want to jot some notes on the provided piece of paper or plastic sheet about questions that contain key information.

 Don't be afraid to take notes on what you see in various questions. Sometimes, what you record from one question—especially if it isn't as familiar as it should be or reminds you of the name or use of some utility or interface details—can help you with other questions later in the test.

Deciding What To Memorize

The amount of memorization you must undertake for an exam depends on how well you remember what you've read and how well you know the software by heart. If you're a visual thinker and can see drop-down menus and dialog boxes in your head, you won't need to memorize as much as someone who's less visually oriented. The test will stretch your recollection of networking concepts, tools, and technologies.

At a minimum, you'll want to memorize the following types of information:

➤ How to diagnose and resolve network problems related to hardware, servers, and client workstations

➤ How to install and troubleshoot the various types of network boards and cables

➤ How to install, set up, partition, and secure hard drives

➤ How to troubleshoot queue-based, Novell Distributed Print Services (NDPS), and network printing

If you work your way through this book and try to exercise the various capabilities of networking hardware that are covered throughout, you should have little or no difficulty mastering this material. Also, don't forget that The Cram Sheet at the front of the book is designed to capture the material that's most important to memorize; use this to guide your studies as well. Finally, don't forget to obtain and use Novell's Test Objectives for Course 580 as part of your planning and preparation process.

Preparing For The Test

The best way to prepare for the test—after you've studied—is to take at least one practice exam. We've included one in this chapter for that reason; the test questions are located in the pages that follow. (Unlike the preceding chapters in this book, the answers don't follow the questions immediately; you'll have to flip to Chapter 14 to review the answers separately.)

Give yourself no more than 120 minutes to take the exam, keep yourself on the honor system, and don't look at earlier text in the book or jump ahead to the answer key. When your time is up or you've finished the questions, you can check your work in Chapter 14. Pay special attention to the explanations for the incorrect answers; these can also help to reinforce your knowledge of the material. Knowing how to recognize correct answers is good, but understanding why incorrect answers are wrong can be equally valuable.

Taking The Test

Relax. Once you're sitting in front of the testing computer, there's nothing more you can do to increase your knowledge or preparation. Take a deep breath, stretch, and start reading that first question.

There's no need to rush—you have plenty of time. If you can't figure out the answer to a question after a few minutes, though, you may want to guess and move on to leave more time for remaining unanswered questions. Remember that both easy and difficult questions are intermixed throughout the test in random order. Because you're taking a form test, you should watch your time carefully: Try to be one-quarter of the way done (20 questions) in at least 30 minutes, halfway done (39 questions) in at least 60 minutes, and three-quarters done (59 questions) in 90 minutes.

Set a maximum time limit for questions and watch your time on long or complex questions. If you hit your time limit, you need to guess and move on. Don't deprive yourself of the opportunity to see more questions by taking too long to puzzle over answers, unless you think you can figure out the correct answer. Otherwise, you're limiting your opportunities to pass.

That's it for pointers. Here are some questions for you to practice on.

Sample Test

Question 1

A customer reports a SCSI disk is not working in a NetWare 4.11 server. What should you check first?

- ○ a. Hard disk read/write heads
- ○ b. Drive spindle
- ○ c. SCSI ID
- ○ d. Disk interleave

Question 2

You've been hired to provide network recommendations for network media in an electrogeneration power facility with high radio frequency (RF) interference. Which type of media should you recommend?

- ○ a. FDDI
- ○ b. Fast Ethernet
- ○ c. ARCnet
- ○ d. Token ring

Question 3

By default, the CLIENT32.NLM is found in which directory?

- ○ a. C:\NOVELL\CLIENT32\INSTALL
- ○ b. SYS:\PUBLIC\win32
- ○ c. C:\NOVELL\CLIENT32
- ○ d. SYS:\PUBLIC\mgmt

Question 4

You're troubleshooting a SCSI drive. What are some potential problems that can be easily checked? [Choose the three best answers]

❑ a. Termination

❑ b. Cable connections

❑ c. Drive speed

❑ d. SCSI ID

Question 5

A user has installed a new CD-ROM drive in a NetWare server but cannot see the drive. What do you recommend the user check or do? [Choose the three best answers]

❑ a. Execute the **CD DEVICE LIST** command to see if the volume name appears.

❑ b. Reinstall the drivers for the CD-ROM drive.

❑ c. Verify that the drive is mounted using the **CD MOUNT** *volume_name* command.

❑ d. Reboot the server.

Question 6

Your network is experiencing network overload I/O problems. What can you do to alleviate the problem? [Choose the two best answers]

❑ a. Upgrade to faster network boards.

❑ b. Divide overloaded network segments with a bridge or router.

❑ c. Install more memory in the NetWare server.

❑ d. Divide overloaded network segments with an active hub.

Question 7

An administrator reports that a drive volume is damaged and asks for your recommendation on how to maintain data integrity during the repair. What should you recommend?

○ a. Unmount the SYS volume.

○ b. Restore all data from tape.

○ c. Run VREPAIR as many times as necessary until all errors are fixed.

○ d. Back up the data before running VREPAIR.

Question 8

A user reports a network printer isn't working. Because you don't really know what the user means by "not working," what are the potential problem areas you should have the user check? [Choose the best answers]

❑ a. Whether the printer cables are connected

❑ b. Whether the printer has toner

❑ c. Whether the printer is on

❑ d. Whether the printer has paper in it

Question 9

Which of the following is not a limitation of IDE drives on NetWare 4.11?

○ a. Older versions of IDE did not support optical drives or tape backup.

○ b. IDE does not support bus mastering.

○ c. IDE does not support disk duplexing.

○ d. IDE does not support overlapped, multitasking I/O.

Question 10

Which of the following are necessary to safely apply a static patch to a Novell NetWare server? [Choose the three best answers]

❑ a. Uninstall all previously applied static patches.

❑ b. Run *patch_name* **SERVER.EXE** at a command line.

❑ c. Rename SERVER.EXE to SERVER.OLD.

❑ d. Copy static patches into the same directory as the SERVER.EXE file.

Question 11

You're troubleshooting a problem with your server and an administrator recommends installing patches. Which patches should you install?

○ a. All currently available static patches only

○ b. All currently available dynamic patches only

○ c. Only the specific patches that are required to fix the problem or are recommended by a Novell technician

○ d. All known and approved patches

Question 12

Which cable category is most commonly used for ARCnet? [Choose the best answer]

○ a. Category 1

○ b. Category 2

○ c. Category 3

○ d. Category 4

○ e. Category 5

Question 13

Which of the following is not a benefit of an electrostatic discharge (ESD) program?

○ a. Happier customers

○ b. Elimination of service calls

○ c. Fewer required on-hand spare parts

○ d. Less computer downtime

Question 14

Which of the following is a false statement regarding ESD?

○ a. ESD events generally cause component degradation rather than immediate failure.

○ b. Normal lifting of your feet can generate up to 1,000 volts or more.

○ c. As little as 20 to 30 volts can damage electronic components.

○ d. Electronic components should always be transported in anti-static bags.

Question 15

You need to access a NetWare support forum. Which of the following tools would you use?

○ a. SupportSource

○ b. The Novell Support Connection CD-ROM

○ c. The Novell Web site

○ d. A Novell Authorized Training Center

Question 16

You need to access the NetWare product manuals. Which of the following tools would you use?

○ a. **www.microsoft.com**

○ b. Novell Support Connection CD-ROM

○ c. SupportSource

○ d. A Novell Authorized Training Center

Question 17

You need access to the most current static patches for your NetWare server. Which of the following tools is the best resource to use?

- ○ a. **www.novell.com**
- ○ b. The Novell Support Connection CD-ROM
- ○ c. SupportSource
- ○ d. A Novell Authorized Training Center

Question 18

You have a network board and you need to determine the correct jumper settings and specifications. Which of the following tools would you use?

- ○ a. The Micro House Technical Library
- ○ b. The Novell Support Connection CD-ROM
- ○ c. The Novell Support Connection Web site
- ○ d. A Novell Authorized Training Center

Question 19

You attempt to connect to a computer on the network but cannot. Other computers cannot connect either. Your network consists entirely of 10BaseT. What are the most likely causes? [Choose the two best answers]

- ❏ a. The computer is off.
- ❏ b. ESD.
- ❏ c. The network cable is not connected to the computer.
- ❏ d. Too many users are logged into the network.

Question 20

What is the suggested value for the setting of the LANalyzer Server Overloads/min alarm threshold?

○ a. 10

○ b. 15

○ c. 5

○ d. 5 to 10 percent above peak

○ e. 5 to 10 percent below peak

Question 21

You receive a "TOKEN-DOS-207: Installation Error=27 Ring Beaconing" error. What is the problem?

○ a. There's a break in the token ring network.

○ b. Tokens are being dropped.

○ c. The token ring adapters are not running at the same speed.

○ d. The IRQ has not been configured correctly.

Question 22

What's the correct expansion for the acronym EISA?

○ a. Extended Internal Speed Adapter

○ b. Enhanced Industry Standard Adapter

○ c. Enhanced Industry Standard Architecture

○ d. Enhanced Internal Standard Adapter

Question 23

Which of the following provide configuration information that's useful when installing network boards in a computer? [Choose the two best answers]

❏ a. FDISK

❏ b. IBM reference diskette

❏ c. NDS

❏ d. EISA Configuration Utility (ECU)

Question 24

Which of the following are valid types of hard disk interfaces? [Choose the best answers]

❑ a. IDE

❑ b. EIDE

❑ c. ESDI

❑ d. SCSI

Question 25

You've just completed a SCSI hard disk installation. The system doesn't recognize the hard drive, although the hard drive appears to spin up. What could be the problem? [Choose the two best answers]

❑ a. Improper SCSI termination.

❑ b. There's no power to the drive.

❑ c. Another computer has the same IPX address as the computer.

❑ d. Duplicate SCSI ID.

Question 26

What's the maximum distance between SCSI cable connectors on a SCSI cable?

○ a. 2 feet (.61 meter).

○ b. 1 meter (3 feet).

○ c. 18 inches (46 centimeters).

○ d. There is no distance limit between SCSI connectors.

Question 27

You're installing a second IDE disk drive on the same disk controller as the existing drive. How should you configure the jumpers for each drive?

○ a. Set the jumpers on both drives to master.

○ b. Change the jumper on the existing drive to master and the new drive to slave.

○ c. Change the jumper on the existing drive to slave and the new drive to master.

○ d. Each drive will obtain a new SCSI ID automatically when the server restarts, so no jumper change is required.

Question 28

You're configuring a new disk drive in CMOS but don't know the number of heads or cylinders. However, you do know the drive size. What drive type should you input for the new drive?

○ a. Type 44.

○ b. Type 46.

○ c. Pick a drive type of the same size or close to the same size as the new drive.

○ d. You cannot install a new drive unless you know the exact drive type.

Question 29

A low-level disk format performs which of the following? [Choose the three best answers]

❑ a. Sets the drive's disk interleave ratio.

❑ b. Tests the drive's read/write heads.

❑ c. Marks bad sectors as bad.

❑ d. Copies system files.

Question 30

A high-level disk format performs which of the following? [Choose the three best answers]

❑ a. Marks bad disk sectors.

❑ b. Assigns sector IDs.

❑ c. Creates the file allocation table for DOS.

❑ d. Creates an empty root directory.

Question 31

Which is true regarding NetWare disk partitions?

○ a. Non-NetWare partitions can be mirrored.

○ b. A partition containing an operating system other than NetWare appears as a non-NetWare partition.

○ c. Two partitions, each containing a NetWare 4.11 installation, can exist on the same physical disk.

○ d. NetWare partition numbering begins with the number 1.

Question 32

Which of the following are true of NetWare volumes? [Choose the two best answers]

❑ a. NetWare allows up to 32 volumes per server.

❑ b. NetWare allows up to 64 volumes per server.

❑ c. The NetWare volumes can total up to 32TB.

❑ d. The NetWare volumes can total up to 64TB.

Question 33

The NWFS.SYS component provides the interface between the local Windows NT operating system and the Novell Client and Novell services. By default, in which directory is the NWFS.SYS file found?

○ a. C:\NOVELL\CLIENT32

○ b. HKEY_LOCAL_MACHINE\Network\Novell\System Config

○ c. C:\WINDOWS

○ d. C:\WINNT\SYSTEM32

Question 34

Which of the following are true of a NetWare volume? [Choose the two best answers]

❏ a. It must exist on a single physical drive.

❏ b. It can span multiple physical drives.

❏ c. It's fault tolerant.

❏ d. It can be the entire NetWare partition.

Question 35

Which of the following is not a benefit of disk mirroring?

○ a. Mirroring allows the failure of a single disk drive in a mirror set with no data loss.

○ b. Mirroring allows the failure of the disk controller without impacting system availability.

○ c. Mirroring is less expensive than disk duplexing.

○ d. Disk mirroring is fault tolerant.

Question 36

Your keyboard locks up while copying files from the system CD-ROM to the SYS volume on a SCSI drive. What can you do to prevent the problem from occurring again? [Choose the three best answers]

❑ a. This is normal and cannot be corrected.

❑ b. Connect the CD-ROM drive to its own SCSI disk controller.

❑ c. Use a parallel-to-SCSI adapter instead of the system SCSI adapter.

❑ d. Install an IDE CD-ROM drive.

Question 37

A user calls and complains he cannot connect to the network, but he could yesterday? Which of the following would not provide valuable information for troubleshooting the problem?

○ a. Asking if any new software was installed

○ b. Asking what changed on the system

○ c. Running the PATCHES utility on the local computer

○ d. Verifying the network cable is connected to the computer's network board

Question 38

You determine that users on a particular subnet are experiencing poor network performance. Which of the following would least benefit network performance?

○ a. Determining and eliminating applications that are not network friendly

○ b. Installing more memory in all network servers

○ c. Upgrading to faster network boards

○ d. Physically dividing subnets with routers or bridges

Question 39

What's the first step for troubleshooting a computer problem?

○ a. Test possible solutions.

○ b. Document the problem.

○ c. Investigate the problem.

○ d. Identify probable causes for the problem.

Question 40

When is the best time to establish baseline parameters for a computer system?

○ a. Before the operating system is installed

○ b. After installing the operating system, but prior to installing any applications

○ c. After the operating system and all applications are installed, but prior to normal user load

○ d. After the operating system and all applications are installed, when under a normal user load

Question 41

Which of the following are valid gateways that ship with NetWare 5 NDPS? [Choose the three best answers]

❏ a. Xerox gateway

❏ b. IBM gateway

❏ c. Hewlett-Packard gateway

❏ d. Novell gateway

❏ e. Microsoft gateway

Question 42

You need to configure a new printer for your network. Which of the following tools can you use?

○ a. PPRINT

○ b. PCONSOLE

○ c. NCONSOLE

○ d. PCONFIG

Question 43

You need to take a printer down for maintenance, but your users are still printing documents. How can you prevent the users from printing to this printer? [Choose the two best answers]

❑ a. Set the File Contents setting to Byte Stream.

❑ b. Set the Allow Service By Current Print Servers setting to No.

❑ c. Set the Allow Users To Submit Print Jobs setting to No.

❑ d. Set the Allow New Print Servers To Attach setting to Yes.

Question 44

Which of the following is not a rule of static prevention?

○ a. Keep humidity less than 30 percent.

○ b. Use grounding straps when working with electronic equipment.

○ c. Store electronic boards in static-shielding bags.

○ d. Keep Styrofoam away from electronic components.

Question 45

You've recently added a new server to your Ethernet network. Other computers are able to connect to the new server. You attempt to connect to the new server from your computer and receive a "FILESERVER NOT FOUND" error message. What is the most likely cause?

- ○ a. Your computer and the server are configured for different Ethernet frame types.
- ○ b. The server is not connected to the network.
- ○ c. The server is not powered up.
- ○ d. The new server's subnet is not terminated.

Question 46

Which of the following are not advantages of token ring networks? [Choose the two best answers]

- ❑ a. Able to use twisted-pair cabling
- ❑ b. Inexpensive
- ❑ c. Fault tolerance
- ❑ d. Easy to manage and administer

Question 47

Which of the following accurately describes a controlled access printer?

- ○ a. It's immediately available to everyone.
- ○ b. It has no security (no NDS).
- ○ c. It has complete NDS security options.
- ○ d. It has no NDS Printer objects.

Question 48

Which of the following is an advantage of FDDI?

○ a. Simple installation

○ b. Inexpensive

○ c. Easy to install and administer

○ d. Fast

Question 49

You're planning to install a new SCSI controller and disk drive. Which of the following are important considerations during the installation? [Choose the three best answers]

❑ a. SCSI disk drives are more expensive than EIDE disk drives.

❑ b. Route SCSI cables as far as possible from sources of electromagnetic interference.

❑ c. Ensure each SCSI device is configured with a unique SCSI ID.

❑ d. Verify proper SCSI termination.

Question 50

You just installed a new SCSI disk drive into an existing computer system. You set the SCSI ID of the new drive to 7. You cannot get the new SCSI drive to boot. What's the most likely cause? [Choose the best answer]

○ a. The SCSI ID 7 is not valid.

○ b. The drive is improperly terminated.

○ c. The SCSI ID of the HBA is set to 7 by default.

○ d. The drive is defective and must be replaced.

Question 51

Your NetWare server's system disk is running disk mirroring. A program is writing information to both drives. During the write operation, the second drive detects a bad sector on the disk. What happens to the data being written to the second drive?

○ a. The disk controller attempts to locate a good sector on the second drive and write the data there.

○ b. The data is not written to the second drive.

○ c. The user receives a drive write failure error.

○ d. The data is written to the Hot Fix Redirection area on the second drive.

Question 52

You have a NetWare server with a 200MB DOS partition. Your company stores critical information in this partition. Your manager wants to provide fault tolerance by mirroring the DOS partitions onto another drive. What must you do to accomplish this?

○ a. Add another drive and a separate disk controller.

○ b. Add a second drive and add that drive to a new mirror set.

○ c. Nothing. Non-NetWare partitioned drives cannot be mirrored.

○ d. Create an additional NetWare partition on the second drive.

Question 53

You're running a RAID 1 configuration (duplexed), and one of the drives fails. What must you do to restore the NetWare server?

○ a. Replace the failed drive and reboot.

○ b. Nothing. The NetWare server automatically switches to the remaining drive.

○ c. Replace the failed drive and drive controller and reboot.

○ d. This failure is not recoverable.

Question 54

You print a document to the printer, but when the document actually prints, it appears as garbage characters. What do you suspect is the cause of the problem?

○ a. A wrong print driver.

○ b. A corrupted print queue.

○ c. Insufficient disk queue space.

○ d. PCONSOLE is not installed.

Question 55

Which of the following is not a commonly used diagnostic tool for trouble-shooting computers?

○ a. WINCheckIt Pro

○ b. CheckIt

○ c. LANalyzer

○ d. Microsoft Diagnostics (MSD)

Question 56

Which of the following are good disaster-recovery plan items for Novell networks? [Choose the three best answers]

❑ a. Maintain at least three copies of each subordinate reference replica.

❑ b. Use Windows Scan Disk to test the integrity of the volumes on the server.

❑ c. Maintain at least three copies of each NDS partition.

❑ d. Make sure the backup software is up-to-date.

❑ e. Make sure the NDS backup is reliable.

Question 57

An MLID is linked most closely to which of the following?

- ○ a. A protocol stack
- ○ b. Network media
- ○ c. A network board
- ○ d. A network board device driver

Question 58

The Link Support Layer (LSL) interfaces between which of the following?

- ○ a. A protocol stack and an MLID
- ○ b. An MLID and a network board
- ○ c. A protocol stack and a network board
- ○ d. A network board and network media

Question 59

Which of the following is the correct description of a disaster-recovery plan (DRP) hot site?

- ○ a. A facility that contains a complete set of hardware and software for the company in a mobile facility.
- ○ b. A facility that contains a complete set of hardware and software for the company off site.
- ○ c. A facility that does not contain all the hardware or software for the company, but the equipment can be brought in within a few hours.
- ○ d. A specialized site for a business that needs to be brought online quickly and can't afford downtime.

Question 60

> Which of the following provides services such as adjusting automatic reconnection levels, file caching, and tracking network resource usage?
>
> ○ a. CLIENT32.TXT
>
> ○ b. NET.CFG
>
> ○ c. C32MODULES.NLM
>
> ○ d. CLIENT32.NLM

Question 61

> Which of the following are not roles of the active monitor in a token ring network? [Choose the two best answers]
>
> ❑ a. Sends out special "hello" packets every seven seconds.
>
> ❑ b. Checks to make sure the ring does not have more than one standby monitor.
>
> ❑ c. It's the last device that joins the ring.
>
> ❑ d. Maintains the master clock.
>
> ❑ e. Handles lost tokens.

Question 62

> What's the first step necessary to set up a NetWare 5 queue-based printing environment?
>
> ○ a. Create the print server and assign the printers.
>
> ○ b. Create the print queue.
>
> ○ c. Specify the volume on which the print queue will reside.
>
> ○ d. Assign the print queue to the printer.

Question 63

You've just completed the installation of a network board in your computer. When you restart the computer, the computer reports a conflict on IRQ 4. Which component is the new network board conflicting with?

○ a. COM1

○ b. Printer port

○ c. Floppy drive

○ d. Keyboard

Question 64

Which of the following is not a type of NetWare patch?

○ a. Static

○ b. Dynamic

○ c. Semi-static

○ d. Semi-dynamic

Question 65

Your junior administrator shows you a file named CONFIG.TXT he found on the SYS volume under SYSTEM. What's the purpose of this file?

○ a. It's a backup of CONFIG.SYS.

○ b. It lists the complete system configuration list generated by CONFIG.NLM.

○ c. It configures the SYS volume on startup.

○ d. It's a system password file.

Question 66

Your manager wants a listing of all known issues related to your current patch level of a NetWare server. Which tool supplies this information?

○ a. Micro House Technical Library (MTL)

○ b. Novell Support Connection CD-ROM

○ c. Novell Support Connection Web site

○ d. A Novell Authorized Training Center

Question 67

Which of the following does not cause an overloaded network?

○ a. Large file transfers

○ b. Server-launched applications

○ c. Inadequate server memory

○ d. Recently added network clients

Question 68

One of your users discovered she deleted critical documents. What can you do to restore them?

○ a. Run VREPAIR as many times as necessary until all files are restored.

○ b. Run DSREPAIR.

○ c. Run WINMSD.

○ d. Restore from backup.

Question 69

NetWare 5 supports drivers with which extension?

○ a. .DSK

○ b. .HAM

○ c. .DRV

○ d. .COM

○ e. .NSS

Question 70

A user has sent a large print job to a network printer and is concerned because of the excessively long time it's taking to print. What is most the likely problem?

○ a. The printer is out of paper.

○ b. The printer is offline.

○ c. The printer has a paper jam.

○ d. The print job is taking a while to spool to the server.

Question 71

A user is printing to a network printer. Although the user never encounters any printing errors, the printer never outputs the print job. What could be the problem?

○ a. The printer is out of paper.

○ b. The printer is offline.

○ c. The user is mistakenly printing to another printer.

○ d. The print server is offline.

Question 72

A user is printing a document, but the printer only prints out garbage characters. What is most the likely problem?

○ a. The wrong print driver is installed.

○ b. The print server has a corrupted print queue.

○ c. The printer has a paper jam.

○ d. The printer has an IRQ conflict with another device.

Question 73

The drafting department uses the **CAPTURE** command to schedule large print files to print every Friday night. On Saturday mornings, the users report that print jobs scheduled in this manner fail to print. What's the most likely cause? [Choose the best answer]

○ a. Full backups occur Friday nights.

○ b. The print servers are shut down for the weekend.

○ c. The printer contains the wrong paper type.

○ d. The print jobs overload the print queue.

Question 74

You attempt to print a 125MB Microsoft PowerPoint presentation. The job repeatedly fails to complete. Other smaller print jobs complete successfully. What's the problem?

○ a. A corrupt print queue.

○ b. Insufficient disk space on the print server.

○ c. The wrong print driver.

○ d. The printer has insufficient memory.

Question 75

Which of the following are valid print queue names? [Choose the two best answers]

❑ a. printq32

❑ b. HP+printerq

❑ c. prINTnoW!

❑ d. prINTnoW

Question 76

RPRINTER repeatedly fails to initialize at a workstation. Which of the following are possible causes? [Choose the two best answers]

❑ a. Insufficient workstation memory.

❑ b. Outdated RPRINTER.EXE.

❑ c. Incorrect RPRINTER parameters in NET.CFG.

❑ d. The printer is offline.

Question 77

Users are reporting that print jobs for a particular printer are not printing. When you examine the print queue, you notice several print jobs queued to print. What can you do to correct the problem? [Choose the best answers]

❑ a. Verify that the printer is on.

❑ b. Verify that the printer is online.

❑ c. Verify that the printer has adequate toner.

❑ d. Verify that the printer isn't jammed.

Question 78

Users are complaining that print jobs are taking too long to print. You currently have one print queue serving a single printer. What can you do to speed up printing? [Choose the two best answers]

❑ a. Replace the existing printer with a high-speed print device.

❑ b. Add another print queue for the printer.

❑ c. Add another printer to the print queue.

❑ d. Add another network router.

Question 79

Which of the following is not a valid component of the NDPS printing system?

○ a. Printer Agent

○ b. Printer object license

○ c. NDPS Manager

○ d. NDPS Broker

Answer Key

1. c
2. a
3. c
4. a, b, d
5. a, b, c
6. a, b
7. d
8. a, b, c, d
9. c
10. b, c, d
11. d
12. c
13. b
14. d
15. c
16. b
17. a
18. a
19. a, c
20. c

21. c
22. c
23. b, d
24. a, b, c, d
25. a, d
26. c
27. b
28. c
29. a, b, c
30. a, c, d
31. b
32. b, c
33. d
34. b, d
35. b
36. b, c, d
37. c
38. b
39. c
40. d

41. a, c, d
42. b
43. b, c
44. a
45. a
46. b, d
47. c
48. d
49. b, c, d
50. c
51. d
52. c
53. b
54. a
55. c
56. c, d, e
57. d
58. a
59. b
60. d

61. b, c
62. b
63. a
64. d
65. b
66. c
67. c
68. d
69. a
70. d
71. c
72. a
73. a
74. b
75. a, d
76. a, b
77. a, b, c, d
78. a, c
79. b

Question 1

The correct answer is c. Over 80 percent of all SCSI-related issues are either SCSI ID conflicts between SCSI subsystem components or incorrect SCSI termination. Although it's possible to have a failure of the read/write heads, the drive spindle, or an incorrectly set disk interleave, they would not be the first things checked. Therefore, answers a, b, and d are incorrect.

Question 2

The correct answer is a. Because the location of the network is subject to high RF interference, any media consisting of current-carrying conductors would be subject to the RF. Fiber-optic cable, which is used in Fiber Distributed Data Interface (FDDI), uses glass tubing and light rather than electrical conductors. FDDI is not subject to RF interference, but Fast Ethernet and token ring are. Therefore, answers b and d are incorrect. ARCnet, although widely recognized as the most resistant copper-based networking technology, is obsolete and is generally not a wise recommendation for a new installation. Therefore, answer c is incorrect.

Question 3

The correct answer is c. The CLIENT32.NLM is found in the C:\NOVELL\ CLIENT32 directory, by default. All other answers represent incorrect locations and are therefore incorrect.

Question 4

The correct answers are a, b, and d. Over 80 percent of all SCSI-related failures are a result of incorrect termination or a SCSI ID conflict. It's also possible, but not likely, for a cable to be upside down or accidentally unplugged. Cable problems are also quite simple to investigate. Although a drive speed problem can certainly impact reliability and usability, without special equipment, it's quite difficult to check. Therefore, answer c is incorrect.

Question 5

The correct answers are a, b, and c. Executing **CD DEVICE LIST** command lists the currently available volumes. This is a quick check to see whether the device is installed. Therefore, answer a is correct. If, for whatever reason, the CD-ROM volume fails to appear in the device list, it necessitates uninstalling and reinstalling the CDROM.NLM. Therefore, answer b is correct. You must mount the drive using the **CD MOUNT** *volume_name* command for the system to recognize it. Therefore, answer c is correct. Rebooting a server is not required for configuring a CD-ROM. Therefore, answer d is incorrect.

Question 6

The correct answers are a and b. Network overutilization is common in all but the smallest of networks. Installing faster network boards reduces I/O of the individual workstations on the network. Therefore, answer a is correct. To reduce the I/O problems, segment the network into subnets using routers or bridges for physical separation. It's also highly recommended to place the users physically close to the resources they frequent. This minimizes the traffic across the routes or bridges and keeps traffic local to the subnet. Therefore, answer b is correct. Installing memory into a server does nothing to reduce I/O. Therefore, answer c is incorrect. Active hubs only connect segments. They do not divide networks as routers and bridges do. Therefore, answer d is incorrect.

Question 7

The best answer is d. Like CHECKDISK for DOS and Windows, VREPAIR does not maintain or correct data integrity; it merely corrects errors in the volume structure. If at all possible, a full backup of that volume is recommended before you unmount it. The question never says the SYS volume was corrupted. It cannot be assumed, therefore, that the SYS requires unmounting. Therefore, answer a is incorrect. The purpose of VREPAIR is to repair drives without restoring from tape. Therefore, answer b is incorrect. Although you should run VREPAIR as many times as required to eliminate all drive errors, the correct procedure is to to regain volume integrity. Therefore, answer c is incorrect.

Question 8

The correct answers are a, b, c, and d. All of these answers are valid reasons why printers fail to print. If you cannot physically see and investigate the printer, assume nothing. Sometimes, the users are so preoccupied with other work they cannot accurately describe symptoms.

Question 9

The correct answer is c. NetWare does support disk duplexing for IDE drives. The remaining answers are indeed limitations of IDE drives in a NetWare environment. Therefore, answers a, b, and d are incorrect.

Question 10

The correct answers are b, c, and d. The application of a static patch alters the SERVER.EXE file. The correct order of steps is to rename the SERVER.EXE to SERVER.OLD. In the event the patch application fails, the SERVER.OLD file is renamed SERVER.EXE and you are back where you began. Next, copy the static patches into the same directory as the SERVER.EXE; then, install static patches from the same directory as SERVER.EXE. Finally, to install the patch, issue *patch_name* SERVER.EXE at a command line. Static patches are cumulative and are not removed once installed. Therefore, answer a is incorrect.

Question 11

The correct answer is d. The best way to ensure the NetWare operating system is free from problems and bugs is to install all current patches. It's not wise to mix and match patches—this generally does more harm than good. Dynamic patches are applied at server startup. Although these patches fix many issues, it's important to apply all patches—static and dynamic. Therefore, answers a and b are incorrect. A NetWare support technician is instructed to make sure you're completely up-to-date on all static and dynamic patches as an initial step in any troubleshooting. He or she will not recommend one patch over another. Therefore, answer c is incorrect.

Question 12

The correct answer is c. Category 3 cable is most commonly used for ARCnet implementations. Category 1 is used for simple communications. Therefore, answer a is incorrect. Category 2 is used for voice and low-speed data. Therefore, answer b is incorrect. Category 4 is used for 16Mbps token ring; and Category 5 is used for 100BaseTX implementations. Categories 4 and 5 are both backward-compatible and will support ARCnet, but Category 3 is most commonly used for ARCnet implementations. Therefore, answers d and e are incorrect.

Question 13

The correct answer is b. Nothing short of a computerless office will completely eliminate service calls. The real goal is the reduction of service calls. Answers a, c, and d are benefits of an ESD program and are therefore incorrect.

Question 14

The correct answer is d. Anti-static bags aren't really "anti-static" at all. Static prevention bags are used when transporting electronic components. ESD generally causes incremental damage to electronic components rather than immediate failure. Therefore, answer a is incorrect. It's also true that simply lifting your foot can generate approximately 1,000 volts. Therefore, answer b is incorrect. Finally, 20 to 30 volts are more than enough to damage sensitive electronic components. Therefore, answer c is incorrect.

Question 15

The correct answer is c. Forums are found on the Novell Web site at **http://developer.novell.com/sitemaps/devsup.html**. Micro House's SupportSource contains detailed information about hardware. Therefore, answer a is incorrect. The product documentation can be found on the Novell Support Connection CD-ROM; however, forums cannot. Therefore, answer b is incorrect. Novell Training Centers provide Novell authorized training but do not support forums. Therefore, answer d is incorrect.

Question 16

The correct answer is b. Novell product documentation is found on the Novell Support Connection CD-ROM. Novell does not distribute product documentation from the Microsoft Web site. Therefore, answer a is incorrect. Micro House's SupportSource contains detailed information about hardware. Therefore, answer c is incorrect. A Novell Authorized Training Center offers training, not product documentation. Therefore, answer d is incorrect.

Question 17

The correct answer is a. Patches are available from several authorized locations, including Novell's Web site and the Novell Support Connection CD-ROM. However, the question asks for the most current resource, and online resources will always be more current than a static CD-ROM. Therefore, answer b is incorrect. Micro House's SupportSource contains detailed information about hardware, not patches for NetWare servers. Therefore, answer c is incorrect. Novell Training Centers are not authorized distribution points for dynamic and static patches. Therefore, answer d is incorrect.

Question 18

The correct answer is a. The SupportSource Micro House Technical Library (MTL) is a great source for technical information regarding configuration settings and technical information. The Novell Support Connection CD-ROM and Web site support an extensive library of information but fail to provide board-level technical information. Therefore, answers b and c are incorrect. Although someone at a Novell Training Center may happen to have this information, the MTL provides this information. Therefore, answer d is incorrect.

Question 19

The correct answers are a and c. Generally, if you cannot connect to another computer on the network, the computer is either down or not connected to the network. There are other possible reasons for this scenario, but of the four offered, these are the most likely. ESD has the potential to damage electronic components. However, effects of ESD are often gradual rather than catastrophic. Therefore, answer b is incorrect. The effect of excessive network load is a reduction in performance, not the inability to connect to the network. Therefore, answer d is incorrect.

Question 20

The correct answer is c. The suggested value for the setting of the Server Overloads/min alarm threshold is 5 per minute. All the other answers represent incorrect values and are therefore incorrect.

Question 21

The correct answer is c. The "Token Ring Beaconing" error indicates that one or more token ring adapters are not running at the same speed as the rest of the adapters, although this is not the only possible cause of this error. A break in the network would preclude data transfer in the network. The beacon error is indicative of incorrect speed settings. Therefore, answer a is incorrect. Tokens don't just fall out of the wire. They are either delivered or result in an error message. Therefore, answer b is incorrect. An IRQ conflict results in an error message on the local machine rather than generating a beaconing error. Therefore, answer d is incorrect.

Question 22

The correct answer is c. EISA is Enhanced Industry Standard Architecture. All other options present incorrect expansions. Therefore, answers a, b, and d are incorrect.

Question 23

The correct answers are b and d. The IBM reference diskette and the EISA Configuration Utility provide configuration information applicable to the installation process of networking components. FDISK is a utility program for low-level configuration of hard disks. Therefore, answer a is incorrect. NDS is Novell's Directory Services and has nothing to do with network board configuration. Therefore, answer c is incorrect.

Question 24

The correct answers are a, b, c, and d. IDE is Integrated Drive Electronics, EIDE is Enhanced Integrated Drive Electronics, ESDI is Enhanced Small Device Interface, and SCSI is Small Computer System Interface. All are valid types of hard disk interfaces.

Question 25

The correct answers are a and d. Eighty percent of all SCSI-related failures are because of improper termination or conflicting SCSI IDs. The question indicates the drive spins up, signifying power is available to the drive. Therefore, answer b is incorrect. Although a duplicate IPX address is a bad thing, it wouldn't prevent drive access. Therefore, answer c is incorrect.

Question 26

The correct answer is c. The maximum recommended distance between SCSI connectors is 18 inches (46 centimeters). Therefore, answers a, b, and d are incorrect.

Question 27

The correct answer is b. IDE and EIDE drives use jumpers to determine the master/slave relationships of the drives. With both these drive types, the drive controller relocates to the drive itself. One drive in a two-drive IDE chain must be designated a master and the second a slave. Therefore, answer a is incorrect. When you're adding a second drive to the system, it's not unusual for the added drive to act as additional storage capacity with the computer's operating system residing on the original drive. It's not necessary to set the original drive to slave and make the data drive master—the opposite is preferred. Therefore, answer b is correct and answer c is incorrect. IDE drives don't use SCSI IDs—SCSI drives do. Therefore, answer d is incorrect.

Question 28

The correct answer is c. When in doubt, guess. More than likely, you'll be able to access the drive by picking a drive type. However, if the BIOS has an AUTO drive type, this solves the problem best. The other place you may reference for drive parameters is the Micro House Technical Library (MTL). Without knowing the correct drive parameters, you cannot determine which drive type to pick. Therefore, answers a and b are incorrect. Although it's preferable to know the exact drive parameters, you should be able to get the drive to work by simply picking another drive of equal size. Therefore, answer d is incorrect.

Question 29

The correct answers are a, b, and c. Low-level formatting of a disk sets the disk interleave ratio, tests the read/write heads, marks any bad sectors, writes data to each sector, creates disk tracks, and assigns sector IDs. Copying system files is a function of high-level formatting, not of low-level formatting. Therefore, answer d is incorrect.

Question 30

The correct answers are a, c, and d. High-level formatting scans the drive and identifies bad sectors, copies the system files, creates the file allocation table, creates an empty root directory, and creates the DOS boot sector. Assignment of sector IDs is a function of low-level formatting. Therefore, answer b is incorrect.

Question 31

The correct answer is b. Any partition other than a NetWare partition is identified as a non-NetWare partition. Only NetWare partitions on a NetWare server can be mirrored. Therefore, answer a is incorrect. You can install different versions of NetWare on the same partition, but you can't install the same version on the same partition. Therefore, answer c is incorrect. All partition numbering schemes begin with 0 as the first partition number. Therefore, answer d is incorrect.

Question 32

The correct answers are b and c. NetWare allows up to 64 volumes per server, with a total disk space of 32TB. Therefore, answers a and d are incorrect.

Question 33

The correct answer is d. By default, the NWFS.SYS file is found in the C:\WINNT\SYSTEM32 directory. The CLIENT32.NLM is found in the C:\NOVELL\CLIENT32 directory. Therefore, answer a is incorrect. HKEY_LOCAL_MACHINE\Network\Novell\System Config is the location in the Registry in which you can find many of the settings that pertain to the Novell Client. Therefore, answer b is incorrect. The C:\WINDOWS directory contains the REGEDIT.EXE file, and much more, but not the NWFS.SYS file. Therefore, answer c is incorrect.

Question 34

The correct answers are b and d. A volume has the capability to span a volume across multiple physical disks as well as to be the entire NetWare partition. The real benefit is the ability to combine small, unused spaces into a single, larger logical device. A NetWare volume can exist across multiple physical drives. Therefore, answer a is incorrect. A volume that spans multiple physical disks is not fault tolerant. A failure of any one of the physical drives results in a loss of the volume. Therefore, answer c is incorrect.

Question 35

The correct answer is b. Disk mirroring uses a single disk controller and two physical disk drives. Data writes simultaneously to both drives, so if a single drive fails, the secondary drive automatically takes over. If the disk controller fails, you have effectively lost access to the disk drives. Disk mirroring allows a single drive failure with no data loss or downtime. Therefore, answer a is a benefit and incorrect. Because disk duplexing requires two controllers and two disks, mirroring is less expensive than duplexing. Therefore, answer c is incorrect. Disk mirroring is indeed a fault-tolerant disk strategy. Therefore, answer d is incorrect.

Question 36

The correct answers are b, c, and d. SCSI CD-ROMs and SCSI disk drives occasionally compete for data transfer on a single cable. The best bet is to put the CD-ROM on its own disk controller. Alternatively, you can use a parallel port to the SCSI adapter and attach the CD-ROM to the adapter. If all is lost on the SCSI CD-ROM, the other alternative is to install an IDE CD-ROM. This problem can be corrected. Therefore, answer a is incorrect.

Question 37

The correct answer is c. Initial troubleshooting steps involve symptom identification and information gathering. Backing off a server patch is completely unnecessary. The remainder of the answers provide valuable data and basic troubleshooting techniques used to solve and understand the problem. Therefore, answers a, b, and d are incorrect.

Question 38

The correct answer is b. The key to the question is subnet. If the problem is restricted to a single subnet, the problem is centered on that subnet and not the server(s). Every computer, whether we realize it or not, has a bottleneck—a limiting piece of the computer system. Whether it's processing, memory, input/output, or disk performance, one of these is the limiting factor affecting overall performance. Adding memory to the servers helps the servers perform better. For any subsequent network request, the servers would simply respond faster and deliver more information in a shorter period back to the network, exacerbating the problem. Answers a, c, and d all help improve network performance and are therefore incorrect.

Question 39

The correct answer is c. When a problem surfaces, the first step is to investigate the problem and gather as many clues as possible about it. A common error even seasoned veterans make is to begin trying solutions before the problem is clearly understood. This is the shotgun approach. Therefore, answer a is incorrect. After you've investigated the problem, identified probable causes, determined a solution, and solved the problem, then, the problem is documented. Documentation assists others affected by the problem to help them quickly solve it. Therefore, answer b is incorrect. Probable cause identification occurs after symptom identification. Therefore, answer d is incorrect.

Question 40

The correct answer is d. Baselines are measurement tools. An analogy of a computer baseline is when you mark a child's height on a doorframe. That mark is periodically evaluated to identify not only change but also the amount of the change over time. The best time to implement a baseline measurement is when everything in a system is configured and under normal user load. It's not possible to establish a baseline until the operating system is installed. Therefore, answer a is incorrect. Until you install applications, the user community can't use them and a baseline measurement is useless. Therefore, answer b is incorrect. Baseline measurements with normal user load are critical. Therefore, answer c is incorrect.

Question 41

The correct answers are a, c, and d. IBM and Microsoft do not ship gateways with NetWare 5. Therefore, answers b and e are incorrect.

Question 42

The correct answer is b. PCONSOLE is used to configure printers. PPRINT, NCONSOLE, and PCONFIG are not valid NetWare programs. Therefore, answers a, c, and d are incorrect.

Question 43

The correct answers are b and c. Setting the Allow Service By Current Print Servers option to No prohibits print servers from using this printer, which eliminates print requests to the printer. Setting the Allow Users To Submit Print Jobs option to No prohibits users from submitting print requests to this printer. File Contents is a description field indicating the data content type of the print job. This is not user configurable. Therefore, answer a is incorrect. Setting Allow New Print Servers To Attach to Yes defeats the purpose of eliminating a print connection to the printer. Therefore, answer d is incorrect.

Question 44

The correct answer is a. Static occurs during periods of low humidity, not high humidity. Think about the number of times you've been shocked during the winter compared to the summer. We rarely get shocked in summertime because the humidity is higher. Humidity levels should be kept in the 70-to-90 percent range to virtually eliminate ESD. The remaining answers are all essential parts of an ESD program and help reduce ESD. Therefore, answers b, c, and d are incorrect.

Question 45

The correct answer is a. The only viable answer given is an incorrectly configured frame type. Using the simple process of elimination, if other computers can connect, it has power and is connected to the network. Therefore, answers b and c are incorrect. SCSI drive chains, not subnets, are terminated. Therefore, answer d is incorrect.

Question 46

The correct answers are b and d. Token ring is second only to FDDI in terms of expense. It's also not the simplest to administer and maintain. Token ring networks can use twisted-pair cabling, and a failure of a device does not bring down the network, making it somewhat fault tolerant. Therefore, answers a and c are incorrect.

Question 47

The correct answer is c. A controlled access printer has complete NDS security options. The other answers describe a public access printer. Therefore, answers a, b, and d are incorrect.

Question 48

The correct answer is d. FDDI is very fast. FDDI is not subject to EMI, it's very secure, and it can transmit over great distances. FDDI requires special tools and training for installation. It's not as easy to install as twisted-pair or coax cable, and it's not easy to administer. Therefore, answers a and c are incorrect. FDDI is the most expensive of the network options. Therefore, answer b is incorrect.

Question 49

The correct answers are b, c, and d. Electromagnetic interference (EMI) can drastically impact data transfer. It's strongly advisable that you route data cables away for EMI-generating components. SCSI devices each require a unique SCSI ID and proper termination. Improperly configured SCSI IDs and termination account for over 80 percent of SCSI-related failures. SCSI components are generally more expensive than IDE components, but this is not a consideration during the installation. Therefore, answer a is incorrect.

Question 50

The correct answer is c. SCSI HBAs are often set to 7 by default. It's highly likely the drive and HBA are using the same SCSI ID. Over 80 percent of SCSI-related issues extend from SCSI ID conflicts and improper termination. The SCSI ID 7 is valid. Therefore, answer a is incorrect. Although the drive being improperly terminated is a valid cause, it isn't the most likely. Therefore, answer b is incorrect. It's also quite possible the drive is defective; however, today's drives offer mean times between failure (MTBF) of 200,000 hours and can withstand several G-forces during nonoperation. Once again, this is not the most likely cause. Therefore, answer d is incorrect.

Question 51

The correct answer is d. In a disk mirroring configuration, if data written to a drive encounters a bad block, the data is immediately written to the Hot Fix Redirection area on that drive. The disk controller is never (directly) involved in this process. Therefore, answer a is incorrect. The data is written to the second drive—unless the Redirection Area(s) is exhausted, which causes a drive failure. Therefore, answer b is incorrect. A bad block failure is completely transparent to the user and no notification is sent. Therefore, answer c is incorrect.

Question 52

The correct answer is c. You cannot mirror non-NetWare partitions. Adding another drive and controller is disk duplexing, not disk mirroring. Therefore, answer a is incorrect. It doesn't matter if you have a million drives, NetWare does not mirror non-NetWare partitions. Therefore, answer b is incorrect. Creating another NetWare partition on the second drive does nothing to help achieve fault tolerance. Therefore, answer d is incorrect.

Question 53

The correct answer is b. In a RAID 1 configuration, a failure of the drive is not noticeable to the users. NetWare automatically switches to the remaining drive. Replacing the failed drive and rebooting will not restore fault tolerance. The INSTALL utility must be used to create a NetWare partition on the new drive. Then, you must mirror it to the existing drive before fault tolerance can be restored. In any case, that's not what the question asked. Therefore, answer a is incorrect. Nothing is wrong with the drive controller. It also doesn't answer the asked question. Therefore, answer c is incorrect. Fault tolerance offers recoverability. Therefore, answer d is incorrect.

Question 54

The correct answer is a. If a printer prints, but prints garbage, you're most likely using the wrong print driver. Installing the appropriate driver will fix the problem. A print queue is a holding spot for print jobs. If the print queue is corrupt, nothing is likely to print. Therefore, answer b is incorrect. If there were insufficient disk space for the queue, the job would never complete from the client. Therefore, answer c is incorrect. PCONSOLE is an administrative tool for managing printers. It would not cause garbled output whether installed or not. Therefore, answer d is incorrect.

Question 55

The correct answer is c. LANalyzer is a tool for investigating networks, and although it can be used to investigate some types of problems on computers, it's not the best tool in most situations and it's seldom used in this way. Answers a, b, and d are all tools used for investigation and troubleshooting of computers and are therefore incorrect.

Question 56

The correct answers are c, d, and e. Subordinate replicas do not contain complete copies of the partition and do not provide any extra protection in numbers. Therefore, answer a is incorrect. Using a third-party desktop utility for Windows is not a good choice for checking Novell volumes. Therefore, answer b is incorrect.

Question 57

The correct answer is d. The Multiple Link Interface Driver (MLID) is a network board driver and directly compared to a device driver. A protocol stack, network media, and network board are components required for network communication; however, they are not directly related to the MLID. Therefore, answers a, b, and c are incorrect.

Question 58

The correct answer is a. The Link Support Layer (LSL) interfaces the protocol stack(s) and the MLID. Both the LSL and MLID exist in the Data Link layer of the OSI model. The protocol stack exists in the Network layer and communicates to the LSL. The LSL talks to the MLID, and the MLID communicates with the network boards in the Physical layer. Therefore, answers b, c, and d are incorrect.

Question 59

The correct answer is b. Because answer b is correct, answer a is incorrect. Answer c describes a warm site and is therefore incorrect. Answer d describes specialized services and is therefore incorrect.

Question 60

The correct answer is d. CLIENT32.TXT and C32MODULES.NLM are made up file names. Therefore, answers a and c are incorrect. The NET.CFG file is a text-based configuration file for management of Novell's Client32. Therefore, answer b is incorrect.

Question 61

The correct answers are b and c. The active monitor checks to make sure the ring does not have more than one active monitor (not standby monitor), and it's the first device that enters the ring (not the last). In a token ring network, the active monitor sends out special "hello" packets every seven seconds, maintains the master clock, and handles lost tokens. Therefore, answers a, d, and e are roles of the active monitor and are incorrect.

Question 62

The correct answer is b. Although it's possible to create the print server first, it's not possible to create it and assign printers without first creating the printers. Therefore, answer a is incorrect. The print queue must be created before assigning a volume. Therefore, answer b is incorrect. To assign a print queue to a printer, both must first be created. Therefore, answer d is incorrect.

Question 63

The correct answer is a. IRQs 3 and 4 are well-known ports for serial ports. If you configured the network board for either of these IRQs, there's a conflict with a serial port. The printer port, LPT1, is usually IRQ 7. Therefore, answer b is incorrect. Floppy drives are almost always IRQ 6. Therefore, answer c is incorrect. Keyboards are often on IRQ 5, although not always. Therefore, answer d is incorrect.

Question 64

The correct answer is d. There is no semi-dynamic patch. Static patches modify the SERVER.EXE file, causing permanent changes to the SERVER.EXE. (To revert to a previous version, you must have a backup.) Therefore, answer a is incorrect. Dynamic patches are easily loaded and unloaded. Novell implements them as NetWare Loadable Modules (NLMs). Therefore, answer b is incorrect. Semi-static patches are one way. They are easily loaded during server operation but require a server restart to unload them. Therefore, answer c is incorrect.

Question 65

The correct answer is b. When a computer loads CONFIG.NLM, it generates an output file named CONFIG.TXT, containing a listing of all loaded modules, configuration files, and listings of the boot and system directories. The file is written to the SYS:\SYSTEM directory. Therefore, answers a, c, and d are incorrect.

Question 66

The correct answer is c. Both the Novell Support Connection Web site and CD-ROM provide listings of available patches and fixes for Novell's client and servers. However, the Web site will always provide the most current information. Therefore, answer b is incorrect. Micro House Technical Library (MTL) does not contain bug or patch information. Therefore, answer a incorrect. Technical Training Centers are responsible for delivery of approved Novell technical training, not the dissemination of patches and fixes. Therefore, answer d is incorrect.

Question 67

The correct answer is c. Although inadequate server memory results in slower server performance, it has no impact on a network. Large file transfers use network bandwidth, resulting in poor overall network performance. Therefore, answer a is incorrect. Server-launched applications, typically in a network that supports thin clients, cause more frequent network accesses over a traditional client/server network. Therefore, answer b is incorrect. If additional network clients gain access to a network, overall traffic increases because of name resolution, broadcasts, and overall increases in resource consumption. Therefore, answer d is incorrect.

Question 68

The correct answer is d. The files must be restored from backup. VREPAIR fixes corrupted disk volumes. Running VREPAIR will not recover deleted files. Therefore, answer a is incorrect. DSREPAIR fixes problems in the NDS database. It does not recover deleted files. Therefore, answer b is incorrect. WINMSD is Windows Microsoft System Diagnostics. WINMSD is a helpful tool for discovering system-wide configurations and parameters, but it's utterly useless for file restoration. Therefore, answer c is incorrect.

Question 69

The correct answer is b. NetWare 5 no longer supports modules with a DSK extension. The more modular HAM drivers are used. Therefore, answer a is incorrect. .DRV and .COM are typical extensions for drivers used on a DOS- or Windows-based machine. Therefore, answers c and d are incorrect .NSS is the extension for the different NSS support modules such as CD9660.NSS. Therefore, answer e is incorrect.

Question 70

The correct answer is d. A print job must completely spool to the print server's hard drive prior to printing. If the file is very large, that would account for the time the application takes to transfer the file to the print server. Answers a, b, and c are all reasons the job would fail to print, not take a long time to print; therefore, they are incorrect.

Question 71

The correct answer is c. If the user fails to receive print job errors, more than likely the print jobs are printing, but possibly to another printer. Ask the user to double-check his or her printer selection. Answers a, b, and d would all generate printer errors and are therefore incorrect.

Question 72

The correct answer is a. Printer problems are categorized as occurring either before or after the print queue. Data is arriving at the printer but appears as garbage characters. This is likely the cause of a corrupt or incorrect printer driver. Reinstalling the driver will quickly eliminate this problem. If there were a problem with the print queue, the print job would never make it to the printer. Therefore, answer b is incorrect. If the printer had a paper jam, nothing would print. Therefore, answer c is incorrect. If the printer had an IRQ conflict with another device, either one or both devices would fail and the user would be unable to print. Therefore, answer d is incorrect.

Question 73

The best answer is a. When a scheduled backup initiates, it can be configured to clear all current connections, including print jobs initiated with the **CAPTURE** command. This results in jobs that fail to print. It's unlikely that a server is shut down for the weekend. Therefore, answer b is incorrect. Although answer c might happen once or twice, somebody would discover the error and add correct paper for the next print run. Because the problem reoccurs, a scheduled job, such as a backup, is a better reason. Therefore, answer c is incorrect. The print queue writes to the print server's hard disk. When the print server's hard disk fills up, the applications printing to it wait until space is available. Therefore, answer d is incorrect.

Question 74

The correct answer is b. For a print job to print, it must completely spool to the print queue. If the print server has insufficient available disk space and never successfully queues, it will never print. If the print queue is corrupt, no jobs print. Therefore, answer a is incorrect. The correct print driver must be installed because the smaller jobs successfully print. Print drivers are selected based on printer type, not size of files. Therefore, answer c is incorrect. A print queue manages the amount of data sent to a printer's buffer. Printers rarely contain a lot of memory. They simply receive the output from the print queue. Therefore, answer d is incorrect.

Question 75

The correct answers are a and d. Valid print queue names can contain alphanumeric characters. Answers b and c are incorrect queue names because they contain nonalphanumeric characters.

Question 76

The correct answers are a and b. Insufficient memory and outdated executables are the most likely culprits. NET.CFG does not contain configuration parameters for RPRINTER. Therefore, answer c is incorrect. RPRINTER initialization has nothing to do with a printer being offline. Therefore, answer d is incorrect.

Question 77

The correct answers are a, b, c, and d. All four are valid troubleshooting tips.

Question 78

The correct answers are a and c. The problem for the users is printer throughput and the print jobs are filling up in the queue. The way to alleviate the problem is to either add a faster printer or add additional printers to the existing print queue. Adding additional queues only further overloads the printer. Therefore, answer b is incorrect. Routers subdivide a network into physical segments. A router doesn't do anything to fix this problem. Therefore, answer d is incorrect.

Question 79

The correct answer is b. There's no such thing as a "printer object license." Answers a, c, and d are valid NDPS components and are therefore incorrect.

Appendix A: Windows Networking

This appendix explores elements of advanced networking. As an administrator, you must understand the complex concepts used to create and maintain a network. It's also important to understand the underlying architectural components from the cable up.

Networking is the connection of computers for the purpose of sharing information and resources. Many of the elements of networking are often misunderstood or poorly implemented in today's networks. Windows NT uses a layered design for its underlying network architecture. The heart of Windows NT, referred to as the *kernel*, is made up of three components: Executive Services, Hardware Abstraction Layer, and the Microkernel. The Executive Services component houses device drivers, the I/O (Input/Output) Manager, the Object Manager, graphics device drivers, the Win32K Windows Manager and Graphics Device Interface (GDI), the Virtual Memory Manager (VMM), the Local Procedure Call Facility, the Process Manager, and the Security Reference Monitor.

The Windows NT network architecture's central component is the I/O Manager. As its name implies, the I/O Manager controls all system input and output. If installed, it manages several Windows NT components, including the redirector, the Multiple Universal Naming Convention Provider (MUP), the Multiple Provider Router (MPR), network providers, network board providers, protocol stacks, and the Network Driver Interface Specification (NDIS) and Open Data-Link Interface (ODI) LAN drivers.

The Redirector

A redirector intercepts and processes network connection requests on behalf of the user. The redirector is similar to a dynamically linked library because it loads and unloads when called by the computer system. When a request occurs for a file that's not local to the calling computer, the I/O Manager intercepts the network request. The redirector then sends the request to the remote server. This transaction occurs at the Network layer of the Open Systems Interconnection (OSI) model. Applications can run in either user mode or kernel mode. The advantage of applications running in kernel mode is that the calling application can call other device driver and kernel mode components directly, without processing an intermediate step. This results in a direct performance enhancement for the computer system. The redirector gives way to the extra advantage of allowing an application to call a single Application Programming Interface (API) for redirecting program calls.

MUP

When a process issues a request for a Universal Naming Convention (UNC) path, the request is serviced by the Multiple UNC Provider (MUP). A UNC path starts with a pair of backslashes, followed by a computer name or IP address, optionally appended with a share name. The following are examples of proper syntax for UNC paths:

```
\\server_name\share_name
\\10.0.0.2\routerbits
\\magnacarta
```

The only required component in a UNC path is the computer name or IP address. Anything following either of these is optional. The MUP keeps a list of paths to all known redirectors and supports multiple redirectors installed on the same computer. When an application requests a UNC path, the request is passed to the MUP. The MUP checks cache to determine whether the request was fulfilled within the past 15 minutes. (The MUP retains filled requests in cache for 15 minutes.) If the requested UNC path is not in cache, the MUP queries all known redirectors and asks them if they're capable of fulfilling the request. The redirector with the best response time to the MUP completes the request. (Note that this architecture creates a potential response time problem if one or more of the configured redirectors has an access problem.)

MPR

The Multiple Provider Router (MPR) works in tandem with the MUP to service I/O requests. If a Win32 API application requests network access, it's filled by the MPR. The MPR works in a similar nature to the MUP. The MPR queries known redirectors to satisfy the network request. It's common for third-party vendors to supply their own libraries for redirector communications.

Network Providers

When an application requests resources, a network provider fulfills it. Microsoft includes network-type specific network providers with Windows NT Server 4. Novell packages network providers with its clients that integrate into the Windows NT environment to satisfy user logon requests, network browsing, Novell Directory Services (NDS), network authentication, and access to NetWare resources.

Network Board Providers

For a protocol to communicate with a network board, it must be bound to the board. Bindings link both services and protocols to lower-layer board drivers in a computer. Once a protocol is bound to the network board, the board is able to communicate using those protocols. Windows NT supports multiple protocols bound to a single network board. The binding interface in Windows NT is NetBIOS and it can bind to several protocols, such as NetBIOS Enhanced User Interface (NetBEUI), NWLink, and Transmission Control Protocol/Internet Protocol (TCP/IP).

When unused protocols are bound to a network board, network I/O performance suffers because unnecessary communication through the other protocols occurs. If the most used protocol is first in the binding list, average connection time decreases. When a connection request arrives, the redirector issues a connection request to each bound transport protocol in parallel. The redirector waits until the higher-priority protocols respond. This generates additional network traffic for every bound protocol (for example, a network board that has both NetBEUI and TCP/IP bound to it). TCP/IP is first in the binding order, and a host makes a request for a network resource. NetBEUI is a more efficient protocol than TCP/IP or Internetwork Packet Exchange (IPX) and will more than likely connect first. Because TCP/IP is the first protocol bound, it ultimately establishes a connection to the resource, and the NetBEUI protocol is dropped. Additionally, the NetBEUI protocol makes an initial broadcast when attempting to establish a network connection, therefore generating more traffic on the network.

When used in a small network, NetBEUI is a fast and efficient protocol. Internetwork Packet Exchange/Sequenced Packet Exchange (IPX/SPX) is not as fast as NetBEUI, but it's easier to configure than TCP/IP. Actually, NetBEUI only requires installation; no network configuration is required because NetBEUI has no network layer. TCP/IP is the protocol used on the Internet; therefore, it's the most widely used. Multiple protocols often exist within a single network. For improved security, it's possible to add IPX/SPX to a network and use proxy servers to access Internet resources. The proxy servers have both TCP/IP and IPX/SPX bound to one (or separate) network board(s). The two protocols act as translators for internetwork communications. A person trying to infiltrate the network using TCP/IP-based tools would have a much harder time crossing the proxy. On the proxy server, IPX/SPX is bound to the internal adapter. TCP/IP is the only protocol bound to the external adapter connected to the Internet.

Note: A network board is also called a network interface card (NIC), network adapter, network card, and network interface board. Novell uses the term network board most often, and Microsoft uses the term network adapter. However, the network board vendors usually call it a NIC.

Binding Optimization

The first step in binding optimization is to uninstall unused protocols. You must understand your network implementation when determining required and unnecessary protocols. If a computer has NetBEUI installed in a routed network, it's a safe bet that NetBEUI is an unnecessary protocol. To remove unused bindings in Windows NT, select Start|Settings|Control Panel and open the Network applet. Next, select the Protocols tab, highlight the desired protocol, and click on Remove. In Windows 95/98, select Start|Settings|Control Panel and open the Network applet. Then, select the Configuration tab, highlight the desired protocol, and click on remove. The binding information is updated in the Registry and you're prompted to reboot to have the change take effect.

Windows accesses protocols in order, as listed in the binding order. Again, it's important to understand the mission of the network. The most frequently used binding should be at the top of the binding list. Let's assume your binding order has NetBEUI first and TCP/IP second. We'll also assume that you need both protocols, but TCP/IP is the most frequently used. To modify the binding order in Windows NT, we again open the Network applet in Control Panel by selecting Start|Settings|Control Panel and double-clicking the Network applet. Select the Bindings tab and click the Move Up or Move Down button to reorder the protocols.

To add a new binding to a network board on a Windows NT Server, you must first add the new protocol. To do so, click Start|Settings|Control Panel, open the Network applet, and select the Protocols tab. Click the Add button and select the desired protocol.

Enabling And Disabling Binding For Network Interfaces

After you add a protocol, you can manage protocol bindings for each interface device. Select the Bindings tab from the Network applet in Control Panel. Using the Show Bindings As combo box, select All Adapters. Bindings are viewed by service, adapter, or protocol. The adapter view shows each adapter and associated bound protocol. To unbind a protocol, simply disable it. Expand the adapter's entry by clicking the + symbol preceding the adapter's name, highlight the desired protocol, and then click the Disable button. This effectively disables the protocol from the adapter.

If you have concerns in your networking environment about bindings and exactly what's going on behind the scenes, Network Monitor is a good starting point for investigation and troubleshooting. Fewer protocols mean less traffic, less exposure to hacks, and less administration.

Protocol Stacks

Computers need a language to communicate with each other—just like people do. Each language has a grammar, syntax, and words—human or computer. Computer communications, which are purposefully designed, are logically constructed around tasks, such as authentication and access, naming, file transfer, and so on. Typically, each task has its own small set of instructions, known as *protocols*. If you group related protocols, they form a *protocol suite*.

To provide extensibility and general utility, the implementation of a protocol suite is generally split into different components: the applications that perform tasks (such as FTP, Telnet, or PCONSOLE, and the lower-level language components, or *protocol stacks*).

Computers on the Internet are able to communicate because of the TCP/IP protocol suite. TCP/IP must reside on each computer attached to the Internet. Other protocols include IPX/SPX, AppleTalk, and Systems Network Architecture (SNA). All these protocols can be represented by a logical model. The most common model used is the seven-layer OSI reference model. Each logical layer of the OSI model more or less maps to one or more layers in an actual implementation.

Each layer, or *level*, of a protocol performs a different function and communicates with the layer directly above or directly below itself. The exception to this rule is the Physical layer. At this layer of the stack, a transmitted packet is transmitted on the physical network media. The Physical layer is the lowest-level layer of a stack.

As a review, the OSI model contains seven layers: Physical, Data Link, Network, Transport, Session, Presentation, and Application. In the broadest sense, Layers 1 and 2 (Physical and Data Link) define a network's physical media and the signaling characteristics necessary to send and receive information across the network medium and to request access to use the medium for transmission. Layers 3 and 4 (Network and Transport) move information from sender to receiver and handle the data to be sent or received. Layers 5 through 7 (Session, Presentation, and Application) manage ongoing communications across a network and deal with how data is to be represented and interpreted for use in specific applications or for delivery across the network.

Each layer concerns itself with a specific element of data transmission. As data moves from layer to layer, header (and trailer) information is added to or stripped from each packet. Each layer concerns itself with a certain aspect of the data and, in effect, insulates the packet from the other layers. This is analogous to placing a letter in an envelope, the envelope in a small box, the small box in a larger box, the larger box in a shipping container, and then the shipping container in a truck. Each layer provides services for the adjacent layer but hides previous information from the remainder of the layers. When the letter arrives at the destination, each container opens in sequence. Therefore, it would be impossible to open the envelope without first opening the small box, and so on. With actual data transmission, when the letter is ready to be sent, it's broken into packets. Individually, each packet would follow the previous process.

If we follow a request sent from an application on Network A to an application on Network B, we see that each layer adds some information to the packet as it's passed layer to layer. Likewise, when the packet reaches the receiving network, information strips itself from the packet as the packet is passed up the protocol stack.

Because the Internet is a network, connections exist between adjacent networks. These connections occur through routers. As your packet moves across the Internet toward the destination computer, the packet has to pass through a router. A router operates at the Network layer. Because a router is a Network layer device, the packet to be received arrives at the Physical layer, passes through the Data Link layer, and arrives at the Network layer. The router determines the correct destination for the packet, repackages (*encapsulates*) it, and passes it to the Physical layer components.

Applications communicate using IPX to manage IPX sockets. IPX routes its packets to the correct application's calling socket. Therefore, if three applications communicate using IPX, each will open a socket connection from the server to the client. When a packet arrives at the destination, IPX routes the packet to the correct socket servicing that particular application. IPX determines the appropriate network segment for the packet enroute to the destination. Microsoft has delivered the NWLink protocol for use by NetBIOS and Winsock applications. NWLink is IPX/SPX-compatible.

NDIS

The Network Driver Interface Specification (NDIS) 5 represents an extension set of functionality to NDIS 4 and NDIS 3.x. NDIS 5 extends previous versions of NDIS, so the basic requirements, services, terminology, and architecture of earlier versions also apply to NDIS 5. The new NDIS 5 architecture is included with Windows 98 and will be included in the Windows 2000 operating systems. Windows NT Server 4 and Workstation do not support NDIS 5.

NDIS 4 added the following features to NDIS 3.1:

➤ Out-of-band data support

➤ A wireless wide area network (WAN) media extension

➤ High-speed packet send and receive

➤ Media sense

➤ An "All Local" packet filter to prevent Network Monitor from using 100 percent CPU time

➤ Miniport binary compatibility across Windows NT and Windows 95/98

NDIS 5 adds the following functionality to NDIS 4:

➤ NDIS power management, required for network power management and network wake up

➤ Plug-and-play support for Windows 2000 drivers

➤ Windows hardware instrumentation support for structured, cross-platform management of NDIS miniports and their associated adapters

➤ A simplified network INF format across Windows operating systems based on the Windows 95 INF format

➤ A deserialized miniport for improved performance on Windows 2000 multiprocessor systems

➤ New mechanisms for offloading tasks such as TCP/IP checksum, IP security, TCP message segmentation, and Fast Packet Forwarding to intelligent hardware

➤ A broadcast media extension required for broadcast components

➤ Connection-oriented NDIS—required for native access to connection-oriented media such as Asynchronous Transfer Mode (ATM), Asymmetric Digital Subscriber Lines (ADSLs), cable modems, and Integrated Services Digital Network (ISDN)

➤ Support for quality of service (QoS) when supported by the media

➤ An intermediate driver support required for broadcast components, such as virtual LANs, LAN emulation, packet scheduling for QoS, and NDIS support over the Universal Serial Bus (USB)

ODI

Before Open Data-Link Interface (ODI) existed, developers had to write specific network drivers for each protocol stack a network board used. These drivers did not coexist well with other drivers and were particularly poor when they supported more than one protocol stack in a single computer. ODI enables network boards to support many different protocols, allowing a network board to support multiple protocols in a single computer as well as to use the same physical network. This implies that instead of requiring developers to code multiple drivers, ODI only requires a single driver to support multiple protocols for a network board.

The components that make up the ODI are the Link Support Layer (LSL) and the Multiple Link Interface Device (MLID). The LSL corresponds to part of the Network layer and part of the Data Link layer, whereas the MLID exists solely within the Data Link layer of the OSI model. The LSL is a communications interface to the protocol stack. An NE2000.COM driver is an example of an MLID. An MLID is a network board driver that supports the ODI specification.

LSL

The Link Support Layer (LSL) communicates with the protocols on behalf of the network board. The LSL is unique to the individual operating system. An LSL from DOS, for example, cannot be used in NetWare 4.11. If a computer has two network boards—one Ethernet and the other token ring—each has an associated network board driver, called an MLID, and each driver communicates through the LSL to a protocol stack. The LSL acts as an intelligent traffic cop to route communication requests to the appropriate protocol stack. The significance of the LSL is that a network board vendor only needs to write a single driver that's capable of communicating with the LSL layer within a specific computer system. The LSL also does not need to be rewritten each time a new network board is added. It's now logical that the LSL lives in the lower half of the Network layer and the upper half of the Data Link layer of the OSI model. DOS loads its LSL using the file LSL.COM.

MLID

A Multiple Link Interface Driver (MLID) is a network board driver. The MLID is coded to interface with the LSL. In the ODI specification, a single MLID is needed regardless of the number or types of protocols serviced by the network board. MLIDs exist only in the Data Link layer of the OSI model. There's nothing "magical" about an MLID. If a new protocol was developed today and the protocol was coded to the interface provided by the LSL, the existing network board driver, or *MLID*, would function normally. When an MLID receives a packet through the Physical layer components, it simply passes the packet to the LSL. The MLID is a "dumb traffic cop." It only routes traffic to a place and doesn't question or peer into the packets at all. MLIDs are often referred to as *ODI drivers*. The NET.CFG file contains configuration data for MLIDs used in a NetWare DOS environment.

During the MLID loading process, the LSL assigns a number to each network board within a computer system. When a protocol registers with the LSL, the protocol is assigned a stack number.

Need To Know More?

 Tittel, Ed and David Johnson. *A Guide To Networking Essentials*. Course Technologies, Cambridge, MA, 1998. ISBN 0-7600-5097-X. Chapter 4, "Network Interface Cards," discusses NDIS and ODI standards.

 www.ftp.com/techsup/ftpsoft/info/ndis.html is the FTP Software site. It provides a great technical support page called "Published FAQs & TechNotes Referencing NDIS" that contains a great deal of NDIS information and facts.

 www.microsoft.com/hwdev/devdes/ndis5.htm contains an article titled "Introduction to NDIS 5.0," which describes what's coming with NDIS 5.0. Take a look at this Microsoft site for an introduction to NDIS 5.0.

Appendix B: Magneto-Optical Drives

This appendix concentrates on the basics of optical drive technology. It covers how magneto-optical (MO) drives work, how they are used, and gives Web addresses where you can learn more. We only mention write once, read many (WORM) drives in this appendix because they're similar in nature to the technologies of MO drives. We will not discuss WORM drives in any detail.

Optical Drive Basics

Magneto-optical (MO) drives are a combination of laser power and magnetics. MO technology delivers rewritable, removable media capable of storing vast amounts of information. When you clean out your hard drives, you decide which items have value and need to be kept and which items need to be thrown away. Some items fall somewhere in between. Data management is certainly no different. When you evaluate data stores, you achieve similar results. Some data is important and needs to be kept, whereas other data may be out-of-date and can be thrown away or stored on external media.

In recent years, it was common practice to simply use a tape drive and move the not-so-important data to a tape. However, storing data to tape has its problems. For example, tape is slow, and the data is stored in sequential order. If the data is written at the end of the tape, the tape drive looks up the data location in the table of contents and then forwards the tape to the storage point.

Data migration is the process of moving data from fast online storage to not-quite-as-fast, near-online storage and, finally, to offline storage, which is where MO storage comes in. MO is nearly as fast as a hard drive and significantly faster than tape. Like tape, the storage capacity of MO can be extended by buying more media. Several MO manufacturers offer magneto-optical juke-boxes, which provide automated retrieval of multiple MO disks.

Most of the MO standards center around the capacity and format of 5.25-inch disks and exactly what makes up a multifunction disk. The most widely used format is based on capacities of approximately 325MB per side (650MB on a double-sided disk). The basic standards that describe MO drives are ISO 9171 (write-once) and ISO 10089 (rewritable).

All the standards allow formatting for either 512KB (for both PC and Macintosh) or 1,024KB per sector (Unix). The capacities are slightly greater at 1,024KB per sector, and vendors frequently state the capacity in terms of the higher number.

How MO Drives Operate

First, don't confuse MO drives with WORM drives. WORM drives don't offer the ability to reuse media, whereas MO drives do. WORM is similar to CD-ROM technology. With WORM, data is written to the media once and only once. MO uses magnetic technology and laser optics to write information to the MO media. MO media contains several layers of a metallic medium sandwiched between layers of Lexan. The Lexan protects the inner layers of media. The laser acts to read and write information, and the magnetics distort the inner media. In a write operation, the laser focuses on a particular area on the media and heats it. The magnetic elements distort the inner media layers to form data points. Once the laser moves away from the focused area, the media is distorted in such a way as to now hold written data. The laser alone reads the data points, albeit at a much lower intensity level. To erase data, the process is similar except the magnetic elements smooth the inner media surfaces rather than distort peaks and valleys.

Why Use Magneto-Optical

MO technology offers some distinct advantages over both hard drives and tape drives. Here are the reasons most often noted:

➤ **Extensibility** You can add extra storage capacity simply by swapping media. Most corporations that use MO use it as intermediate-level near-online storage prior to migrating data to slower tape. Network-connected jukeboxes allow multiple computers to read and write data remotely.

➤ **Speed** *Fast* is a relative term, but MO performs in the 20-to-50 milli-seconds access time range. Small Computer System Interface (SCSI) drive arrays report in the sub-10 milliseconds access time range, and tape response is in the several hundred milliseconds to several seconds or minutes access time range.

➤ **Access** MO drives are randomly accessed, unlike tape drives, which are sequentially accessed. This access method improves speed and reduces device wear.

➤ **Maintainability** Because MO drives don't use traditional read/write heads like hard drives, drive head crashes are impossible. The media is on par with CD-ROM media in terms of longevity. The MO media can be reused several hundred thousand times without data loss.

➤ **Backups** MO subsystems allow data backups at near hard drive speeds. Compared with tape systems, MO delivers consistently faster network backups.

➤ **Media life** MO media manufacturers indicate that the life expectancy of their media is well over 10 years. Although the technology will certainly change during that time, the media itself expects a longer life.

➤ **Multiple data types** MO media places no restrictions on file formats. It's capable of storing anything normally stored on a hard disk.

MO also has a few disadvantages when compared with other media types:

➤ **Price** If we compare MO subsystems with tape subsystems based on price, tape subsystems are cheaper. MO systems are comparable in cost to hard disk storage. You must make a determination about the usefulness of the data and timely response to a user's data requests.

➤ **Compatibility** Although there are International Organization for Standardization (ISO) and American National Standards Institute (ANSI) standards for MO, that doesn't mean every manufacturer follows them. Buyers should beware when selecting a MO manufacturer.

➤ **System use** Current MO drive media is 5.25 inches. This makes the physical drive size too large to fit in a standard laptop. As technology improves, we should see smaller MO components.

Need To Know More?

 www.research.ibm.com/research/nmt.html is an online article recognizing the three IBM scientists who discovered magneto-optical technology. The IBM researchers who were honored at White House ceremonies are Praveen Chaudhari, Jerome J. Cuomo (retired), and Richard J. Gambino (retired).

 www.polyu.edu.hk/Datapro/toc06159.htm is a Web site that offers extensive information related to the magneto-optical technology as well as links to manufacturers' Web information.

Appendix C: Memory Core Dump

Memory core dumps in computer systems are pictures of a computer's memory contents at the time the dump occurs. NetWare 5 and NetWare 4.11 require setting parameters for manual recovery mode. Memory core dumps are often large, and their sizes depend on the quantity of physically installed memory. Core dumps may occur programmatically, manually, or by responding to system prompts following a server abnormal end (abend).

A core dump is useful as a troubleshooting tool, but often as a last resort. For example, if a server displays errant behavior without generating error messages, a core dump provides internal system details to technical staff for evaluation. Another scenario would be during a server crash—politely referred to as an *abend*—when the option to create a memory dump is not presented. Should a forced memory dump ever be required and the server is running properly, press the left Shift, right Shift, Alt, and Esc keys at the same time. Should the keyboard not respond, issue a nonmaskable interrupt (NMI) against the CPU to force a memory dump. The preceding key sequence launches the debugger. After the debugger is open, type ".c" in the debugger to start a memory dump copy.

Prior to creating the dump file, you must be sensitive to the dump file's size requirements. NetWare versions 3.12 and newer allow you to write the dump file to any DOS-mappable local or network drive. You can copy memory dumps to floppy disk, a local disk drive, a network path, or the local parallel port. Remember that the size of the core dump will closely equal the amount of physical RAM in the computer. If you're running NetWare 3.11, you'll need to use a NetWare Loadable Module (NLM) called HDUMP.NLM. This NLM is available from the Novell Support Connection site (**http://support.novell.com**), and it allows you to write the memory dump file to a DOS local or network drive rather than to floppies.

If your server has a modest amount of physical RAM (for example, 256MB), writing the memory dump file to floppy disk will take some time. Dumps to floppy disk should only be considered if the physical RAM is small or you have no other option. The two preferred methods are to dump to a local hard drive or to a network drive. Dumping to a local hard drive should be your first choice. When this is completed, the dump file (COREDUMP.IMG) can be compressed and sent for evaluation. There is no restriction on the method of data transfer when sending the file. Dumping to a network drive requires a bit more effort than dumping to a physical local disk drive. This method must be somewhat premeditated. The server must have an additional network board installed prior to the abend event with a Virtual Loadable Module (VLM) client or NETX.COM bound to the board. Additionally, the network connection must be kept connected for the additional network board. NETALIVE.NLM provides such a service. To configure the server for such an event, follow these steps:

1. Restart the server as a NetWare client.

2. Connect to a NetWare server on the network.

3. Map a network drive to the now-connected server and verify sufficient space to contain the memory dump file.

4. Execute SERVER.EXE from the DOS partition.

5. Maintain the secondary network board's server connection using NETALIVE.NLM.

Core dumping to the parallel port is often an overlooked option. It's quite simple to implement but requires the addition of extra hardware. To implement the parallel port method, you need a parallel port hard disk drive. Any device where the device's drivers can load from a CONFIG.SYS file would constitute a valid backup mechanism. If you have several servers you want to make parallel port dump-capable, follow this plan:

1. Attach the parallel device to the server and reboot.

2. After the server boot gets past the DOS-based portion, you may remove the drive from the parallel port.

3. NetWare still assumes, although incorrectly, the device is still connected. You may then move on to the next server.

4. When a server abend occurs, simply reattach the drive and export the core dump file to the parallel device.

Another potential solution to the core dump size problem is to use NetWare 5 and/or the third-party product Alexander LAN. Both of these allow stripping the cache buffers before dumping memory. Alexander LAN has additional capabilities, including an improved debugger that allows isolating a single thread (in the case of an errant NLM, the NLM may then be unloaded and reloaded without downing the server) and is an outstanding crash-analysis tool. The analysis tool is simple to use and understand and does an excellent job of determining the cause of an abend. It also has the capability to package the crash analysis (with a runtime viewer) to send the crash to Novell, Alexander LAN, or any third-party developer for additional help. Alexander LAN runs on NetWare versions 3.11 through 5.

Handling Server Abends

What really happens when a server abends, and what should you do when one occurs? When a server abends, it attempts to deliver the cause and time of the abend. The message "Abend in process *NLM_name*.NLM" indicates that *NLM_name*.NLM caused the failure. In reality, that message is often symptomatic rather then exacting. Another process calling or passing information to *NLM_name*.NLM may actually trigger the abend but cause the failure in *NLM_name*.NLM. To attempt to avoid abends altogether, try the following:

➤ Verify that all static and dynamic patches are current.

➤ Verify that the drivers on all network boards are current.

➤ Analyze the abend, such as the time of the event, event repeatability (that is, can you reproduce it by cycling the monitor power switch?), and what conditions exist when the abend occurs.

If the abend events continue to occur, make sure you do the following:

1. Find out where the fault originated.

2. If the abend was generated by a processor exception, figure out which type of processor exception. If it was generated by software, go to the next step.

3. Gather troubleshooting information. Remember to do the following:

   ➤ Document all screen information.

   ➤ Launch the debugger and press the ? key to record all NLM and function screen information.

➤ Press the R key to record the running process information.

4. Determine what the state of the operating system was when the abend occurred.

5. Attempt to restart NetWare. If these steps don't work, you need to contact Novell Technical Support. They will request the following information, so it's best to prepare it ahead of time:

➤ The version of NetWare you're running.

➤ The frequency of the abends.

➤ When the first abend happened, what the most recent change to take place on the network was that might have affected the server. Here are some examples:

➤ An upgrade of local, server, or host software

➤ A change of hardware

➤ Additional users on the system

➤ More traffic on the network

➤ A changed system configuration

➤ The use of new features, such as printing, security, or IP address pools.

➤ The hardware used, including information such as server make, model, and specification, as well as the amount of memory.

➤ The network board used and the version of driver.

Additionally, you'll want to locate a copy of CONFIG.NLM (preferably the latest). If no CONFIG.NLM output is supplied, you should at least supply a copy of all NCF files, including AUTOEXEC.NCF from the SYS:\SYSTEM directory and the STARTUP.NCF file. If AUTOEXEC.NCF calls any other NCF files, be sure to supply those as well. Also, supply version numbers of all NLMs loaded. Executing the **MODULES** command at the server console will give you this list.

In NetWare 4, NLMs can be loaded in protected rings. In theory, the server can load an NLM in a protected ring to ensure it does not abend the server. All new NLMs should be loaded in protected rings during testing. Different levels of rings perform different levels of checks. The more checks made, the slower the NLM operates. Certain other commands, such as the following, can be typed at the NetWare 4 console to protect the server against abends:

```
SET READ FAULT EMULATION=ON
SET WRITE FAULT EMULATION=ON
```

These commands will check every read and write to and from memory. If any NLM attempts to read/write information to an address out of its allocated memory space, NetWare reports it to the main console screen rather than abending the server.

 Novell has an excellent Abend Recovery Tool. You can download this file by accessing the TID titled "Abend Troubleshooting Guide." Search **http://support.novell.com** for TID 2927789.

Systematic Response

Every problem has a solution. The trick to finding the answer lies within six troubleshooting steps:

➤ **Investigate.** This is a reconnaissance mission. The mission is not to engage the enemy but rather to gather as much information as possible. When you're troubleshooting, the trick is to gather pertinent information. The previous section lists the information Novell requires to understand your environment.

➤ **Identify causes.** Two options exist when identifying possible causes: You can either build a list or eliminate possibilities. If the problem just surfaced, it probably isn't the hard disk you added two years ago. However, if you just upgraded a static patch this morning and the abend occurred 20 minutes after that, you've identified a possible cause.

➤ **Test your guesses.** This step contains two smaller steps. First, identify which solutions should fix the problem and then test the solutions in a controlled manner. Let's say you determine three possible solutions, and one solution seems the most likely; however, it will take four hours to test. The remaining two solutions take five minutes each to test but are not as likely to fix the problem. Good judgment says to try both five-minute solutions first because of the brief amount of time it takes to test them.

➤ **Use a debugger.** If the problem is not obvious or insufficient information is available for diagnosis, try a LAN analyzer or send a core dump to Novell for evaluation.

➤ **Implement the solution.** After you've done your homework, it's time to implement the fix. Be cognizant of change in management processes and always be able to restore in case of failure.

➤ **Document everything.** We all forget this step; however, documentation may prevent your lesson learned from being another's lesson learned. This step is the most important and the most neglected. Because of business pressures and increasing workloads, it's also the easiest to skip.

Need To Know More?

 www.ftp.com/techsup/ftpsoft/info/tn-nx0102.html is FTP Software's Web site. It has an excellent section on server abends and troubleshooting.

 http://support.novell.com/search/ is Novell's Support Connection Knowledgebase, which contains the latest static and dynamic patches.

 novell.netware4.abend is an Internet newsgroup that's a central source for excellent discussions on NetWare abends.

 http://developer.novell.com/research/appnotes/1995/june/04/ index.htm is an excellent article titled "Abend Recovery Techniques for NetWare 3 and 4 Servers."

 www.alexander.com is a third-party NetWare developer that provides an enhanced debugger and assistance with server crash analysis. The Web site also contains a trial download of the product.

Appendix D: IPX/NETX

The Internetwork Packet Exchange/NetWare shell (IPX/NETX) network client is a predecessor to the currently available Novell clients. NETX and IPX are generally found in NetWare versions 3.11 and earlier. IPX, or more accurately *IPX.COM*, is the network transport portion of the IPX/SPX protocol stack. NETX is the NetWare shell. These two components work in harmony to provide network connectivity for older Novell clients. To be considered a client/server application, an application must use software on both the client and the server for communication. For example, mainframe terminals are not strictly speaking client/server-based, because all the processing is done on the server. The mainframe terminal only permits viewing of the information provided to it by the server.

Understanding IPX.COM

IPX.COM is Novell's Internetwork Packet Exchange protocol. This protocol serves as an interface for the actual network board. The following is taken from RFC 1132:

> "IPX is a proprietary standard developed by Novell derived from Xerox's Internet Datagram Protocol [6] (IDP). Defining the encapsulation of the IEEE 802.2 Data Link Layer Standard over IPX in terms of yet another 802.X Physical Layer standard allows for the transmission of IP Datagrams as described in RFC 1042 [7]. This document will focus on the implementation of that RFC over IPX networks."

IPX is a datagram protocol. It operates at the Network layer of the Open Systems Interconnection (OSI) reference model. *Datagram* is another name for packets transferred in a connectionless communication. *Connectionless* implies that packets of data are sent from a source host to a destination host without any prior setup of the connection, and without the manual monitoring of the packet exchange by both the source and the destination hosts. The source computer simply assumes that the destination computer can handle any information it sends. The destination receives the packets and resequences them.

Novell installs IPX support on the workstations along with the workstation requester software, such as the DOS Requester or OS/2 Requester. Current versions of the software include the Novell Open Data-Link Interface (ODI), which provides a way to load multiple protocol stacks, such as IPX and TCP/IP, side-by-side. The Requester software is basically a redirection utility that looks at commands issued by the user and either sends them to local operating systems or sends them out over the network to the network operating system. If requests are destined for the network, the Requester software packages the requests in an IPX packet and hands it to the network boards, which send the packet as a bitstream.

Here are the valid switches for IPX.COM:

➤ **IPX -d** This switch displays potentially available hardware configurations of the network board.

➤ **IPX -i** This switch displays information about the currently installed IPX stack.

➤ **IPX -O**x This switch permits changing the configuration option number for the network board.

Understanding NETX

NETX.EXE, which you might find as NET2.EXE, NET3.EXE, or NET4.EXE, is the NetWare shell. NETX.EXE determines whether client requests are handled on the client using DOS or sent to a particular network server. When connecting to the network, NETX attempts a connection to the first server responding to its connection request. NETX is capable of connecting to other servers either by using the **ATTACH** command or processing a **LOGIN** request. NETX is a terminate-and-stay-resident (TSR) application. It was later replaced by Virtual Loadable Modules (VLMs) and is currently replaced by Client32.

There are large differences between VLMs and NETX. A VLM is a DOS redirector, doing most of its work underneath DOS. The NETX shell intercepts connection requests prior to DOS seeing them. A VLM is modular, allowing selective loading of its components; NETX is ancient, and the whole thing must be loaded. VLM will perform a large degree of memory management on its own, whereas NETX requires configuration.

Troubleshooting IPX And NETX

On occasion, IPX or NETX will act up and prevent a network connection. This section offers a troubleshooting guide for correcting the inability to establish a network connection:

➤ **Eliminate the obvious.** Most network connectivity problems are hardware- rather than software-related. Check all cabling, replace the cable for verification, and remove and reset the network board. You can correct a significant number of errors with this step alone.

➤ **Verify frame types.** If you're running Ethernet, the Ethernet frame types must match. There are four Ethernet frame types, three of which (802.2, 802.3 or Ethernet RAW, and Ethernet_II) are commonly used. Depending on the version of the client used, the default frame type changes. Windows 95/98 and NT do not allow auto-frame typing.

➤ **Verify settings.** If physical network connectivity isn't the problem, check the settings of the network board. Every computing device in a computer must have a unique interrupt request (IRQ). If the network board comes with diagnostic software, run it. The diagnostic software tests communication to and from the board as well as checks for potentially conflicting settings. Some diagnostics even provide a ping utility that tests from one workstation to another.

➤ **Bypass the redirector.** COMCHECK.EXE is an excellent diagnostic tool that bypasses NETX. Use this to determine whether a reliable physical connection exists. This, of course, only works with the DOS version of the client.

➤ **Load network drivers manually.** Often, drivers fail and don't provide useful error messages. Load them manually in the following order: LSL, network board, IPXODI, and finally NETX.

➤ **Use a protocol analyzer.** It's often easier to see what's happening by directly viewing the network conversation (or the lack thereof) to determine the problem's location than to use any other method.

Need To Know More?

 www.networkcomputing.com/1008/1008ws1.html is a Web site that's useful if you're converting from IPX to IP. The Network Computing section offers a planning guide for executing the conversion.

 http://sunsite.auc.dk/RFC/rfc/rfc1132.html contains RFC 1132, "A Standard for the Transmission of 802.2 Packets over IPX Networks."

Appendix E: Disaster Recovery

At some time, devices and services on a network will fail. Hardware cannot run forever, and when operating systems and software change, problems surface. These problems range from minor annoyances to major disruptions in business activities. Additionally, most major losses of data are not caused by the actions of people—they are caused by earthquakes, floods, tornadoes, and other natural disasters. In this appendix, we'll address some techniques for disaster planning and recovery, and cover disaster-recovery items that are applicable to a Novell network.

Planning And Recovery

Disaster-Recovery Planning (DRP) has been around since the late 1960s, but companies only recently began to implement disaster-recovery plans as part of their backup plans. Techniques and services range from backups of critical data to complete off site systems and services.

The degrees of disaster recovery services are typically categorized as follows:

➤ Hot sites

➤ Cold sites

➤ Warm sites

➤ Mobile and specialized facilities

➤ Internal solutions

Hot Site

Hot sites are the most involved and expensive types of disaster-recovery services, but they also provide the most insurance. This service is for organizations that cannot suffer from any extended downtime. These sites are fully equipped with all the hardware and software needed to run the daily activities of an organization. These sites are usually equipped to allow an organization to move its activities to the site and to occupy it for several weeks. After that time, the organization is then moved to a cold site or a mobile facility.

Cold Site

A *cold site* can handle occupancy for several weeks but isn't equipped with the hardware, software, and other elements needed by an organization to operate. This type of facility allows a company to operate its business after it has moved in its equipment and set up operations. A cold site is a cheaper alternative than a hot site—as long as an organization can afford to be out of operation while it's being relocated to the disaster-recovery facility.

Warm Site

A *warm site* facility's features and functions operate somewhere between a cold and hot site. A warm site is usually equipped with the organization's equipment, or it can be brought in within 24 hours. The components, however, have not been customized for the organization. This facility allows an organization to be back in operation in less time than it takes when using a cold site facility (and the cost is lower than at a warm site facility).

Mobile And Specialized Facilities

A *mobile facility* usually contains the organization's equipment and allows the organization to resume operations after the facility is in place. An advantage of this type of disaster-recovery plan is that employees do not need to relocate. However, the organization must be able to handle the downtime while the mobile facility is moved in and activated.

Specialized facilities are usually designed as disaster-recovery plans for certain types of organizations. These organizations cannot handle downtime and have unique needs or equipment. Examples of these include telephone companies, security trading, and delivery operations.

Internal Solutions

The last category is *internal solutions*. An internal solution is one in which an organization develops and maintains its own disaster-recovery solution rather than using an external solution supported by other organizations.

Most organizations develop and use their own disaster-recovery plans. These plans can range from the typical back up of data to complete hardware and software redundancy. The plan that is developed should include people from all aspects of the company's business. It's vital that proper and up-to-date documentation of the organization's procedures is performed, and that an accurate and complete inventory exists of all hardware, software, and other necessary equipment. Copies of the disaster-recovery plan and all supporting documentation should be kept off site, so if a disaster occurs, the disaster-recovery plan isn't part of the disaster. Whichever plan is used, it's important that the employees are familiar with the plan and can actually perform the actions required. Improper training of key personnel on disaster-recovery activities can lead to no disaster-recovery plan. It's also very important that the disaster-recovery operations are tested occasionally and that the testing process itself doesn't cause a disaster.

The objective of recovery after a disaster is to enable the company to resume business as soon as possible and in as normal a manner as feasible. Depending on the degree of failure and the breadth of the disaster-recovery plan, this can range from no downtime to a few days of downtime. Organizations that lack a disaster-recovery plan of some type and suffer a major loss may not be able to resume business at all.

Disaster-Recovery Planning For Novell Networks

Hardware and software failures that occur in Novell networks can cause either minor or major disruptions in service. Additionally, there are many large organizations that rely on Novell networks that have disaster-recovery plans ranging from recovery for the occasional hardware and/or software failure to total loss of facilities because of a natural disaster. This section covers items that Novell considers important parts of a disaster-recovery plan.

Backups

Every network should have a good, reliable data-backup system in which the data backups are stored off site. This backup-system should back up all critical data and Novell Directory Services (NDS). Test the backup system on a regular basis to make the sure the information backed up is recoverable and the backup process runs smoothly. Also, keep the backup software and hardware up-to-date and easily replaceable.

Replicas

If your network has three or more servers in an NDS tree, you should have at least three replicas of each partition. This way, if one server fails, the others can maintain NDS while corrective actions are executed. Make sure the master replicas are not placed on either side of a slow communication link. This ensures that if you need to perform an operation that requires the master replica, the replicas will stay in sync and up-to-date.

Make sure that all the replicas are healthy and that a master replica exists for each partition. If a server goes down, it may not be replaced for a long time or at all. Make sure that all master replicas that server was holding are re-created using one of the read/write replicas. Also, it's very important that time is synchronized on the network. If time is not in sync, any changes made to the tree may be applied improperly.

 Make sure you are aware of some of the NDS disaster-planning suggestions.

Need To Know More?

 Search the Novell Online documentation, using the keywords "disaster recovery", "replicas", and "partitions" for more information on topics covered in this appendix.

 http://support.novell.com is where you can find the following list of TIDs that contain topics related to this appendix. At Novell's support Web site, go to the Knowledgebase and perform a search using the following TID numbers:

➤ **TID 2950668** Disaster Recovery

➤ **TID 2940806** NDS Disaster Planning For WAN

➤ **TID 2940396** Disaster Recovery With Server Specific Info

 www.infosecuritymag.com/campb.htm is a link from the ICSA Web site (www.icsa.net). It contains a DRP article titled "Planning For Success; Preparing For Failure."

 www.infosecuritymag.com/gearing.htm is another related document titled "Gearing Up For Disaster Recovery."

Glossary

10Base2—See *Thin Ethernet*.

10Base5—See *Thick Ethernet*.

10BaseT—One of the most popular IEEE 802.3 Ethernet standards. In a 10BaseT network, each device is attached to a central device called a concentrator or hub. The physical network topology is a star, whereas the actual path the data travels (the logical topology) is a linear bus topology. 10BaseT is sometimes referred to as twisted pair Ethernet.

100BaseT—See *Fast Ethernet*.

1000BaseT—See *Gigabit Ethernet*.

1000BaseX—See *Gigabit Ethernet*.

5-4-3 rule—This rule applies to Ethernet running over coaxial cable. It states that a network can have a maximum of five cable segments with four repeaters, with three of those segments being populated. The rule is intimately connected with end-to-end packet transmission times across repeaters; following this rule prevents late collisions on shared media.

802.2—The IEEE specification within Project 802 for the Logical Link Control (LLC) sublayer within the Data Link layer of the OSI reference model.

802.3—The IEEE specification within Project 802 for Collision Sense Multiple Access/Collision Detection (CSMA/CD) networks, more commonly called Ethernet. CSMA/CD means Ethernet users can attempt to access the medium any time it's perceived as "quiet," but they must back off and try to transmit again if they detect any collisions once transmission has begun.

802.5—The IEEE specification within Project 802 for token-ring LANs, which maps a circulating ring structure onto a physical star and circulates a token to control access to the medium.

abend (abnormal end)—A system crash. An abend usually occurs because a checking procedure has detected a condition that would potentially damage the integrity of the system's internal data.

active monitor—The computer in a token ring network responsible for guaranteeing the network's status.

alarm—A warning in LANalyzer for Windows (LZFW) that can be set to go off when a preset threshold is met.

ANSI (American National Standards Institute)—The U.S. body responsible for many current terminal and data communications standards. It represents the U.S. on the Consultative Committee for International Telegraphy and Telephony (CCITT) and the International Organization for Standardization (ISO).

ARCnet (Attached Resource Computer Network)—An inexpensive and flexible network architecture created by Datapoint Corporation in 1977 that uses the token-passing channel access method.

ASCII (American Standard Code for Information Interchange)—The eight-bit character system that's the standard for transferring data between systems.

ATM (Asynchronous Transfer Mode)—A packet-switched networking architecture based on Broadband Integrated Services Digital Network (B-ISDN) technology. ATM provides connection-oriented, unreliable service over virtual circuits using fixed-length (53 byte) packets called *cells*.

attenuation—The degradation or distortion of an electronic signal as it travels from its origin.

AUI (Attachment Unit Interface)—A type of universal media connector for Ethernet cables.

AUTOEXEC.NCF—The server batch file that launches modules and configures NetWare during startup. AUTOEXEC.NCF is stored in SYS:/SYSTEM and is launched after STARTUP.NCF.

autoreconfiguration—In a token ring network, this is the process that takes place if a problem occurs when an active station is brought online and the station attempts to reconfigure itself and tries to rejoin the ring.

AWG (American Wire Gauge)—A nonferrous (such as aluminum or copper) wire measurement standard. The diameter of the wire is measured and the larger the number the thinner the wire.

bandwidth—The range of frequencies that a communications medium can carry.

base memory address—The memory address at which the transfer area between the computer's main memory and a network board's buffers begins. This address is bounded by the size of its extent.

baseline—A measurement of network performance over time against which current performance can be measured.

beaconing—A signaling process employed by nodes on a token ring network to indicate that a serious error has occurred. The error may involve the node itself or it may involve the node's nearest active upstream neighbor (NAUN). The beaconing process causes all normal network transmissions to be suspended until the error condition is corrected.

bindery—The flat database used in NetWare 3.x and earlier versions to contain User, Group, Print Server, and Print Queue objects. An NDS container can emulate a 3.x bindery, thus allowing services to establish a bindery connection for backward compatibility.

BIOS (Basic Input/Output System)—Software built into a computer system that acts as the interface between the operating system and the hardware.

browser—The client-side software that's used to display content from the Web, also called a *Web browser*.

Category 1 through 5—The EIA/TIA designations for unshielded twisted pair (UTP) cable are described in terms of categories, labeled Category 1, Category 2, and so on.

CAU (Controlled Access Unit)—An intelligent hub, used in token ring networks, that can participate in network management functions.

CDM (Custom Device Module)—The NetWare Peripheral Architecture (NWPA) driver component that is specific to storage devices.

cladding—The nontransparent layer of plastic or glass material inside fiber-optic cable that surrounds the inner core of glass or plastic fibers; cladding provides rigidity, strength, and a manageable outer diameter for fiber-optic cable.

CLIENT32.NLM—One of the three main components of the Novell Windows 95/98 client. The CLIENT32.NLM is found in the C:\NOVELL\CLIENT32 directory.

client—A computer on a network that requests resources or services from some other computer.

CMD (Compatibility Mode Driver)—The virtual network driver that implements Compatibility Mode, which is a tunneling technology that puts an IPX stub inside the IP packets to provide IPX application compatibility.

coaxial cable—A type of cable that uses a central solid wire surrounded by insulation. A braided-wire conductor sheath surrounds the insulation, and a plastic jacket surrounds the sheath. This type of cable can accommodate high bandwidth and is resistant to interference.

collision—A condition that occurs on Ethernet networks when two nodes attempt to broadcast at the same time.

CONFIG.NLM—A NetWare utility that creates a text file that contains items such as the contents of the STARTUP.NCF and AUTOEXEC.NCF files, what NLMs modules are currently running, and more. This is a useful tool to use when documenting the server's hardware and software components.

ConsoleOne—The NetWare management utility that uses a Java GUI environment to allow you to perform basic administrative functions on NDS objects, access the file system, and edit NetWare configuration files within a Java text editor. ConsoleOne can be run on the server or on a workstation. (However, the workstation version has limited features compared to the server version.)

contention—A channel access method in which computers vie for time on the network.

controlled access printer—A printer that can be used only by NDS-authenticated users with sufficient rights. Controlled access printers have corresponding NDS objects. Contrast this with *public access printers*, which have no security and no corresponding NDS objects.

CRC (cyclic redundancy check)—A mathematical recipe that generates a specific value, called a checksum, based on the contents of a data frame. The CRC is calculated before a data frame is transmitted, then is included with the frame; on receipt, the CRC is recalculated and compared to the sent value. If the two agree, the data frame is assumed to have been delivered intact; if they disagree, the data frame must be retransmitted. CRC errors are also called *CRC/Alignment errors*.

crosstalk—A phenomenon that occurs when two wires are laid against each other in parallel, and signals traveling down one wire interfere with signals traveling down the other, and vice-versa.

CSMA/CD (Carrier Sense Multiple Access with Collision Detection)—A method in which collisions are detected by monitoring the transmission line for a special signal that indicates a collision has occurred.

DHCP (Dynamic Host Configuration Protocol)—A protocol that dynamically assigns IP addresses to hosts in a network. DHCP allows each host machine to request an IP address from the server and return the address when it's done.

diagnostic software—Specialized programs that can probe and monitor either a system or a specific system component to determine if it's working properly and, if not, try to establish the cause of the problem.

DIP (dual in-line package) switches—An electrical circuit that consists of a series of individual two-way switches contained in a single chip. A DIP is an integrated computer circuit that features two parallel rows of pins of equal length, offset approximately 1 cm.

Directory Map object—An object that contains a reference to a file-system directory on a NetWare volume. It can be used with the **MAP** command in login scripts to point to file-system resources.

disk driver—A module that allows the server to communicate with the disk and other storage devices installed on the server.

disk duplexing—A fault-tolerant disk configuration in which data is written to two hard disks, each with its own disk controller, so if one disk or controller fails, the data remains accessible.

disk mirroring—A redundancy feature that duplicates all information on one drive (or drives) onto another drive for fault tolerance in the event of drive failure. Disk mirroring, also known as *RAID level 1*, may be implemented in either hardware or software.

disk striping—A feature that creates a single, logical volume out of two or more physical drives by interleaving logical disk blocks on the physical drives. Disk striping improves performance for file access.

disk striping with parity—A fault-tolerant disk configuration in which parts of several physical disks are linked in an array, and data and parity information is written to all disks in this array. Should one disk fail, the data may be reconstructed from the parity information.

DMA (direct memory access)—A technique for addressing memory on some other device as though it were local memory directly available to the device accessing that memory. This technique lets a CPU gain immediate access to the buffers on any network board that supports DMA.

driver—An abbreviation for "device driver," which is a small program that mediates between an operating system and the hardware device it knows how to access.

early token release—A feature on a 16Mbps token ring network in which the transmitting device doesn't wait for the token frame to come back from the destination device. Instead, as soon as it finishes sending the data, it sends out a free token.

EIA/TIA (Electronic Industries Association/Telecommunications Industry Association) Commercial Building Wiring Standard—A standard for wiring in commercial buildings. The EIA is an industry trade group of electronics and networking manufacturers that collaborates on standards for wiring, connectors, and other common components.

EIDE (Enhanced IDE)—An enhancement to the IDE standard that was developed to support drive sizes greater than 528MB and higher data transfer rates (up to 13.3Mbps).

EISA (Extended Industry Standard Architecture)—A 32-bit PC bus architecture that is backward-compatible with the older, slower 16-bit ISA bus architecture.

EMI (electromagnetic interference)—A form of electrical interference caused by emissions from external devices, such as transformers or electrical motors, that can interfere with network transmissions over an electrical medium.

ENS (Event Notification Services)—A procedure that creates specific messages assigned by a network manager regarding any printer functions, such as print queues and other actions.

ESD (electrostatic discharge)—The transfer of the charge caused by static electricity between bodies at different electrical potentials.

ESDI (Enhanced Small Device Interface)—The more powerful replacement for the ST-506 drives that allows for a larger storage capacity and faster data transfer.

Ethernet—A type of shared-media LAN that uses a bus or star topology and packet switching, and is based on contention-oriented media access.

Ethernet cards—Network boards that provide Ethernet services for computers.

Ethernet II—The Ethernet frame type used by TCP/IP.

Fast Ethernet—Ethernet that operates at 100Mbps by limiting the time it takes for a bit to be sent. Fast Ethernet can't be run on a cable longer than 100 meters between the repeater and the sender. Also, there can be no more than two repeater hops. Also called *100BaseT*.

fault tolerance—The capability of a computer to work continuously, even when a component failure occurs. Fault-tolerant systems generally have redundancy on most, but not all critical components, but retain single points of failure. The term fault tolerance is often abused and misinterpreted to mean failure proof.

FCC (Federal Communications Commission)—The U.S. government communications regulatory agency. Among other responsibilities, the FCC regulates access to broadcast frequencies throughout the electromagnetic spectrum, including those used for mobile computing and microwave transmissions. Where these signals cover any distance (more than half a mile) and require exclusive use of a particular frequency, an FCC broadcast license is required. Many wireless networking technologies use so-called "unregulated frequencies" set aside by the FCC that do not require such licensing, but they must be shared with others (individuals or companies) using the same frequencies.

FCC ID—An identification number that is provided by the FCC and is found on labels of hardware devices.

FDDI (Fiber Distributed Data Interface)—A network communications protocol characterized mainly by its use of fiber media for data transmission and high-speed throughput (100Mbps).

fiber-optic cable—Cable that uses light to transmit signals and is, therefore, immune to electromagnetic interference (EMI) and electronic eavesdropping.

firewall—Software and/or hardware that regulates access to the network to protect both information and computers from outside threats.

fragment error—A packet error that is generated when incomplete packets that result from collisions (and are less than 64 bytes in size—or fragments) are transmitted. Fragment errors can also occur from packets that have an invalid Frame Check Sequence (FCS) value.

Frame Relay—A protocol specification and a type of public data network service that provides efficient Data Link layer functions on permanent and switched virtual circuits.

FTP (File Transfer Protocol)—A TCP/IP protocol used to transfer data between remote machines.

gateway—A link between two dissimilar networks that acts as a translator between the systems.

Gigabit Ethernet—A form of Ethernet that supports data transfer rates of 1000Mbps. Also called *1000BaseT* and *1000BaseX*.

GUI (Graphical User Interface)—An operating environment that uses icons, buttons, and other visual elements rather than commands to perform certain functions.

HAM (host adapter module)—The NetWare Peripheral Architecture (NWPA) driver component that is specific to host adapter hardware.

HBA (Host Bus Adapter)—An adapter board or disk controller that adds a bus so peripheral devices can connect to the CPU.

HCSS (High Capacity Storage System)—In NetWare, this extra storage method employs a jukebox (an optical disk library) to increase the storage capacity of the NetWare file system.

hexadecimal—A mathematical notation for representing numbers in base 16; 10–15 are expressed as A–F; 10h or 0x10 (both are notations to indicate the number is hexadecimal) equals 16.

HFS (Hierarchical File System)—The Apple Macintosh file system.

high-level formatting—This process occurs on a hard drive after partitioning, and it double-checks the success of the low-level format and scans the drive for bad sectors a second time.

hop—The distance traveled by a packet between routers or other network devices as it moves along to its final destination.

Hot Fix Redirection Area—The space on a NetWare partition that is reserved for data from a bad block.

HP Gateway—One of several gateways for NDPS services to legacy printers. The HP Gateway was developed by Hewlett-Packard specifically for its printers. Other gateways include the Xerox gateway and the Novell gateway, the latter of which is generic and may be used with any brand printer.

hub—The central concentration point of a star network.

IBM 8228—A Multistation Access Unit (MSAU) that allows a maximum of eight attached active devices.

IBM Type 1 through 9—These numeric cable designations represent the grades of cabling recognized by IBM's cabling system. Types 2 and 9 are the most commonly used networking cables, and Type 3 is voice grade only—unsuitable for networking use.

IDE (Integrated Device Electronics)—One of the two major types of hard disks currently sold (the other is SCSI). IDE's controller electronics are a physical part of the disk. IDE uses only run length limited (RLL) encoding for its drives.

IEEE (Institute of Electrical and Electronics Engineers)—An engineering organization that issues standards for electrical and electronic devices, including network interfaces, cabling, and connectors.

ILD (injection laser diode)—A device used in fiber-optic cable to produce light.

impedance—The resistance a metal-based cable has to the transmission of signals. Impedance is a primary cause of attenuation in cables.

INSTALL.BAT—The name of the file used to begin the installation of NetWare 5. To begin the installation, simply type "INSTALL" at the DOS prompt.

intraNetWare—The operating system developed by Novell in 1996 that combined a Netscape browser, a Web server, TCP/IP support, and NetWare 4.11. All of this, and more, is now included in NetWare 5.

IP (Internet Protocol)—A Department of Defense (DoD) Internet layer protocol that provides connectionless, nonguaranteed service to move packets across an internetwork.

IPX (Internetwork Packet Exchange)—Modeled after Xerox Corporation's Internetwork Packet protocol, XNS, IPX is a protocol that operates at the third layer (Network layer) of the OSI model to move packets across an internetwork.

IPX/SPX (Internetwork Packet Exchange/Sequenced Packet Exchange)—The native protocol stack for NetWare networks. SPX provides reliable connections, operates at the Transport layer of the OSI model, and relies on IPX for lower-level network functions.

IRQ (interrupt request)—Any of 16 unique signal lines between the CPU and the bus slots on a PC. IRQs define the mechanism whereby a peripheral device of any kind, including a network adapter, can state a claim on the PC's attention. This claim is called an "interrupt," which gives the name to the lines that carry this information. Also called a *hardware interrupt.*

ISA (Industry Standard Architecture)—Originally an 8-bit PC bus architecture, ISA moved up to 16-bit with the introduction of the IBM PC/AT in 1984.

ISDN (Integrated Services Digital Network)—A digital communication service that uses special adapters on regular phone lines that can differentiate between digital and other types of data transfer. ISDN lines can transfer data at up to 1.536Mbps.

ISO (International Organization for Standardization)—A Geneva-based organization that sets standards for data communication.

ISP (Internet Service Provider)—A commercial organization that provides customers access to the Internet, usually for a fee.

jabber errors—An error that occurs on a network when packets are greater than 1,518 bytes and have invalid CRC and/or Frame Check Sequence (FCS) values.

Java—Sun Microsystems' cross-platform programming language.

jukebox—A system of multiple drives set up on a mechanism that swaps optical disks when another optical disk is needed, just like the music jukeboxes popular in the 1950s.

jumper—A tiny plastic-coated metal connector used to connect pins located on the rear of a hard drive.

jumper block—A collection of two or more sets of jumper pins, or a special connector designed to make contact between two or more sets of contiguous jumper pins at the same time.

kernel—The base of most operating systems. The kernel provides just the core functions deemed critical for the operating system. Further functionality is added by additional program modules. Kernels are generally classed as either a microkernel or macrokernel, based on the core functions included.

Knowledgebase—A selection on the Novell Support Connection Web site that contains technical information documents (TIDs).

LAN (local area network)—A collection of computers and other networked devices that fits within the scope of a single physical network. LANs provide the building blocks for internetworks and wide area networks (WANs).

LAN driver—A file containing software code that provides a communication link between the operating system and the network board.

LANalyzer—A software protocol analyzer produced by Novell.

LED (light emitting diode)—A device used in fiber-optic cable to produce light. LED uses a semiconductor diode that emits light when a charge passes through it.

low-level formatting—The hard disk formatting process in which the physical layout of the tracks and sectors on a drive are determined. Low-level formatting completely and permanently deletes all information from a drive.

LZFW (LANalyzer for Windows)—A software protocol analyzer product that is produced by Novell and is available as a component of Novell's ManageWise product. LZFW works on Ethernet and token ring networks.

MAC (Media Access Control)—A level of data communication in which the network interface can directly address the networking media; also refers to a unique address programmed into network adapters to identify them on any network on which they might appear.

magneto-optical—A type of drive that combines laser power and magnetics. This technology delivers rewritable, removable media capable of storing vast amounts of information.

ManageWise—A product designed by Novell to provide network management services, including documentation and monitoring functions.

MCA (Micro Channel Architecture)—IBM's proprietary 16- and 32-bit computer buses, originally developed for its PS/2 PCs, formerly popular on its midrange RISC/6000 computers. MCA is superceded by PCI in its four variations.

memory core dumps—Pictures of a computer's memory contents at the time the dump occurs.

MFM (modified frequency modulation)—An encoding scheme used on ST-506 drives that writes data onto hard disks under 40MB.

Microsoft GINA—The module that provides the ability for developers to replace pieces of the login process with their own.

MSAU (Multistation Access Unit)—A multiport wiring hub used on token ring networks that can connect as many as eight nodes. Sometimes abbreviated as *MAU*.

MTL (Micro House Technical Library)—An extensive collection of hardware information found on the SupportSource CD-ROM.

Multimode Graded Index fiber-optic cable—One of the three types of fiber-optic cable in use today. Multimode Graded Index fiber-optic cables vary the refractive index of the cladding gradually so the signal remains more in the glass or plastic cable. The cable types range from 50 to 100 microns in diameter and can therefore be used for longer distances.

Multimode Stepped Index fiber-optic cable—One of the three types of fiber-optic cable in use today. Multimode Stepped Index cable is typically found in older installations of fiber-optic cable and the thickness ranges from 50 to 100 microns in diameter. These Multimode Stepped Index fibers do not have optimized cladding refractive indexes so the signal can bounce around more, which increases signal propagation delay.

NDIS (Network Driver Interface Specification)—A specification for network-board drivers developed by Microsoft and 3Com. The drivers for the Novell Client support this specification.

NDPS (Novell Distributed Print Services)—A service that provides administrators the ability to control printing through NDS. It also provides bidirectional communications between control points, management applications and workstations, and network printers.

NDPS Broker—This NDS object is created when you install NDPS. It provides three basic NDPS services: the Service Registry Service (SRS), the Event Notification Service (ENS), and the Resource Management Service (RMS). Also called *Broker object* and *NDPS Broker object*.

NDPS gateways—In NDPS printing, this gateway is used to integrate NDPS and queue-based printing. There are three types of NDPS gateways: HP, Xerox, and the default Novell gateway.

NDPS Manager—An NDS object that is a repository for NDPS Printer Agents. You must create an NDPS Manager in NDS before you can create Printer Agents that reside on file servers.

NDS (Novell Directory Services)—Novell's directory service that stores information on the network resources and regulates their access. NDS is a hierarchical distributed database that is X.50x compliant.

NetBEUI (NetBIOS Enhanced User Interface)—An enhanced set of network and transport protocols built in the late 1980s (when earlier implementations became too limiting for continued use) to carry NetBIOS information.

NetBIOS (Networked Basic Input/Output System)—A venerable set of application programming interfaces (APIs) designed by IBM in the late 1970s to provide easy access to networking services; NetBIOS remains a popular networking interface.

NetWare Administrator—NetWare's graphical utility for managing NDS databases. Also called *NWAdmin*, although it's not a trademarked term. The executable for NetWare Administrator is NWADMN32.EXE and is located in the SYS:\PUBLIC\WIN32 directory.

NetWare Client Requester—One of the three main architectural components of the Novell Client for Windows 95/98, also called the *DOS Requester*. The NetWare Client Requester provides services such as adjusting automatic reconnection levels, caching of files, and tracking the different network resources used. These activities are provided by CLIENT32.NLM, which is located in the C:\NOVELL\CLIENT32 directory, by default.

NetWare Expert—A component of LANalyzer for Windows (LZFW) that provides a program for network troubleshooting. The program uses artificial intelligence techniques to provide network recommendations.

NetWare partition—In NetWare 5, the NetWare partition is the partition created from which you will create NetWare volumes. NetWare partitions and NDS partitions are not the same.

network board—A circuit board installed in a computer to allow it to communicate with other workstations on a network. Also called a *network interface card (NIC)*, *network adapter*, *network card*, and *network interface board*. Novell uses the term network board most often; however, vendors usually call it a NIC.

NIC (Network Interface Card)—See *network board*.

NIOS (NetWare Input/Output Subsystem)—One of the three main architectural components of the Novell Client for Windows 95/98. NIOS provides the interface between the local Windows 95/98 operating system and the Novell Client and Novell services. This functionality is provided by the NIOS.VXD file, which is located in the C:\WINDOWS\SYSTEM directory, by default.

NIOS.VXD—The file that provides the functionality for NIOS. It's located in the C:\WINDOWS\SYSTEM directory, by default.

NLM (NetWare Loadable Module)—One of several types of NetWare server executables; the other types include CDM, HAM, LAN, and NAM. Each executable has a specific function, with the NLM being the most common form.

NMI (non maskable interrupt)—An interrupt that comes from some device or process that the system cannot determine from where it's coming. NMIs cannot be disabled by other interrupts.

Novell Client—The Novell package that provides connectivity to a Novell network.

Novell Support Connection—A collection of information about various Novell products provided by Novell on its Web site. There's also a CD-ROM version, which requires a subscription.

NSS (Novell Storage Services)—An enhanced file system that overcomes many of the limitations of the traditional NetWare file system.

NWFS.SYS—One of the four main architectural components of the Novell Client for Windows NT. The NWFS.SYS component provides the interface between the local Windows NT operating system and the Novell Client and Novell services. NWFS.SYS is located in the C:\WINNT\SYSTEM32 directory, by default.

NWGINA (NetWare Graphical Identification and Authentication)—The Novell GINA that replaces the Microsoft GINA so users can access Novell resources.

NWLink (NetWare Link)—A set of protocols developed by Microsoft that behaves like IPX/SPX.

NWPA (NetWare Peripheral Architecture)—The current NetWare architecture for storage devices. The NWPA drivers contain two types of modules: the Host Adapter Module (HAM) and the Custom Device Module (CDM).

ODI (Open Data-Link Interface)—Part of the Novell protocol suite; it provides the capability to bind more than one protocol to a network board.

ODINSUP (ODI NDIS support)—A 32-bit ODI LAN driver that uses the ODI NDIS interface.

optical drives—A drive that uses a laser to store information on media optically instead of on a magnetic head. Optical drives are generally removable and have the advantages of being stable and long lasting. Technically, CD and DVD are optical drives, although the term is usually reserved for high-speed read/writable drives.

oversize errors—An error that occurs on a network when packets are greater than 1,518 bytes and do not have any incorrect CRC or Frame Check Sequence (FCS) values.

parity—Redundant segments of data used to provide fault tolerance for information. Also, a disk-storage configuration in which additional data is stored, therefore, in the event of a single drive failure, all data can be reconstructed.

partitioning—The process of dividing a hard drive into logical sections. This process usually occurs after low-level formatting.

PC Card—Another way to refer to a Personal Computer Memory Card International Association (PCMCIA) card. See *PCMCIA*.

PCI (Peripheral Component Interconnect)—The PCI standard was developed to replace the EISA/ISA and MCA buses. It features high-speed, automatic configuration, direct access to memory, and other performance enhancements. The original specification operates at 32 data bits with a bus speed of 33MHz, but has been enhanced with double-width or double-bus speed, or both.

PCL (Printer Control Language)—A page description language (PDL) developed by Hewlett Packard in 1984. PCL has become an unofficial standard for printing, competing directly with Adobe's PostScript.

PCMCIA (Personal Computer Memory Card International Association)—Also called a *PC Card*, this credit card sized network board provides a way to tie peripherals into a computer bus without opening the computer and plugging the board into a connector on the motherboard. PCMCIA cards are commonly used on laptop computers.

peripheral—A device added to a standalone computer or a network to extend its capabilities. Examples are printers, modems, external CD-ROMs, and scanners.

plenum—The area between a false ceiling and the true one in most commercial buildings. It's used to circulate heating and cooling air. Many types of cable, including networking cable, are also run through this space.

Port Handler—A component of queue-based printing that provides communication between the Print Device Subsystem and the printer.

preemptive—When referring to operating systems, preemptive is used to describe an operating system that decides which service can use the processor and for how long. In a preemptive system, the operating system can take control of the processor and prevent all services from running.

print queue—The temporary storage location (logical and/or physical) for documents sent to the printer that are waiting to be printed.

Printer Agent—The component of NDPS that provides the functionality that in the past was provided by the Print Server, Print Queue, and Printer objects. This entity must be created before an actual NDPS printer can be created in NDS.

Printer object—An object in the NDS structure symbolizing a physical printer.

promiscuous mode—A setting on some types of network boards that allows the board and drivers to see all the packets on the transmission media—not just those destined for the device.

propagation delay—Signal delay that is inherent in the media used or created when a number of repeaters are connected in a line. Because of this, many network architectures limit the number of repeaters on a network.

protocol—A rigidly defined set of rules for communication across a network. Most protocols are confined to one or more layers of the OSI reference model.

protocol analyzer—A hardware or software entity that analyzes the traffic on a network. LANalyzer is a software-based protocol analyzer.

public access printer—An NDPS printer that is accessible to anyone on the network. Public access printers have no NDS objects or security. Compared to controlled access printers, which do have security.

Pure IP—A new feature of NetWare 5 that allows you to run a network without IPX.

queue-based printing—The NetWare printing system that allows you to manage a network printing environment. You must configure three objects in NDS to use queue-based printing: the Print Queue, the Printer, and the Print Server objects.

RAID (Redundant Array of Inexpensive Disks)—Multiple drives linked via hardware or software, used to increase reliability. There are six recognized levels of RAID, with additional levels being developed. The exact features depend on the RAID level used.

repeater—A networking device that strengthens a signal suffering from attenuation. Using a repeater effectively doubles the maximum length of the network.

RFC (request for comment)—A procedure in the Internet community that involves the submission of a series of documents that contain protocol descriptions, model descriptions, and experimental results for review by experts.

RG (Radio Government)—The coaxial cable designation that reflects coaxial cables' original use as a conveyance for radio frequency data and signals. The cable designation for thinnet (10Base2) is RG-58, for CATV RG-59, for ARCnet RG-62, and for thicknet (10Base5) is either RG-8 or RG-11.

RJ-11—The four wire modular jack commonly used for home telephone handsets.

RJ-45—The eight wire modular jack used for twisted-pair networking cables and also for PBX-based telephone systems.

RLL (run length limited)—An encoding scheme used on ST-506 drives, among others. RLL uses a combination of compression and error-checking code to provide higher data density and greater reliability than previous methods.

RMS (Resource Management Services)—This regulated system provides centrally located resources to the rest of the network. Resources include drivers, printer definition files (the other PDF file type), fonts, banners, and so on.

router—A networking device that operates at the Network layer of the OSI model. A router is able to connect networks with different physical media and also can translate between different network architectures, such as token ring and Ethernet.

SAP (Service Advertising Protocol)—The protocol used by file and print servers on Novell networks to inform computers of the services available.

SCSI (Small Computer System Interface)—One major type of hard disk currently sold (another is IDE). SCSI is a high-speed, intelligent, parallel-drive standard in which the electronics are separated from the physical drive.

server bottleneck—When a server slows operations because a particular task or activity is using too many resources and/or the hardware or software is not capable of meeting the demand.

server console—The NetWare 5 screen used by the network administrator to interact with and monitor the server.

server overload error—An error that occurs when the number of "Request Being Processed" or "Server Busy" packets sent by a busy server to clients that request its services goes over a certain number per minute. The suggested setting for the Server Overloads/min setting is five.

SERVER.EXE—The name of the kernel on the NetWare 5 server.

sheath—The outer layer of coating on a cable; also called the *jacket*.

single mode fiber-optic cable—One of the three types of fiber-optic cable in use today. Also called *monomode*, single mode fiber is very thin, with a diameter of less than 10 microns, where 1 micron is about 1/25,000 of an inch. These thin fibers produce very little signal bounce and, therefore, have the greatest bandwidth of the three fiber types.

SMS (Storage Management Services)—Novell's suite of services that allows information on NetWare volumes to be archived and retrieved. Typically, SMS is used to send data to and retrieve data from a tape drive.

SMTP (Simple Mail Transfer Protocol)—The current standard protocol for Internet and other TCP/IP-based email.

SNA (Systems Network Architecture)—IBM's native protocol suite for its mainframes and older minicomputers; SNA is still one of the most widely used protocol suites in the world.

SNMP (Simple Network Mail Protocol)—A Department of Defense (DoD) Process/Application layer protocol that specifies a process for collecting network-management data between devices.

spooler—A temporary file location on a hard drive or in RAM, usually used for output such as printing. *Spool* is an abbreviation for Simultaneous Peripheral Operation On Line. There's little practical distinction between a spooler and print queue.

standby monitor—A computer in a token-ring network that monitors the network status and waits for the loss of signal from the active monitor, so it can take over that role.

STARTUP.NCF—One of the two boot files for the NetWare server (the other is AUTOEXEC.NCF).

STP (shielded twisted pair)—A cable with a foil shield and copper braid surrounding pairs of wires that have a minimum number of twists per foot of cable.

support pack—Also called *service packs*. A support pack is a collection of fixes for various Novell products. The support packs are usually categorized by operating systems patches, device driver updates, and NetWare Loadable Module (NLM) updates.

SupportSource—A utility by Micro House that contains detailed information about various types of hardware. SupportSource costs more than $1,000 for a yearly subscription.

SVGA—See *VGA*.

SYS volume—The mandatory name of the first volume on a NetWare file server. The SYS volume must be a traditional NetWare volume.

TCP/IP (Transmission Control Protocol/Internet Protocol)—A protocol suite created by the Advanced Research Projects Agency (ARPA). This transmission protocol suite is the standard used for Internet communications.

termination—The process of closing off or ending a cable.

terminator—A specialized end connector for coaxial Ethernet networks. A terminator "soaks up" signals that arrive at the end of a network cable and prevents them from reflecting off the end of the cable back onto the network, where they would interfere with *real* network traffic.

Thick Ethernet—Coaxial cable with a diameter of 1 centimeter, used to connect Ethernet nodes at distances as far away as 1,000 meters. Also called *thicknet* and *10Base5*.

Thin Ethernet—Coaxial cable wire with a diameter of 10 millimeters, used to connect Ethernet nodes at a distance of about 300 meters. Also called *thinnet* and *10Base2*.

TIDs (Technical Information Documents)—Documents on Novell's Support Connection Web site or CD-ROM that contain information about various Novell products and technical issues relating to them.

token—In a token ring network, the token is a special type of packet that consists of a 3-byte Media Access Control (MAC) frame. The token is similar to a permission slip that allows a device to transmit when it has the permission.

token ring—IBM's version of a LAN. A token ring network consists of stations connected serially, each receiving information sequentially around a closed network ring.

topology—The physical layout of a network, including the cabling, workstation configuration, gateways, and hubs.

traditional NetWare volume—A NetWare volume that uses a 32-bit interface and file allocation tables (FATs) to organize the storage space. The size of the files on a traditional NetWare volume is limited to a maximum of 4GB each, and volumes can be no larger than 1TB each. (This limitation is not practical because of the memory requirements involved.)

transceiver—Literally, this compound word takes the beginning of transmitter and the end of receiver. Therefore, a transceiver combines the functions of a transmitter and a receiver, and integrates the circuitry needed to emit signals on a medium, as well as receive them, into a single device.

TSR (terminate-and-stay-resident)—A program that loads into the memory of a computer and is always accessible by simply entering a preset key combination. TSR technology was required by DOS limitations and has little relevance to modern operating systems.

twisted-pair cable—A type of cabling where two copper wires, each enclosed in some kind of insulating sheath, are wrapped around each other. The twisting permits narrow gauge wire, otherwise extraordinarily sensitive to crosstalk and interference, to carry higher bandwidth signals over greater distances than would ordinarily be possible with straight wires. Twisted-pair cabling is used for both voice telephone circuits and networking.

undersize errors—An error that occurs on a network when packets are less than 64 bytes, but do not have any invalid CRC or FCS values.

Unicode—Standardized by the Unicode Consortium, Unicode is a 16-bit system used to encode characters and letters from many different languages.

Unix—An interactive, time-sharing, operating system developed in 1969 by a hacker to play games. This system developed into the most widely used industrial-strength computer operating system in the world, and it ultimately supported the birth of the Internet.

UPS (Uninterruptible Power Supply)—A battery-backup system that supplies power in the event that building power is lost and can, in some cases, shut down a server gracefully to prevent data loss. UPSs come in two primary flavors: standby and online. Manufacturers constantly battle over the two competing types but for most network engineers, there's little practical difference between the two.

URL (Uniform Resource Locator)—An addressing system used to locate files on a network or the Internet (for example, **www.lanw.com**).

vampire tap—A hardware clamp used to connect one cable segment to another by penetrating the insulation of the cable segment without cutting it.

VESA (Video Electronics Standards Association)—A group committed to the standardization of VGA monitors.

VGA (Video Graphics Adapter)—The minimum standard for modern monitors. VGA displays at up to 640 by 480 pixels at 16 colors. Super VGA (SVGA) adheres to no one standard, but expands on the number of pixels or colors, or both.

VLB (VESA local bus)—Also called *VL-Bus*, VLB is a bus provided by the Video Electronics Standards Association (VESA) committee to handle 486 processors. VLB slots were backward-compatible with both ISA 8-bit and 16-bit cards. However, VLB systems have disappeared in favor of PCI or Accelerated Graphics Port (AGP) slots—another video-only bus connector.

VLM (Virtual Loadable Module)—Utilities or programs that perform communication and other services between workstations and servers. This is the basis of Novell's 16-bit client that preceeded Client32 for access from DOS and Windows clients to the NDS tree.

volume—The fundamental unit of NetWare server storage space.

Volume object—An NDS object that represents a corresponding physical volume.

VREPAIR—A NetWare utility used on traditional NetWare volumes to fix volume problems and remove name space entries from the file allocation table (FAT) and directory entry table (DET).

WAN (wide area network)—A network encompassing a large geographical area.

Web browser—The client-side software that's used to display content from the Web. Also called simply a *browser*.

Index

CERTIFIED CRAMMER SOCIETY

A breed apart, a cut above the rest—a true professional. Highly skilled and superbly trained, certified IT professionals are unquestionably the world's most elite computer experts. In an effort to appropriately recognize this privileged crowd, The Coriolis Group is proud to introduce the Certified Crammer Society. If you are a certified IT professional, it is our pleasure to invite you to become a Certified Crammer Society member.

Membership is free to all certified professionals and benefits include a membership kit that contains your official membership card and official Certified Crammer Society blue denim ball cap emblazoned with the Certified Crammer Society crest—proudly displaying the Crammer motto "Phi Slamma Cramma"—and featuring a genuine leather bill. The kit also includes your password to the Certified Crammers-Only Web site containing monthly discreet messages designed to provide you with advance notification about certification testing information, special book excerpts, and inside industry news not found anywhere else; monthly Crammers-Only discounts on selected Coriolis titles; *Ask the Series Editor* Q and A column; cool contests with great prizes; and more.

GUIDELINES FOR MEMBERSHIP

Registration is free to professionals certified in Microsoft, A+, or Oracle DBA. Coming soon: Sun Java, Novell, and Cisco. Send or email your contact information and proof of your certification (test scores, membership card, or official letter) to:

Certified Crammer Society Membership Chairperson
THE CORIOLIS GROUP, LLC
14455 North Hayden Road, Suite 220, Scottsdale, Arizona 85260-6949
Fax: 480.483.0193 • Email: ccs@coriolis.com

APPLICATION

Name: _____

Address: _____

Society Alias: _____

Choose a secret code name to correspond with us and other Crammer Society members. Please use no more than eight characters.

Email: _____

CORIOLIS HELP CENTER

Here at The Coriolis Group, we strive to provide the finest customer service in the technical education industry. We're committed to helping you reach your certification goals by assisting you in the following areas.

Talk to the Authors

We'd like to hear from you! Please refer to the "How to Use This Book" section in the "Introduction" of every Exam Cram guide for our authors' individual email addresses.

Web Page Information

The Certification Insider Press Web page provides a host of valuable information that's only a click away. For information in the following areas, please visit us at:

www.coriolis.com/cip/default.cfm

- Titles and other products
- Book content updates
- Roadmap to Certification Success guide
- New Adaptive Testing changes
- New Exam Cram Live! seminars
- New Certified Crammer Society details
- Sample chapters and tables of contents
- Manuscript solicitation
- Special programs and events

Contact Us by Email

Important addresses you may use to reach us at The Coriolis Group.

eci@coriolis.com

To subscribe to our FREE, bi-monthly on-line newsletter, *Exam Cram Insider*. Keep up to date with the certification scene. Included in each *Insider* are certification articles, program updates, new exam information, hints and tips, sample chapters, and more.

techsupport@coriolis.com

For technical questions and problems with CD-ROMs. Products broken, battered, or blown-up? Just need some installation advice? Contact us here.

ccs@coriolis.com

To obtain membership information for the *Certified Crammer Society,* **an exclusive club for the certified professional.** Get in on members-only discounts, special information, expert advice, contests, cool prizes, and free stuff for the certified professional. Membership is FREE. Contact us and get enrolled today!

cipq@coriolis.com

For book content questions and feedback about our titles, drop us a line. This is the good, the bad, and the questions address. Our customers are the best judges of our products. Let us know what you like, what we could do better, or what question you may have about any content. Testimonials are always welcome here, and if you send us a story about how an Exam Cram guide has helped you ace a test, we'll give you an official Certification Insider Press T-shirt.

custserv@coriolis.com

For solutions to problems concerning an order for any of our products. Our staff will promptly and courteously address the problem. Taking the exams is difficult enough. We want to make acquiring our study guides as easy as possible.

Book Orders & Shipping Information

orders@coriolis.com

To place an order by email or to check on the status of an order already placed.

coriolis.com/bookstore/default.cfm

To place an order through our online bookstore.

1.800.410.0192

To place an order by phone or to check on an order already placed.